MW00584124

The Congressional Journal of
Barber B. Conable, Jr.,
1968–1984

The Congressional Journal of Barber B. Conable, Jr., 1968–1984

Edited by Bill Kauffman

Foreword by Albert R. Hunt

University Press of Kansas

Published by the University Press of Kansas (Lawrence, Kansas 66045), which
was organized by the Kansas Board of Regents and is operated and funded by
Emporia State University, Fort Hays State University, Kansas State University,
Pittsburg State University, the University of Kansas, and Wichita State University.

Publication made possible, in part, by funding from The Dirksen Congressional
Center.

Library of Congress Cataloging-in-Publication Data

Names: Conable, Barber B., author. | Kauffman, Bill, 1959– editor.
Title: The Congressional journal of Barber B. Conable, Jr., 1968–1984 / edited by
Bill Kauffman.
Description: Lawrence : University Press of Kansas, 2021. | Includes index.
Identifiers: LCCN 2020042510
  ISBN 9780700632091 (cloth)
  ISBN 9780700632107 (epub)
Subjects: LCSH: Conable, Barber B.—Diaries. | Legislators—United States—
Diaries. | Legislators—New York (State)—Diaries. | United States. Congress.
House—Biography. | United States—Politics and government—1969–1974—
Sources. | United States—Politics and government—1974–1977—Sources.
| United States—Politics and government—1977–1981—Sources. | United
States—Politics and government—1981–1989—Sources.
Classification: LCC E840.8.C65 A3 2021 | DDC 328.73/092—dc23
LC record available at https://lccn.loc.gov/2020042510.

British Library Cataloguing-in-Publication Data is available.

Printed in the United States of America

10 9 8 7 6 5 4 3 2 1

The paper used in this publication is acid free and meets the minimum
requirements of the American National Standard for Permanence of Paper for
Printed Library Materials Z39.48-1992.

Contents

A photo gallery follows page 180.

Foreword

The best beat in Washington for a reporter is not the White House, radiating glamour and power. It is Congress, where in good times and bad the nexus of policy and politics is omnipresent and the extraordinary diversity of America is on display.

Those 535 men and women represent every region and economic, social, and political stratum of the country. Watching this political melting pot try to reach consensus on huge issues—war and peace, taxes, health care—is to understand the value and the challenges of a representative democracy. It is often unruly, sometimes cowardly. Winston Churchill reminded us that democracy is the worst form of government except for all the others. Important legislation involves complex challenges and competing claims.

Above all, it is about people. I covered Congress for ten years and tried to stay in touch during subsequent decades. There were formidable figures in those times: Kennedy, Dole, Pelosi, Kemp, Moynihan, O'Neill, Baker. None shaped my knowledge of legislative politics better than Barber B. Conable, a less recognized Republican lawmaker from upstate New York who served in the House from 1965 to 1985. His colleagues cited him as the most respected member of that body; he was a close associate of Gerald Ford and George H. W. Bush and had many Democratic admirers. For seventeen years he kept a journal, periodically musing about big events in an era that included Vietnam, Watergate, political realignment, and major changes in entitlements and taxes, where he played a key role. He had a gift for expression and astute insights. These writings were rendered in real time, not retrospectively, when we usually try to make ourselves look better. They illustrate Bismarck's admonition that there are two things one should not watch being made: sausage and legislation. What one author called the dance of legislation is not a ballet.

Taxes, Conable's forte as the leading Republican on the powerful House Ways and Means Committee, seem arcane to many, but ultimately they boil down to who gets what and why. Conable reveled in the drama of getting there. He hated the familiar mantra, "If you have to explain anything, you're in trouble." To his constituents, colleagues, and journalists, he was a great explainer.

Conable wrote about the machinations of major tax measures in 1975, 1977, and 1981; trade and pension bills; the National Commission on Social Security Reform (of which he was a member); and the overall climate of the body politic on Capitol Hill. He never shied away from his personal, often partisan, views but captured the crazy quilt of politics: the bill is dead on Monday, revived on Tuesday, taking lethal flak on Wednesday, recovering on Thursday, a deal on Friday. Compromises or concessions that seemed impossible last week are this week's panacea.

The 1982–1983 Social Security Commission, led by Alan Greenspan, was a classic exercise. Conable thought a deal was critical for the solvency of the Social Security Trust Fund, but it seemed politically impossible, given the sensitivity of the issue and the differing priorities of the chief protagonists: President Ronald Reagan and House Speaker Thomas P. ("Tip") O'Neill agreed on little. In his journal, Conable pronounced the effort doomed on January 13, 1983. Two days later, he marveled at the political and personal dexterity and skill that produced a deal. Given the fiscal future America faces after the catastrophic COVID-19 pandemic, policy makers would do well to read this account.

Conable had an acute sense of the human dynamics of legislating, as well as an appreciation of his fellow politicians and the role the good ones played. He was particularly high on Republican representatives such as Minnesota's Bill Frenzel, Wisconsin's Bill Steiger, Ohio's Bill Gradison, and, earlier, John Byrnes of Wisconsin. He admired them not because they were fellow moderate-conservatives but because they were smart, serious legislators. Similarly, his disdain for a right-wing bomb thrower like Phil Crane of Illinois was based on the fact that Crane was a prancer, not a performer—"a waste of time."

Conable overrated the achievements of the often-heralded Wilbur Mills, Ways and Means chairman during Conable's first eight years on the committee (Mills enjoyed institutional powers that his successors did not have). And he chronicled the evolution of a successor chairman, Democrat Dan Rostenkowski of Illinois, from committee errand boy for Chicago's Mayor Daley to shrewd legislator—a politician from head to toe.

Here I digress to tell a story that Barber would have loved: A House-Senate conference committee was hammering out the two chambers' different versions of the historic 1986 tax reform bill, which cut rates, long sought by conservatives, and slashed loopholes, the dream of liberals. The conference leaders, Rostenkowski and Republican senator Bob Packwood of Oregon, agreed not to include anything that was not contained in one of the two versions of the bill. One day Packwood asked if he could slip in a very minor measure pertaining only to his home state. When the House chair thundered his objection, the senator backed down, explaining that it was just a favor for an old friend. Well, replied the wily Rosty, if that was the case, then it would be okay. The next day

Rosty got Packwood to accept a much larger extraneous measure, no doubt for an "old friend."

Conable had a knack for brilliantly sizing up his colleagues from the opposition. He showed a grudging affection for a political hack like Jimmy Burke of Massachusetts, who boasted that he voted for every appropriations bill and every tax cut and voted against every debt ceiling increase. When an incredulous Conable suggested that this was not entirely logical, Burke replied, "Do you think this place is on the level?" Conable did think so, and he admired those Democratic colleagues who thought so too: California's Jim Corman, Florida's Sam Gibbons, and Illinois' Abner Mikva, who possessed a "sparkling ability," according to Conable. In contrast, Ohio Democrat Wayne Hays, a power in the House, repulsed him: "His whole personality reeks of corruption." Sure enough, Hays was soon caught up in a scandal and forced out of office. Conable also understood the mediocrity of senior members such as Oregon's Al Ullman, Mills's successor as Ways and Means chairman, and ranking Republican Herman Schneebeli of Pennsylvania.

The president he dealt with most often was Richard Nixon. He never much liked Nixon personally but respected his intellect and backed many of his policies; one of those scorekeeping tabulations had him voting with the president more than any other member of Congress. Conable worried about Vietnam and the duplicity surrounding the war, but the retired marine colonel thought it would be a mistake to get out. (He was among the best and brightest who were mistaken about that.) On domestic issues, from taxes to revenue sharing to trade, he was with the administration. An exception was civil rights, which he consistently championed.

There are some gaps in Conable's journal, most notably involving Watergate and the Nixon impeachment, which dominated politics for a year and a half. In early 1973 he decried the break-in and some of the idiots surrounding the president. A year later there was hope among Republicans in Congress that Nixon might resign—Conable dismissed that possibility—and idle talk of contingency plans in case of impeachment. But, perhaps because it so pained him, he ignored the topic for long stretches in his journal.

I can fill in some gaps. While covering the Ways and Means Committee for the *Wall Street Journal*, I talked to Conable constantly. Initially these conversations were mostly about legislation, but as 1973 advanced, Watergate loomed more and more. I was convinced that if it ever came to impeachment, Conable would be one of the most influential Republicans in the House on the issue. Foolishly, I misplaced the notes from those interviews. Some were short discussions in the committee room; others were longer sessions in the Speaker's lobby off the House floor. Best of all were our conversations in his office, where he loved to show off his latest Native American arrowheads or his doodles, which were so good that President Reagan requested one. He would tell stories about his district and talk a lot about taxes, Washington politics, and, increasingly, Watergate.

By the late summer of 1973, he knew the Watergate scandal had enveloped the president. In the fall Nixon tapped Barber's friend Gerald Ford, the House GOP leader, as vice president. Still, as Conable told Ford, the key was for Nixon to lay Watergate to rest, admit his mistakes, and move on. By the start of 1974, there was escalating concern. Barber told me—during background conversations—that Nixon was a crook and deceptive to the core. He thought Nixon was going to bring down the Republican Party with him.

Conable had a kind of neoromantic view of his party as personifying small-town, Main Street values and as being the pillar of rectitude. He knew there were exceptions, but the Democrats—excluding his friends—were the party of big-city machines and southern courthouse politics and corruption. Nixon was changing that view, and it infuriated him. (Conable disliked fund-raising and paying homage to special interests; only in the Watergate-infected campaign of 1974 did he hold fund-raisers at $35 a head.) Yet he feared that impeaching a president for the first time in more than a hundred years could set a dangerous precedent and inflict great harm on a nation already divided by Vietnam and a souring economy. Somehow, he thought we would muddle through it, but that gave him no pleasure.

By late spring, there was a sense—although he would not say it—that Conable was moving closer to accepting the inevitable impeachment declaration while hoping against hope that it would go away. He repeatedly said that it had to be bipartisan, and both the Senate Watergate panel and the House Judiciary Committee were moving that way. The reservations were cracking.

I spent time early that summer covering the Judiciary Committee and was writing a story about who the central figures would be when an impeachment bill came to the House. At the top of that list was Conable because it seemed clear that a dozen or so Republicans and perhaps a few Democrats would look to him for guidance. In the end, of course, it never came to that because Nixon was forced to resign.

I must tell one minor anecdote to set the record straight. In early August, when the so-called smoking gun came out showing the president's complicity, Conable wrote that he told ABC correspondent Sam Donaldson that the "only issue is the orderly transfer of power" to Jerry Ford. He first told me that same thing in the Speaker's lobby with a mixture of anger and relief. I remember nervously running up the stairs to call the Dow Jones business wire with the news that Nixon was through. But of course, ABC carried a lot more weight than the Dow Jones ticker.

Conable never spoke to Nixon again and was uncharacteristically bitter: "No man did more damage to my enjoyment of public service than Richard Nixon. I hate the bastard. I just hate him."

Conable's journal reflects the different perspectives from the Capitol and from the White House; the distance is far greater than those sixteen blocks on Pennsylvania Avenue. Conable worked with five presidents. He had little to say about Lyndon Johnson. The other four, viewed with varying degrees of respect, all appeared to be out of touch, listening to a cacophony of voices and depending, for better or worse, on nonelected staff. He had great admiration for Reagan's chief of staff Jim Baker, but much less for most of the others. His criticisms of Jerry Ford and George H. W. Bush were based on supportive concern. His first vote in 1965 had been to dump Charles Halleck of Indiana, the incumbent House Republican leader, in favor of Ford. But he often questioned the legislative and political strategies of the presidents he served. Sometimes he was right, but sometimes he was just seeing the issue from his side of Pennsylvania Avenue.

He was taken with the elder Bush the moment he arrived in the House, two years after Conable. He saw a future leader, maybe a future president. When Bush was running in the Republican primaries in 1979, however, he thought it was not going well. "So far he has caught on only like a tame fire," Conable worried in his journal. In addition to Ronald Reagan, Bush was running against Senate Republican leader Howard Baker of Tennessee; Bob Dole of Kansas, the vice-presidential candidate four years earlier; and former Texas governor and treasury secretary John Connally, a Democrat turned Republican. In that heavyweight field, Bush was the runner-up and impressive enough to become Reagan's vice president.

Conable saw Jimmy Carter as exceptionally bright but in over his head as president. When the president proposed a luxury tax on yachts forty feet or larger, Conable asked him, "Do you know how many thirty-nine-and-a-half-feet yachts will be built?" Conable was a man of genuine decency, and only rarely did a mean or petty streak surface. For instance, after riding on Air Force One, he complained about the food, blaming it on Carter's ineptitude.

Reagan perplexed him more than the others. He supported most of the president's policies on taxes and trade, while occasionally chafing at his lurches to the right. He thought Reagan was lazy but had a good mind "sealed inside an envelope of anecdotes." Pessimism about a second Reagan term was a factor in his retirement. Conable was relatively young (sixty-two) and at the peak of his influence. He was worn down, however, by perpetually being in the minority, with no end in sight. He knew there were prestigious academic opportunities and lucrative corporate opportunities available to him.

I was sure he would return to public life. In the noblest sense, Barber was a patriot. In 1942, immediately upon graduating from Cornell University, he joined the Marine Corps and fought in the Pacific. The scars of Iwo Jima never left him. After the war, he got his law degree, practiced for a while, and reenlisted during the Korean War. After practicing law, he fell in love with public service and spent two years in the New York senate before being elected to Congress. He would have been a good choice to become Reagan's treasury secretary until Jim Baker took the job. The State and Defense Departments were set, and few other positions were commensurate with his considerable skills.

A year and a half later, in a surprise move, Conable was named president of the World Bank, despite having no financial or business background. In typical fashion, he threw himself into the job, traveling the world with his wife, Charlotte—a women's studies scholar—to understand the needs in developing nations. Five years later, he left to rave reviews. The liberal *Guardian* newspaper wrote that this conservative politician had taken the bank "by the scruff of the neck, totally reorganised its often sclerotic bureaucracy and persuaded the US Congress to double the amounts the bank could disburse to developing nations." Millions of struggling poor people around the globe were the beneficiaries.

But Conable's congressional legacy is his most profound accomplishment, and that is why his journal is so valuable. I cannot think of a single member who served entirely in the minority with such a large a presence. The journal illuminates his intellect, his commitment, and his appreciation of principled pragmatism. He never compromised his integrity but never considered compromise a dirty word. The perfect should not be the enemy of the good. As a Republican in a Democratic-run House, sometimes the good he sought could not be achieved. He would gripe to colleagues, to reporters, and in his journal. But he would bounce back. In our many conversations, one of his favorite expressions was not to get caught up "in the passions of the moment." A policy intellectual, he had a zest for his job. He would sometimes grab associates—and reporters—by the lapels and get right in their faces, almost like Lyndon Johnson did.

Because Conable took governance so seriously, he could be pompous. After one successful forum, he wrote that he was "swelling up like a self-important toad and croaking like a frog." Some thought him arrogant; he was smarter than most, and he knew it. But I have never spent time with a more thoughtful and generous politician. He championed public financing of congressional campaigns not only because he hated soliciting contributions and the conflicts this might raise but also because it was a distraction from representative government.

In our many conversations he would occasionally pick my brain on politics or even try to elicit a little gossip. I covered the 1976 and 1980 presidential campaigns, and he was curious about Carter and Reagan; in the early summer of 1980 he asked if I thought Bush should be Reagan's running mate. But this was a very one-sided process; I learned far more from him than he did from me. Around the office, reporters would ask me, "What does HR think?"—a reference to "highly respected," a cliché I used too often in describing Conable. I cherished our many conversations.

I think he would be miserable in today's Washington, out of sorts with the mainstream of his party, uncomfortable with a sham legislative process, and horrified that a man like Donald Trump could occupy the White House. Politics goes in cycles, and maybe someday we will see his like again.

When he left Congress in 1984, his service and contributions were praised by fellow New Yorker, Senator Daniel Patrick Moynihan: "Some men meet standards, others set them. Barber Conable has been one of the others."

Albert R. Hunt

Acknowledgments

Jane Conable Schmieder's question, "Well, whaddaya think?" got this project rolling. Without her initiative, it would not have happened. I thank her and her siblings—Anne (whose spelunking through the family scrapbooks provided the photos for this book), Emily, and Sam—for entrusting me with their father's journal.

Bob Merry and Al Hunt were sources of great assistance and encouragement; David Congdon saw the book's potential. Jim Fleming's fine biography of Mr. Conable stands as an essential companion to this work. Scott Alexander Wood smoothed the process of transferring photos from the family scrapbooks to this book. Cindy Hagelberger of the Alfred C. O'Connell Library went above and beyond, as did Isobel Ellis of the *National Journal*. The support of the Dirksen Congressional Center made possible the index. I am also grateful to Linda McLaughlin for her cheerful assistance in identifying transcriptionists and to Ellen Parker for her comradeship in a long ago summer. The staffers who typed these journals are the unsung heroes of the project: in addition to Linda McLaughlin, profuse and very belated thanks to Joanne Burton, Joanne Peartree, Marian Wallace, Sigi Woolbert, Sharon Wells, Dorothy Maneri, Mary Matthews, Marci McDonald, Janet Klinger, Susan Morris, Sue Connolly, and Lynn Smith. If I have missed anyone, please let me know and I'll right that wrong in the paperback edition!

As always, my wife, Lucine, our daughter, Gretel, and my parents, Joe and Sandy, were my anchorage and my delight. Finally, I owe a debt of gratitude to the late Richard Fenno, my professor, mentor, and friend, who chaired the selection committee that sent me to Washington in the summer of 1979 as an intern for Barber Conable. In 1981 Professor Fenno's letter of recommendation was, I am certain, critical in securing my position on the staff of Senator Daniel Patrick Moynihan. In ways subtle and profound, his assistance changed my life. Richard Fenno died on April 21, 2020, as I was writing this introduction. Like Barber Conable, he was the best of the breed.

Editor's Introduction

Barber Benjamin Conable, Jr., was "as highly and widely respected as any member of Congress in the last half of the twentieth century," according to Richard Fenno, the late dean of congressional scholars and author of the classic *Home Style: House Members in Their Districts*.[1]

Conable was a rectitudinous rural intellectual of the sort once produced by the muck-spattered gentry. He grew up reciting Browning and Gray with his father as they milked the cows. He was a small-town lawyer and a youthful pacifist who enlisted in the Marine Corps and fought at Iwo Jima, yet he never exploited his heroism for political gain. Though he served twenty years (1965–1985) in the US House of Representatives, Conable was so deeply rooted in his district that he became the avatar of rural western New York.

A Republican pragmatist with a localist streak, Conable was a self-described "Jeffersonian" and "decentralist" who nevertheless believed strongly in the two-party system.[2] He was the ranking Republican on the Ways and Means Committee during the Carter administration and Reagan's first term, his party's spokesman on tax policy, and a father of Nixon-era revenue sharing. Although he would solidify his reputation as a moderate Republican, mostly for his support of the Equal Rights Amendment and various civil rights measures, Conable was parsimonious on budgetary matters and a relatively strict constructionist with respect to the Constitution. Unshakably honest, Conable refused campaign contributions greater than $50, joking that he could be "bought cheaper" than anyone in Congress.[3]

For seventeen of his years in the House, Barber Conable kept a journal in which he recorded his thoughts, actions, opinions, and doubts. He spoke this commentary into a Dictaphone while driving to and from Capitol Hill and also on the long drive between Washington, DC, and his home in Alexander, New York. Comprising upward of 400,000 words, Conable's journal is literate,

1. Richard F. Fenno, Jr., *Home Style: House Members in Their Districts* (Boston: Little, Brown, 1978).

2. Barber B. Conable, Jr., *Congress and the Income Tax* (Norman: University of Oklahoma Press, 1989), 105.

3. Brooks Jackson, "Lawmakers' Success with Fund Dinners Hinges on Lobbyists," *Wall Street Journal*, February 25, 1982.

searching, ruminative, brutally frank, self-lacerating, sometimes amusing, some-times dripping with asperity. There are no advertisements for himself therein, nor is there a hint of self-aggrandizement. The journal is a unique entry on the sparsely populated shelf of congressional diaries, containing the impressions of a very bright, hardworking, conscientious representative surrounded by some men and women of talent and quality, some dullards, some blowhards, and on every side overweening ambition.

This is how Congress works, or how it worked from the late 1960s through the mid-1980s. We read about the hashing out of differences, the personalizing of conflicts, the workhorses and the showhorses. We learn, from an angle of vi-sion not found in any civics text (is there such a thing as a civics text anymore?), how a bill becomes (or does not become) a law.

The journal includes keenly drawn portraits of the lions of both the House and the Senate of his era: Daniel Patrick Moynihan, with whom Conable had a relationship of mutual admiration and occasional exasperation; John Anderson, who exhausted Conable's initial admiration; Jack Kemp, whom Conable never admired (you can almost see him roll his eyes and sigh ruefully whenever the frenetic Kemp makes an appearance); longtime Ways and Means Committee chairman Wilbur Mills, the shrewd Arkansan whose slow-motion dissolution ended in embarrassing scandal; and a cast of hundreds. Conable is thoroughly bipartisan in his evaluations. There are both Republicans (Bill Frenzel of Min-nesota, Bill Steiger of Wisconsin) and Democrats (Abner Mikva of Illinois, Jim Corman of California, Richard Bolling of Missouri) whom he esteems through-out, and there are others—Democrat Sam Gibbons of Florida is a particularly interesting case—whom Conable comes to value only after extended exposure.

He draws incisive portraits and issues candid assessments of the Republican presidents with whom he worked. Conable endorsed his home-state governor Nelson Rockefeller for the Republican nomination in 1968, considering Rich-ard Nixon "a plate of warmed-over hash," yet, to his mortification, he became a key Nixon ally.[4] His support of Nixon, he told me, was due to the president's "decentralist" bent, as evidenced by his promotion of revenue sharing (discussed extensively in these pages), but Conable's later disillusionment was severe and irrevocable. He refused to answer Nixon's postpresidential missives and spoke harshly of his dishonesty.

We follow Gerald Ford in these pages from his position as House minority leader to the vice presidency (Betty Ford blamed Conable for her husband's

4. Conable Journal, July 19, 1968.

ascension) and then the presidency. Conable supported Ford over Ronald Reagan for the 1976 GOP nomination, and he would consistently underestimate Reagan's political appeal and prospects—the wish perhaps being father to the thought. He was chairman of the national steering committee for his former Ways and Means colleague George H. W. Bush's 1980 presidential campaign, and Conable's excitement at Bush's selection as Reagan's running mate was palpable. Bush's failure as vice president to assume a more forceful role as a voice of moderation disappointed Conable, and their relationship would suffer a break in later years when Bush was president of the United States and Conable was president of the World Bank, a post to which Reagan appointed him in 1986. Conable would say of Bush, "He thought I should be supporting an American agenda; I thought I was there to help the poor people. So I got the reputation of not being a team player, and that was the one thing George wouldn't stand for."[5]

Barber Benjamin Conable, Jr., was born November 2, 1922, in Warsaw, New York, a village of 4,400 and the seat of Wyoming County, where cows have long outnumbered people. A collateral ancestor, Samuel Conable, Jr., had settled in Warsaw in 1817, eventually building a woolen manufactory. Samuel's mother, Sarah, was the daughter of Thomas Crafts, one of the "True Born Sons of Liberty" and both a participant in and a supplier of the Mohawk dress for the Boston Tea Party. Samuel Sr. and Sarah bore the surname Cunnabell, which the subsequent generation shortened.[6]

Samuel Jr.'s brother, Rufus Conable, and Rufus's wife, Sophia, made the trek from New England to western New York in 1821. Rufus was a farmer and tavern keeper; his son Benjamin Barber Conable farmed and was a partner in a lumber and building materials company with, among others, Augustus Frank, a Civil War–era Republican congressman from Warsaw and an influential promoter of the Thirteenth Amendment.[7]

In the next generation of what had become one of the leading families of Wyoming County, Barber Benjamin Conable, Sr., would graduate from Cornell University in 1901, receive his law degree from New York University, and

5. "N.Y. Rep. Barber B. Conable Jr. Dies," *Washington Post*, December 2, 2003.

6. For a genealogy of the Conable family, see Anita Ripstein, "The Conables of Wyoming County," *Historical Wyoming* 30, 3 (January 1984): 57–67.

7. Michael Vorenberg, *Final Freedom: The Civil War, the Abolition of Slavery, and the Thirteenth Amendment* (New York: Cambridge University Press, 2001), 183.

set up practice in the village of Warsaw. He married Agnes Gouinlock, who bore three sons, the youngest being Barber Benjamin Conable, Jr. In 1923 Barber Sr. was elected Wyoming County judge. He would serve in that position for twenty-eight years—the longest tenure in the history of the county until it was surpassed by his son John, who was elected to succeed his father in 1951 and did not leave office until thirty-two years later. (Barber's eldest brother, William Gouinlock Conable, was an attorney and Buffalo-area civil rights activist who died in 1966.) The Conable family lived, appositely, on Jefferson Street.

Young Barber hated his forename. He was teased by classmates with an old nursery rhyme:

> Barber, barber, shave a pig!
> How many hairs will make a wig?
> Four and twenty that's enough
> Give the Barber a pinch of snuff.

Still, its distinctiveness would come in handy for the candidate. During Barber's first congressional race, a barbershop quartet of young women sang for him, and even late into his career, some of his less attentive constituents were sure they were represented by a nice lady named Barbara.

Conable's native Warsaw had been singed by the fires of what became known to historians as the "burned-over district" of upstate New York, a hotbed of numerous reform movements in antebellum America. The Conable family was touched by those flames. In 1839 Warsaw hosted a convention of the New York Anti-Slavery Society that laid the groundwork for the formation of the abolitionist Liberty Party; Warsaw-based Seth Gates and Augustus Frank were among the most ardent abolitionists in Congress. Coincidentally, Barber Jr.'s daughter Jane Conable Schmieder practiced law with partner Charlotte Smallwood-Cook—who was married to Barber's cousin Ned Smallwood (the small-town web is tangled)—in the two-story Italian villa–style residence that had once been the home of Congressman Frank. Barber's mother and his grandmother, Margaret Gouinlock, were suffragists; his grandmother was a close friend of Susan B. Anthony's. "So I came by [my feminism] honestly," he said. "I wasn't just being a milquetoast for my wife's enthusiasm."[8]

---

8. Bill Kauffman, *Dispatches from the Muckdog Gazette: A Mostly Affectionate Account of a Small Town's Fight to Survive* (New York: Henry Holt, 2003), 111.

Barber Sr. drilled his boys in the fundamentals of civic and personal responsibility, although his lessons were leavened with a dollop of agrarian eccentricity. Barber Jr. recalled that his father recited Walter Scott's *The Lady of the Lake* and other verses from memory while milking the cows: "My father thought it was good for a young man's character to have to clean out the stables. Our cows used to give better to iambic pentameter. They were the most productive cows in Wyoming County."[9]

Barber Jr. attended Cornell, where he majored in medieval history and helped organize the antiwar America First Committee. Like his father, he was a pacifist who opposed US involvement in foreign wars. Among his notable America First classmates at Cornell was future novelist Kurt Vonnegut, who in later years "used to lobby me about getting more deductions for authors."[10] (Even socialists prefer their taxes to be as low as possible.)

Conable graduated from Cornell in 1942 at the age of nineteen, enlisted (over his father's "bitter" objections) in the Marine Corps as a private, and went ashore at Iwo Jima as a second lieutenant on February 19, 1945, his father's birthday.[11] He told biographer James Fleming that he remembered thinking, as he landed on the beach at the base of Mount Suribachi, "My God, I'm going to be killed on my father's birthday." He suffered not even a scratch.[12] After the war, Conable earned a law degree at Cornell, serving as editor of the *Cornell Law Review* and graduating first in his class.

Following Conable's unhappy stint with a prestigious Buffalo law firm (he "hated" corporate tax law[13]) and an eighteen-month detour as a Stateside intelligence officer during the Korean War, he and his new bride, Charlotte Williams, a Buffalo native and Cornell graduate, moved to Batavia, New York, twenty miles north of Warsaw. Batavia, the seat of Genesee County, was a burg of just

9. Laurie Bennett, "Before There Was an Attica, There Was a Judge Conable," *Rochester (NY) Times-Union*, January 7, 1984.

10. Bill Kauffman's interview with Barber B. Conable, Jr., March 9, 1999. See also Bill Kauffman, "The Power Broker Who Came Home," *American Enterprise* 10, 6 (November 1999).

11. Conable interview, March 9, 1999.

12. James S. Fleming, *Window on Congress: A Congressional Biography of Barber B. Conable Jr.* (Rochester, NY: University of Rochester Press, 2004), 30. Conable said he was one of two Iwo Jima veterans to serve in Congress; the other was Richard C. White (D-TX). Conable Journal, February 19, 1970.

13. Fleming, *Window on Congress*, 38.

xxii Editor's Introduction

under 18,000 souls. Brother John had been elected judge in neighboring Wyoming County, and Barber "wasn't about to put myself in the position where all my life I'd have to practice in my brother's court."[14]

The newcomer jumped into civic affairs as if he were auditioning for a role in a Sinclair Lewis novel. He was active in the Boy Scouts, the United Fund, the Chamber of Commerce, and, critically, the Rotary Club. In short order he was named to the Republican city committee, and "within three months I was selected chairman of the city committee because nobody wanted it."[15]

After Barber and Charlotte bought a circa-1830 hybrid Federal–Greek Revival home in Alexander, a town south of Batavia, he agreed to serve as Genesee County campaign chairman in the 1960 election. Two years later he refused to reprise his role. "I won't be campaign chairman if that old bastard Austin Erwin is on the ticket," he told party chairman Jim Beach, "because he's a crook." Beach warned Conable that he would be throwing away his career if he challenged Erwin, the powerful chairman of the state senate's Finance Committee. Conable, with the support of the *Batavia Daily News* and "a bunch of young punks from the Republican committee," tossed his hat in the ring.[16] In announcing his candidacy in April 1962 he explained: "I consider myself a conservative, and while I acknowledge that no governmental problem is simple, I can generally be expected to favor that course which encourages responsibility in our localities, rather than vesting additional power in our distant seats of government." He also pledged "not to use my public position for private gain."[17]

Erwin backed down from the challenge, and Conable was elected to the state senate after routing an Erwin protégé in the GOP primary. In his maiden race, Conable won 329 of the 346 votes cast in Alexander—a ringing endorsement from his neighbors.

Two years later, in the teeth of Barry Goldwater's landslide defeat in the presidential race, Conable was easily elected to the US House of Representatives, succeeding GOP backbencher Harold Ostertag. Barber Conable distinguished himself almost immediately by reviving a practice that was seemingly as dead as the peruke and the snuffbox: writing one's own newsletter to constituents. He explained: "In Kierkegaard's phrase, you try to get to a truth that's true for

14. Bennett, "Before There Was an Attica."
15. Conable interview, March 9, 1999.
16. Conable interview, March 9, 1999.
17. "Batavia Attorney Announces Candidacy for State Senator Opposing Long-Term Official," *Batavia (NY) Daily News*, April 17, 1962.

you. That's particularly true in politics. One way to have an unsuccessful political career is to imitate somebody. So I tried to develop my own formula, and it involved writing my own newsletter, which I did every three weeks and wrote every word of it myself."[18] Conable sent these newsletters not to everyone in his district, as is typical, but only to those "who were interested in Congress" and had requested to be placed on the mailing list. At its peak, these numbered about 30,000 recipients.[19] Senator Daniel Patrick Moynihan (D-NY) once said that he admired Conable above all members of Congress in part because of Conable's newsletters, which contained none of the usual self-promoting guff. They were pedagogical, introspective, even confessional. (Moynihan tried to emulate Conable in this respect, but he lacked the discipline.)

The new congressman also cut a distinctive profile in his fund-raising practices. As early as 1966 he proposed to cap congressional campaign spending at ten cents per constituent, which would have meant about $45,000 per candidate.[20] He set a strict $50 limit on donations to his own campaigns because he was appalled by the contributions-for-favors relationship between lobbyists and some members of the Ways and Means Committee. Conable's interest in campaign finance reform eventually led him to assume the leadership of the small GOP faction that supported the public financing of congressional candidates' campaigns. His Republican critics noted that Conable had no need for a large war chest because he had only one difficult race in his entire career: in the Watergate-tainted year of 1974, when feisty Rochester vice mayor Margaret "Midge" Costanza made an energetic and well-financed but ultimately unsuccessful run against him (she outspent Conable nearly two to one).

Barber Conable joined the House Ways and Means Committee in 1967 in his second term. He was widely regarded as a promising young man and was labeled a moderate, although that limp term does not do justice to Conable's blend of fiscal frugality, institutional reformism, burned-over district social liberalism, hardheaded realism, solicitude for Main Street, constitutional federalism,

18. Conable interview, March 9, 1999. Congressman Morris K. Udall (D-AZ), whom Conable admired, apparently also wrote his own newsletters. See *Education of a Congressman: The Newsletters of Morris K. Udall* (Indianapolis: Bobbs-Merrill, 1972). Others who followed this outdated practice included Senator Paul Simon (D-IL) and Congressman John J. Duncan, Jr. (R-TN).

19. James S. Fleming, "The House Member as Teacher: An Analysis of the Newsletters of Barber B. Conable, Jr.," *Congress and the Presidency* 20, 1 (Spring 1993): 55.

20. Fleming, "House Member as Teacher," 67.

xxiv Editor's Introduction

and strong preference for local and voluntaristic solutions rather than top-down programs. He insisted that "the Republican Party is a middle class and not a business party."[21] Very quickly he became a leader of the free-trade bloc in a party that, in its pre-Reagan incarnation, retained a substantial and traditionally Republican protectionist wing. He would serve his entire career as a member of the minority party in the House, a source of discouragement for him, especially under the Ways and Means chairmanship of Dan Rostenkowski (D-IL), whom Conable regarded as a wily politician but a petty man and a bully.

In *Federalist*, no. 52, James Madison wrote that a member of the US House of Representatives should have "an intimate sympathy" with the people he represents. Conable, by dint of lineage, upbringing, and disposition, had an almost mystical connection to his district—in particular to its rural and small-town inhabitants.

Political scientist Richard Fenno, who disguised Conable as "Congressman H" in *Home Style*, grasped his placedness right from the start. They met in November 1964, when Fenno, a professor at the University of Rochester, was on assignment for the *New York Times Magazine* to profile newly elected representatives. (The magazine, which Gore Vidal called the mausoleum of American prose, killed the piece.) Conable explained his politics at their first meeting: "We're all decentralists up here. We don't trust the big cities and the impersonal government way off somewhere. We like our local institutions."[22]

Traveling with Conable in the spring of 1970, as he was researching what became *Home Style*, Fenno discerned the congressman's essence: "From the time we spent driving through the district during that first visit, I picked up something more basic and more permanent—his attachment to a place—and to the values and practices of that place." As Conable drove Fenno from the city of Rochester, whose western edge made up about one-third of his district, into the countryside, he spoke of what home meant to him. Fenno writes:

> His comment to me about his identification with the rural people of his district was almost poetic in nature, because it came just as we left the four-lane superhighway . . . and turned onto the two-lane road to (small town) Byron. . . . Suddenly, he said, "It must be terrible to be without roots, without a place to

21. Conable Journal, February 5, 1975.

22. Richard F. Fenno, *The Challenge of Congressional Representation* (Cambridge, MA: Harvard University Press, 2013), 17. See also Bill Kauffman, "When Richard Met Barber," June 17, 2013, www.frontporchrepublic.com.

call home. I have a profound sense of identification with these rural people. . . . I worry about the rootlessness of our people, about the changes that are taking place in our values which were, after all, pretty durable." Soon, he brightened and said, "It won't be long now. Here are the Byron suburbs! Those are Gerald Britt's beets growing over there. He grows 3 percent of all the edible beets in the United States."[23]

Conable had an aw-shucks side, but it was authentic, not a politician's calculating put-on. Fenno writes: "During my first visit Conable displayed another personal behavior pattern that distinguished him from every elective politician I would ever know. It was a distinctiveness related partly to shared rural, small-town values/expectations and partly to his self-confidence in connecting with his constituents. Not once in all our time together did a staff person accompany us—not in the car and not at any event."[24]

Though popular, Conable was never completely comfortable in those parts of his district encompassing the city of Rochester and its suburbs. He explained:

> In the urban area, I'm a captive of the party. I go to rallies and stand up and make platitudinous pro-party solidarity statements. I'm not allowed to be independent, to be myself. People in the rural areas wouldn't be satisfied with this. They expect whole relationships with people, not fragmentary relationships the way city people do. I like whole relationships, and that's why I do so much better in the rural area than in the urban area.[25]

"I'm a country boy and Rochester is a sophisticated enclave," he once said to me, wink in eye and tongue in cheek. This habitue of the opera and the theater, this reciter of poetry—not doggerel—from memory, this avid listener of Schubert, Mozart, Haydn, Verdi, and Beethoven was no slack-jawed yokel.[26]

As the years went by, the plaudits for Barber Conable piled up. A *National Journal* profile remarked: "House members, lobbyists and journalists speak admiringly of him, more because of his intellectual brilliance than because of his expertise."[27] Bob Woodward and Carl Bernstein wrote in *The Final Days*, "he

---

23. Fenno, *Challenge of Congressional Representation*, 24.

24. Fenno, *Challenge of Congressional Representation*, 27.

25. Fenno, *Home Style*, 156.

26. Stephen Wigler, "Conable, the Music Man," *Rochester (NY) Democrat and Chronicle*, July 17, 1981.

27. Quoted in Edward C. Burks, "Republicans Turning to Conable as Their Spokesman in Congress," *New York Times*, January 21, 1978.

was regarded by his colleagues as almost puritanical in his standards of personal and political conduct, a man of unquestioned integrity."[28] George Will concluded, "There has never been a better congressman."[29]

Conable declined to seek reelection in 1984, for reasons explained later, but he never gave a thought to stepping into the meretricious role of lobbyist. He said:

> Now why would I stick around Washington? That's what many of my colleagues do: they stay there and practice law or lobby. . . . And that's one of the most foolish things in the world. There's nothing deader than a dead politician. I recall my dear friends Wilbur Mills and Al Ullman coming to lobby me after they had gone to their rewards one way or another, and I would duck into doorways to avoid them because they would be asking me for things that I knew they didn't believe in. They were pure mercenaries.[30]

The "toughest job" he turned down, he said, was an endowed chair at Harvard in the Kennedy School of Government. "I seriously considered that for a long time, and finally I said to my wife, 'You know, here I am, sixty-one years old. I was asked to buy a very expensive house in a Boston suburb, get a great big mortgage, buck a whole new traffic pattern, establish a whole new set of friends, start on a whole new career I don't know whether I'd be any good at.'" A year and a half later he was offered the presidency of the World Bank. It was, he said, an "opportunity to be useful on a global level . . . so I did accept that."[31]

Upon leaving the World Bank in 1991 after a single five-year term, Conable returned home to Alexander, although he remained active as chairman of the executive committee of the Board of Regents of the Smithsonian Institution and as chairman of the National Committee on US-China Relations. For the next dozen years he moved seamlessly between worlds: one night he might be chairing the Smithsonian board, and the next night he and Charlotte might be discussing how much to spend on toner cartridges with fellow members of the Holland Purchase Historical Society—the "Hysterical Society," they jokingly called it. Conable manned the cash box at the society's annual yard sale. As museum director Patrick Weissend joked to him, Conable was qualified for this job by virtue of having been "a teller at the World Bank."[32]

28. Bob Woodward and Carl Bernstein, *The Final Days* (New York: Simon & Schuster, 1976), 154.

29. George Will, "An American House of Lords," *Newsweek*, June 4, 1984.

30. Conable interview, March 9, 1999.

31. Conable interview, March 9, 1999.

32. Patrick Weissend, Holland Land Office Museum newsletter, December 2, 2003.

By his count, Conable gave ten to fifteen talks a year on local history and culture. They were witty, informative, extemporaneous, and, of course, gratis. By long tradition he continued to read the Declaration of Independence every Fourth of July at the Genesee Country Village and Museum (upstate New York's Williamsburg). Most Saturday mornings, he kept his date for "coffee with the boys" at Genesee Hardware, as he had since 1952. Proprietor Karl Buchholtz had long ago propelled him into the Batavia Rotary Club. He also planted 187 varieties of trees on the three acres behind his home in Alexander. "I'm a tree hugger," he confessed.[33]

The last time I saw Barber Conable, he spoke plaintively about the ephemeral nature of his legislative accomplishments, likening them to footprints on a sandy beach, washed away by the tide, with nary a sign that they had ever been there. His most lasting achievement, he said with bemusement, seemed to be his authorship of the provision in the 1978 tax bill that effectively legalized home brewing and made him the legislative father of the microbrewery revolution. Conable never mentioned this in his journal, and when two journalists asked him about it a quarter century later, he said simply, "I did not consider it a big deal."[34]

Barber Conable died on November 30, 2003. Charlotte passed in 2013. The Conable plot is adjacent to a pasture in the western verge of the Alexander Village Cemetery, on whose board of trustees Barber served. "He wanted the Schmieder cows to come to his funeral," said his daughter Emily. The couple is commemorated with a black marble bench on which is incised the message "Reach Out!"

Every May the village of Alexander is brilliant with the flowering crab apple trees that line its streets. These were a gift from Barber Conable. As his daughter Jane explained, "He loved Alexander. He was so enormously attached to that place as his home that he wanted to give it a beautiful gift and pay it back, at the same time making it more beautiful with its own special identity."[35]

---

33. Rebecca Borders and C. C. Dockery, *Beyond the Hill: A Directory of Congress from 1984 to 1993* (Lanham, MD: University Press of America, 1995), 79.

34. Patrick Flanagan and Rick Armon, "Toast Barber Conable for the Homebrewing Boom," *Rochester (NY) Democrat and Chronicle*, August 27, 2002.

35. Howard B. Owens, "Alexander's Crabapples in Bloom, a Legacy Gift to the Village from Barber Conable," May 11, 2015, thebatavian.com.

In 1968 Congressman Conable began to keep a journal that was a more personal, much franker version of his newsletters. I shan't spoil the insights and revelations to come, but I will note what is not included here. Though he began the journal in 1968, he didn't really hit his stride until 1969.[36] I think it took him a while to get used to using a Dictaphone. As a result, the excerpt from 1968 is very brief, limited to his assessments of Ways and Means chairman Wilbur Mills (D-AR); John Byrnes (R-WI), the ranking Republican on the Ways and Means Committee; and George H. W. Bush (R-TX), who impressed Conable and figures prominently in later entries. Likewise, the 1984 entry is spare, for he commented very little during his final year in Congress. He was tired; twenty years was quite enough.

Removing redundant material was hardly sufficient to pare this journal down from its original 400,000-plus words to a publishable length. So I have excised accounts of Conable's foreign travel and, because these subjects were not within his legislative bailiwick, cut most of his occasional comments on foreign and military affairs. In this regard, he was something of a Kissingerian realist, an advocate of trade with the Soviet bloc, and an unenthusiastic supporter of the war in Vietnam, despite his pacifist beginnings. He took pride in being able to speak Japanese and occasionally visited the Japanese embassy. Likewise, I have largely omitted remarks about local politics and accounts of the decennial wrangling over redistricting. I have retained some of his dismissive comments about Frank Horton, the time-serving fifteen-term Republican congressman from the adjoining district, whose absence of principle would frustrate Conable for the duration of his service. Horton was useful, however, as a negative example: the kind of congressman Conable would not, and could not, be.

Perhaps someday the full journal will be available online. In the meantime, those interested can consult these volumes in the Rare and Manuscript Collections at Cornell University in Ithaca, New York.

On April 29, 1975, after showing the Watergate-related portions of the journal to Bob Woodward and Carl Bernstein, Barber Conable wrote, "Perhaps I will have to be more careful about the way I write these entries, although it

---

36. For the record, Barber Conable kicked off these journals on March 13, 1968, with a discussion (not excerpted herein) of the Ways and Means Committee's hearings on the Johnson administration's proposed tax on international airline tickets—the so-called travel tax. The irrepressible Martha Griffiths (D-MI) blamed chairman Wilbur Mills for promoting this ultimately unsuccessful idea, saying that Mills "didn't have 100 people in the Little Rock district who were interested in travel anywhere."

would seem to me that the great value of them is in their candor and their honesty." Thankfully, he never became more circumspect.[37]

I was aware of the existence of Conable's journal; he had occasionally read excerpts to me, as he had to his biographer and to other guests. But when Jane Schmieder, one of the four Conable children, asked me in 2018 if I would like to be the first person to read it in its entirety, I jumped at the chance. We were delighted when David Congdon and the good folks at the University Press of Kansas agreed to its publication in edited form.

The typeface of the bound originals was too light, and there were too many scribbled editorial interpolations by Conable, to permit the pages to be scanned. So, during my second read-through, I retyped them from scratch, omitting repetitious and other material that obviously would not make the final cut. With the greatly appreciated assistance of Bob Merry, who covered the Ways and Means Committee in the Conable era for the *Wall Street Journal* before going on to serve as president and editor in chief of *Congressional Quarterly*, I carved the journal down to just over 150,000 words.

Mr. Conable dictated these entries, but he did not type them, nor did he divide them into paragraphs. Therefore, I felt free to break up what are, in the journal, often overly long paragraphs. I have corrected obvious typos and a handful of factual errors, regularized punctuation (one or two of his excellent transcriptionists had an aversion to the comma), and, in some instances, excised words or phrases he overused (for example, *completely*, *apparently*, and *of course*). Missing material within the text is denoted by ellipses, although, for the sake of readability, I have dispensed with ellipses at the beginning and end of paragraphs. I have checked and rechecked my transcription, but I take full responsibility for any elisions or mistakes.

Barber Conable seems to have envisioned from the start that his journal would someday be published, or at least made public. As early as April 5, 1968, before his first evaluation of his Ways and Means colleagues, he wrote that he made "such an analysis with some trepidation, confident that it will not be used until long after most of the people involved have left the scene."

37. Published congressional diaries are few and far between. One contemporaneous example is Donald Riegle's chatty and not overly revealing account of life in the House from April 1971 to March 1972. Riegle, a liberal Republican from Michigan, switched parties and was elected to the Senate in 1976 as a Democrat. He served three terms and left office under the cloud of the Keating Five scandal. See Donald Riegle with Trevor Armbrister, *O Congress* (Garden City, NY: Doubleday, 1972).

A dozen years later, he confided, "I am sure that this has been one of the few unique contributions of my service in Congress."[38] More than half a century after he first spoke into his Dictaphone, the extent of that contribution may finally be judged.

Each journal year begins with a paragraph set in sans-serif font in which I summarize the events of that year in Conable's congressional life. This is followed by italicized paragraphs providing a retrospective gloss. The journal entries begin after the writing hand glyph.

38. Conable Journal, February 12, 1980.

The Congressional Journal of
Barber B. Conable, Jr.,
1968–1984

In the only excerpt included from 1968, Conable makes the first of several assessments of his Ways and Means colleagues, evaluating Chairman Wilbur Mills (D-AR), ranking minority member John Byrnes (R-WI), and a promising freshman Republican named George H. W. Bush (R-TX). This entry was made on April 5, 1968, the day after the assassination of Martin Luther King, Jr. King's murder does not go unmentioned in the journal, nor does its most immediate legislative consequence: House passage on April 10 of the Fair Housing Act of 1968. Conable was one of seventy-seven House Republicans to support the bill, although he notes on April 9, "The sad thing [is that] I don't expect the bill will accomplish anything. It's typical open housing red herring, the problem being de facto economic segregation and not discriminatory segregation."

Barely a year into his membership on the Ways and Means Committee, Barber Conable offered tentative evaluations of the men and women with whom he served. He was dazzled by Chairman Mills—a judgment he would revise, gradually and then sharply, over the next six years. He was still feeling his way, shrugging over some of the less active members. Of Missouri Democrat Frank Karsten he observed, "I don't believe he would recognize me if he were to meet me." And he confessed that some colleagues, such as Republican Harold Collier of Illinois, are "hard for me to figure out."

Nevertheless, certain themes emerge that run throughout the journal. He was impatient with ideologues: he called Missourian Tom Curtis, the second-ranking Republican on the committee, "a man of considerable ability and high intelligence who reduces his effectiveness a great deal by the uncompromising and frequently academic positions he takes." He was dismissive of those who lacked diligence, contemptuous of those he regarded as demagogues (Democrats Jim Burke of Massachusetts and Charles Vanik of Ohio would never cease to disgust him), and he cut a break to the witty and independent-minded (e.g., Democrat Martha Griffiths of Michigan).

His dictated prose in this early entry lacks the felicity and ease, as well as the force and compactness of expression, of later entries, but hey, you try achieving a concinnity of spoken style while talking into a Dictaphone in Rock Creek Parkway traffic.

April 5, 1968

This might be the appropriate time, since I have not had the opportunity to do it previously, to review the makeup of the Ways and Means Committee and to discuss the personalities that comprise it. It is an excellent committee, but I must admit that the main reason for its excellence is the excellence of its leadership and not the individual members, many of whom are not diligent in their work or particularly perceptive in their understanding of the more technical aspects of the Ways and Means Committee's responsibilities.

Of course, first of all the Ways and Means Committee has to be understood in terms of the towering personality of Wilbur Mills. Wilbur Mills is treated by the president frequently as a petty, rural politician, and certainly the New York papers are in accord with this view, feeling that anyone who concerns himself with his constituency is somehow not fit to serve in a position of power in the Congress. Wilbur is particularly sensitive to his constituency. He is proud to consider himself one of them. His constituency is a provincial constituency, being mostly countryside in the vicinity of Little Rock, Arkansas. But Wilbur Mills is a man of tremendous mental power and a man of great character and certainly his stature and his contributions cannot be described as provincial in any sense. Although he is a graduate of Harvard Law School, Wilbur Mills, I should judge, is a man of narrow interests. He has traveled very rarely, as the papers constantly pointed out during our deliberations on the travel tax, and he tends to react to social pretension. He works constantly and worries about the quality of what he does. When he spoke at my request in the Rochester area in May of 1967 he did three complete and different versions of the speech he gave before he finally delivered it. It proved to be a thoughtful and detailed analysis of government fiscal policy.

Wilbur Mills has a very precise mind and a very detailed memory. He has been chairman of the Ways and Means Committee since 1958, I believe, and in that entire time there is nothing that has passed this committee or the Congress without it bearing his stamp of approval. Since he feels personally responsible for everything before the committee, he is very thorough in his analysis of it and in his study of the background of it before we ever get to the point of discussing specific legislation or the position the committee should take with respect to proposals made by the executive branch. His memory serves him in very good stead and he is frequently recalling with witnesses appearing before the committee what they said in 1961 or what we did in 1959 in respect to similar questions. He is a tactful man with a very strong tactical sense and a high degree of political sensitivity. Generally he votes the straight Democratic line, although he represents a southern constituency and frequently deviates on matters of civil rights and more volatile urban programs. He seeks and gets a fierce loyalty from members of his committee on both sides of the aisle, and frequently at election time takes steps to assure the reelection of Republican committee members as well as Democratic members.

Some of the less diligent Democrats resent the nature of his leadership, which leaves them quite helpless. They don't come to meetings regularly and so they are terribly dependent on his judgment. When he takes their support for granted and tries to seek consensus with the Republicans, they feel they are being neglected. In no case, however, are they really able to stand up to him effectively, and he knows quite properly that they will have to rely on his judgment all the way, as well as his sense of what is necessary in the form of compromise, in order to achieve the unanimous support of legislation, which Wilbur, being a consensus man, always desires.

I shudder to think what would happen to the committee if we suddenly had to rely on the leadership of one of the lesser Democrats, a man who is not aware of the historical development of the tax code or the rationale behind some of the complex areas of legislation in which we are asked to work. We are all terribly dependent on Wilbur Mills's personal judgment and his sense of personal responsibility.

John Byrnes is the ranking Republican. He comes from Green Bay, Wisconsin, and has been in the House of Representatives since the late 1940s.[1] A very fine looking man, he was the victim of polio and has a badly atrophied leg which nevertheless does not seem to have affected his personality. John is a popular member of the House and quite respected for his abilities. I think justly so. He has a close working relationship with Wilbur Mills, and these two seem to share a lively mutual respect, which is probably the primary factor responsible for the comparatively nonpolitical atmosphere of the committee. John would make an excellent chairman, although I think he would have to take a stronger line and provide a greater degree of leadership than he does as ranking minority member. He is as careful as Wilbur Mills and only slightly less patient. Although he has a nasal voice and a tendency to overgesture in speaking, he is nevertheless a very effective speaker largely because of the force of his intelligence. He has the reputation of being extremely conservative, but if this is so, I must be an extreme conservative myself because I find myself frequently in agreement with the point of view he expresses. Although he may have very strong feelings, John Byrnes

1. Byrnes took office with the 79th Congress in 1945.

has a tendency to temper his positions by a feeling of responsibility for what the committee does. For instance, he feels a stronger responsibility to get agreement with Wilbur Mills than other Republican members of the Ways and Means Committee feel. Frequently John does not take a clear or a strong position on matters where we have anticipated he would.

The last and most junior [Republican member] is George Bush of Texas, a freshman, but a man who has conducted himself so adroitly during his first term, including his wangling the first claim as a freshman on the Ways and Means Committee since 1904, that he has no opposition by the Democrats for reelection. This is an incredible thing for Texas, which, if it is a one-party state, is one party on the Democratic side. George and I have been the most regular in our attendance since 1966 of any members of the committee, with the exception of Wilbur Mills and John Byrnes. George is extremely bright, a Phi Beta Kappa from Yale and the son of Prescott Bush, a former senator from Connecticut. He was for several years president of Zapata Off-Shore Oil and came to Congress with impeccable credentials as a businessman. He will obviously be a leader of our party and a leader of his state.

In his early forties and personally very attractive in every way, George also has the faculty of little-boy winsomeness that makes him popular almost everywhere. He is quick and has the knack of getting to the root of most every matter that comes up, although I sometimes find him being distracted by the many projects he has going. George relies on me to some extent to explain technical things to him that he does not wish to make the effort to understand himself, but I do not relate this in any patronizing way since I believe George can understand anything he wants to. George is certainly one of the most popular members of the committee on both sides and I will be surprised if he does not go far in politics.

I like my work on the Ways and Means Committee. It gives me a sense of being a participant in the best legislative sense of the word. Because of the nature of our leadership, anyone with a valid idea to contribute to the cause of legislative draftsmanship is heard and can be assured that his idea will be judged on its merits. There is very little partisanship and the work is thoroughly done. . . . Although service on the committee does not give a Republican the same stature it gives a Democrat, it nevertheless is considered to be a first-class assignment in the House, and I find my colleagues frequently envying my opportunity to serve in such a significant arena. Since we present our legislation on a "take it or leave it" basis to the House (under a closed rule), I find more than the usual interest among my colleagues in the internal workings of the committee and in what the committee is doing with respect to specific issues known to be in front of the committee. Wilbur's tireless work to achieve consensus rarely leaves them disappointed.

In the year of the moon landing (Conable was among the minority of members of Congress who didn't bother to attend the launch), the Ways and Means Committee explores the contentious sublunary subject of tax reform. Buffeted by special-interest pressures, committee members rise (Chairman Mills, California Democrat Jim Corman) and fall (Louisiana Democrat and House majority whip Hale Boggs) to the occasion. Conable begins his third term by assuming a leadership role in the GOP reform bloc whose previous paladin was an aggressive Illinois congressman named Donald Rumsfeld. While sailing on the presidential yacht *Sequoia*, Conable speaks bluntly about Richard Nixon's remoteness from Congress and wonders whether he will be blackballed by the White House.

In 1969 Conable emerged from backbench obscurity, scoring prominent appearances on the Today *show, on the* Huntley-Brinkley Report, *and in the pages of the* Washington Post. *His spoken prose grew more confident, mirroring his lengthening stature in the House.*

He was frank, perhaps even disrespectful, in his discussion with Nixon aide and Republican elder Bryce Harlow, expressing the frustration of younger Republicans who chafed under the leadership of Eisenhower-era figures. But the role of Young Turk was not unfamiliar to Conable, who began his political career in 1962 by challenging a corrupt state senator and a superannuated local GOP establishment.

We meet a cast of characters with whom he will contend and sometimes ally over the course of his career: pompous Oregon Democrat Al Ullman, Chicago machine pol Dan Rostenkowski, irascible Florida Democrat Sam Gibbons (about whom Conable will do the most complete volte-face), unprepossessing Pennsylvania Republican Herman Schneebeli, liberal Republican orator John Anderson, impish Nixon aide and later Democratic senator from New York Pat Moynihan, and Conable's congressional next-door neighbor and Republican hack extraordinaire Frank Horton.

We also get the first hint of Conable's melancholy, a disappointment in his own performance that will recur throughout the years.

January 16, 1969

I returned to my office on the second of January and made an effort to meet and get to know the new Republican congressmen, particularly those from the Northeast. They appear to be a somewhat older group than one might expect, but there are some men of caliber among them. Generally speaking, the three new ones from New York, Ham Fish, [Martin] McKneally, and [James] Hastings, will be sympathetic additions to the delegation. . . . My assessment of Ham Fish is a cautious one. He obviously is an aristocrat, a condition to which I personally react, but I have been pleased by his willingness to grapple with the problems initially presented to us. I believe him to be a serious-minded man of average intelligence who wishes to do a good job and who will therefore doubtless work harder than the average to do the right thing.

The issue which provided the inauspicious launching pad for the 91st Congress was that old chestnut, the seating of Adam Clayton Powell.[1] I felt pretty well committed personally, by the Constitution, to his seating, but I also felt he should be punished within the framework of our power to police our own House. The issue was broached by H. R. Gross [R-IA] that Adam stand aside during the swearing-in of the House members. Carl Albert [D-OK] immediately moved his seating following the oath of the rest of the group, and Emanuel Celler [D-NY] opened the debate with an outrageous speech (on the basis of which I suspect Manny is at last beginning to lose his powers) in which he first completely repudiated the report of two years ago of the special committee which he chaired in investigating the seating of Adam, saying that we had no power to do what he had recommended at that time . . . [and] by his entire performance he demonstrated a completely untypical slovenliness of speech and fuzziness of approach which made us think the issue was not of importance to him.

John McCormack [D-MA], who had at the outset given a nostalgic and maladroit speech which unconsciously irritated the young men in the group with his emphasis on being a *members'* Speaker rather than a *people's* Speaker, made several rulings during the course of the debate which also led a number of people to comment on how the old man was slipping. Between them, these two elderly gentlemen must have driven away a number of uncertain votes who

---

1. On March 1, 1967, the House had refused to seat Powell for various financial and personal misdeeds. The US Supreme Court ruled in *Powell v. McCormack* (1969) that the exclusion had been unconstitutional. Powell would be defeated for reelection in 1970 by Charles Rangel.

would otherwise have voted for the seating and punishing of Adam, but who, in their anger at the mishandling of the matter by the leadership, took the easy course and voted in effect to exclude him altogether. He nevertheless was seated by a fairly wide margin, fined $25,000 (which is to be deducted monthly from his pay, thus making it unnecessary for any court to issue process for the collection of the fine), and stripped of all seniority.

SOS has started out with a bang. . . . [2] Our second speaker for the breakfasts was Bryce Harlow, Nixon's first appointment to the White House staff and his choice for congressional liaison. Bryce shocked me by spending more time talking about Eisenhower than Nixon. He obviously is a nostalgic type.

The maneuvering within the Republican Conference with respect to the Research and Planning Committee has been intense and extensive. The adversaries are John Rhodes [R-AZ] and Don Rumsfeld [R-IL]. Rumsfeld early staked his claim to the chairmanship; he is an activist and overbearing young man and an intensely intelligent bundle of ambition. I have been trying to help him, although I told him long ago that his problem would not be his own election but rather his election to something significant. The decision of what to do about Research and Planning has been postponed, and every postponement works to his detriment because it strengthens the opposition to Research and Planning as a force in the Republican Conference. The older members of the House, being the ranking minority members of the committees, would much rather have a direct personal relationship with Richard Nixon through the committee structure than they would through an inevitably youth-dominated series of independently operating task forces not necessarily closely related to the committee structure.

January 31, 1969

I find there is some bad blood between Wilbur Mills and John Byrnes (at least resentment on John's part) over trade. John feels that Wilbur, speaking for himself, uses the possibility of restrictive quota legislation to try to force voluntary restraint on the part of importing countries with respect to the areas of trade which are problems only for Wilbur. . . . John has dairy, fur, and meat problems in his own district and these, of course, are ignored by Wilbur, who, apparently

---

2. SOS, which Conable called "part of the hidden leadership of the House Republican Party," consisted of mostly moderate Republicans who met on Wednesday mornings for off-the-record breakfast gatherings with "journalists, ambassadors, and other political types." Interview with the Honorable Barber Conable by William A. Syers, February 1, 1985, Securities and Exchange Commission Historical Society.

speaking for the committee, talks about the need for restraint in the textile field. John, sitting next to me on the floor of the House during one quiet period this week, sounded quite upset and used a good deal of profanity about how little the chairman could be trusted on these matters. I have a tendency to look at such conversations as having a significance beyond what appears on their face, and as suspicious as I am of my relations with John Byrnes anyway, it occurred to me that it was not beyond the realm of possibility that John was warning me not to deal with the chairman as directly as I normally do.

February 3, 1969

After dictating the last entry on the way to work Friday morning, I arrived and casually checked the *Congressional Record*. In the summary of the day's events Thursday, I discovered that appointments had been made, and among them were listed appointments to the Joint Economic Committee. Thinking I had been bypassed because I had received no notice, I turned to see who had been appointed by the Republicans and discovered my name among those listed. This is the first time I knew of the appointment. Apparently, Jerry[3] had submitted the appointments in writing and had failed to tell me about it. I immediately called him on the phone to thank him for the appointment, and he apologized by saying that Jo Wilson, his able secretary, had been ill and he had been unable to send out the usual letter of notification.

During the day I was visited by Mary McInnis of Don Rumsfeld's staff and another member of his staff on temporary assignment to the congressional reorganization problem. This meeting was a surprise, but it was apparently prompted by Don Rumsfeld's absence in Japan for the entire month of February. . . . The decision had been made, apparently, that I was to be the one to head up the initial securing of cosponsors, the filing, and the public relations attending the issuance of the congressional reorganization bill to be backed by Rumsfeld's Raiders during the 91st Congress. . . . [4] I have no real objection to this, since I strongly support congressional reorganization, but I am repeatedly amused by efforts to use me as a type of respectable figurehead for efforts which

3. House minority leader (and later vice president and president) Gerald Ford (R-MI).

4. The Rumsfeld's Raiders' reform proposals included "improved minority staff ratios on committees . . . a rational division of committee jurisdictions, and restraints on the power of committee chairmen and their monopolization of information and policy decisions." Geoffrey Kabaservice, *Rule and Ruin: The Downfall of Moderation and the Destruction of the Republican Party, from Eisenhower to the Tea Party* (New York: Oxford University Press, 2012), 259.

are not considered completely respectable by some members of the House. One of the major reasons for this amusement is that all my life I have had this kind of problem: I am not much of an initiator, and the brilliant people disdain the fuzziness of my mind, but I do seem to be the sort of person to whom people turn to "head things up," and it is not a role completely without embarrassment.

February 28, 1969
I find continually that few people attend the hearings of the Joint Economic Committee, I suppose mostly because they are busy people engaged in other pursuits of a more immediately pressing nature. [Chairman Wright] Patman [D-TX], [Senator William] Proxmire [D-WI], [Representative Henry] Reuss [D-WI], [Representative William] Brock [R-TN], and [Senator Charles] Percy [R-IL] are diligent in their attendance. Patman is impossible; he insults anyone vaguely connected with interest rates or banking and spends very little time listening to the remarkable amount of information that is put before the committee. Proxmire and Reuss are both excellent, showing inquiring minds and very good grasp of the details of America's economic life. Brock continues to impress me as a man of high articulateness and no small amount of intelligence. Percy, who sits next to me, tends to show up about the time he is reached for questioning and asks questions which are obviously well prepared and carefully thought out by his staff. He is a very handsome, smooth person.

George Bush is having real doubts about whether he should run for the Senate in 1970 against [Ralph] Yarborough. He has had several long talks with me about this, yearning for the job but wondering whether or not he can win. . . . His chances as a non-Texan leaning moderate in a state which has virtually no moderation in its makeup would seem to me to be rather bad, and so I have generally tended to discourage him from going for the Senate.

I have had an unhappy exchange over a speaking engagement this week. Some time ago the Republican National Committee asked me to speak at a supper dance to be held by the Richmond County Republicans on Staten Island. The request was said to have come from state senator John Marchi, who is an old friend from state senate days. I readily agreed to do it because it was Friday night of this week, the day after I was already committed to speak to the Tax Forum in New York City. Unfortunately, however, on Wednesday John Marchi announced himself for mayor of New York, thus indicating that he was going into a primary contest with John Lindsay. There is no reason why I should become involved in a dispute between two friends so far from my home base, but I felt obliged to honor the commitment made to the county Republican organization.

I saw John Lindsay, however, at a Port Authority of New York breakfast on Wednesday morning. I went up to him and asked him if I could speak to him privately and told him that I found myself in this position. I wanted him to know that while I was honoring the commitment, I was not going up there with any idea of endorsing Marchi or cutting up Lindsay in any way. His response was, "Barber, if you are a friend of mine you will endorse me in that speech." I said to him that he didn't seem to understand that I was going to be introduced by John Marchi, that Marchi was an old friend of mine, and that such an act would be impolite on my part. His response was, "I have told you what I think you will do if you are a friend of mine." After which he turned away. I am aware of John's reputation for arrogance, but his rather brutal handling of what I thought was a modest embarrassment made me angry enough so that I even toyed with the idea of going up and endorsing Marchi. I saw Lindsay again at luncheon the same day with the New York Republican delegation with the governor,[5] and he was perfectly cheerful, friendly, and made no further reference to the matter.

March 7, 1969

Sam Gibbons of Florida, the most junior Democrat, is proving to be extremely obstreperous, vocal, and partisan. . . . I find a considerable resentment building up on our side of the committee against his constant comments about everything, and at the close of our executive session on the debt ceiling I asked Wilbur Mills what he thought of the new member from Florida. Wilbur said, "Oh, Sam will be all right after he gets to understand the traditions of this committee. He just doesn't know yet that we don't like to fight like that about everything."

I have not reported finally on the outcome of my speech at Staten Island last Friday night. The affair was a supper dance beginning at nine o'clock. I went to John Marchi's house first, where he was having a few friends in for cocktails, and had a pleasant discussion with him, renewing an old friendship and reconvincing myself that he was a fairly decent sort of low-key, reasonable man rather than the type who could be expected to run for mayor of New York City. The affair itself dragged on at some length, and I was finally put on to speak at a quarter to twelve in a large hall in which there were 300 drunk people in one end and 300 drunk people in the other end. . . . I cut down a twenty-five-minute speech to about eight minutes, thus making it wildly incoherent, and nobody noticed. I said two or three nice things about John Marchi but of course did not refer in any way to the mayorship race. During the dinner before I spoke, the deputy

5. Nelson Rockefeller.

mayor, Robert Sweet, came in representing John Lindsay and sat opposite me. He said to me several times in different ways that he understood John Lindsay had campaigned for me when I was first running for office. I explained that this was not true, but he did not seem to accept it as a fact and was obviously primed before he came to put maximum pressure on me to keep me from saying anything nice about John Marchi.[6]

April 3, 1969

The death and burial of Eisenhower after such a long struggle left me feeling some guilt, although I was somewhat relieved that the poor old man could finally be through with his ordeal. My feeling of guilt was related to his complete lack of relevance to my own political career. All around me were friends who knew Ike personally, while I have never met him.

There were two ceremonial opportunities in connection with his funeral: the first was the lying of his body in state in the Rotunda of the Capitol, while the second was the actual funeral at the National Cathedral. My wife and I attended both of these, more as spectators to ogle the great and the near-great who came from far and wide to attend the funeral than as participants in the funeral ourselves. Charles de Gaulle looked old and paunchy and had bags under his eyes, thus creating the appearance of humanness that one does not get from his Olympian public image. When the shah of Iran first came into the Rotunda and I had not yet been able to identify him, except from a distance observing his many self-anointed medals and his brilliant red sash, I told my wife that he was at least a Romanian drum major judging from his appearance. My wife was outraged when another congressman in front of me turned around and said, "No, I think it is a Mexican general."

May 15, 1969

On Tuesday of this week I attended a luncheon put on by the officers of the Chase Manhattan Bank (excepting only the president, David Rockefeller) at the Carroll Arms restaurant on Capitol Hill for several influential legislators who could inform the bank officers about what was to be expected in the field of tax reform. These sober and serious gentlemen assembled at a very luxurious luncheon and basked in expectation, whetted by the arrival of Senator Russell Long [D-LA], chairman of the Senate Finance Committee; Hale Boggs

---

6. Marchi narrowly defeated Lindsay in the Republican primary, but Lindsay, running on the Liberal and Independent lines, was elected mayor in November.

[D-LA], second ranking Democrat on Ways and Means; Senator Gene McCarthy [D-MN], also of the Senate Finance Committee; and Jack Gilbert [D] and myself, representing the New York delegation on the Ways and Means Committee. The lunch completed, the senior vice president, who was in charge of the program, said: "Well, let's have some dialogue now. We're interested in finding out what we can do about tax reform and participating in whatever exchange you gentlemen may think would be helpful."

Russell Long and Hale Boggs were having a loud exchange immediately to his left and paid no attention to his call for dialogue. He tried it once more tentatively, and then one of his underlings crept around behind my chair and whispered in my ear that he hoped since I was the only Republican present I would take the position of the administration and start things rolling by making a few remarks. I immediately stood up [and] did exactly that, saying that I did not feel the administration's proposal would do much more than stimulate the necessary work of the Ways and Means Committee; that the Ways and Means Committee would doubtless draw the bill; that I thought there was a head of steam back of tax reform, as the chairman had said on several occasions; and that, if I were to guess, it would be that there would be some significant tax reform presented to the Congress this year, although probably not before the necessary extension of the surtax.[7]

I sat down and Hale Boggs got up with an air of some heavy sarcasm, saying, "There ain't going to be any tax reform." He then proceeded to say that he had been in Congress for more than twenty years and knew a good deal about tax reform efforts in the past—they all came to nothing—that people had been sold a bill of goods about the value of tax reform, and that he could see the whole thing sputtering out and coming to nothing—from his vantage point, a good thing. Russell Long leaped up and took the floor and immediately demonstrated that he was plastered almost beyond all coherence. He told a long series of pointless and punchline-less anecdotes about "niggers," drunk popes, long poker sessions with Hale Boggs, and his great admiration for Gene McCarthy, who, he said, had voted for him in his hour of travail. He talked for about twenty minutes, and time was fast approaching when I would have to leave. The bankers were getting quite restless, apparently not knowing how to handle the chairman of the Senate Finance Committee when he was in his cups. Finally, Russell turned

7. The Revenue and Expenditure Control Act of 1968 had imposed a temporary 10 percent income tax surcharge on individuals and corporations, expiring June 30, 1969. It was extended at a 5 percent rate through June 30, 1970.

to Gene McCarthy, introduced him as his dearest friend, and with tears in his eyes, sat down.

Gene McCarthy got up, told a tasteless anecdote derogatory of the president, denied that he had voted for Russell Long on the first ballot . . . then stated that Wilbur Mills had made his usual annual speech about tax reform and that was the end of that. He said what happened in taxes would be dictated by economics and not by any reformer zeal, and he generally agreed with Hale Boggs that the whole effort was an abortive one doomed to failure. When he sat down, I got up and left, since I was expected to go to Brookings that afternoon to participate in one of their forums.[8] I understood from Jack Gilbert later that Russell Long took the floor again for another twenty minutes and that they finally adjourned at 2:30 without any serious discussion of tax reform or any opportunity for the dialogue that had brought all these distinguished corporate bank officers to Washington.

May 24, 1969

On Tuesday of this week we had our [Ways and Means] public hearings with administration witnesses urging the extension and reduction of the surtax and the repeal of the 7 percent investment tax credit. The witnesses were the secretary of the treasury,[9] the chairman of the President's Council of Economic Advisers,[10] and the director of the Bureau of the Budget.[11] There was the usual political honking whenever we have a hearing, with particularly colorful demagoguery going on by Jim Burke [D-MA], Charlie Vanik [D-OH], and Joel Broyhill [R-VA]. Joel, of course, uses every opportunity he can to abuse Pride Inc. and other poverty programs and activities in the District of Columbia. I leaned over to him in the middle of his long speech and said, "Joel, this is the Ways and Means Committee and not the District of Columbia Committee." He answered, "It's a forum, isn't it, and look at all the press."

Jim Burke gave a long lecture to the secretary of the treasury about how the people had been waiting long enough for tax reform and the administration had better get behind it. I overheard John Byrnes saying to him after he was through, "Look out, Jimmy, or somebody's going to figure out how long you've been on

8. The Brookings Institution, a Washington, DC, think tank at which Conable frequently spoke on tax matters.

9. David M. Kennedy.

10. Paul W. McCracken.

11. Robert P. Mayo.

the Ways and Means Committee with nothing having been done in this area, and you'd better stop calling attention to the inaction that has been going on. It was all during Democratic administrations."

June 5, 1969

On Thursday morning, the day following the president's speech at the Air Force Academy in which he had, at least by implication, attacked those who wished to throw off all responsibility as the new isolationists and in which he had also been critical of those who were taking unrealistic views toward defense (reserving, of course, the right for those who wished to criticize unnecessary defense spending to do so), I had planned originally to go to Ways and Means. . . . At about a quarter of ten, apparently Douglas Freckling, the fine young minority staff member on the Joint Economic Committee, called Harry [Nicholas, Conable's chief of staff] to say that Proxmire was distributing a press release and was planning to attack the president's speech of the day before.

There were no other Republicans available, so I ran all the way over to the hearing, getting there just as Proxmire was starting to read his press release which charged the president with trying to intimidate Congress on the issue of national defense. . . . I was not prepared but decided I would jump in anyway . . . pointing out that the president had made ample allowance in his speech for the work of the committee and that there was no reason to be intimidated by the president's contributions to the dialogue on defense. I didn't know it, but the entire exchange was photographed and later appeared on Huntley-Brinkley[12] that evening. The chairman, Mr. Proxmire, kept coming back all during the morning to this particular issue, and I always went after him when he did it. I don't believe I was particularly effective, but at a time when not much is happening in the Congress, it seems to have caused some impression, as my picture was in the *Washington Post* the next morning and there were references to it on television. At the end of the morning, Proxmire, who apparently felt that he had gotten the better of the exchange, leaned over to me and said, "You know, I'm glad you came on this committee. Things have been dull as hell around here."

June 13, 1969

This entire week, Wilbur Mills was ill with diverticulitis. . . . His absence this week put considerable pressure on Hale Boggs, who delighted in telling the papers that he was acting chairman of the committee, and who was catapulted into

12. The NBC nightly news program.

a statesmanlike role by Richard Nixon, a man who knows when to flatter and whom to flatter. Hale hasn't had much idea of the legislative work of the committee for some time, showing up only for votes and participating in the most partisan manner possible. He showed his weakness in any discussion of legislation this week, trying to hasten Larry Woodworth[13] along in ways quite unusual to the experience of the committee and constantly evoking from John Byrnes the statement, "Now wait a minute, let's take a look at this. It should be discussed."

On Thursday, a meeting of the congressional leaders was held at the White House, Mr. Nixon now having got sufficiently exercised to be worrying about the surtax. Apparently, Hale Boggs suggested a very obvious sweetener for the tax package, namely the low-income allowance, which would take up to five million people at the poverty level off the tax rolls completely. This was an obvious sweetener if you want sweeteners, because it affected only about $665 million of revenue, while giving a liberal Democrat something to point to in the package of which he could be proud and which did not represent solely an unpleasant duty. The president, apparently waiting for such a suggestion to be made, grabbed it and ran with it. . . . I suppose this sort of thing has to be done by a president who must deal with the different party in congressional relations, but it, of course, generated some sourness on our side, and many of us felt that the loss of such a sweetener to the tax reform package later on could have serious implications there. It now appears that the Ways and Means Committee will try to bring out the final package, including surtax extension and reduction, the repeal of the 7 percent investment credit with transitional features, the extension of the excise tax, and the low-income allowance. There is still some doubt whether there are sufficient votes to pass this package in the House, but apparently a decision has been made to go with it.

Jim Corman [D-CA] came to my office Friday afternoon . . . and we had a long, serious talk about this. Jim has been a regular tower of strength among the liberals on the Ways and Means Committee, saying that he felt it was absolutely imperative such a package pass and fearing that the low-income allowance is not enough to get the Democratic votes needed to pass the package. He felt that we would be better off saving the low-income allowance for some other purpose and extending the surtax only for six months, thus giving those people who are symbolic reformers the opportunity to say to their people, "We didn't even extend the surtax all the way, because we wanted to keep some lever over reform." I call them symbolic reformers because many of them have no idea

13. Director of the Congressional Joint Committee on Internal Revenue Taxation.

what reform entails and would think we had done a great job of tax reform if we simply reduced the oil depletion allowance from 27½ percent to 15 percent, paying no attention to all the other tax havens which are less notorious but perhaps of greater economic significance. The basic trouble with Jim's concern about this group is that the chances are, if they are mollified in some way, they will find some other excuse to vote against tax reform.

I passed on his suggestion to John Byrnes, feeling that John should know that this option was open if we didn't have the votes on the package the White House helped put together with Hale Boggs's help on Thursday. John was inclined to be impatient about this, but John, being a thoughtful man, may think further on it once the idea is in his head. Jim Corman tells me that he is in considerable difficulty with the liberals from California, who are telling him, "We put you on the Ways and Means Committee to be a liberal, and now on the first issue you have sold out to Wilbur Mills and the Republicans, going along with an extension of the surtax without sufficient protection for the reform effort." . . . I have considerable respect for him and was grateful that he chose me to come around to speak to.

June 17, 1969

Sunday morning I took my family to the White House for religious services. It was much the nicest thing we have done at the White House since we have been in Washington. Norman Vincent Peale[14] was introduced in a brief, quiet introduction by the president. I would judge that there were about 150 people there, mostly families and mostly unidentified. I did recognize the chief justice,[15] the ambassador from Ceylon, five or six congressmen and senators, the attorney general,[16] and Secretary and Mrs. Romney.[17] We had the good fortune to be seated in the front row on the left side of the East Room, and so it seemed as though my family were on display. Norman Vincent Peale gave an excellent simple sermon that even my children liked. After the service the president demonstrated that he had been briefed on those who were going to be present.

14. Popular Protestant minister and author of the best seller *The Power of Positive Thinking* (1952).

15. Warren Burger, who had been confirmed as chief justice on June 9 but would not be sworn in until June 23.

16. John Mitchell.

17. George Romney, secretary of the Department of Housing and Urban Development, and his wife, Leonore.

He introduced me to Norman Vincent Peale with the statement, "This fellow has been saying some nice things about us in a committee where we are having a hard time." I was amused to see [Senator] Bob Griffin [R-MI], who was, of course, responsible for the disappearance from the high court of Abe Fortas, talking with great vivacity with the new chief justice. I asked Bob afterwards if Warren Burger was a good friend of his and he said, "I've never met him before. He seems like a nice man." I suspect that Warren Burger should be a good friend of his whether he has met him before or not.

Monday has seen the return of Wilbur Mills to the committee, although he apparently did not know which way his troops were marching and so he chose to sit in the back row rather than assume the leadership from Hale Boggs. Hale demonstrated how ill equipped he was to lead the Ways and Means Committee by everything he did during the next days. He was impatient, unconcerned about details, inclined to be heavy-handed in his dealings with his own people, and also inclined to fly off the handle without much cause.

The big fight was on the low-income allowance, which Hale Boggs had put into the package at the White House meeting and which Nixon had grabbed not because he was for it but because he wanted it to appear to be a Democratic package. But it seems that the liberal Democrats were furious at Hale for working out such a package, so these people who could normally be expected to be for anything like the low-income allowance, designed to take poverty-level people off the tax rolls, were all fighting it as vigorously as they could on the grounds that it should be part of the reform package. I felt this way myself, and when the vote came, I hesitated, expecting John Byrnes to jump in with some concern as to how I was going to vote. I did vote with all the other Republicans to retain the small-income allowance, although I believe very few of us were enthusiastic about it. As I understand the motivation behind the group, everyone was afraid that if it was defeated in committee, it would let the Democratic leadership off the hook on voting for the surtax package. Wilbur voted against it, but Jim Burke, trapped in his own rhetoric after speaking for the low-income package, then voted against it and asked to have his remarks stricken from the record. He tried to explain his remarks away later in conversations with [Richard] Fulton [D-TN] and Gilbert, and I could hear them giving him a real tongue-lashing.

When the surtax extension itself came up, [Al] Ullman [D-OR] first moved to extend it only for four months until October 1. This was quite easily beaten, with only seven or eight Democrats voting for it. Corman moved to extend it for six months until January 1 and started to move effectively to get Democratic support for his position. It brought the chairman to his feet. He moved over to the table (we were meeting in the small room off the floor) and delivered a tub-thumping, sidewinding speech promising once again that he would back fully comprehensive tax reform legislation and that we would have it out by August. He was so effective that no roll call was asked for on Corman's motion, and it was defeated on a voice vote. Once again, Wilbur seemed to know exactly the time to put the pressure on his colleagues and saved himself for the moment of maximum peril to the package.

June 21, 1969

[Earlier in the week at Ways and Means] Martha Griffiths [D-MI] was the only liberal member of the committee who was present. I walked over to Martha and said, "Where are all the reformers today?" Martha said, "They think reform is dead and that we are just spinning our wheels here." I asked her, "Are they basing that solely on the inclusion of the low-income allowance in the surtax bill?" Martha answered that that was only one indication—that everything else added up to the fact that there wasn't going to be any tax reform bill. She then led an attack on the three top members of the committee, saying that Hale Boggs was telling everyone (this I can attest to myself) that tax reform was just a lot of talk and that he was doubtful that anything would come of it. John Watts [D-KY] also has his skepticism and his reluctances, and she says that nobody trusts the chairman on this issue. Then she said to me, "Barber, I don't think I can get you three Democratic votes on any item of tax reform anyway. So many people have points of sensitivity." I told her that if this were so, then tax reform was indeed dead but that I didn't believe it. I said that the great bulk of the people on our side were in favor of it, and of course, there were some things that for political reasons people like George Bush and Joel Broyhill could not and would not vote for, but they would each help with all other areas of the package and that there was a general support. She said, "Well, I'll continue to come to meetings but I think we are just spinning our wheels."

On the floor that day, during the one-minute period, Hale Boggs promised the House as a whole that there would be a tax reform bill, giving such unctuous assurances that I felt it difficult to believe he is the same man who has been saying the exact opposite at private meetings he has been going to.

On Thursday we met at eleven o'clock to bring out the bill itself. Most of the Democrats were there that day, but they came only to vote against the bill. Nine of them voted against reporting it, including Jim Corman, who apparently has felt too much pressure from the liberal delegation in California to be able to vote for the package with the low-income allowance in it. Phil Landrum [D-GA] made a speech against the "demagogic" low-income allowance and was among those voting against the bill. Dan Rostenkowski [D-IL] was voted for it by the chairman by proxy but probably would have voted that way anyway. The other Democrats voting for the bill were the chairman, Boggs, Watts, Burke, and [Omar] Burleson [TX]. All Republicans voted for it.

George Bush had a very disturbing experience with Walter Hickel, the secretary of the interior. George went down to see him about regulations affecting offshore oil drilling and felt that he was making some perfectly innocent and proper requests in the interests of improving his relations with Hickel. Hickel blew up at George as though George were a representative of the oil industry and berated him personally at the top of his lungs in the Interior Department restaurant, to the extent that George finally threatened to leave if Hickel did not treat him more politely. George was deeply disturbed by the affair and told me that he had barely been able to sleep the night following the incident because of his concern about what he had done to stir Hickel's animosity to the extent that was expressed. Apparently, Hickel has a very bad temper, and George thinks as a result of the incident that he is unfit to be a public official.

July 9, 1969

The great effort of the last few days has been to get the surtax through, and now that it has been accomplished, there is every appearance that it may come to nothing in the Senate.

On Thursday morning I was on the *Today* show on NBC debating Charlie Vanik before forty million people about the surtax. All my friends told me to look out for Vanik—that he would hog the camera if I gave him a chance—and the result was that I was rather more warmed up than I needed to be and created the appearance of going after Charlie personally more vigorously than was necessary. He sat back quite quietly and espoused the cause of the little people and left me dangling on the end of the limb of fiscal responsibility. My assessment of my performance was that it was not very good, and this assessment seems to have been confirmed by staff and family and the roughly fifty letters of mostly complaint I received from all over the country. I must say that the complaint by others than those interested in my performing well was mostly addressed to the substance of my remarks. There can be little doubt that the surtax is not the most popular device for extorting money from the citizenry that ever was devised by government. Surprisingly, I had very little constituency reaction as I moved around the district that weekend, and more people seemed to have been proud to see me on the *Today* show than were upset by the substance of my remarks.

The vote was nerve-rackingly close, and I kept track of it after the second round began for the leadership. We ended the second round seven votes behind, but as a result of changes in the well and those who held back until the last minute to see if they were needed, we were able to win the final vote with 210 to 205.

Frank Horton[18] was one of twenty-six Republicans who held out against the surtax, announcing that he was doing so because reform had not been coupled with it. His real reason, doubtless, was the surprisingly unanimous opposition of organized labor. . . . I feared, because of the vehemence of the leadership's assessment of Frank's disloyalty in this respect, that some retaliation might be taken against Rochester, and so I shortly thereafter wrote the head of the GSA[19] to let him know that the federal building in Rochester is located in my district, rather than in Frank's. . . . The Rochester press, at least on the front page, gave wide dissemination to Frank's view that he has courageously withstood a great deal of pressure generated by political leaders and, by inference, that I had caved in to that pressure. The editorial in the [*Rochester*] *Times-Union* supported me, but I doubt if anyone ever reads editorials.

The following Tuesday morning we reconvened in the Ways and Means Committee with a new sense of urgency about tax reform. Wilbur, John Byrnes, and Hale Boggs had all made so many protestations of sincerity with respect to tax reform that there is little doubt the Congress has every right to expect us to bring out a comprehensive and effective tax reform bill. . . . It has been my own impression all along that if we didn't have the courage to vote [for] a needed fiscal measure like surtax extension, it was very questionable that we would have the courage to vote for as complex a measure as comprehensive tax reform. . . . The problem with so many of the liberals who profess to oppose the surtax is that they are not true liberals but "formula men" who react to the pressure of whatever special interest happens to be pushing on them at the moment. . . . There is little doubt that a comprehensive tax reform bill will bring out almost every special interest in the country in opposition, since there is virtually no one who does not have some vested interest in the tax structure as it now is. I intend to do my duty, and I hope the committee will as a whole, but the results of the surtax vote, close as they were, signal real trouble for tax reform.

18. The Republican representing the district immediately east of Conable's and a source of frequent exasperation to him.
19. General Services Administration.

July 16, 1969

We are going right at the central problems now—not resolving them easily and not solving them quickly in most cases, but at least making a serious effort to resolve them. It is tiresome work, and tempers are short on occasion. You can't even tell which casts of characters are with the program because there is such a mixed bag of motives that people are saying things they actually do not mean, depending on their view of whether or not tax reform should ultimately pass. George Bush has said several times, "Let's go after the timber resources and see if we can flake Al Ullman off" or "I think we dropped Landrum on that one." George, I suppose, is assuming that he cannot vote for a tax reform bill which includes substantial changes in oil. I find him wistfully hoping that he can vote for a bill occasionally, however, and I don't believe he is locked in on anything. . . . It is interesting to observe the personalities of the members under the stress of major decisions of this sort.

Last Friday morning I went over in the corner with Jim Corman and sat and talked with him at some length. I told him that, as he knew, I was in favor of tax reform but that I was uncertain what the proper posture should be for anyone who really was in favor of tax reform. He assumed the role of a cheerleader and started giving an "all the way" sort of speech. I said to him, "You know darn well that if we follow on the course we've been following this week, a tax reform bill will not pass. Your own liberals will be running for the hills if we bring such a bill to the floor because of the pressure the special interests will bring to bear on them. John Byrnes leaned over to me the other day and said that if we kept on this course, a man who voted against the bill would be a 'national hero.'"

Corman took the attitude that this was not the way he saw it at all. He said that if something was done with the oil depletion allowance, he would guarantee to me that 90 percent of the liberals would not dare do anything but vote for it. . . . Corman is one of the most interesting members of the committee because of his high intelligence. His statements about the liberals not running away from tax reform, however, would have the ring of greater assurance with me if he had not himself been so responsive to pressure on the surtax once his California liberal delegation started pushing on him for apparently having joined the Republicans and Wilbur Mills in wanting to do a responsible thing.

John Watts has become quite a strong antireformist in his attitude to individual issues. After one speech I made about the alternative tax,[20] John came back to

20. The alternative minimum tax, which was included in the Tax Reform Act of 1969, was

me and said, "You're not against the capital gains, are you—are you?" and looked very distressed. I had previously made a strong speech in favor of the capital gains generally, but he seemed to be very upset about any deviation from the very conservative viewpoint he had himself. Martha Griffiths has been saying very little and has been assuming her usual sardonic pose of amused watching while the conservatives kill the reform bill. I must say that her pose has not squared with the facts. John Byrnes has made a number of very sensible contributions and has himself been, I think, one of the most consistent and strongest of the reformers, although his positions are not as far out as other people's. Herman Schneebeli [R-PA] has also been doing a very good job and has been participating very actively. I have been surprised by the extent of Joel Broyhill's knowledge and shrewdness. There's no question about it: Broyhill really understands what is going on, and although he appears to spend a good deal of his time looking after his particular interests, his intelligence is quite penetrating.

This committee work has been quite a drag. . . . I am no longer able to contribute very much simply because of my drowsiness and my need for a change of pace. . . . I have been disappointed with my contributions to this debate and have been less effective than I usually am in the committee. The rather earthshaking decisions that we have been making and some of their possible consequences have bothered me to the point where I have not been sleeping very well at night.

July 27, 1969

Al Ullman, incidentally, has been the source of some amusement during this debate on tax reform, in that he personalizes everything he does. He takes himself terribly seriously and always starts his comments with some reference to himself, his ability to understand what's going on, his solution for the problem, his difficulty in resolving the issues in his own mind, or something of this sort. He obviously feels his contribution is more important than it actually is. Both John Byrnes and Wilbur have referred a number of times in my hearing to the fact that Al Ullman has "come along nicely" and that he is making a valuable contribution to the committee. I wish he weren't so stuffy.

August 1, 1969

This past week has seen the completion of the tax reform bill, with all the maneuvering and agony and effort such a completion entails. At the beginning of

---

an "add-on tax" to ensure that high-income individuals who made extensive use of deductions and tax preferences did not escape taxation.

the week we didn't think such a consummation was possible, and indeed, there were times during the week that we despaired that we wouldn't be able to finish.

The week saw a steady deterioration of Hale Boggs's condition. . . . He was voluble in the extreme, putting in his two cents every time any point was to be made and constantly moving around the room, spending at least a quarter of his time on the phone giving orders to people. The chairman showed the patience of Job in dealing with Hale, occasionally getting irritable with him but never telling him to shut up and sit down, as almost everyone else in the room wished he would. Frequent reference was made to the fact that Hale was not a "well man." And it seemed unlikely that he could be drunk during the entire period of our deliberations. He acted like a man on pep pills with his mind constantly speeding, somewhat disoriented about his surroundings. The last full day of deliberations, when we were trying to decide how to divide up the scrawny melon we had been able to put together into some form of tax relief, he had a protracted fight with well-meaning members of the staff, requiring them to put up on a blackboard all sorts of figures that were meaningless to anyone but him and the particular staff member he happened to be dealing with at the time. When we got all through and Hale was briefly out of the room, one of the members of the committee moved that Hale Boggs's blackboard be preserved and presented to the Smithsonian Institution as a grisly relic of our week.

It was easy to see which of our members were most accessible to lobbyists because Al Ullman and John Watts constantly brought in exceptions which they tried to have incorporated into the law—occasionally with some success. Ullman and Rostenkowski led a major effort to take all efforts to tax the exempt interest on municipal bonds completely out of the bill, and in this they had the strong support of Herman Schneebeli, Jim Utt [R-CA], Joel Broyhill, Rogers Morton [R-MD], and Charlie Chamberlain [R-MI]. John Byrnes hunkered in there like a block of granite, and I became closer to John than I have at any time since I have been in the committee as a result of my supporting his position on this.

The chairman also proved himself quite capable of heavy-handed action when it became necessary to impress on the "exceptors" his feeling that he would rather have no bill at all than a bill which left substantial loopholes. At one point, Martha Griffiths said to me that she felt on tax reform she could count only on John Byrnes, me, and "maybe the chairman." Martha herself made very few contributions, sitting there with a sardonic look on her face and apparently expecting the worst with respect to each issue that came up. Jim Burke made several impassioned speeches mostly unrelated to the subject (he tried to impose a 10 percent excise tax on "the fat-cat magazines") and, aside from that, protested on numerous occasions that he had every intention of being reasonable, a word he loves to use. Generally speaking, he seemed to be supporting the chairman better than I would have anticipated. Rostenkowski apparently had his orders from His Honor the Mayor,[21] and anything he tried to do was closely related to what he conceived to be in the best interests of Chicago. He did not participate actively except with respect to the taxation of municipal bond interest.

John Watts was constantly being ingratiating in his obvious way, coming around and asking me questions like, "How's my pragmatic friend?" or [saying] "I'm so sorry you can't go fishing with us this next week," apparently hoping that I would support some of his particular pets like hobby farming or depletion. When I disappointed him, he became progressively less amiable, although I'm sure he is pragmatic enough not to let this sort of disappointment affect what has been heretofore a friendly relationship.

George Bush continued to perform very ably, although of course he continued to take the position also that he was foreclosed by his connection with the oil interests from supporting any reform which did substantial damage to the oil industry. It was in the oil industry that we had our one failure: we took intangible costs out of the section on limited tax preferences, much to my disappointment. . . . I personally would have favored reducing the depletion allowance a little less if that were necessary to get at intangible drilling costs, which I consider a major manipulative device and probably of more economic concern to the oil industry than depletion. If we are honest, we will have to acknowledge that it is still possible for a wealthy man handling his oil development properly to escape taxation. In no other field can that be said.

On the final day the Senate passed a six-month extension of the surtax, and Wilbur received a note in the middle of the afternoon from [Senate majority leader] Mike Mansfield [D-MT] saying, in effect, "Six months—take it or leave it." Wilbur blew his stack and used more profanity than I have heard him use and said out loud, "I am going to teach that man a lesson. He may know a lot about foreign affairs, but he's got to learn that it's the House that writes tax bills."

August 7, 1969

[Wilbur Mills] said that while he had been willing to compromise on the surtax, the attitude of the Senate had made it impossible for him to do anything else but to teach [Mansfield] a lesson. He then had all the provisions that had been included in the surtax, including the 5 percent extension from January 1 to July 1,

21. Chicago mayor Richard J. Daley.

1970, added to the reform bill by a motion by Martha Griffiths. After that had been accomplished, he expressed some satisfaction that now the Senate would have to go into conference, and "we'll sit there until Easter if necessary to get them to accept these surtax provisions as part of the reform bill."

August 13, 1969

On Thursday of last week, we completed the tax bill. . . . It is obvious that we have not struck a blow for tax simplicity but have, through a whole series of compromises, tightened the tax law with respect to those tax preferences which were the reason for the head of steam behind tax reform. There was considerable complaint from the House that the individual members did not have the time to analyze and test the large number of proposals included in our package, but when the chips were down and the members were called upon to vote, only 30 voted against the bill while 394 voted for it. Even Charlie Vanik gave up at the last minute and stated that he would support the bill, voting for it (as everyone expected he would), despite his grousing about our failure to increase the personal exemption.[22]

On Friday night Hale Boggs had a garden party which was announced to be for members of the Ways and Means Committee and all the staff involved in the work on the reform bill. I assume that by this gesture Hale hoped to heal over any scars which might result from his abrasive manner during the consideration of the bill. I stayed that night for the express purpose of going to the party, not because I wanted to but because it was my fear that none of the other members of the Ways and Means Committee would go and that it would be apparent that Hale was being snubbed by his colleagues. Although I would have liked to snub him myself, it has seemed to me that Hale was not in complete possession of his faculties, and I suspect that he is a rather more sensitive man than his gruff behavior would indicate. As it turned out, Jack Betts [R-OH] and Al Ullman came to the party as well, although the other twenty-two were absent. . . . Hale pulled me aside and said he wanted to apologize if his manner had been overbearing and abrasive during the consideration of the bill, called me a states-

---

22. Major provisions of the Tax Reform Act of 1969, which would be signed into law by Richard Nixon on December 30, 1969, included the extension of the surtax (at 5 percent) until June 30, 1970, increases in the personal exemption and minimum standard deduction, lowering of the maximum income tax rate from 70 percent to 50 percent, establishment of an alternative minimum tax and the low-income allowance, and repeal of the investment tax credit.

man, and thanked me for coming to the party. On Monday he was back at his overbearing worst on the floor of the House, intruding in a District of Columbia bill in a manner which was quite unlike his usual smooth performance. There is a growing concern about him in the House and an almost certainty that there is something wrong with him.

October 10, 1969

On Thursday night about fourteen Republicans, a mixed bag, went on the *Sequoia*.[23] Initially, it appeared there were only going to be three of the very junior White House staff members on the *Sequoia*, but after we had gone down the river for about three-quarters of an hour, a small boat moved alongside and Bryce Harlow and a couple of other minor staff aides came on board. We sampled the usual fine cuisine of the White House, and then one of the staff members suggested quietly to E. Ross Adair [R-IN] that, as the senior man present, he might get up and make a toast to Bryce and suggest that Bryce answer questions or engage in discussion.

Ross did this, and Bryce immediately responded with a long, reminiscent talk about comparisons of the Eisenhower and the Nixon administrations, saying his usual courtly and flowery things and making it sound as though God's in his heaven [and] all's right with the world. I finally interrupted him and, with all the pent-up frustration of a man trying to ruin his relations with the White House, proceeded to tell Bryce as bluntly as I could that all was not right with the world and that one of the great problems was that he and the president didn't seem to know who was in Congress at this point.

I then looked around the room and told him that of the fourteen people present, people he had described as "stand-up guys" in the Republican Party in the House, only three had served during the Eisenhower period. I told him that I had never met Eisenhower and that I was in a central position in the House because of my committee assignments; that to me, Eisenhower was a historic person and not the warm personal friend that I am sure Bryce thought of him as. I said if he continued to try to build the loyalties of this administration on the mystic bonds of memory that just weren't there, the administration was doomed to failure; that he should understand that better than half the members of the Republican Party in the House had no reason to think of Nixon as anything but the president, rather than as Eisenhower's vice president who [had] finally made good—the apparent manner in which Bryce Harlow thought of him. I told him

23. USS *Sequoia*, the presidential yacht.

that the president had better start making some effort to establish a personal relationship with the majority of the members of his own party in the House and described a conversation with one member of the 91st Club[24] who had refused to go along with the president on pollution, saying, "Nixon? Who's Nixon?" when I tried to argue that he was tied inextricably to Nixon whether he liked it or not.

I made a total of two long speeches of an extremely blunt nature to Bryce, while everyone else was very polite and either sat there nodding their heads or remaining silent. On the way back to the car, both Ross Adair and Clark Mac-Gregor [R-MN], who had said nothing during the evening, walked with me and told me I had done the right thing. . . . I am sure they were thinking they were glad they had been politic enough to remain silent. As I shook hands with Bryce on the way out, I told him I hoped I had not offended him, and in fact, I had been paying him a compliment by being blunt. He rejoined that he was not offended but [said] "Oh, God, you made me feel old!" . . . It will be interesting to see if I am blackballed at the White House for having been too pointed in my remarks.

Wednesday noon I debated Proxmire again at Brookings on the tax reform bill. This was the first time I really had the good senator at a disadvantage. He is not thoroughly familiar with the provisions of the tax reform bill, and I have talked to businessmen so much about it that I have developed a patter that is somewhat sensitive to their sensitivities. As a result, I was much more confident and voluble than usual, and Senator Proxmire seemed hesitant to express any strong opinions, something that rarely characterizes his approach to anything. All in all, I had a good time swelling up like a self-important toad and croaking like a frog.

November 7, 1969
George Bush has all but locked himself in on running for the Senate in Texas next year. I deeply regret this decision of his because he is so atypical of Texas politics, coming from Houston and being a transplanted northerner in the bargain, but George has stars in his eyes and he is convinced he can beat Yarborough. Bill Brock is also announced and running in an effort to beat Senator [Albert] Gore [Sr.] of Tennessee. There are other congressmen who are expecting to run for the Senate, and it illustrates what I think is one of the great deficiencies of the House of Representatives: that it is not a sufficiently high-level group to retain

24. Consisting of those members first elected to the 91st Congress, which was seated in January 1969.

its leadership, much of which goes on to other opportunities, leaving behind a level of mediocrity which is not in the country's best interest. I have become more and more convinced that the greatest service I can perform is by staying in the House and doing as good a job as possible there, rather than chasing off after political will-o'-the-wisps in the hope that I can somehow achieve a position of greater preeminence.

Wednesday noon I debated at Brookings with Senator Gore, talking before a group of businessmen about tax reform, as I had previously done against Senator Proxmire. Apparently, Senator Proxmire felt ill at ease in talking about this subject with me, and so Senator Gore was brought in for the Senate Finance Committee for the second in this series of debates. Gore does not impress me favorably. He is obviously a man who considers himself very important, and he speaks ponderously, slowly, and without any regard for detail and without any great regard for fact. He spent a large part of his time calling the House bill on tax reform a "rich man's" bill, something that doesn't square with the facts. . . . I went right after him on every point that came up, and I was not surprised when he decided he had to leave early, leaving the field to me for the last half hour without contest.

November 21, 1969

The most exciting thing on the floor of the House this week was the foreign aid authorization. There were innumerable amendments offered, and the one which I could not understand was one adding $54 million for F-4 fighters for Taiwan. The president did not ask for this authorization, and I am frank to say I was perplexed by the pressure Jerry Ford generated in getting people to switch their votes until it passed by the narrowest of margins. I asked [Rogers] Morton if this was based on the lobbying and political contributions of Mrs. Chennault,[25] and Rog said he was sure that was not the case. There was a good deal more to the operation than meets the eye, and Jerry Ford referred ruefully to my failure to support him on this issue.

I am somewhat perplexed to find how much Jerry Ford pushes me nowadays to vote in the way he is voting. Perhaps this is part of his new responsibility as a result of having the Nixon administration in the White House. Always before, I have had the impression that he couldn't care less how I voted, and certainly I am not more inflexible on party voting now than I was earlier. I must confess

25. Anna Chennault, Chinese-born wife of "Flying Tigers" aviator Claire Chennault and a strong supporter of Nixon and Taiwan.

that I do not like being pushed and tend to resist pressure of this sort, despite my natural "tame" instincts.

December 12, 1969

The emotional bit of legislation on the House floor has been the extension of the Voting Rights Act, which was effectively blocked by a coalition of Republicans headed by Jerry Ford and the southern Democrats. John Anderson [R-IL] worked actively on the other side, and about forty Republicans, myself included, did not support our leader. The White House did some lobbying on the bill, although I must say their pressures on me were modest. There was no justification for the Ford substitute, which, although it extended voting rights to the entire country, very much watered down the enforcement provisions of the bill with respect to those southern states where [there] has been traditional deprivation of constitutional rights in the voting area.

I have refused to acknowledge that there is [a southern] strategy until this point. I find it difficult to justify it and was particularly upset to find my party moving in this direction. It seems as though we have done enough in the South. We, of course, have an obligation not to exclude this section of the country, but the major issues simply must not be tilted toward the particular biases of the South, or what could be a national strategy will become, in fact, a regional one. . . . The voting rights bill has worked very well in the South, operating to enfranchise at least a million Negroes who on any historical basis probably would not have been able to vote during the four years of operation of the Voting Rights Act.[26]

December 22, 1969

Jerry Ford has been doing a poor job of communicating with the rest of the Republicans. . . . John Anderson has broken with him on at least three occasions that I can think of, speaking actively against the House Republican leadership's cause and usually taking with him about fifty or sixty of us. . . . I have heard some muttering about John's unwillingness to follow the leadership, particularly among the southerners, and I sought the opportunity to talk privately with him on Friday, urging him to balance his positions and his postures with sufficient care so that he won't find himself unceremoniously dumped from the leadership. The fact is that all moderate and reasonable people rely on John to express their

---

26. The Voting Rights Act Amendments of 1970, signed into law by President Nixon on June 22, 1970, extended the act for five years.

views, to touch their consciences, and, in general, [to] provide a degree of independence seemly to a great political party. His problem is not one so much of position as of posture, because John has always been insensitive to the crosscurrents of political thought in our Republican group. This is one reason why I was not enthusiastic about him as conference leader, despite my admiration for him; his leadership, immediately following that of Mel Laird's,[27] has been startling. Mel always had his finger on everything that was happening and had remarkable lines of communication running out in every direction possible. Mel also was a moderate, but a much more devious one and one much more able to find an acceptable tone of political leadership. John is usually the last person to know when something is happening because he is an introvert and much inclined to live the life of the mind rather than the hurly-burly of political discourse.

Last Wednesday we had an SOS breakfast with Pat Moynihan[28] from the White House. He proved to be a most ingratiating rascal, smashing graven images in every direction and trampling the sensibilities of all those present. He still describes himself as a Democrat in most unabashed fashion. Rog Morton tells me that he rode down to the White House afterward and Moynihan expressed astonishment at the liveliness and intellectual capacity of our group. He also tells me that Moynihan, for all his oddball characteristics, is a great personal relief to him in the White House that otherwise must be characterized as full of earnest dullards. I suspect Pat Moynihan is quite able to adjust his point of view to his audience, so that he can manage to insult almost everyone on their own terms.

27. Wisconsin Republican who was appointed secretary of defense by President Nixon.
28. Then counselor to the president.

Conable takes on the seniority system, irritating those ranking committee members who have achieved their status on the basis of longevity rather than skill, smarts, or congeniality. "Vindictive elders" lurk. He emerges as the leader of the small free-trade bloc within the Ways and Means Committee that stands against Chairman Wilbur Mills's textile quota bill. A rift deepens between House Republican moderates and conservatives, and, somewhat to his surprise, Conable is identified as a leader of the moderate-to-liberal wing. Acknowledging that he has become something of a "cause man," Conable takes up revenue sharing on behalf of the Nixon administration, despite the opposition of Ways and Means chairman Mills and ranking Republican John Byrnes. The Rayburn building's gymnasium, site of cross-ideological paddleball friendships, is thwacked with controversy.

As his profile rose, Barber Conable faced a choice: ascend into the House GOP leadership or concentrate on his Ways and Means and Joint Economic Committee assignments. Should he be a legislator or a politician? Instead of choosing one or the other, he decided to do both for the moment, although Conable was surprised to find that the disaffected right wing of the House Republicans regarded him as a moderate or perhaps even a liberal.

He sensed, too, that he was "clearly identified as a rebel" by the leadership, whose foot-dragging on House reform measures he lamented. Minority leader Gerald Ford's caution frustrated Conable, who urged an aggressive reformist agenda.

Members came and went. In 1970 Conable's friend George H. W. Bush ran a losing campaign for the US Senate, a race that Conable had urged him not to make. Though Bush was at loose ends, uncertain of his next step, he would reappear.

February 13, 1970

For the first time at SOS I brought up the issue of congressional reorganization, largely because I was perplexed by the large number of Democrats who are bringing public assaults on the seniority system in connection with their frustrations over the continuation in office of [Speaker] John McCormack. This loss of discipline on the issue of reorganization is very likely to destroy any chance of bringing the Rules Committee's reorganization bill to the floor of the House, and unless it arrives on the floor of the House we will have no focal point on which to base a major effort for congressional reorganization. I found the sentiment in SOS, though somewhat lukewarm, almost unanimously in favor of trying to exploit this reorganization politically, and I am very seriously considering making a strong one-minute statement on the floor of the House and accusing the Democrats of headline hunting at the expense of John McCormack and, in so doing, seriously damaging any kind of chances for institutional reform.

It looks more and more as if this is going to be a political issue in the 1970 congressional elections, and as if we are not going to actually accomplish anything in the way of substantial reorganization this year. The frustration of the young Democrats is acute in relation to their leadership. I cannot feel that they are very serious about congressional reorganization, and if they are, whether they are sufficiently disciplined to achieve it. Incidentally, I have talked with Gerald Ford about this, telling him that I was not the leader of the Rumsfeld Raiders[1] and telling him that I did not view our efforts as an assault on leadership but a necessary step toward making our institution more responsive. He professed to agree with me and said that this could be politically exploited in the elections but kept insisting that I check everything with H. Allen Smith [CA], the ranking Republican on the Rules Committee, who is well known to be no friend of reorganization. Jerry will be no ally in this effort because of his commission that he has to deal with the ranking minority members, some of whom could have achieved the positions they have only through seniority.

March 26, 1970

I have been having an interesting time with the Task Force on Seniority to which I was appointed by Jerry Ford and Bob Taft.[2] The task force is well balanced, reflecting all viewpoints, I would judge, although I suspect the advocates of change are more numerous than the standpatters, thanks to Jerry Ford's lack of

---

1. Rumsfeld had joined the Nixon administration in 1969, serving first as director of the Office of Economic Opportunity.

2. This nineteen-member GOP task force, headed by Conable, was appointed on March 19, 1970, and issued its recommendations on October 13, 1970. Its central recommendation—that ranking Republican members be chosen by secret ballot—was adopted on January 20, 1971. Norman Beckman, "Congressional Information Processes for National Policy," *Annals of the American Academy of Political and Social Science* 394 (1971): 155.

knowledge about the attitudes of some of the middle-class members like myself. I called a meeting two days after the appointment of the task force, and we discussed the various means for gathering suggestions, ordering studies by the Library of Congress, etc., and also agreed to send out a letter to all Republican members of Congress asking for their suggestions on alternative means. Shortly after the letter went out, Les Arends [R-IL] came up to me on the floor and asked me what the idea was of sending out such a letter. I said I thought it was part of my job to find out what other members of Congress thought about it. He said, "I thought we'd buried that whole thing when we appointed the task force." I said that I didn't understand my mission to be one of interment but a study and reporting mission. He said, "Well, you aren't going to get a letter from me with my suggestions in it. I can tell you what to do in two words—forget it." Coupled with the attitude Jerry Ford has—which he has expressed a number of times to me, just to be sure that I heard him—that "the burden of proof is on those who want to make some change," it would seem that our leadership is going to demonstrate some reluctance if we don't bring in the right kind of report.

April 10, 1970

[A] grand total of ten members[3] have responded [to the request for ideas about reforming the seniority system] and so I have started going around and asking people, particularly the younger members, to write me a letter setting out their views. There seems to be a considerable reluctance to do it. The sensitivity of this issue leads people to resist getting out on a limb, feeling that anything they say will be used against them by vindictive elders. They are happy to talk to me personally about it, but this leaves me largely without any base from which to operate. . . . I am afraid I am going to have to do a good deal of maneuvering and exercise a leadership that is not in me if I am to shepherd this particular project along to the point of any satisfaction.

April 17, 1970

Washington is beautiful this week with the cherry blossoms out, and the early flowering shrubs that are coming into full bloom. The traffic is intolerable as people ogle the advent of spring.

Chairman Mills has done one thing which has caused me a good deal of concern. Early in the week he filed in the House a bill which established quotas on

---

3. Of the 192 Republicans in the 91st Congress.

textiles and footwear, the items of import causing the most trouble.[4] Although he has talked this game before, he has never previously taken steps which indicated he was very serious about trying to push quotas as an instrument of national policy. At the time he did this he apparently announced [it] at a meeting of a number of textile executives, and among them were some Rochester people. He told these people, the owners of Hickey-Freeman[5] and some apparel manufacturers, that it was important to get me to cosponsor the bill. He said nothing to me about this, but of course, these people called me and expected me to cosponsor it. I did not talk to them directly, but Harry said he would take it up with me and notify them. We decided not to cosponsor the bill under any circumstances, since my rhetoric and my instincts are all on the side of free trade rather than this type of restriction.

In an effort to buttress my position, I called Louis Eilers, the president of Eastman Kodak,[6] and asked him what the interests of that great company were and explained my predicament. Although not taking a strong position with me, he left me in no doubt that Eastman Kodak . . . was sympathetic to the problems of its customers in the apparel field and that therefore Eastman felt some type of restrictive trade might not do a great deal of damage. It was my feeling that Eastman, as a worldwide film monopoly, might be more afraid of retaliation than of trade, and so I had hoped that I would get a fairly firm statement from him in favor of retaining a historic path toward freer trade. I am disappointed about Eastman's position on this, but I am not likely to change my own position very much, since it personally seems to me that restrictions on trade are particularly foolish at a time of galloping inflation, competition being a major device by which we hold our prices down.

May 1, 1970

I must confess that I have been low in my mind during this spring. There is no particular reason for this except that I have been working hard and taking on too many political assignments of a dubious nature with probable questionable results. . . . Things certainly are not happy in the nation, and this is bound to affect anybody who feels emotionally involved in the nation's affairs. I still do not feel close to Nixon in any way and support him as strongly as I do only because I can't think of any feasible alternative. After five years in Congress, I have yet to

4. H.R. 16920, which had 184 House cosponsors.
5. A Rochester-based manufacturer of men's suits.
6. A Rochester-based manufacturer of cameras and photography-related products.

be invited to a state dinner or to find my way into the Oval Office, whatever that is. I have never attended a bill signing except for Lyndon Johnson's Cold War GI bill at which more than a hundred congressmen were present. If I were not so busy, I would feel quite detached from the administration, but in all intellectual honesty, I would have to acknowledge that they need me as much as they need anybody other than the leadership because of the positions I have and because of my lack of doctrinal or other hang-ups which might limit the support I can give. I suppose the most anyone can hope for ultimately is to be helpful.

May 18, 1970

It is very difficult to recall the events of the past week because of the tremendous volume of generalized activity regarding the Cambodian affair.[7] A great many students have come to see me or members of my staff. They were higher-caliber students than those visiting during previous protests, well organized and obviously prepared to be polite and to listen as well as to make their pitch. . . . They traveled in small groups with at least one constituent usually among their group to give them an opening in their approach to a congressman. Some congressmen refused to be very civil with them, but for the most part, they were the type of kid that was very difficult to exclude and also quite difficult not to like, since they used such a reasonable approach. We received a tremendous amount of mail during this period also, running at least ten to one against the president's decision in Cambodia. The mail showed signs of being almost entirely organized mail, with repetitive phrases and in many cases simply a signature on a clipped coupon or a mimeographed form letter. I wrote a letter to the president delineating my limited support of the Cambodian venture and then mimeographed the letter to send to some 3,000 people who had written about the Cambodian affair. It will not satisfy the critics, but at least it expresses my position.

The Rules Committee has apparently cleared the reorganization bill that [it has] been considering and [is] prepared to send it to the floor sometime in the not too distant future.[8] H. Allen Smith, the ranking Republican on the committee, accused me today of having not shown good faith in my relation-

---

7. The joint US–South Vietnamese invasion—or "incursion," as President Nixon called it—of the neutral country of Cambodia, bordering Vietnam.

8. This package of reforms, enacted as the Legislative Reorganization Act of 1970, was most notable for opening all House and Senate committee hearings (except those of the appropriations committees or those dealing with national security) to the public and for eventually leading to the installation, in 1973, of electronic voting machines.

ship to this bill, saying that I had sent a general letter out criticizing the bill before I had even seen it. I was confused by what he was saying and asked my staff to find out if such a letter was being circulated with my name on it. It appears that it was not, but that he had confused a letter from Phil Ruppe [R-MI] with being something I, myself, had generated. Apparently, judging from this, I am very closely identified with the opposition to the establishment in the Republican Party. Although Smitty called my office and apologized for his error after he had checked it, it left little doubt in my mind that I am clearly identified as a rebel in the eyes of the elder members of the Republican establishment in the House.

In the same connection, John Rhodes has spoken to me twice since the last task force meeting. . . . John, it appears, was appointed to the task force because of his outspoken opposition to doing anything about it. Since he is generally a reasonable man, I am surprised at the vehemence of his opposition and the thinness of his veiled warnings to me that I had better not be progressive on this assignment.

Of the sixty-six people who have so far answered the questionnaire we sent out three weeks ago, better than a margin of three to one favored some degree of change in the operation of the seniority system with respect to the House Republican rules. We are going to face something of a crisis on this issue when the reorganization bill hits the floor because the bipartisan majority of younger members of the House may very well want to enact House rules relating to seniority binding on both parties, rather than relying on the party rules to be changed. I am not sure what the appropriate posture for the chairman of the task force should be on that one.

May 21, 1970

One of the most interesting things happening this week has been the announcement of the retirement of John McCormack. I was in the Ways and Means hearing when the word came that Mr. McCormack had just held a press conference announcing his retirement. Because there were no other Republicans there, I sat next to the chairman. I leaned over to him and said, "Mr. Chairman, I hope you're not going to leave us as a result of this change in leadership." He answered, "Barber, if you were chairman of Ways and Means, you wouldn't give it up to be Speaker either." He went on to say that he had known John McCormack's decision for three weeks and that he had told Carl Albert [D-OK] he would support him. He said that Carl Albert would win easily with fairly broad support but that below Carl, it was absolutely impossible to predict. He seemed to think that Ed Boland of Massachusetts had a good chance for one of the leadership jobs. I asked him what was going to happen to Hale Boggs, and he said he didn't know—that he was awfully afraid Hale would be "badly hurt." He brushed off the possibility that Morris Udall [D-AZ] would be a strong candidate for one of the leadership positions and refused to explain his feelings on that. I would personally think that Udall would have a good chance for something. He did say that he thought Udall was considerably brighter than his brother, the former secretary of the interior.[9]

The Ways and Means hearings have continued all week, and I find myself getting in deeper and deeper trouble with the labor bloc and the special-interest business bloc by my obvious prejudice against the quota legislation we are considering. It is difficult for me not to telegraph my feelings in my questioning, and the free traders are beginning to consider me as somebody they've got to talk to and encourage, since I seem to be one of the only committee members espousing this general viewpoint. I don't really feel as open and shut in my attitudes as my questioning would appear, and I just make a greater effort to preserve some balance here in my questioning. It is upsetting to me, however, that all the colleagues with whom I have made so much common cause in our other hearings seem to be so clearly protectionist in their views.

June 13, 1970

On Friday of this week I attended Ways and Means for the first time all week long. They have been involved in a very heavy schedule of witnesses appearing mostly in behalf of this or that industry getting some quota protection on imports. Apparently, I was tired because I had a bad set-to with Jim Burke. Jim interrogated a witness from the aerospace industry who was advocating the retention of the greatest possible degree of free trade, and after cutting the man up in small pieces, Jim was kicking the pieces around on the floor at embarrassing length. When I was recognized, I urged my friend from Massachusetts, whom I complimented on his effective advocacy in the interests of his region, not to berate witnesses to the point where it would affect the free exchange of ideas, which is so necessary at a hearing. I pointed out that his statements for not voting for further funds for the aerospace industry or for the SST [supersonic transport] unless the industry involved started showing some concern for the problems of other industries sounded too much like logrolling, which I am sure he was not attempting to do. He, of course, took serious umbrage, and I am

9. Stewart Udall, secretary of the interior from 1961 to 1969.

afraid I offended him badly by implying that he had gone too far in his abuse of the witness.

Dick Wilbur of our staff reassured me that I had been tactful in the way I had put my assault on Jim's tactics, but I have serious misgivings about it in that respect. I also waited until Jim was out of the room and then went over to the chairman, telling him, "Mr. Chairman, I want to apologize for having blown my cool about Jim's method of questioning. I realize it will not help relations in the committee and I regret having done it." Wilbur [Mills] in his usual fashion agrees with everyone, and so he said to me, "I am glad you did it. Jim has been going too far in expressing his point of view." Wilbur himself would never attempt to shut off any line of questioning, however unfair, and he may have been glad that I did it, but I rather imagine that he simply is following his usual politic course of agreeing with everyone. I shall try to get Jim's agreement on Monday to take the entire exchange out of the record of the hearings.

June 18, 1970

I had a particularly alarming talk with Bill Scherle [R-IA], who told me about a group of "at least fifty" conservatives who meet regularly at Costin's Restaurant in Washington under the leadership of Sam Devine [R-OH] and who have dedicated their efforts over the next few months to bringing John Anderson [R-IL] down as chairman of the Republican Conference. I don't know why John is so much a target for them, except he sometimes espouses liberal causes, and whenever he does, he gets not only good attention by the press but proves to be a most effective champion. Thirdly, anyone who conceives of John as a dangerous liberal must be quite a dangerous conservative himself.

Bill acknowledged that I was probably not a conspirator myself but implied that I was at least a dupe of the left wing. Despite this, he kept referring to the liberals as "you guys," and this by itself alarmed me enough so that I brought it up at SOS, asking if we did have a large group of conservatives who considered themselves disenfranchised. The older members there said, in effect, "Barber, you are a nice guy. Quit worrying." I do worry about any organized effort to get John Anderson, although I am sure the numbers in Sam Devine's group are nowhere near as impressive as Bill Scherle would like me to think.

We have had a rumbly week on the floor. There was the voting rights extension and the postal reform foreclosing much of the other work. The voting rights extension was particularly troublesome to me because I favor the simple extension of the Voting Rights Act more than the administration's watered-down proposal, and somewhat earlier this measure was amended in an irresponsible way by the Senate to add the eighteen-year-old vote on a legislative basis, something I have consistently said could not be done, although I have sponsored a constitutional amendment for an eighteen-year-old vote.[10] I was shocked to find how many of my colleagues said, "Of course it is not constitutional, but the right political vote is to pass it and let the courts take care of it." To me, this is a dereliction of our oath of office, and I cannot understand a congressman who would take such an attitude. I have to acknowledge that my strict constructionism gets me in trouble more than it helps me and seems to be such a minority view that it does no good for the country. Generally speaking, I don't think young people have much to look forward to, no matter how much they vote, if there is not somewhere a stable bedrock like the Constitution, supported by all who must deal with it, for the protection of their rights. I would hate to leave the protection of black minority rights, for instance, to the tender mercies of the majority in this country at this point.

July 11, 1970

We have been in executive session [in Ways and Means] during this period, moving quite briskly toward a sharply protectionist type of trade bill. The chairman has had a short fuse and seems out of sorts about the whole affair, but his condition has not made him circumspect; it has made him appear to want to plunge on ahead, taking half-formed decisions as completed ones, and acting as though he wanted to get an unpleasant duty behind him. I still feel that he is trapped in his own rhetoric, required by an oratorical commitment to take a position he knows in his heart is foolish.

John Byrnes's position, on the other hand, remains inscrutable. He has said all along that he wants to have a "free-market mechanism" that will trigger in tariffs or quotas on a large number of goods established by imports, rather than going the route of the special quota on textiles and footwear called for by the Mills bill. John's position is a rational one if you deem protection a desirable legislative goal, since it demonstrates that protection should not be based on political clout but rather on economic factors related to imports. The big trouble with John's position from Wilbur's point of view is that in order to include textiles and footwear in any kind of a general triggering formula, the trigger has to be a hair

10. The US Supreme Court, in *Oregon v. Mitchell* (1970), struck down the congressional imposition of an eighteen-year-old voting age in state and local elections. In response, the states ratified the Twenty-Sixth Amendment, which guaranteed eighteen-year-olds the right to vote in federal, state, and local elections.

trigger, which means that a large number of items will have to be protected. For anyone who is basically a free trader like Wilbur, this is an undesirable result: he would much prefer to have the frankly political Mills bill and not try to justify the quotas imposed on any rational economic basis. A further complication of his position is the almost certainty that if we send such a political bill to the Senate, it will come back bedecked with all kinds of special quotas protecting each individual senator's special interest. The chairman could keep control of the bill in the House of Representatives, but he has demonstrated time and again that he cannot control a bill in the Senate.

The four free traders who seem to be emerging in the course of our deliberations are Sam Gibbons, Jim Corman, and me and, to an only recently discovered extent, Jerry Pettis [R-CA]. Sam, Jim, and I have twice discussed ways in which we could limit the march to protectionism. Sam is, as usual, the lightning rod drawing the ire of all the other members by his loquaciousness and his insistence on interrupting and personalizing. Corman is, as usual, tactful and very effective and considerably more persistent than I. I have several times made somewhat protracted and generalized emotional outpourings about quotas being a poor response to the protectionism of the Japanese, and some of my friends have implied, as a result, that I am a "Jap lover."

July 21, 1970

Yesterday in the Joint Economic Committee I heard an illuminating exchange between George Shultz, the director of the Office of Management and Budget, and Chairman Wright Patman. Mr. Shultz and Dr. McCracken[11] were sitting at the witness table when the chairman came in and sat down. The chairman was, as usual, oblivious. Mr. Shultz went up to him and extended his hand and said, "Mr. Chairman, I'm George Shultz." The chairman said, "Oh, George. How nice to see you again. Now, let's see, where are you now? Are you still in Chicago?" George said, "No, Mr. Chairman, I am one of your witnesses today." The chairman said, "Oh, that will be interesting." John Stark,[12] who had also heard the exchange, rolled his eyeballs upward, looked at me, and said, "It's a bad day at Black Rock."

Last week was engaged in the reorganization bill having a leisurely launching on the floor of the House and the trade bill getting an abrupt and unhappy denouement in Ways and Means. The chairman continued to press vigorously

---

11. Paul McCracken, chairman of the Council of Economic Advisers.
12. Staff director of the Joint Economic Committee.

for a conclusion, although I believe he was holding his nose as he did it. . . . The John Byrnes "trickering" amendment (John has always mispronounced the word "trigger"), which would result in the inclusion of all products affected by imports, was adopted. The knowledgeable people seemed to be downgrading the impact of this device, saying that the formula John and the chairman have chosen will exclude most small businesses rather than including most. I am skeptical about it. There has been a reaction from the liberal press of the Northeast establishment, of course, to this bill, as could be predicted. I predict it will also see delayed but substantial reaction from American business once they realize the extent of its protectionism, since most American businessmen (I hope, at least) are still willing to compete in the world market.

I brought the matter up at the 89th Club[13] last night, expressing myself quite forcefully on it, and had the entire group, which is mostly southern oriented, descend upon my neck with hobnail boots. The only one in the group who seemed to agree with me was Chester Mize [R-KS], who is probably the weakest of the congressmen in our group. I intend to oppose the bill in its present form, and I am somewhat amused to find that President Nixon apparently is also alarmed by it. At a press conference late yesterday afternoon he said he would veto the bill if it came to him with anything but textile quotas in it. I don't know what he expected, once he opened the door to quota legislation, but I suspect that Secretary of Commerce Maurice Stans is beginning to realize that he has been somewhat naïve about the whole business.

July 23, 1970

The night before last, I went down to the White House with all the Republican congressmen whose names [began with the letters] A [through] L to be photographed with the president for campaign purposes. We were taken in through the Cabinet Room to the Oval Office, standing in line and moving one at a time to sit behind the desk chatting with the president while the photographers did their worst. Inevitably, we all got a few moments to chat with the president—something I had never been able to do before, except in a very limited amount of time available in passing through a reception line. I started out by saying, "Mr. President, this is the first time I have been in the Oval Office, and I must say it is very attractive. I like where you work." He said—bringing his long, lugubrious face up against mine—"You've never been in here before?" in

---

13. Republican members first elected to the 89th Congress, which was seated in January 1965.

such a way that I responded, "Yes, but I'm not complaining; I simply wanted to say that I think it is an attractive place." He said, "Barber, we've got to look into this." I immediately switched to talking about the reorganization bill and the trade bill. "I'm afraid," he said about the latter, "that it had better not be loaded up too much or I'll have to veto it." I said, "Mr. President, many of us think it is already too loaded."

Afterwards, we went upstairs to a reception, and when the photographing had been completed, Bill Timmons[14] came up to me and said, "You son of a gun, you've got me in real trouble with the boss." I said, "Well, Bill, what in the world did I say?" And he said, "He told me he wanted a full explanation from me as to why you had never been in the Oval Office before." I said to Bill, "Did you explain to him that I had never been invited?" He said, "But your class was down here." I said, "You remember that—I was off speaking for the Republican National Committee." He said, "Well, what shall I tell him?" And I said, "Well, tell him the truth. He shouldn't really be surprised that I've never been in the Oval Office if he's never invited me."

I found. . . . Mrs. [Pat] Nixon very chatty and relaxed and not a bit self-conscious. Something about the Nixon women makes them appear to be considerably tenser than they are, and Mrs. Nixon has a disarming directness which makes any great sympathy for her martyrdom seem misplaced.

July 31, 1970

This afternoon Wilbur Mills put on a singular performance. We had felt that the trade bill was all locked up by the protectionists and that Wilbur was forced to acquiesce in their plan by his rhetorical entrapment. [At] the beginning of this week, the drafted bill, based on the tentative decisions, was presented to the committee for consideration and presumably for reporting to the floor of the House in substantially the wording drafted. The end of the week finds us with only a few pages of progress and obviously wide disagreement about whether or not the bill should be reported. I had prepared for use earlier in the week a tentative minority report which I designed as a comparatively short piece, punchy in nature and not very statistically involved. I showed it to Corman, Gibbons, and Pettis, presumably the only other members of the committee who might be expected to join me in something of a denunciatory nature.

Friday afternoon, after having asked to go off the record so that no copy of his remarks could be made, Wilbur Mills launched into a very long analysis of the

14. Assistant to the president for legislative affairs.

bill, saying, as he had said privately earlier in the week, that he has never had a bill that has been vetoed and that he doesn't propose to have this one vetoed. He then proceeded to say that there were some sections in the bill that he, himself, could not stomach and that it would be impossible for him to support the bill in its present form. He singled out John Byrnes's "basket clause," about which we have had a great deal of discussion during the week, saying that he was convinced that the arithmetic formula involved in the basket clause would become a pattern for retaliation. He made it clear that he wanted to back up on the bill and sounded like a pristine free trader, uttering cries diametrically opposed to the earnest speeches against the free traders that he made almost daily during the public hearings and that have characterized his general remarks during the formulation of the tentative decisions.

Jim Burke leaned over to me and said that he was going out to get a glass of milk for his ulcer. Phil Landrum got red in the face and talked about how the committee must not behave in such a manner as to bring down ridicule upon it at this stage in the proceedings. Jack Betts walked out of the room, and Herm Schneebeli sat staring directly ahead, drumming on the table. In short, the complacency of the protectionists evaporated almost instantly. John Byrnes, still pushing earnestly for his basket clause, said to me on the floor a little while later, "I won't insist on my basket clause if the chairman will take out the quotas on textiles and shoes," and winked at me as though that was what he was driving for all along. That may have been his motivation, but I suspect that John is preparing a fallback position in case the chairman is serious about taking a turn toward a more liberal trade policy than that embodied in the tentative bill.

The four of us who have been opposing the bill do not know what to think or do at this point, and I suspect that the abrupt change in direction may not be as real as it is apparent. In all possibility (and John Byrnes has suggested this to me), the chairman is frightening the majority of the committee who favor a protectionist type of bill, giving them a weekend to worry about what's going to happen next, then suggesting a compromise position that they will eagerly grab rather than see the whole thing go down the drain. With the free traders he can claim that he has salvaged something from the earlier bill, which would have been a considerably greater disaster than what he will come out with finally. With the protectionists, he will say that he has saved the bill by understanding the onslaught expected from the executive branch and the free traders and by compromising the more irritating provisions. In this way, he may have a chance of appearing to be a hero to both sides while compromising a very bad bill.

I suspect we are viewing another Mills tour de force: a complex tactical course which will permit him to protect his position with almost everybody concerned and to prevent any major disaster of a legislative nature, even though other forces impelling us toward such a disaster are very strong ones. I may be giving him more credit than he deserves, but I suspect not.[15]

August 15, 1970

I have been having some twinges of leadership during the last couple of weeks. John Anderson, chairman of the Republican Conference, came to me and asked me to be thinking of people who might be able to take [John F.] Bibby's place as executive director of the Research Committee, Bob Taft's[16] policy-type committee. I asked him why he wanted me to concern myself about it, and he said it had occurred to him that I was the logical person to succeed Taft in this leadership role. He said I was the kind of person who should do it because I had exhibited a degree of "balance" in my views of the country. I told him I was flattered by the suggestion, but I had grave doubts whether anyone from New York State could in fact be elected to anything by the conference. He did not press me, and of course, John Anderson is the wrong person in the leadership to be advancing my candidacy because he himself is somewhat beleaguered by the more conservative elements of the Republican Party.

If I could be sure of success, this would probably be a good time for me to make a move into the leadership, because there is a dynamic about such things that makes the opportunity less likely later, once it has been turned down. Many people would consider it presumptuous of me to make such a move after only three terms in the House, just as it was presumptuous to go on the Ways and Means Committee after one term and then to go on the Joint Economic Committee after two. Of leadership jobs, I would probably prefer to have this one, since it would involve work other than status and would not be as circumscribed as the Policy Committee by tradition. Since it is part of the leadership by vote of the conference early in the 91st Congress, the Research chairman would meet at the White House in policy and strategy meetings with the other members of the leadership.

In another sense, though, it would be particularly damaging to me to aspire to a position of this sort and not get it, either because of the unpopularity of New York, or because of my brashness and comparative inexperience, or because I am somewhat more liberal than the center of gravity in the Republican Party of

15. The bill was voted out of committee by a margin of 17–7, with nays cast by Conable, Corman, Gibbons, Pettis, Vanik, Ullman, and Bill Green [D-PA]. Schneebeli voted present.

16. Taft would be elected to the Senate in November 1970.

the House, or because some other stronger candidate aspired for the job and got it. I recall the disastrous impact it had on Al Quie [R-MN] and his reputation for him to announce for chairman of the Republican Conference only two days before the vote[17] and then secure only eight votes for the job, despite his general effectiveness as a congressman and as a person. One cannot ignore questions of strategy in making a decision, as Al did.

I also have the general philosophical question which still bothers me about whether or not I should try for the opportunity for political leadership when I have such a strong legislative position already foreclosing so much of the political activity a congressman must conduct in his home district if he is to survive. I can be an effective, influential congressman, regardless of leadership, because of the legislative position I hold. I will be a less effective legislator if I aspire to political leadership in the House.

September 17, 1970

After I get through with reorganization, task force, and trade, it appears likely to me that I will want to try to organize some revenue-sharing activity. I don't know why I'm getting to be such a "cause" man, but it seems to me that revenue sharing is the way of the future and we would do well to try to hasten the future along, in view of the crisis in local and state governments. I will endear myself to neither of the leaders on the Ways and Means Committee if I take up the cudgels of this cause, since John Byrnes recently has come out expressively against it after two years of muttering about it. Wilbur, of course, has always been vocal in his opposition to a division of the spending authority.

Night before last I attended a dinner for Mel Laird at Airlie House, in which he was presented with a "Statesman in Medicine" award. This award refers back to Mel's service on the [Departments of Labor and Health, Education, and Welfare] subcommittee of the Appropriations Committee. I sat not far from John Byrnes, who had, as usual, a little more to drink than was discreet and who was complaining in a loud voice that members of the Ways and Means Committee get no awards but only the opprobrium that goes with taxing people, and that if you want to be considered a statesman, you have to spend the money. There is a good deal to what he says, and I find occasional flashes of bitterness among my colleagues on the committee that we are not sought after the way Appropriations Committee members are in the executive branch and in Washington society. Somebody has to do the dirty work, and we are it.

17. At Christmastime 1968.

September 29, 1970

Ever since we completed with surprising success the reorganization bill, I have been working quite hard on the Task Force on Seniority report. Our proposal there is admittedly a compromise. It involves selection by the Republican Committee on Committees[18] of the ranking minority member or committee chairman without regard to seniority (although it is assumed that seniority will normally be the criterion) and his nomination individually to the Conference of the Republican Party for a yes or no secret ballot, with a "no" ballot by the majority of the members automatically assumed to recommit the nomination to the Committee on Committees for a new nomination. The task force is getting it from both sides on this proposal, and some of the members, although admittedly only a few, are saying that we did not go far enough and that this is purely a cosmetic change. The more serious opposition is by those who benefit from the seniority system, particularly the members from Ohio. This delegation is reacting with its usual patronage-oriented view, saying the whole proposal is a conspiracy to take away some of Ohio's six ranking minority members.

I have the members of the Republican Conference divided up among the members of the task force for a careful whip check. Although the response is coming back three to one, I am disappointed by the large number of people who are opposing such a statesmanlike opportunity for modification of the seniority rule. Worse than that, Jerry Ford and the leadership seem to be backing up in a surprising way as they get under pressure from a few of their old friends.

Out in Illinois last weekend I was at the same affair that Rog Morton was speaking at, and he seemed to be responding with such caution about how we should put over a decision until after the election, and I asked him in exasperation, "Rogers, are you presiding over a settlement house or a political party?" I find it difficult to believe that our party leaders would base their party policy on their desire to protect a few old men instead of giving the party itself an issue demonstrating vitality and working very much to the advantage of young challengers for old Democratic incumbents.

The trade bill has been put over until after recess. In a strictly no-guts operation, the Democratic leadership has decided that we are going to recess somewhere between the ninth and sixteenth of October and come back for a lame-duck session after the election, which will be neither responsible nor responsive.

---

18. Consisting of one member from each state that has at least one Republican representative.

October 14, 1970

Although the Democratic weakness in the leadership has been . . . apparent to everyone, I have had some experience of weak Republican leadership during the pre-recess period. Our [Task Force on Seniority] report . . . was ready three weeks ago, and at least two weeks ago we had a clear indication through a whip check that a margin of almost three to one among the Republican membership supported the proposal. I gave my report to Jerry, who has supported the proposal all along, and asked him when he would like to have a conference on it. He began to hedge, feeling heat from the Ohio delegation. . . . Finally he told me that he felt that he should not make the decision about what to do with the report himself, but have a meeting of the nine members of the Republican leadership in the House and let them make the decision.

We met in Les Arends's office with all the members of the leadership, and Rog Morton as well, present. Bill Cramer [R-FL] was not there, being in Florida campaigning, and Dick Poff [R-VA] had to stay on the floor because of a Judiciary Committee bill going at that time. Dick Poff would not have come anyway because he always avoids standing up and being counted, and in this case, he used the excuse that it might appear that he was looking for Bill McCulloch's [R-OH] ranking minority position on the Judiciary Committee. . . . John Anderson, who has not been enthusiastic about the report because he felt that it did not go far enough, pressed for a conference, as did Rogers Morton and Bob Wilson [R-CA]. Jerry took the position that he wanted simply to send a letter to all Republican candidates for Congress describing the proposal. I urged taking some official action so that we would have something more than a proposal to point to.

It was finally decided that the Republican leadership would endorse the idea "enthusiastically" and that Jerry would hold a press conference announcing that the plan would be recommended for adoption at the beginning of the 92nd Congress. This course was favored over a conference, and frankly, I acquiesced in the decision finally because of some fear that during the three days of meetings this week there would be widespread absenteeism and that therefore the result could not be predicted. . . . John Rhodes, a member of the task force, proved to be the most lacking in courage of any of the leaders, wanting to run away the minute there was any controversy. Bob Taft was embarrassed by his membership in the Ohio delegation and so took the position that he would not object to whatever was decided, but he wanted to express the Ohio view. At the meeting I pressed Jerry for a decision on when he would have his press conference, and it was decided that he would have it yesterday, Tuesday the thirteenth, at 2:30 in the afternoon.

Two o'clock came and no Jerry Ford; 2:30 I went up to the press conference and told them that Jerry was en route from Miami, where he had been speaking that morning. Finally at three o'clock Jerry's staff contacted me and said they thought I ought to go ahead with the press conference. . . . I tried to get some other members of the Republican leadership to come up and handle the press conference, saying that I would help them, but they all had some excuse for not coming and did not want to be involved. . . . I am somewhat resentful of having been made apparently the sole proponent of this plan and of having been put in the position of setting Republican policy when the leadership should have been doing it themselves. I have no doubt that I have made a number of enemies and identified myself as something of a revolutionary to the older group. This would not have been necessary if there had been any joint assumption of responsibility by those who have the position which permits them to make decisions.

Dick Cook of the White House liaison staff came to see me and asked me if I would be willing to serve as the prime cosponsor of the administration's revenue-sharing bill on the first day of the 92nd Congress. I, of course, assented readily, having decided that I would make revenue sharing my next cause. I am convinced that it is the wave of the future and the only thing ultimately that will save the vitality of our democracy.

It occurs to me that I have never yet in my journal mentioned an institution which has a good deal of use in the House of Representatives and which most congressmen feel for silly reasons to be quite furtive about. That institution is the Rayburn building gymnasium. Actually, I get down there comparatively rarely, since it is difficult to sandwich a paddleball game in between meetings of the Ways and Means Committee and the Joint Economic Committee. At a time like the past two weeks, when Ways and Means has had only an occasional meeting, I get down to the gym at least three times a week and participate actively in the fierce paddleball games that characterize the gym activity. . . . It is difficult to generalize about the roughly one hundred congressmen who use the gym regularly except to say that it obviously does not include Manny Celler [D-NY] and Flo Dwyer [R-NJ].[19] A spirited camaraderie grows up among the competitors in the paddleball games, who use the three courts quite without regard to political association, ideological view, or geographical distribution. Congressmen by nature are competitive, and the paddleball courts, providing a very quick way to get vigorous exercise in competitive surroundings, vent a good many of the frustrations that congressmen feel as they work in their large

19. At the time, Celler was eighty-two years of age and Dwyer sixty-eight.

groups under circumstances which require more cooperation sometimes than is comfortable.

Veteran political enemies seem to be able to put their differences aside and to associate quite comfortably as partners on the paddleball court. Congress is a human institution, and the paddleball courts in the gymnasium are a net plus for its humanity. It is difficult to imagine the violence of the reaction a month or so ago when Hatfield-McGovern[20] came up on the floor of the House and Don Riegle [R; switched to D in 1973] (a young man from Michigan completely without any relieving grace of humor or perspective in the intensity of his feelings) spoke directly to the galleries, claiming that the reason more congressmen were not on the floor to discuss that vital matter was that they all had run over to the paddleball courts to avoid their obligations for peace in the most irresponsible manner possible. The result was that, at the time of the next quorum call, a number of photographers went down to the escalators coming up from the subway from the Rayburn building into the Capitol and photographed a number of congressmen coming along to respond to the quorum call, including a number who had not been on the paddleball courts, as Riegle had charged. There was a good deal of bitterness about Riegle's remarks, and it added to the furtiveness of those congressmen who thereafter wanted to go and get some exercise at some point during the day. Many of them made a joke of it, saying things like, "How about coming over to the library with me to do a little research?" or "Have you been over to the Botts Committee yet?" (Herb Botts is the man in charge of the gymnasium.)

My own campaign has been singularly lackluster, and I have heard virtually nothing from my opponent, a young science teacher from Spencerport.[21] It is difficult to look forward to the next three weeks as anything but drudgery when the competitive element is not present. . . . The candidacy of [appointed senator] Charles Goodell [R-NY] continues to be a disaster, and the other night I went so far as to go to supper with Clifton White, [Conservative Party candidate James] Buckley's campaign manager, although I made it quite clear to him that I was not in a position to endorse Buckley, despite all the assurances he gave me that Buckley was in fact now ahead not only of Goodell but also of [Democrat Richard] Ottinger. Although Buckley is obviously doing well, I still find it hard

20. A measure calling for the withdrawal of all US military personnel from Vietnam by June 30, 1971.

21. Richard N. Anderson. Conable was reelected with 66 percent of the vote to Anderson's 30 percent, with a Conservative Party candidate taking the rest.

to believe that a third-party candidate can win in a state like New York. . . . I find myself resenting in undiminished earnest the extent to which Goodell is a polarizing factor in this election: if you are for him, you are a left-winger; if you're against him, you are a right-winger; and if you try to fudge in any way, you are a mealymouthed politician.[22]

November 16, 1970

We reconvened today for an irresponsible and unresponsive lame-duck session. The motivation for it has dissipated with the elections, since it appears that the 92nd Congress will be a carbon copy of the 91st.

Over on the floor there was a great deal of backslapping and handshaking as everyone greeted everyone else back for the lame-duck session. I had a long, somber talk with George Bush, who looked at me from deep-sunk eyes and talked only about what a sour outlook he had on life and how he really was finding it very difficult to face up to the options that are open to him now that he has been defeated for the Senate in Texas.[23] Incidentally, he doesn't seem to blame anyone about that, even though the papers have been liberally assigning blame to the president and vice president for their having stirred up all the rural Democrats in Texas and gotten them to the polls in record numbers.

November 17, 1970

This has been a tense day, with most of the activity directed toward consideration of the trade bill tomorrow. George Shultz has picked up the ball at the White House and is spending a great deal of time working on this measure. I met with representatives of different trade groups in the morning and was originally taking the position that I would not get myself involved in the House Republican strategy meeting due to come off at 12:30 between George Shultz, Jerry Ford and the leadership, and John Byrnes. Jerry called from the White House, however, saying he wanted me to be there. It became rather apparent that the White House considered me their fair-haired boy, and I have had worried phone calls from them almost every hour on the hour. My position has been that I am against quotas but that I will be willing to compromise if, in the process, the president will take a firm position on the trade bill and that position will be an improvement over the Mills bill. John Byrnes, of course, supports the

---

22. Buckley won the three-way race with 39 percent of the vote.

23. Bush was defeated by Lloyd Bentsen by a 54 to 46 percent margin. Bentsen had bested incumbent Ralph Yarborough in the Democratic primary.

Mills bill and feels the White House has intruded on this matter forcefully only after long, mushy leadership in which it was not clear what the president did want. I asked George Shultz to talk with Jerry Ford and take the position that I was not being cooperative in accepting the textile quotas so that Jerry could ask me to move and be enlisted in the cause in such a way that I would be in a position to make some concession to him.

This strategy all fell through when I had to go to the meeting in the early afternoon. John Byrnes took the position that the Republican Party was entitled to take a posture apart from his stand on the trade bill but that the entire Republican side of the Ways and Means Committee must be involved and that the president could not decide on a motion to recommit himself. . . . He would much prefer a straight motion to recommit.

November 30, 1970

Despite the great lapse of time since my last journal entry, the trade bill issue is not yet decided in the Senate. We did better in the House than we anticipated, getting 165 votes against the bill on final passage and 173 on a straight motion to recommit. The motion to recommit was handled by Harold Collier [R-IL] and represented the success John Byrnes had in turning back the White House initiative to delineate the president's position on trade.

The chairman and John Byrnes were both vigorous and effective [in debate on the floor]. I had to speak in the district that night but came back the next day and spoke for about twenty-five minutes against the bill, using no notes and rambling rather badly, at least according to my wife, who sat in the galleries and who is fully honest about such matters. A number of people were interested in my speech because my position had become so widely known on the bill and because I was such a unique member of the Ways and Means Committee. Most of the emotional oratory was on the other side. Neither John nor Wilbur seemed to be angry with me for fighting the committee's consensus, and both complimented me on my speech afterwards. Apparently, I have come out of this thing without their everlasting enmity, something that I do not believe Sam Gibbons has accomplished. Sam continues his abrasive ways, happy and unconcerned about his relations with other members of the committee and thus largely without influence.

December 21, 1970

The leadership race in the House continues to be a mystery to me. Jerry now tells me that there is going to be a major move to end the Research Committee, although he says he still favors its retention. Failure of anyone to come into the race against me leads me to believe this is a most serious possibility, and so I have asked John Erlenborn [R-IL] to get together a group of friends, and a whip check has been taken among the members trying to determine their attitude toward the Research Committee. This check does not disclose any widespread antipathy to the committee, and so I have to feel that opposition is vested in the same old group of senior and conservative members who generally oppose anything to do with activity or the possibility of jurisdictional dispute.

With respect to the race for chairman of the Republican Conference, John Anderson has put together an organization which is working very hard to counter the tough campaigning against him Sam Devine is doing. Sam sent out a letter last week saying that he was not running against anybody but *for* a job. This letter came a little late because the general discussion of this race has been entirely along the lines that it was a "Get Anderson" movement. They still think the conservatives, who claim at least eighty commitments for Devine, are talking a lot tougher than anything they can deliver. Bob Stafford [R-VT] is now clearly the man to beat for the vice chairmanship, since he has been campaigning vigorously and his membership on the Armed Services Committee has permitted him to put together a group of prime backers which includes some well-known elder conservatives.

Since the Research job will be the last one to be voted on, I therefore think it is quite probable that I will have at the end some opposition. I am considered in the moderate group in the House . . . and if Anderson and Stafford both win, there will be an argument that balance is needed in the leadership and that I cannot provide that balance. Also, those who are defeated for the more distinguished positions up the line will have a fallback position running for the Research Committee job, which will create a stampede for the disappointed, despite the fact that they have not campaigned for the research job previously. With this in mind, I am continuing to see individuals and urge their help for this job. I consider it more important as time goes on because it is quite obvious there is dissatisfaction with the function of the Research Committee, and a wise person with a little ambition who takes over the job will have the opportunity to do quite a bit of researchering.

The other night we all went to the White House for a Christmas reception, and I was surprised to find the detail of the president's memory and knowledge of what goes on in Congress. I introduced him to my wife, saying, "You remember my wife, Mr. President," and he said, "That is not your wife, Barber, that is your daughter." When I introduced her to him the first time at the Sunday church services at the White House at which Dr. Norman Vincent Peale spoke a year and a half ago, I introduced my three daughters and then added, "and my daughter, Charlotte." The president remembered that, even though it was an incident of modest humor—typical reception-line small talk. He also said to me, "Jerry tells me you are a sure thing to be elected to the leadership this year," to which I replied, "Nothing is sure in politics," and he said that he understood it was as sure as anything could be and that he would look forward to having me attend the Tuesday morning breakfasts.

I listened carefully because the next person in line behind us was Jolane Edwards, passing through the line without her husband. The president said to Jolane, "I understand your husband is running for the vice chairman's job in the Republican Conference. I certainly wish him good luck." Jack [R-AL] does not have a very good chance of winning, and so in each case, the president was saying properly what he thought he could say about the actual state of facts. We marvel that he knows as much about the Congress as he does, in light of his obvious isolation from opportunities to learn firsthand what members of Congress are doing and thinking.

Elected to the House GOP leadership, Conable begins regular meetings with Richard Nixon, whom he finds a puzzlement. The Joint Economic Committee is an arena of grandstanding and posturing, and Conable is quickly sick of it. Conable carries the ball for the administration on revenue sharing but goes his own way on the SST and campaign finance reform. Wilbur Mills is dreaming of the White House, but Conable is pushing him for the Supreme Court. Flattering press coverage is a mixed blessing for the congressman.

Though in only his fourth term in the House, Conable was achieving a certain emi-nence. In leadership meetings at the White House, he was anything but obsequious, even adopting a lecturing tone toward President Nixon. Conable approved of Nix-on's occasional decentralist initiatives, and in championing the president's revenue-sharing proposal, he defied Chairman Mills and ranking minority member Byrnes.

He was now quoted regularly in the national press, and his candor had a double edge: it attracted reporters but sometimes crossed the border into indiscretion. To the relief of the press, the discreet held no charm for Conable.

His opinion of Mills evolved. Mills the pragmatic legislator, the seeker of consen-sus, the crafter of veto-proof revenue bills had seemingly been replaced by Mills the panderer, the troller for votes in what Conable considered a preposterous and vain-glorious bid for the presidency. The "nonpartisan colossus standing astride the House of Representatives" was collapsing into something much less impressive: a politician in pursuit of office.

January 23, 1971
The day dawned cloudless, politically speaking, on the twentieth, and we com-pleted our entire work in one day while the Democrats took the day after, the twentieth and the twenty-first, to wind up their business. John Anderson beat back a major challenge to his chairmanship of the conference by a vote of 89–81, and Stafford defeated Jack Edwards for the vice chairmanship by a vote of 85–82. Rather than doing away with the Research Committee, the reluctants moved procedurally in an effort to defer consideration of it. H. Allen Smith

made a motion to this effect, and he was supported in it by Doc Hall [R-MO], John Rhodes, and a few others, although Jerry Ford stood up and made the main defense of the Research Committee, saying also that he wanted the chairman of the Research Committee, "whoever he may be," to be in the leadership. Surprisingly, Al Cederberg [R-MI], whom Jerry Ford had told me was opposed to the committee, stood up and criticized the past work of the committee but said that it should be continued. A voice vote was taken, and it appeared to have the support of the conference by about three to one, and so no division was demanded. The time came to vote for the chairman, but nobody else was nominated but me. John Erlenborn nominated me, and Bill Steiger [R-WI] seconded it, saying, to my surprise, that I wished to rehabilitate the committee, saying also he was embarrassed by Charles Goodell's tenure in the chairmanship. I certainly would have urged him not to have said anything of this sort if he had asked me.

Almost immediately after we laid to rest the issue of the Research Committee, its chairman, and whether or not its chairman would be in the leadership, the issue of seniority came up. I made a short report, as requested, and yielded the floor as soon as I was through. Strangely enough, most of the apparent opposition came from some three members—Phil Crane [R-IL], Ben Blackburn [R-GA], and Dan Kuykendall [R-TN]—although the major presentation against the report of the task force was made by Dave Martin [R-NE] of the Rules Committee. Fortunately, then Page Belcher [R-OK], ranking minority member of Agriculture, got up and made a wandering and disjointed speech in his whining voice, acting as though he were a good deal more senile than he is and saying that the proposal should be studied to death, deferral rather than downright rejection being the proposed route, and that set the stage for the final speech summing it up, which came from John Byrnes.

Jerry had asked John to speak, and John rose and made a very eloquent talk to the effect that he had been in Congress twenty-four years and he certainly didn't want to have his leadership of the Ways and Means Committee based solely on the fact of survival. He wanted to have legitimacy before his constituents as a selected committee leader rather than a senior committee leader. The boys cheered for him when he was through, and again on a voice vote it was apparent that we had at least three to one in favor of the proposal. I went out and faced the press, and the questions were all along the line of my having had a double victory, although it was so late in the day that the papers the next day barely gave notice to it in light of Democratic actions and struggles.

That night at home during supper, I was called to the phone and the president himself congratulated me on my selection to the leadership and chatted with me about the seniority issue. It was heady stuff. I don't think moving into the leadership after three terms in the House is unprecedented, but it obviously is going to take some adjustment for the establishment to have me there. For instance, no seat was saved for me at the leadership tables during the State of the Union address, although some of the senior ranking members were there, a fact which I noted with amusement but did not make a point of, since I would rather sit back with the boys anyway. Amusingly, the president has apparently adjusted more quickly than my colleagues to this fact; I have been invited to the White House three times in the first two days of next week, twice for leadership meetings and once for breakfast.

Carl Albert was elected to the Speakership . . . and his initial moves seemed to destine us to a rather partisan time. At the formal opening he gave a cliché-ridden speech nowhere near as graceful or appropriate as Jerry Ford's in present-ing him. One of the first acts of the new leadership of Albert, Boggs,[1] and Tiger Teague [D-TX][2] was to take away the investigative staff prerogatives (one-third of the staff money) guaranteed to the minority party by the Reorganization Act of 1970.

January 26, 1971

Yesterday morning began with a nonbreakfast meeting of the House and Sen-ate Republican leadership at the White House. . . . Both Bob Stafford and I, the newest members of the leadership, were the first to arrive, indicating our uncertainty about the time factors in driving to the White House, our eager-ness, and our excitement at being in the group. We went in the northwest gate on Pennsylvania Avenue, were checked off a list at the gate, and ushered in the front door of the West Wing by the marine guard. We sat in the lobby reading the *Washington Post* and chatting while other members of the House and Sen-ate leadership showed up. Those present were Jerry Ford, Les Arends, H. Allen Smith, John Rhodes, Bob Stafford, Dick Poff, and Bob Wilson and I from the House side (John Anderson was ill with a heavy cold) and Senators Norris Cot-ton [NE], Margaret Chase Smith [ME], Hugh Scott [PA], Bob Griffin [MI], Peter Dominick [CO], and Bob Dole [KS]. For some reason, the vice president did not show up, although a place was left for him. The president sat in the cen-ter of the oval table with his back to the Rose Garden, and I sat diagonally across from him, between Bob Stafford and Bob Griffin. Members of the president's

1. Hale Boggs had been elected House majority leader.
2. Olin "Tiger" Teague was chairman of the House Democratic Caucus.

staff, including Clark MacGregor,[3] Murray Chotiner, Ron Ziegler, Bill Timmons, Bryce Harlow, William Safire, and a couple of people I didn't recognize, sat around the outside of the room.

The president came directly from the Oval Office, and we all stood up as he entered the room. He exchanged some pleasantries, mentioned the fact that there were new leadership people there and that he wanted to welcome them. During the course of his remarks, he seemed to look at Bob Stafford and me more than at the others. The remarks were to the effect that there had been a good reception to his State of the Union address and that he thought the Democratic reaction was likely to be just that—nitpicking. . . . He said, "We'll let the Democrats have the lobbies; let us be in favor of moving." He said also, "I am sick of the dime-store New Deal attitude of Republicans generally," which he described as an attitude saying that we really favored the basic New Deal–type proposals made by the Democrats but weren't in favor of putting as much money in them as the Democrats would. He said, in effect, here is a bold new course where we can come out for something and . . . not nitpick in the usual Republican manner. He showed a good deal of political sensitivity in the course of his remarks, seeming to relate most of the issues involved to the politics of the situation, something that will surprise no one about Richard Nixon.

Following this opening statement, there were some exchanges with some of the senior members present, and then he asked George Shultz[4] to talk about the budget. George did, showing a chart which converted actual deficits to full employment deficits or surpluses. And George gave a scholarly little talk in uneconomic terms about the inflationary impact of a full employment budget as opposed to an actual cash budget. This raised some issues. I was one of the first to say, in effect, the following: Mr. President, I can see two political perils in the substantial deficit that you apparently are recommending in connection with the new full employment approach. The first is that you are assuming a continued high level of unemployment in order to justify a substantial deficit. It seems to me the Democrats can make some political hay with the assumption of a substantial unemployment rate going well into fiscal 1972. The second problem has to do with a more immediate and practical question. I do not know, but I assume that since this is a unified budget you are talking about being in deficit, that it also includes a substantial run-up in the trust funds, and therefore that it will be

---

3. After losing a US Senate race to Hubert Humphrey in 1970, MacGregor served as Nixon's liaison to Congress.

4. Director of the Office of Management and Budget.

necessary to raise the debt ceiling, which applies only to the general treasury, by an even greater amount, thus raising all the old issues of credibility and permitting the Democrats, again, to talk about the deficit actually being much more than it is on a unified budget basis.

The president dealt with these issues briefly, again talking from a political viewpoint, and then asked George to comment. It stimulated a good deal of further comment from members of the leadership, John Rhodes jumping in and agreeing that I had put my finger on a couple of sore points. Thus it went, with further discussions dealing with revenue sharing[5] and the consolidation of departments,[6] which the president proposed in his State of the Union address. He said that we would make every effort in the leadership meetings to be through by 9:30, henceforth, and to deal with preferably only one issue at each meeting, but this particular meeting went until slightly after 10:00 a.m., when Jerry Ford and Hugh Scott had to face the press and give their impressions of the meeting.

At 11:20 I left [an orientation meeting for new House members at which Conable spoke] to rush over to the Joint Economic Committee, which is having hearings. . . . It was announced that [Senator Stuart] Symington [D-MO] has left the committee and that Hubert Humphrey [D-MN] will take his place. Martha [Griffiths] said to Senator Proxmire, the new chairman, "Mr. Chairman, I am going to insist on firm enforcement of the five-minute rule in light of the new membership" and got a big laugh from it. Following the meeting, Bill Widnall [R-NJ] asked me to come to his office and talk with him, with an air of great mystery. I did and was appalled to find him saying that he was in bad shape physically as a result of arthritis in his hip and that he was going to have to depend on me very heavily to uphold the honor of the House Republicans in connection with the Joint Economic Committee. He described me as the "white hope" of the committee and said he hoped I would not get too bogged down with other things because he was going to have to depend on me greatly. I just moaned a little.

5. In his State of the Union address on January 22, 1971, Nixon had called for "a new partnership between the federal government and the states and localities—a partnership in which we entrust the states and localities with a larger share of the nation's responsibilities, and in which we share our federal revenues with them so that they can meet those responsibilities."

6. Nixon had proposed to reduce the number of cabinet departments from twelve to eight, retaining State, Treasury, Defense, and Justice and consolidating the others into new departments of Human Resources, Community Development, Natural Resources, and Economic Development.

January 30, 1971

My new job has added to my labors, and I have been somewhat concerned about my capacity to handle it. I missed virtually all Joint Economic Committee activity this week, with the exception of [New York governor] Nelson Rockefeller's appearance before the committee yesterday morning. He was there to make a big pitch for revenue sharing, which he did very well. The hearings, which are being conducted by Chairman Proxmire, are on the "crisis" of the American economy, and the imbalance in the witnesses invited by Mr. Proxmire scarcely masks a lurking partisan interest. I am continually appalled by the distinguished economists who lend themselves to a primarily partisan effort. Anyone who thinks economics is a science should listen to a master of innuendo like [Walter] Heller or [John Kenneth] Galbraith, pointing with alarm or expressing dismay, criticizing and always dealing his barbs at Republicans and compliments at Democrats.

I have had trouble getting the Research Committee together. Jerry asked me to check all people I was appointing (and that constitutes seven in addition to the leadership who make up the membership on Research) with each member of the leadership. I decided it was desirable to choose a group that would be fairly conservative, in view of the nature of the opposition in our organizing conference to the Research Committee, and the list I chose was generally acceptable to the leadership, although H. Allen Smith of California objected to one freshman member originally on the list because he was an "eager beaver." Nobody would consider H. Allen Smith an eager beaver or likely to be a friend of one. In any event, I replaced the offending youngster with another youngster who would not offend.

February 9, 1971

The Cabinet Room is an impressive room taken up largely with a large oval table facing out on the Rose Garden. Over the fireplace, which seems constantly to have a fire in it, is a large portrait of President Eisenhower. At the other end of the room, on the wall which is toward the Oval Office, are two large portraits, one of Teddy Roosevelt and the other of Woodrow Wilson. There is a pad of note-size paper with "The White House" printed simply at the top, and a mechanical pencil sits on each pad. These are scattered around the table, one at each chair. Coffee is served during the period before 8:00. The president arrives at 8:00 sharp and proceeds immediately to the center of the long side of the table, which places him with his back to the Rose Garden. The senators in general, with the exception of Bob Dole, sit at the end of the table toward the fireplace.

I sit diagonally across the table from the president, with Bob Stafford, the vice chairman of the conference, on my right, and Bob Griffin, the whip of the Senate Republicans, on my left.

The president usually opens the meeting with a modest statement of some sort. This morning he asked immediately for Henry Kissinger to give us a briefing on Laos, where the intrusion of South Vietnamese troops to cut the Ho Chi Minh Trail is presently in progress. He said that he would then turn to Secretary [of Health, Education, and Welfare Elliot] Richardson, who was present, for a description of the administration's health program.

Henry Kissinger proceeded to talk for thirty-five minutes about the Laos operation, not only giving us the details about the operation itself but answering an extensive number of questions from those present. . . . At 8:35 the president took over and held forth on the Vietnam War, continuing Kissinger's briefing and fielding further questions until 8:55, at which time Secretary Richardson took over.

Richardson spoke with assurance but did not appear to have a great deal of hard information, and from this I quickly drew the lesson that the president was pushing him for a medical program for which he was not sufficiently researched.[7] The president said that there would be a statement on this important part of his administration's program for this year on February 17. I think the time between now and then will have to be taken up largely in preparing a program, and I found among those present following the presentation that there was general dismay that the program had not been sufficiently thought out. I myself asked the second set of questions following Richardson's presentation. First I asked if this had been carefully checked with Wilbur Mills and John Byrnes, saying that it was my increasing feeling that very little would be achieved in the Ways and Means Committee over the dead bodies of Wilbur and John. There was no direct answer to this, but the president stated that last year Wilbur Mills had said that one of his major goals this year was to get some adequate health legislation. That was not, of course, to say that the president or Secretary Richardson had checked with the chairman about the details of this particular proposal.

The second question I asked was what the cost would be, pointing out that it was obviously a mandated insurance program which would have to be financed

7. Nixon had proposed, in his State of the Union address, a "program to insure that no American family will be prevented from obtaining basic medical care by inability to pay." The centerpiece of this program, which was effectively dead on arrival in the Democratic-controlled Congress, was employer-provided health insurance.

out of the payroll tax, and I stated that the public was viewing payroll taxes with increasing disfavor in light of the economic burden they represented to business at a time when the cost of labor was rising sharply and productivity was not going with it. Secretary Richardson tried to answer me that the tax for the mandated health insurance would not be imposed upon the employee but [on] the employer only, but I interrupted him and said that it was classical economic theory that any burden imposed upon a payroll, since it raised the cost of labor without increasing its productivity, in fact reduced the bargaining power of the employee and that it was the total burden on payrolls that I was concerned about. The only satisfactory answer I got on this, and only partially satisfactory at that, was that a large percentage of those people who are employed in the larger concerns now are covered by some sort of health insurance program for which the employer carries the major burden. Of course, small businesses and businesses with narrow profit margins are not included among those that presently furnish health insurance, and this aspect of the president's program, whether it is thought through or not, disturbs me at this point.

I did not get as clear an impression of a man on top of the issues as I did at the first meeting I had with the president. It seemed to me that not only the secretary of health, education, and welfare but the president himself was quite short of details with respect to the health program and was inclined to fall back on general principles and aphorisms about the American health delivery system. It would seem entirely consistent to me that the president of the United States was so involved in the big picture that he would not have time to come to grips with details, but the impression I had at the first meeting was that he concerned himself with almost every aspect of his work, and not just with the outlines of his major responsibilities.

February 20, 1971

Yesterday . . . was an interesting day because [chairman of the Federal Reserve] Arthur Burns appeared before the Joint Economic Committee, and Arthur Burns always supplies textbook testimony for whatever subject he is testifying about. My initial impression of this man was that he was a celluloid-collar type and that his ponderous way of speaking reflected a ponderous personality. I was wrong. He sets the tone for every answer he presents with a careful definition of the parameters of his answer and incisively set[s] out the most definitive answer of which he is capable. He has an excellent sense of humor. . . . In short, he is a delightful witness and obviously a remarkable man.

When he appeared before the committee, most of the committee members were there. I did not ask exciting questions, but it was primarily because I was so enthralled with the testimony that I did not have time to ponder my questions carefully. Hubert Humphrey simply threw his hands up in the air and made a ten-minute speech, a kind of campaign speech for the benefit of the little working man and the rural areas of our country. Martha Griffiths got off on her usual tangent and cross-examined the great man about small bank failures, something he was not qualified to talk about but which he took very seriously and promised to investigate for her. The chairman, Senator Proxmire, was somewhat more subdued than usual and did not make his usual innuendos in his opening statement, apparently confident that Arthur Burns would call him on it if he did.

[Secretary of the Treasury] John Connally appeared before the Ways and Means Committee this past week, speaking for two days in hearings in executive sessions on the raising of the ceiling on the national debt. I have had considerable misgivings about Mr. Connally, feeling that his appointment was only a "clever" one and that he was designed primarily as a captive Democrat in a Republican administration for the purpose of trying to improve political relations with the majority party in Congress.[8] My initial reaction was confirmed by his appearance as a junior version of LBJ, complete with Texas accent, unctuous manner, and occasional cuteness. I must say, however, that his performance on the debt ceiling was more than just clever. Despite the fact that he could not have been familiar with the subject matter of the hearing, he himself handled the questions, with [Undersecretary] Charlie Walker relegated to the backseat rather than whispering in his ear, and Connally showed the sense of timing and the ability to negotiate which marked him as a professional in his dealings with our complicated committee. He also showed considerable patience and a willingness to meet questions head-on in a way that was not at all reminiscent of [his predecessor] David Kennedy, a man who usually gave the impression of wanting to run away when a tough question came along. All in all, I have to express some grudging admiration for Connally's obvious abilities in the field of congressional relations, and I find an increasing expectation that his appointment will be one of the key appointments of the Nixon administration.

We have had virtually no success in securing Democratic cosponsorship of the revenue-sharing bill. Hugh Carey [D-NY] and I have exchanged a carping set of correspondence relating to the Democrats from New York and their phony political response to revenue sharing: the creation of a "task force on federal-

8. Connally had been confirmed as treasury secretary on February 11, 1971.

state sharing" which permits them to claim they are doing something without sponsoring the president's bill. I told Hugh I would join such a task force if it was clearly constructive in its thrust and not intended simply as a roadblock for what I considered to be a major government initiative through the revenue-sharing proposal. He wrote me back in some haste and some impatience, expressing the defensive attitude the Democrats must feel on this issue. I think we will let the correspondence stop where it was, since it is obvious that the bulk of the New York Democratic delegation are not going to go along with anything led by Richard Nixon.

March 19, 1971

The SST issue was up this week,[9] and it proved to be a very distressing one for the members of the Republican leadership. Almost two weeks ago, when asked about it at a Republican leadership conference, the president said, "Yes, I'm for it all the way."

It became an issue to Jerry Ford which aroused him more than almost any issue I have seen since I have been in Congress. On the floor of the House, Jerry gave a very intense speech obviously prepared at some length and delivered with such fierceness that he became all confused about whether it was the yes or the no vote that was wanted on a particular amendment under consideration and had to be corrected by Frank Bow [R-OH] in the middle of his speech because he was creating confusion.

I sensed that I was not alone among the Republican leadership in having a long history of voting against the SST. But I did not know the dimensions of the problem until Jerry called a leadership meeting the day before the vote. It became apparent that five of the nine members of the Republican leadership were not going to vote for the SST. . . . H. Allen Smith gleefully offered to resign from the leadership rather than vote for the SST. Bob Stafford said that he had a television program on and couldn't stay but that he'd think it over. Dick Poff said that he was afraid if he voted for the SST people would interpret it as being a sale of his vote in the interest of getting a judgeship. John Rhodes expressed his uncertainty and said he would think about it also. I met Jerry head-on, argued about the merits, and made everybody angry by saying that this should not

9. The supersonic transport (SST) airplane, funded primarily by the federal government and secondarily by the airline industry, had been under development since the late 1950s. Critics, a mixture of fiscal conservatives and environmentalists, charged that it was an egregious example of corporate welfare.

be the kind of political issue it was being made and that it appeared to me the president cared more about Scoop Jackson of Washington[10] than he did about his own party if he was expecting us both to support the myriad vetoes that will be necessary in the defense of the budget later in the year and the SST.

Jerry and I carried the burden of the debate in the meeting, which resolved nothing, and all five members of the leadership ultimately voted against the SST. Fortunately, the margin was slightly larger than would have been effected if all the members of the leadership had voted for the project.[11] I resented the issue from first to last and got the tightness in my stomach that always indicates to me that I am worrying about the vote too much.

Jerry has been very nice to me. I'm afraid he felt that I was being disloyal in not supporting him, but unfortunately, compromise was not possible on either side.

The White House, on the other hand, did not press on me at all with respect to the issue. I was called to a briefing by Kissinger the morning of the vote and thought that perhaps I would be taken in for a direct confrontation with the president in the course of the briefing, but the issue was not raised at all, and Dick Cook, the most effective arm-twister in the White House ménage, when he saw me shortly before the vote, said, "Barber, I'd better stay away from you, you're doing too much for us in other things for me to want to get involved about the SST." Well, the whole thing was an unhappy business.

John Ehrlichman[12] invited me to lunch at the White House this past week and showed considerable interest in the work of the Research Committee, and I enlisted him for assistance and consultation as the year progresses. He is an earnest, well-intentioned man with very quick perceptions, and his efficiency and matter-of-factness make him seem almost a caricature of the executive's right-hand man.

March 31, 1971

The chairman has been mentioned several times in the past week for president on the Democratic ticket in the upcoming election, and although he disclaims

10. Senator Henry "Scoop" Jackson (D-WA), a prime supporter of the SST, was sometimes known as "the senator from Boeing."

11. The House voted by a margin of 215–204 to cancel federal support of the SST. Gerald Ford's dogged lobbying helped revive the SST in May by a narrow vote of 201–197, but the Senate ultimately killed it on May 19 by a vote of 58–37.

12. White House domestic affairs adviser.

any interest, it's apparent to all who know him that he is tickled by the attention and the suggestion. Jim Burke, in particular, is playing the role of sextant on this issue, referring to it with glee and saying that he is going to put up billboards and things of that sort. . . . The chairman does have a substantial ego and enjoys flattering references that are made to him in the press. . . . He enjoys recognition; he does not seek power because he has ample power where he is at present.

April 23, 1971
I am getting a little sick of people coming around and interviewing me about Wilbur Mills. It seems that every national newspaper and magazine is doing a feature article on the chairman, and since he is such a mysterious and sometimes contradictory figure, they are consulting with members of the committee a good deal about it. Unfortunately, the *National Journal* put out an article at the beginning of this week[13] reporting a poll of committee members, former members, staff people, lobbyists, and executive branch people indicating that they considered me the most active and influential member of the committee after Wilbur and John, and the result of this article is only to confirm potential students of the committee and the chairman in their determination to talk to me about what goes on there, something that I would be more comfortable with a greater degree of anonymity about. So far, I have not had any unfortunate quotes attributed to me with respect to the chairman's personality or his modus operandi, but I am usually so frank that sooner or later I will be in bad trouble with him for shooting off my mouth. Most of the people who interview me are people who want to hang on to my own goodwill if I am the flapping mouth type and easily accessible, and so they protect me from my own sometimes innocent indiscretions.

May 5, 1971
[Wilbur Mills] is obviously relishing the talk about him running for president, and the other morning when I came into the Ways and Means Committee room, he was sitting there reading with great absorption a *New York Times* article which professed that the South was to have a major role in choosing the next president. I persist in the belief that he is enjoying the recognition primarily and is not terribly serious about running for president because any major leadership role of that sort, president or Speaker, would be quite different from the type of leadership in which he has excelled. Far-flung responsibilities with respect to very diverse

13. Frank V. Fowlkes and Harry Lenhart, Jr., "Two Money Committees Wield Power Differently," *National Journal* 3, 15 (April 10, 1971): 784.

groups such as the national Democratic Party would put the chairman into an ulcerous condition very quickly, with his thin skin and his penchant for worrying. He enjoys the role of being the man of mystery, the power behind the throne, and doubtless his efforts to encourage support for the presidency at this point are designed to put him in control of a bloc of influence with which he can be a power broker. In other words, nature, politics, and Wilbur Mills all abhor a vacuum.

May 25, 1971

The president put out a statement embracing and congratulating the committee on the. . . . Social Security benefits increase,[14] against which all of the Republican members of the committee voted for reasons of fiscal responsibility. John Byrnes was furious and kept referring to the president as "Tricky Dick" in his discussion with Jerry Ford and others about how the president had sabotaged members of the committee. John also wrote the president a personal letter in which he said that he would discuss the contents of the letter with him at his next personal meeting to be sure that he had read it.

John's relations with the White House seem to go from bad to worse, with neither side caring particularly. This, of course, leaves me in an increasingly embarrassing position as a man who is, for the most part, supporting the administration and is halfway down on the seniority list of the committee and not a bit anxious to get at cross-purposes with my committee leader, whose qualities of mind I considerably admire. The only conclusion that can be drawn is that the White House is not good at its congressional relations, despite the heroic efforts of Clark MacGregor. Clark himself is much upset about the Social Security blunder, but of course, he cannot keep his hand on everything that is going on at the White House, and so the blunders continue.

June 2, 1971

Yesterday the Ways and Means Committee hearings began on revenue sharing. The day before yesterday Jerry Ford chose to have a press conference early in the morning to kick off revenue sharing, having with him Murray Weidenbaum of Treasury[15] and the other members of the House Republican leadership. . . . I got down there early and told Jerry that Wilbur had made a statement the day previous in which he had said that they were going to give revenue sharing a nice quiet funeral. I said to Jerry, "If you want to catch a little attention at this

14. A 5 percent increase, beginning June 1972.
15. Assistant secretary of the treasury for economic policy.

press conference, you might say in effect that you don't know in what capacity the chairman was speaking. You could say that if he is speaking as an undertaker, he underestimates the vitality of the corpse; if he is speaking as an executioner, he underestimates the political consequences of destroying a proposal with so many friends. In any case, it won't be a quiet funeral." Jerry said, "That's good; can I use it?" And I said sure. He did try to use it and got all tangled up on it, but I noticed that the 11:00 TV had him talking about Wilbur as an executioner and as an undertaker.

John Connally was the lead-off witness yesterday at the hearings. He had laryngitis and obviously didn't feel very good, so the sparkle wasn't there. He showed himself amenable to possible suggestions for improvement, but the chairman and John Byrnes led off with undisguised displays of hostility. As soon as Connally finished his general statement, the chairman said that he had done remarkably well with a very weak proposal. I had stopped over at John Byrnes's office on the way to the hearing to find out what was going on, and John said he didn't know that anything was going on, but in the middle of the afternoon, after I had made what Connally described as an ardent and eloquent statement in behalf of revenue sharing (he said he thought we ought to change places, since I'd make a better witness than he would), Larry Woodworth, the executive secretary of the Joint Committee on Internal Revenue Taxation and one of the closest confidants of the chairman, sitting in his usual place back of the desk, said to me quietly, "Barber, if I were you, I'd stay on this issue and you may very well get almost everything you want." I said, "Larry, do you know something about this that I don't know?" He answered, "Oh, now, Congressman, you know everything." I said to him, "Larry, don't brush me off on this; is something going on?" He said, "I just want to repeat: you sit tight and keep cool and you may be surprised how well you'll come out on this."

I reported this conversation to Jim Cannon,[16] Governor Rockefeller's salve man who was in the audience, and Jim repeated to me a story that he had said earlier, which I hadn't believed: that when the governor called Wilbur Mills last week about revenue sharing, he was surprised at how mollifying the chairman was in contrast to the public statements he was making about revenue sharing. The first time Jim told me about this, I was inclined to brush it off as the chairman's usual politeness and anxiety to be friendly with someone like Nelson, to make him feel that they were in the same ballpark, but now I'm not sure that

16. Special assistant to Governor Rockefeller for federal, state, and intergovernmental affairs.

there isn't more going on than meets the eye. The chairman certainly has not hewed to his usual pattern of leaving loopholes open, but maybe I just don't recognize a loophole when I see it.

Yesterday the Democrats defeated our first attempt to pass one of the special revenue-sharing proposals, this one relating to manpower training. The vote on the whole had indicated that we might win it, but the vote on final passage was then delayed for two weeks while Carl Albert put his personal reputation at stake with a large number of Democrats who had defected on the rule vote. In a sense, I'm almost glad that Carl Albert won this one, because he has certainly lost almost everything he has tried to succeed with up to this point in the 92nd Congress. It is bad for a Congress to be as leaderless as this one has been, and certainly Carl has been not only ineffective but almost counterproductive for his causes. This victory came hard on the heels of the debacle of the Albert House Office Building. He wanted to replace the authorized Madison Library Annex, adjoining the Cannon House Office Building, with the fourth House office building but was rebuffed on Monday of this week by the Appropriations Committee, almost none of which were willing to go along with this suggestion. If the Republicans were good politicians, they would have kept it alive in order to clobber Carl politically on what must be one of the worst exercises of judgment on the part of the legislative leader.

July 25, 1971

Since my last journal entry, I have been spending most of my time . . . waiting for the chairman to decide when the time has come to kill revenue sharing. He has said several times, "I guess we'll start voting on this tomorrow—that is, deciding what we won't want to do." By this, he means that he still opposes the administration's plan, but his own plan has not seen the light of day as yet. John Byrnes has been needling the chairman three times a day, saying to him, in effect, "We read in the papers about the Mills plan. What *is* the Mills plan? When are you going to disclose it to the rest of us, as you have to the newspapers?" The chairman says, "John, I'll let you know when I have thought of the Mills plan," or reacts with impatience to John needling him. Nothing is decided, and nothing is apparently about to be decided after several weeks of executive session. We meet only in the mornings, since the chairman almost always has speaking engagements in the afternoon and evening which take him out of the usual pattern of committee work. We find out more of his intentions from reading it in the paper in response to questions asked him at his speaking engagements than we do from the work in the committee.

I have no reason to believe that more than six members of the Ways and Means Committee, and those all Republicans, will vote against a motion to kill or table the administration bill. All the Democrats, knowing the strength of the chairman's feeling about this issue and wishing to support him in the political kick on which he has now embarked, would vote dutifully to kill the administration bill, even though many of them favor one form or another of revenue sharing. If I were to guess right now what the probable strategy of the chairman will be, it would be that he will try to table the administration proposal shortly before the August recess begins on August 6, at the same time instructing the staff to do some drafting on a general revenue-sharing plan to be called something other than revenue sharing, probably bypassing the state government level and reflecting the Democrats' concern about the cities rather than the counties. By letting the recess intervene between the killing of the administration's plan and the generation of the "Mills plan," he will make it clear that it is not a Nixon initiative that is aiding the cities and that in fact revenue sharing is dead, to be supplanted by his own particular type of plan. The newspapers are giving a great deal of attention to him, and as a side effect, they are interviewing me a good deal since I seem to be the noisiest spokesman on behalf of the administration. I continue to say variations on my theme that what we come out with finally will look like a rose and smell like a rose but that for purposes of politics, we will have to call it a pansy.

I have also been stepping up the decibel rating of my criticisms of the chairman as he has himself become more and more openly critical of Richard Nixon and of the administration for its "uncooperative attitude." The chairman seems to be relishing his role as a presidential candidate. There no longer seems to be much doubt that he considers himself to be a serious candidate, although he plays cat and mouse with those who ask him directly. I understand he has a great many speaking engagements scheduled between now and December and that most of them are before politically sensitive forums. His role as a presidential candidate, incredible as it seems, is bound to affect in unconstructive ways the work of the committee. Instead of a nonpartisan colossus standing astride the House of Representatives, Wilbur Mills is becoming something less than a colossus and uncolored partisan. Those Republicans who have considered him an ally up to this time because of his normal conservatism and because of his quest of the consensus rather than the partisan advantage I hope will reassess their positions, since the error of their ways should be by now apparent to them.

The talk of the country and therefore the Congress also since the last journal entry is the president's decision to go to Peking, following Dr. Kissinger's successful mission to set up the invitation.[17] Last Tuesday morning we had an interesting White House meeting on this subject and on the subject of the economy. . . . I had hoped to be able to tell the president that it was my conclusion from moving around my district last weekend that the great bulk of the people support his diplomatic initiative with respect to China, but when he completed his own explanations of what Kissinger had said [earlier in the meeting], he moved immediately to discussion of the economy. On this discussion, John Rhodes, John Anderson, Peter Dominick, and, to some degree, Bob Griffin raised strong, articulate, and persistent objections to what was described as administration policy by George Shultz.

Talking with Clark MacGregor later, I learned that the president left the Cabinet Room, went back to the Oval Office, and said to Clark, "What kind of people are those legislative leaders? I pulled off the coup of the century with respect to China, nobody says a good word about it, and in fact Dominick expresses his dismay about the abandonment of Taiwan, and they spend all their time berating me about an economic condition which is nowhere near as bad as the Democrats are trying to paint it."

If only Nixon was not such a loner, preferring to sit and look at a yellow sheet of paper on which he can scrawl his thoughts rather than mingling with the people that must support him if the administration is to be successful. The White House is a great leadership weapon, the cynosure of all eyes and the ultimate environment in which to flatter the followers. But he ought at least to do it for a greater percentage of his own people. He ought to do it for the press, too.

August 6, 1971

I am getting into a thing with other members of the leadership again about the women's Equal Rights Amendment. It seems politically very bad for us to line up behind amendments which are, at best, subterfuges in reducing the effectiveness of the amendment. Bob McClory [R-IL] was the only member of the Judiciary Committee who voted against such amendments on the Republican side, and he came to see me and John Anderson. It now appears that the two of us, and possibly Bob Stafford, will be the only members of the leadership to support the Equal Rights Amendment, once again making us look like a liberal clique in the leadership. I do not feel like that great a liberal, and yet I am constantly promoting a schism within the leadership of the Republican Party on

---

17. On July 15, 1971, President Nixon announced in a televised address to the nation that he would visit the People's Republic of China the following year. He did so in February 1972.

issues that are interpreted as liberal-conservative issues to the membership as a whole, the conservative elements of which have a very vague idea about what it is to be conservative.[18]

September 7, 1971

I reread *The Education of Henry Adams* during the recess and found it considerably more charming, and more comprehensible, than the first time I read it back in college.

October 4, 1971

We continue to struggle with the rules of the new ball game on Ways and Means since the chairman has started running for president. His votes on the floor are incredible in terms of the old Wilbur, his approach to committee work is distracted and shows obvious evidence of partisanship, his well-known tendency to tell everyone he is talking to what he wants to hear rather than the facts of life has become obvious even to those persuaded of his statesmanship, and old relationships are by the boards.

Of even greater interest is the way he is handling future program work by the committee. We have now not only completed hearings but two months of executive sessions on revenue sharing, and yet it is obvious he does not intend to take it up again for the rest of the year. He has announced that on October 18 we will begin our hearings on health insurance but will not deal with any executive sessions on this subject or anything else before we adjourn the first session of the 92nd Congress.

When the committee reconvenes in early 1972, he will have two major items ready to go. One of them is coveted by organized labor, the other by the central city machines. These are two elements of the Democratic coalition which have some potential support for him for president, as yet unrealized, to add to the already realized support from the South. I am currently mixing my metaphors in saying that Wilbur has stars in his eyes, holes in his head, and is going to wind up with egg on his face.

Danny Rostenkowski told me today that he thought the chairman was really interested in taking the Speakership away from Carl Albert and that his presi-

18. The House passed the Equal Rights Amendment (ERA) on October 12, 1971, by a vote of 354–24, after stripping it of the amendments added in the Judiciary Committee. The Senate approved the ERA in March 1972, at which time it was sent to the states for ratification.

dential campaign would build him up to a point where he would be not only a power in the Democratic Party but a power in the Congress. It is widely speculated that he is interested in the vice presidency, something which carries very little responsibility with it but involves a nice recognition after long years of heavy responsibility in a comparatively unheralded congressional slot. I incline to the latter view, that it is recognition he wants, and so I have been urging the people at the White House, without notable success, to consider appointing Wilbur to the Supreme Court. Dick Poff bowed out this past weekend, smashing his long dreams of a Supreme Court or circuit court judgeship in a splurge of bitterness because he did not have enough votes in the Senate possibly to break a filibuster directed at him for his long-expressed civil rights views.[19] The chairman's position on civil rights is not much better, but you can be sure it is more equivocal than Poff's, and, as a southerner and strict constructionist, he would meet the president's requirements for the Supreme Court, while his appointment would remove the major impediment to the president's program in the Congress.

Clark MacGregor has said to me, "But Barber, we would then have Al Ullman, who would be just as bad as the chairman." I have said to Clark in response that Al Ullman has nowhere near the commanding reputation of the chairman, his influence on either the committee or the Congress, or the capacity to deal with John Byrnes on the same terms as the chairman does. Also, Al Ullman is not running for president. I tried to put this bee in John Connally's bonnet this morning, but he did not return my call. I would say the same thing to the president if I were to see him, but we have not had a leadership morning meeting now for three weeks. In any event, I doubt the White House would have the wisdom to appoint Wilbur to the Supreme Court, even if Wilbur were to turn out to be interested. I know this: the pipsqueak American Bar Association would never dare claim that Wilbur was unqualified for high judicial office, despite the long years he was a county judge in Arkansas, unless they are willing to say that anyone in government office is disqualified from holding one of the great jewels of the judiciary.[20]

October 13, 1971

Last Thursday night I went to Buffalo to serve as master of ceremonies at Jack Kemp's [R-NY] fund-raising dinner at which Spiro Agnew spoke. It was poorly

19. Poff was appointed a justice of the Supreme Court of Virginia in 1972.
20. On October 22, 1971, President Nixon nominated William Rehnquist and Lewis Powell to the Supreme Court.

organized, with Jack himself largely without understanding of the details and apparently so full of adrenaline that about all he could do was walk around on the wall. His wife, Joanne, appears to be a very fine politician, helpful and intelligent. Spiro gave a graceful and clever speech, comparatively low-key if you are to contrast it to his public image as a fire-breather, although the *Buffalo Evening News* felt obliged to have a knee-jerk reaction about his criticism of the press. Charlie Goodell came to Buffalo that night and met with Mayor [Frank] Sedita in an obvious effort to draw play away from Spiro. Charlie apparently has not only lost his dignity but his intelligence.

November [no date] 1971

We have an issue facing us which is potentially very divisive in the Republican leadership: that is the issue of election reform. John Anderson has assumed a leadership position with respect to this issue, trying to get together a bipartisan coalition, the Democrats headed by Mo Udall, for the purpose of getting through some sort of an election reform measure.

Recently I have come to realize how far out of phase with my colleagues I am in my own election financing practices. I raise most of my money in contributions of $10 or less, having raised $16,000 or so in this manner for the last election. I accept no more than $50 from any individual source. I will not even take an honorarium at this point in excess of $150. I can run my campaign on a total of $25,000 or less, in contrast to a large number of my colleagues, who spend as much as a quarter-million dollars on a campaign. I have not had major labor union money put in against me, nor have I had a very creditable candidate in the last two elections. As a result, I am in a very poor position to judge the problems of my colleagues and to construct an election reform system which will be acceptable to them sufficiently that it has any chance of passage. Therefore, my role in this particular issue has subsided, and I am glad that other people like John Anderson have come forward to assume the leadership. Be that as it may, I have been politically willing, even anxious, to join him now that he has something going of a bipartisan nature.

The agitation on this issue started some time ago, and a meeting of the House Republican leadership was called to consider whether or not we should take a position. At that time we did not, as a result of what was said. I made an emotional speech in which I said that we were unfit to be called a political party if the only way we thought we could win elections was by buying them. Jerry was upset with my attitude, and after John Anderson had had a bipartisan meeting last week, at 4:00 in the afternoon Jerry unexpectedly called a leadership meeting scheduled for 5:00 in the whip's office. I was sitting on the floor at that time and I was not even invited to attend the meeting, nor did I hear about it until afterwards. Clark MacGregor was there and read the riot act to John Anderson, saying that his efforts to compromise the issue were not appreciated and that there were certain things that would cause the White House to oppose any bill as long as they were included in it.

From the report that John Anderson gave me later, I would judge that the momentum for the White House's late involvement in this issue was coming from Secretary of Commerce Maurice Stans, one of President Nixon's major fund-raisers.[21] I came back from a $500-a-plate dinner in Rochester a little over a week ago. Secretary Stans, who had spoken at the dinner, got Frank Horton and me together on the Eastman plane that was bringing us back and told us how essential it was that the president not have limitations imposed on the contributions that could be made to his campaign. His position was that 40 percent of the money Nixon raised in 1968 was from contributors of more than $10,000, while the Democrats get their money from a wide range of union activities, the organization of which can be divided up so that no one group gives any very substantial sum of money.

November 30, 1971

Last night Jerry Ford had us meet with a man by the name of Richard Scaife, an heir to the Mellon fortune and a controller of the various Mellon foundations which function in the quasi-government area. The meeting was a dinner meeting at the Capitol Hill Club, and to me, it was somewhat distasteful because of the obsequiousness of the Republican leadership in attendance when confronted by all that money. There is something obscene about extremely wealthy men with political ambition, or at least manipulative ambition, who have very little to give to any subject except the power of their wealth.

December 8, 1971

Looking back over the year, I cannot find any great satisfaction in my service in the House, although I continue to be challenged by the opportunities that were presented. I have performed badly on the Research Committee assignment, and if I am offered the opportunity to be in the leadership again after the 1972 elec-

---

21. Stans, finance chairman of the Committee to Re-elect the President (CREEP), helped raise more than $60 million for the campaign. He was indicted but acquitted on charges of conspiracy, obstruction of justice, and perjury.

tions, I am not sure I will take it. The major reason I have performed badly is because of the pressure of Ways and Means Committee work. This committee has also detracted from my work on the Joint Economic Committee, which continues to seem like a publicity forum rather than a really constructive part of the work of the Congress. John Byrnes seems to take me increasingly into his confidence about Ways and Means Committee work, and looking back, I can see now that change in my role on Ways and Means followed the article by the *National Journal* in which I was erroneously identified as the third most influential member of the committee. The article created an expectancy with respect to my service on Ways and Means that affected both the other committee members and people who have to deal with the Ways and Means Committee, particularly those who cover its activities for the press.

I have apparently identified myself to members of the press quite independently of this article as a man who talks very frankly about the personalities on the committee, and the great consternation generally about the chairman's role as a political candidate has led increasing numbers of press people to seek me out for my analysis of what it means in terms of committee action and in terms of the chairman's own future in politics. Because the chairman is such a sensitive man, and because he has such pervasive feelers out in the Congress, most of the members of the committee are unwilling to say anything about him except the most glowing assessment of his capacities. I continue to admire the chairman as a man of great ability, but I try to view him objectively and to assess the impact of what he is doing on the committee itself, and this is apparently quite enough to keep me in trouble with him and in demand by the press. My candor will be my undoing yet.

Conable's laudatory press clippings and sharpening profile feed resentments by some GOP colleagues. Wilbur Mills uses Ways and Means to further what Conable (and voters) regards as his will-o'-the-wisp presidential ambitions. Conable admits to misgivings about Herman Schneebeli, the heir apparent to John Byrnes as ranking minority member on Ways and Means. Stirrings of a political midlife crisis? Revenue sharing, the first major piece of legislation in which Conable has played a central role, is enacted after a fierce battle. Another easy reelection campaign is the calm before the Watergate storm.

The more ludicrous Wilbur Mills's presidential candidacy became, the further the chairman drifted from the shrewd statesman Conable had once admired. Despite being in the minority, Conable saw himself as a defender of the integrity of the Ways and Means Committee, and he was concerned that the chairman was staining its reputation.

Conable lamented Nixon's remoteness from Congress and his apparent indifference to the fortunes of any Republican but himself. He slipped into garrulity at White House meetings, partly in response to the reticence of other members of the leadership. Why, he wondered, don't they speak up?

His latest evaluation of his Ways and Means colleagues was more incisive but also much harsher than the previous one, perhaps due to a wave of autumnal melancholy and his sense that Ways and Means was a "faltering committee."

January 7, 1972

I went home for a week during the recess and found the usual problems of a congressman at home. One's accessibility is learned by his neighbors, and any little problems that have been stacked up awaiting the moment preoccupy the congressman's time. Far from getting a rest, I came back to Washington after the holidays feeling that I needed a vacation from the home front.

[John Byrnes's announcement of his retirement] got nice notices in the paper by the *New York Times* and some of the other knowledgeable journals that are aware of John's importance to the committee. Eileen Shanahan quoted me extensively in her story of the retirement and, as a matter of fact, since no one else was around, pretended to have interviewed three or four members of the committee when in fact everything she said was something she had derived from me.

Nobody seems to know much about Herman Schneebeli, and so a number of reporters have asked me about him following John's announcement and Herman's apparent accession to the top place on the committee. It has come back to us from lobbyists that Herman does not want to be the ranking minority member, and I think he will have a tough time doing it because it is a considerable responsibility. He is basically a bright man and a decent man, and so if he is willing to make the effort, he will be able to do the work and certainly would do it far better than many other possible choices on the committee. His impulsiveness and stubbornness will be his greatest problems, and he will have to learn a lot. I think the man who will suffer most by John's retirement is Wilbur Mills because it will very much increase the burdens on the chairman. He used to have John's good mind as a counterfoil or a check on his own complicated thought processes. As for me, I shall be number four on the committee, low enough to require additional responsibility, with a high expectancy because of the good publicity I've had this year, but without the real authority of being a member of the conference committee. It is there, of course, that legislation is written.

January 21, 1972

[At a political event in Rochester] I sat next to Rockefeller at the dinner table and chatted with him throughout the evening. He said several things that were of interest. (1) That he had not made any deals on congressional districts in order to get the by-now famous letter from Wilbur Mills assuring that there would be revenue sharing and early in the session.[1] He did say they made some deals with some legislators on legislative redistricting in order to get votes for his interim tax measures. (2) That Wilbur's back really was bad and that he had even gone so far as to talk with Wilbur's doctor about it. He refused to speculate about what Wilbur's plans on the presidency might be and evidently did not want to accept the postulate that the chairman's bad back was really cold feet and that we could not count on the chairman's coming back to take control of the

---

1. According to Rockefeller biographer Richard Norton Smith, Mills agreed to put in writing the outline of a revenue-sharing plan after receiving a phone call over the Christmas recess from Hugh Carey in New York City, who said that he was "here with the governor" and that "reapportionment is coming up." Richard Norton Smith, *On His Own Terms: A Life of Nelson Rockefeller* (New York: Random House, 2014), 613.

revenue-sharing effort very quickly. (3) It appears that he still intends to retire in 1974, although he says the papers pushed him into announcing that he would be a candidate again. I suspect he was already having lame-duck troubles, with his state government splitting up into cliques of those intending to succeed him. (4) He said that he was relishing his feud with John Lindsay and told me gloatingly that he had really unloaded on Lindsay that day in a speech in Albany. (5) While [Lieutenant Governor] Malcolm Wilson was speaking, he leaned over to me and said that Malcolm sounds more and more like a right-winger, doesn't he? (6) As for himself, he said that he was planning to keep his options open. He laughed and winked knowingly at me when he said this.

February 14, 1972

I continue to get unfortunate publicity indicating that I am going to be the real leader of the Republican side of the Ways and Means Committee this next year. There will be three people senior to me, and Herm Schneebeli will be the ranking minority member. I like Herm and I have pledged him my support in every way, so he does not seem to worry about any effort to short-circuit his leadership by me. Harold Collier and Joel Broyhill are another matter, however. They both act grumpy at any suggestion that I have any more influence than my modest position on the seniority scale would justify. Joel is particularly unpleasant about this, since he has always resented the activity of my Task Force on Seniority.

Kevin Phillips, the columnist, asked me if I would do an interview with him about fiscal policy since I would be the fiscal expert of the Republican side of the Congress after John Byrnes's departure. I wrote Kevin and said that I was having a little problem with my colleagues and that I would prefer not to. I feel rather strange to be turning down opportunities for expressing influential opinions like this, but I really feel that a low silhouette is a wise idea in this human institution when I am being ascribed influence I am unlikely to be able to wield. Maybe someday I will be able to accept the theory that I have influence whether I deserve it or not. In the meantime, I would prefer to improve my relationship with my colleagues.

February 24, 1972

The White House asked me if I would go around and talk to Wilbur and see what I could do to get him off the dime on revenue sharing. . . . I got to the chairman's office and found him closeted with a bunch of oilmen, I suppose talking about campaign donations. In about twenty minutes he let me in and I stated that my purpose was to find out what I could do to help on trying to resolve the modest differences between the administration and the Mills bill on revenue sharing. His answer was, "Just sing out at meetings as you usually do, Barber." That was about the level of his helpfulness, and he appeared quite unwilling to assign to me any role as a resolver of difficulties. I tried to talk with him about substantive matters, but he also did not wish to do that, but instead wanted to talk to me about how many Republicans in New Hampshire he had persuaded to vote for him and how he was rising in the polls there. He presented a very good picture of a man hooked on the vanity of his ambitions.

Wednesday of this week, Wilbur thunderstruck us all by appearing during a one-minute session on the floor and saying that he was in favor of a 20 percent benefit increase in Social Security. He asked that the Senate substitute this for the 5 percent benefit increase in the H.R. 1 bill that is presently stalled in the Senate as a result of Senate objections to welfare reform. He said that as a conferee he would cheerfully accept the 20 percent increase, possible because of the overfunding of the system. He did not spell out that actuarial assumptions had been wrong, although he indicated this and inferred that taxes could actually be reduced at the same time a benefit increase was paid.

Immediately after the delivery of this thunderclap, I crossed the House floor and said to the chairman that his proposal was incredible. His reaction was, "Barber, you check with your actuary friends and they will tell you that it is not only possible but desirable to make these changes." I said that I was sure it was possible but I questioned whether it was either desirable or sound. I repeated that I thought coming from him it was an incredible proposal, and he then put his finger on my chest and said, "Listen, your fellows downtown are going to propose this anyway."

A proposal relating to the actuarial assumptions had been made in 1971 by the Advisory Council on Social Security, but up until now, the committee has not taken it seriously. I still believe that is what he is talking about when he says the administration is going to make such a proposal, because a check made with the responsible people in the administration doesn't indicate anything of the sort.

At the beginning of the session this morning, I raised the issue of Social Security again, saying that I was appalled to think that the committee would supinely accept the Senate action on this without holding any hearings and that I thought any such fundamental change in the assumptions of this system should be carefully considered by the committee rather than accepted out of hand on the say-so of a board which the committee has never had any respect for. For the first twenty minutes of the beginning of the session I pressed the chairman for hearings, and he finally said that he would have somebody in to talk about it. This was as far as I got on the hearings, and so I went over and sat next to him and said, "Mr. Chairman, I am going to go to the floor this noon and call for hearings on this issue. I want you to know about it because I really think it is essential to the integrity of the House and the integrity of the Social Security system."

His response was, "Don't oppose me on the 20 percent, Barber, or I'll pull the rug out from under you. If you want to go to the floor on this, of course, go ahead and do it." I went ahead and, in a one-minute [speech] which Carl Albert gaveled down before it was completed, made a very mild statement asking for hearings and consideration of alternative ways of improving the benefits if it was decided that our actuarial assumptions of thirty-seven years standing have been incorrect.

John Byrnes was not here, going instead to Florida yesterday to play golf and evidently starting the whole tapering-off process that is involved in shifting burdens to others on retirement. Herm Schneebeli and Jack Betts thought I should not risk offending the chairman by doing the things I have been doing on this, but I am quite in the frame of mind now to challenge the chairman on almost every political gimmick and gesture that he comes up with. One of the things that concerns me most about the Social Security gambit is that it is so transparently political and so related to the New Hampshire primary that it could damage the credibility of the committee, his own credibility, and in all probability the credibility of government itself with respect to a very central part of the security protection for older Americans.

April 9, 1972

[The chairman's] distraction was almost complete as the New Hampshire primary came along. It became increasingly clear that he was making a major effort, expending a substantial sum of money raised from lobbyists, and hoping to achieve a major breakthrough via the write-in route following a television blitz. I do not recall the exact percentage he received, but it was somewhere around 6 percent.[2] He professed to be delighted with this and, I believe, in fact was delighted, having rationalized the smallness of the figure in view [of] the modest personal effort he made in the campaign.

Nelson Rockefeller called him the following morning and quite cynically told

2. Mills won 4 percent of the vote in the March 7 New Hampshire primary. He withdrew from the race after receiving 3 percent of the vote in the April 25 Massachusetts primary.

him that he was the real winner, since he received twice the write-in vote the newspapers had been predicting. Wilbur was delighted with Nelson's call and repeated it to me at least three times, apparently feeling that Nelson was more perceptive than those who were inclined to minimize his success. My suspicion that Nelson's interest in revenue sharing prompted his call more than his pride in the chairman's achievement in New Hampshire was confirmed by Jim Cannon, Nelson's representative here, who has been so diligent and so effective in shepherding the revenue-sharing proposal along. The chairman's apparent interest in his political ambitions continued through to the Florida primary, where he again expected a substantial write-in but got virtually none, all the conservative support going to [George] Wallace there. Since that time, his interest has fallen off and his interest in some legislative achievement in the committee has increased proportionately.

Although he paid greater attention to the legislative side, he began to treat it as though it were an unpleasant duty to be accomplished, pushing for decision without relish and apparently looking for almost any decision to resolve the issue. He showed a remarkable tendency to compromise and made an effort to accommodate a wide range of views, apparently for the sake of accommodation and not to achieve some result that he had in mind.

[In the revenue-sharing hearings], several of the other members of the committee were virtually filibustering against anything. Corman, in particular, took an attitude which would indicate, on the face of it at least, that he was willing to support some form of revenue sharing, looking for the points he felt in some cases should be embodied into law, then, after the final draft was being prepared, indicating in unmistakable terms that he was bitterly opposed to the final result. . . . Gibbons's behavior followed more clearly a purely filibuster pattern, since he has been from the outset bitterly opposed to any form of revenue sharing, although this did not prevent him from making long and disputatious speeches about issues that had been decided previously. He continues, as always, to cause a great deal of irritation among other members, even those who agree with him.

Herm Schneebeli also continued to take a very active and very negative role in revenue sharing, although about a week before we completed the pre-draft of decisions that had to be made, Nelson Rockefeller called Herman and asked him to shut up. Strangely enough, Herman did it, saying to me that he thought Nelson Rockefeller was one of nature's noblemen and had thought so ever since he roomed with him at Dartmouth, and saying also that was the least he owed to Nelson, although he was not in a position to change his views about the undesirability of revenue sharing.

I seem to talk altogether too much at [White House leadership] meetings, and I am beginning to feel sensitive about it and will ask my colleagues if I should make a greater effort to be quiet. So far, they have been patient with me and said that my contribution has been worthwhile. I am appalled, constantly, at the extent to which the Republican legislative leaders meet with the president and then sit and listen rather than giving him any feedback on his relationship with the Congress. It seems to me that we can give him valuable political advice, despite his political expertise, since he insists on isolating himself to such a large degree.

On March 21 I was asked by the Council of Economic Advisers to get together a group of five interested congressmen to meet with the vice president of Romania and two members of the Economic Planning Council of Romania to talk about a most-favored-nation status for Romania. This group of officials had met with the White House and State Department officials, as well as talking with interested senators, and I arranged for the meeting at 5:00 in the room under the front steps of the Capitol. I included among those in attendance Herman Schneebeli, Sam Gibbons, Henry Reuss, and Peter Frelinghuysen [R-NJ]. The vice president, Mr. [Manea] Manescu, proved to be quite a self-confident gentleman, and for the most part, the meeting was a love feast, since those present, with the possible exception of Herman Schneebeli, were generally favorable to expansion of East-West trade.

Herman, incidentally, made something of an ass of himself by some of his remarks about the expense of campaigning in the US ("what does it cost you fellows in Romania to run for office?") and by his statements indicating that he thought the whole meeting was ridiculous since all the decisions in Romanian foreign policy would be made in Moscow, in any event. He showed not only a complete lack of understanding of Romania's special position between the East and the West, but he also expressed himself without tact and without any thought of the impression his remarks might make upon those present. . . . I finally moved in and tried to keep him from participating by recognizing other people when he wanted to blurt out further undiplomatic observations. I'm beginning to generate some real misgivings about Herman as a Republican leader of the Ways and Means Committee, although I don't believe anything can or should be done about it in light of the alternatives. I wound up the meeting with the Romanians, pointing out to them that they had some responsibility if they expected special treatment by the American government.

During the past month I have been home a good deal of the time, missing virtually no weekends, and I do not develop any feeling of political problems for me personally from my constituents. There is a very tentative feeling about the state of the nation generally, but little blame apparently attaches to me personally. My newsletter continues to be a major bridge between me and my constituents. My opponent[3] was announced this past week and on the face of his record, at least, promises little beyond the usual nominal run. He is a college professor, a Department of Languages member at the Rochester Institute of Technology, whose residence is on the far edge of my district in the county of Ontario. A labor leader this past weekend described him to me as another one of those radical college professors. I am now trying to find out something about his background and affluence so that I can judge what political insurance may be necessary to protect my incumbency.

I am continuing my personal idiosyncrasy of accepting no contributions beyond the $50 amount I set previously, and I am deriving the usual amount of enjoyment from watching lobbyists' faces as they come in and offer me contributions substantially in excess of that amount. The rule is probably a silly one; I have been criticized by Gerald Ford for doing this on several occasions, since he feels it reflects on other members of our party and on our colleagues. I have told Jerry that I consider the Republican Party to be altogether too preoccupied with money, but I realize that my position is considerably happier than that of many of my colleagues, since I have not as yet had to spend major amounts of money in the kind of political campaign that has been waged against me.

My friend Dick Bishop, a Washington lawyer, has asked me if he could raise money for me, that being an apparent hobby of his, and I have told him after a good deal of negotiation that I would permit contributions to be made in my name to the Republican Congressional Campaign Committee to be held in a fund there subject to designation by Jerry Ford. I neither want to have such money expended in my behalf nor subject to my own designation, since this would be a subterfuge and would negate any possible advantage to me in having somewhat higher standards of money-raising than many of my colleagues do. Tom Benton, my staff member in Darien, New York, will be running my campaign again this year, and he has already sent out the usual letters asking for contributions of $10 and less from a large number of my constituents who receive my newsletter regularly.

In the past I could always say, "Next year I will be more influential because I can capitalize on greater experience and perhaps move myself into a more influential role in the House." It is now apparent to me that I probably have

3. Terence Spencer.

one of the most central positions in the House of Representatives and that my powers are at their peak. Despite this, my personal activity and energy seem to make very little difference, while I have an expectancy which is not potentially any greater than the role I am already fulfilling. This, coupled with the kind of doubts generated by John Byrnes's retirement and the reasons for his retirement, has led me to wonder whether I want to spend the rest of my life beating my head into this brick wall. I certainly have not developed any further political ambitions or any desire to run for any other type of office. I still would be terribly bored by a judgeship, and I am sure I have no administrative abilities which would lead me to seek an executive job of some sort. But at forty-nine years of age, I cannot really look forward as a Republican to the exercise of any greater influence in the House than I now exercise, and my employability in some outside role diminishes with each passing year as my age goes up into the fifties. These feelings are tentative, but they are disquieting, and I imagine they will become overpowering after I have a few more terms of office behind me.

April 24, 1972
The revenue-sharing bill, now known as the Community Assistance Act but still called "revenue sharing" by all, was voted out by the committee as expected. Corman's wife had unexpected breast surgery (nonmalignant, as it turned out) and so he was not there for a rearguard action, but John Byrnes rose to high dudgeon and finally released a press statement calling it a "triumph of expediency over responsibility," while Sam Gibbons also continued his abrasive ways to the bitter end. The final vote to send it to the floor was 17–7, with Joe Waggonner [D-LA] abstaining. His performance was equivocal throughout, and I'm sure he has arranged to be recorded for or against once he has fully plumbed the quid pro quos. I am sure that Joe will prove as wily a quarry on every Ways and Means issue presented to him during his tenure as personal and political profit can suggest.

The committee report is due tomorrow night. I feel I should write some supplemental views to the majority report if only because of the role I've played, but perhaps that is a vainglorious posture. I can be sure that John Byrnes will upbraid the chairman for his turnabout, making it clear that the chairman is not the natural parent, no more than the stepfather, and even an unnatural stepfather at that. John, at least, has been the soul of integrity throughout, and he seems to bear me no rancor despite our disagreement and his intense dislike of the final product. For my part, I feel increasing affection for his indignant honesty and increasing sorrow at the prospect of his departure.

May 10, 1972

I was going to do a journal entry yesterday but I was so depressed by the president's decision to mine the harbors of North Vietnam and to blockade its coast, and by the general war news from Vietnam, that I thought it would be better to wait until this morning driving to work to express my concerns. I think I would have supported strongly the blockading of the North Vietnam coast four or five years ago. I recall asking Lyndon Johnson this on several occasions at White House briefings early in his term, and his answer was always that such action would involve "third parties," meaning the Russians, and that he was unwilling to have a confrontation with the Russians. At that time, we had half a million men in Vietnam and were suffering very heavy casualties. Now we have a tenth that number and the issue is the collapse of South Vietnam rather than the protection of American troops. I suppose American troops are endangered by North Vietnamese action there, but it is difficult for me to believe they could not be removed summarily if the South Vietnamese collapse proceeded. I see no real indications this is happening at the present time.

What has depressed me much more than the substantive matters has been the manner of the president's decision. The possibility of this action, at least to my knowledge, has not been seriously discussed with anyone either in the Congress or in those parts of government not directly concerned with military action. I am amused to think that my modest elected position in the House puts me in a group that is known as the "leadership." This gives us the privilege of sitting once every two weeks with the president in the Cabinet Room and hearing briefings, rather than the privilege of participating in any leadership decisions. When major changes of policy of this sort occur without any advance warning, I find myself wondering if my credibility is a reasonable price to pay for this modest status. I feel that I have little choice but to support the president at this point; but the thought also occurs to me that after the crisis has passed, if it does, I should take the steps to remove myself from the leadership, since my presence there means only the loss of my independence, not the opportunity for any input into the decision process.

Nixon continues to treat Congress as though it was irrelevant. I don't like to think this because there is a good deal of dislocation and discomfort involved in service in the Congress, and I have been doing it for eight years now under the illusion that what we do does make a difference in the running of the country. I guess I've said enough to indicate that I am uncertain, depressed, and wondering about the nature and the significance of my role, as well as seriously questioning the manner of decision exercised by my leader in the White House.

[George] McGovern rolls on in the primaries. I find it very difficult to believe that the Democratic Party will nominate him, and yet he certainly will be one of the two probable nominees as the convention is called to order early in July. Rumors persist that Chairman Mills is slated to be Senator [Edward] Kennedy's running mate and that the increasing impasse between Humphrey and McGovern is playing into the hands of the Kennedy-Mills ticket. To me, that seems almost as incredible as the chairman's candidacy in the first place.

May 18, 1972

Yesterday I attended in the morning a meeting of the Rules Committee, which was considering a rule for the revenue-sharing bill. I had heard rumors that it was not going well there as a result of John Byrnes's impassioned plea the day before yesterday against revenue sharing and his persistent efforts with members of the Rules Committee, which I had been noticing myself on the floor of the House. John seemed to be moving from one Republican member of the Rules Committee to the next, sitting next to him and talking earnestly with him—I presume about revenue sharing. When I arrived yesterday morning, Jack Betts was testifying earnestly but without too much fire or persuasion. After he completed his testimony, arguing that he was a fiscal conservative and that this was a fiscally conservative measure because it would reduce the role of the bureaucracy, he was extensively interrogated by almost every member of the Rules Committee, almost each one sounding like an advocate against the bill in the course of this interrogation. Chairman Mills was nowhere present, although I understood that he made a reasonable and consistent pitch for the bill before John Byrnes launched his major campaign against it.

I had left word that I wanted to testify, just in case, and after listening to what they were doing to Jack Betts, I decided that I would testify even though I had no prepared remarks. I wound up making the strongest spontaneous pitch of which I am capable, showing a fairly high decibel rating and fearing after I had completed that I had overdone the passionate oratory. I was further shocked by having almost no interrogation of any sort. Jim Burke followed me, also speaking for the bill, and I stood around for a while listening to him and [was] surprised to find that he received almost as extensive an interrogation as Jack Betts had. I assumed I had done poorly, but Frank Elleaser of Associated Press slipped me a note saying, "You were good. You almost persuaded even me." John Anderson told me over the phone shortly afterward that I had given one of the strongest statements he had heard before the Rules Committee.

I am floored by the vigor of the opposition to this measure, which seems to be of a much deeper philosophical nature than I anticipated from our committee debate over formula, more a nitpicking operation than the ultimate attitudes expressed before the Rules Committee. Jerry called a meeting of all the Republican members of the Rules Committee for this afternoon. I told him that I thought it would be a disaster if this last possible Nixon initiative for the 92nd Congress was killed by action of the Republicans on the Rules Committee. What stimulated me to bring this concern to Jerry's attention was a statement by Jim Burke that if this bill was killed, it would be killed by Republican opposition and that it was another example of the Republicans not supporting their president.

May 28, 1972

Last Friday, as expected, George Shultz came in and spent about one half hour in my office just chatting over some of the thoughts that occurred to him as he took over the Treasury Department, some of the developments on the Hill, even reading my news column for the day, which I had just finished, and giving me some comments on it. The news column, incidentally, was about Vietnam, and I felt somewhat nervous about it because I was once again coming to the conclusion that there was no real alternative to supporting the president, but I dwelt at some length on the point of view of the antiwar movement. George thought that I dignified them too much, saying that they were not a sufficiently numerous group, at least to the extent that they represented a vocal element, that we should worry about their support. I told him that I did not worry about their support but felt that their point of view had to be answered.

On Tuesday the revenue-sharing bill was voted out of Rules under a closed rule by a vote of 8–7. I was elated and surprised at the five Democratic members of the Rules Committee who held together for a closed rule.[4] I thought the bill should be rammed onto the floor and passed as quickly as possible, feeling that a majority of the House would prefer to keep the low silhouette with a closed rule and that there should not be any great problem about sustaining it on the floor, despite the inevitable muttering about a closed rule which always attends a controversial piece of legislation. But only a couple of hours after the Rules Committee action was announced, Carl Albert said that it would be put off for at least two weeks and let it be known that he thought the votes were not there to sustain such a rule. The theory seems to be that he felt extensive lobbying in the interim by the mayors and governors would save a day which otherwise would be lost.

---

4. Permitting no amendments on the floor other than those proposed by the reporting committee.

June 30, 1972

June has been a tough month and my mental state has not been such that I wish to record much of it in journal form.

I spoke to the Genesee Community College[5] commencement, braving a rather cool atmosphere following my disclosure to the college officials that I planned to vote against the Higher Education Act.[6] They had reason for upset at my position because the community college movement would benefit considerably from grants made under the Higher Ed Act. My reason for voting against it was, of course, related to what this bill does to the whole philosophy of education and, in particular, to the emphasis it puts on open enrollment for colleges at a time when we have major tax revolts brewing around the country against the financing of elementary and secondary education.

My mother has had a severe stroke, so I spent a good deal of time sitting in the hospital, lending out for an occasional speech and returning to worry about her condition.[7]

On Tuesday the thirteenth I attended a stag dinner for Prince Sultan, the defense chief of Saudi Arabia and the son of the king of Saudi Arabia, at the Georgetown Club. Apparently, Mel Laird invited me as a gesture of friendship, and I found the environment one of Oriental intrigue and mysterious burnooses. That morning we had had a very interesting meeting at the White House in which the president showed comparatively little appreciation of domestic matters and waxed eloquent only about his concept of the world, thus disclosing the difficulty he was having coming down from the [Moscow] summit,[8] but just at the end launched into an extensive discussion of his view of George McGovern and why George would be tough to beat this fall. He demonstrated his usual paranoia about the press and predicted the press would urge George to change his position to accommodate the middle voter, in sharp contrast to the manner in which ten years earlier they had forced the public to recall everything irresponsible that Barry Goldwater had ever blurted out in the course of his irresponsible rhetoric. I talked with Hugh Sidey about the president's remarks about George McGovern and found that Hugh repeated what I had told him almost verbatim in his editorial in *Life* magazine the following week.

5. In Batavia, New York.
6. The Education Amendments of 1972, which amended the Higher Education Act of 1965.
7. Agnes Gouinlock Conable died on March 6, 1975, at age eighty-nine.
8. Held May 22–30, 1972.

On Tuesday the twentieth of June I had to fly with my wife up to vote in the New York State primaries. Once again, the virtue of not endorsing candidates in primaries was graphically illustrated by the crushing defeat of everyone I had endorsed in the legislative races in my area.

Wednesday the twenty-first of June saw the beginning of the great revenue-sharing debate, eight hours of it. The day was first given to the inevitable and intense discussion of the closed rule, which many people considered the most critical part on revenue sharing. Many people who had told their governors and mayors that they were for revenue sharing were unwilling to vote for a closed rule, either because of the general antipathy which is building up against a closed rule or because they were not basically in favor of revenue sharing. The problem with opening the rule would have been the efforts that would have followed to change the distribution formula and to make the whole process subject to Appropriations Committee annual review.

H. Allen Smith, our ranking man on Rules, controlled the half hour allocated to the Republicans. He opposed the closed rule. He allowed fifteen minutes to Jerry Ford, John Anderson, Dick Poff, and Les Arends, all of whom supported the closed rule and supported revenue sharing. The other fifteen minutes he divided between himself and John Byrnes, who made his expected effective speech against the closed rule, which he has supported so often when he favored the merits of the bill. Smitty even refused to let Jerry sum up, and I had an angry and emotional exchange with Smitty about this, being personally subdued by Jerry Ford, who felt that he had the votes and didn't want to see me or anyone else rock the boat by personal encounters with the opponents. On the Democratic side, the debate was controlled by Bill Colmer [D-MS], who also opposed the closed rule, and the chairman, Wilbur Mills, in support of the closed rule, [who] gave a comparatively lukewarm performance. Nevertheless, the vote carried for the closed rule by 223–185, and everyone relaxed in anticipation of substantial success of revenue sharing.

The next day completed the debate. I took about half an hour and answered a number of questions, I think performing adequately. I performed without notes, as usual, and tended to ramble a little too much, but otherwise my talk seemed to be well received and was courteously listened to. The motion to recommit was controlled by John Byrnes rather than the minority leadership, and he decided the best opportunity would be to try to knock out the retroactivity in the bill, which, under its terms, was to take effect on January 1, 1972. Although I had some effect in urging this position for Republicans in personal lobbying on the floor, the threat did not materialize, and the motion to recommit was defeated by a vote of 241–157. Passage followed by a margin of 274–122.

Curiously, I felt surprisingly little elation on the final passage of revenue sharing. For one thing, I was somewhat embarrassed by the extent to which members of Congress voted for revenue sharing for the wrong reasons. The usual wrong reason was the kind induced by Nelson Rockefeller: that it would make the job of local and state officials easier and that they had been improvident in their expenditures. Lots of congressmen were sincerely afraid of their local officials. I also felt very little elation because of the chairman's attitude generally. I am convinced he still opposes revenue sharing but has been taking a political posture on the matter, thinking it will help his incredible presidential ambitions. The final and probably most important reason for lack of elation is my conviction that the bill will never come to fruition in the 92nd Congress. I quite anticipate, in view of the delaying tactics that have been used by the Democratic leadership in bringing this to a vote, that the bill will die ultimately for lack of completed action. The way for the Democrats to do this will be for them to make major changes in the Senate and then go to conference in the postconvention period with Wilbur and John dominating the House scene and Wilbur no longer feeling the press of his presidential ambitions. The issues in the two versions of the bill will become impassed, and obstructionism will make it quite easy for uncompleted action to deny Nixon this major domestic initiative and this sound federalist tactic.

On Friday the thirtieth we had a shocking performance on Social Security. The Senate, on a deal whipped up by Wilbur Mills and Senator Frank Church [D-ID], added a 20 percent Social Security benefit increase to the debt ceiling bill we had passed and sent to the Senate earlier this month. The Senate dawdled with it until the temporary ceiling was due to expire as of June 30, then sent it back to us with the SS amendment in a move that John Byrnes said on the floor held the whole government hostage to this political gambit.

A couple of days before this happened, and after it was apparent that it was going to happen, Wilbur wiggled his fingers at me on the House floor and I went over to talk with him briefly. He said to me, "Barber, I think you should get Bob Ball[9] and Jack Veneman[10] up to your office and satisfy yourself that the Social Security increase is an appropriate one." I said, "Mr. Chairman, you promised us that you would have somebody in to speak to the committee about this, and the issue is not whether I am personally satisfied or not but whether we are using appropriate legislative procedure and allowing sufficient public safeguards

9. Commissioner of Social Security, 1962–1973.
10. Undersecretary of health, education, and welfare.

in the changing of a major institution of public reliance like the Social Security system." He said, "Well, there isn't going to be time for that sort of thing. I can't help it if the senators are irresponsible about this." I told him I continued to be disappointed with his attitude on this, and the conversation ended.

John Byrnes felt as I did that this was a shocking procedure, and I found it pleasant indeed to be able to associate myself with him again after the rather bitter fight we had on revenue sharing, the opposition to which he had put more of himself into than any other issue since I have been on Ways and Means. Very little time was available for debate when the conference report came in, and the atmosphere was a surcharged one because of the political intensity of any vote on Social Security. The chairman made very little effort to justify his position on anything but the most blatant political grounds, at least in my view, and John Byrnes responded with a dignified and extremely effective speech. John wanted me to say something, and I spoke, myself, in opposition to the 20 percent increase, pointing out that if we were to accept an actuarial windfall of the dimension the chairman was suggesting, we should consider other possible uses for the money in the Social Security system than the across-the-board 20 percent benefit increase. My language was intemperate, and I delivered the speech badly. It would have been better if I had not spoken at all from the point of view of the atmosphere in the chamber, because I referred to the process as being one of "shabby politics, demeaning to the Congress." John offered a motion to recommit with instructions to increase the benefits by only 10 percent, saying that the other 10 percent should be considered as a possible source of the reforms that were included in H.R. 1 and were in some ways more desirable than a straight benefit increase.

That motion to recommit with instructions was lost by a vote of 253–83, and I was proud of the fact that it was mostly Republicans who voted for the motion to recommit. On final passage, I joined a lunatic fringe of 35 members who voted against the 20 percent benefit increase as opposed to the 302 who voted for it.

I really feel that I allowed my bitterness and antipathy to the chairman and his tactics to sway my judgment in my approach to this measure. Certainly it would have been better for me politically to have voted in favor of the 20 percent benefit increase in the light of the obvious favorable vote for it that was to be expected. I simply could not swallow the remarkably cavalier approach to such a central institution, so in need of reform, so contributory to the regressive tax structure, and so likely to be adversely affected by short-term political considerations, when we were asked to vote on a bill of this magnitude without any hearings by a responsible committee of the Congress. I am sure that vote will be used against me a good deal in the future, but I am also certain that it was morally a completely justifiable vote.

July 26, 1972

We had a leadership meeting at the White House with the cabinet last Friday evening. . . . The president is obviously savoring the political campaign with McGovern, although he professes not to be overconfident about his prospects. He spoke first, then called on Clark MacGregor, then Hugh Scott, then Jerry Ford, then [Secretary of State] Bill Rogers, and then Mel Laird. About halfway through I turned to Bryce Harlow, the presidential adviser, who was sitting next to me, and asked him if the president wasn't going to call on the vice president for some remarks. Bryce pulled an envelope out of his pocket and wrote on the back of it, "4 to 1 he doesn't," showing it to me and then putting it back in his pocket. The president not only did not call on Spiro for remarks, he did not refer to Spiro and, as far as I could tell, he did not ever look at him. I told my wife, home in Alexander that night, that Spiro had had the course and it appeared probable that he would not be on the ticket. The next morning [Ron] Ziegler[11] announced that Spiro would be on the ticket, thus gratifying my wife with the sure knowledge that her husband was on the inside and could interpret clearly the signs and portents from on high.

Ways and Means has done very little since we came back. . . . The chairman has been subdued—a member of his staff said to one of my friends that the word was "chagrined"—by the complete failure of the Democratic Convention to notice either his great services to the party or his availability for a candidacy of some sort.[12] I suppose he has reason for bitterness, but any of his friends could have told him that he was not going to get off the ground as a great national leader on other than the legislative level. I personally feel that he has sold his country out for considerably less than a mess of pottage. I find it very difficult to look him in the eye or to feel comfortable in the light of his fallen status and his apparent lack of either integrity or judgment.

August 18, 1972

Herman Schneebeli gives increasing evidence of being a difficult leader for the Ways and Means Committee next year. He gets most of his exercise jumping at

11. White House press secretary.

12. Mills tallied 34 votes (just over 1 percent of those cast) for president on the first and only ballot at the Democratic Convention that nominated Senator George McGovern.

conclusions and shows himself to be not only impulsive but headstrong once he has assumed a position. He has told me that he considers me to be a moderate and constructive fellow and that he intends to rely on me, Pettis, and [Donald] Brotzman [CO] for collective assistance to his leadership next year. . . . I think he is going to be a babe in the woods in his relations with both Wilbur Mills and the White House. He simply worships the chairman, and although he has expressed dismay at the chairman's springtime aberrations, he constantly gives him the benefit of the doubt and assumes that he will return to his old, lovable, responsible self next year.

August 25, 1972

The week before the recess we had a regular White House leadership meeting to discuss the economy primarily, but also touching on such subjects as busing and tax reform. I found the group present very much inclined to want to defend the tax system and thus permit George McGovern to cast them in the role of friends of the affluent. I gave the president a lecture about this, saying that it was very poor strategy not to support tax reform and that I hoped someone in Treasury was working on a proposal that could be announced in due course so as to deny McGovern the class struggle bit for which he dearly yearns. Just because demagogues magnify tax inequities, we Republicans need not magnify by maladroit defense a system the credibility of which is constantly suspect when tax burdens are so heavy.

The president at least acquiesced in my suggestion, but I must say that at the meeting in general he seemed considerably more confident about his ability to flatten McGovern than he did at the earlier breakfast meeting a couple of weeks before, when he warned everybody about overconfidence. In this light I might add that immediately following the convention, where he gave a speech that was very bad in comparison to Vice President Agnew's, he rushed off to several hard-line engagements where he did himself further political damage. I don't know how we are going to get a cork in him if he is so confident of his political prowess. He is a good president but a bad politician, and if it is possible to snatch defeat away from George McGovern (a heroic feat!), he'll do it.

September 7, 1972

On Thursday morning the president called a leadership meeting at the White House. He opened the meeting by saying how proud he was of the work that the members of the leadership had done at the national convention in Miami. He then went around the room, referring by name to each member and what he had done. When he got to me, he pointed his finger at me and said, "What happened to you?" I answered, "I wasn't invited, Mr. President," although this was not strictly correct because I had been asked by John Rhodes early in the game to serve on the Platform Committee and as an executive member of that committee, provided I was willing to be a delegate. I didn't wish to run against any of my local political leaders, and so I declined to serve as a delegate or member of the Platform Committee for this reason. When I answered as I did, however, the president realized that he had put me in a boat, and so he brushed it off with a smile, saying, "Well, probably you are too young to serve this year, anyway."

I found myself quite surprised that the president noticed that I did not participate in the convention, since I am never sure that he knows who I am, and since he had himself not been at the convention for long. I came right back to the office and wrote a letter to each of my county chairmen, saying that the president had commented unfavorably on my nonparticipation at the national convention and that therefore I was requesting them to permit me to serve as a delegate in 1976, assuming I am still a member of the Congress. I said that I was making this request of my county chairmen at this time because I realized it was not a request that could be made at the last minute in the light of the commitments they would have to make.

The Watergate bugging affair is on the TV and in the press almost daily, and it seems from the comments I have heard back home it is beginning to impinge on the consciousness of the American voter to a slight degree.[13] The general tendency has been, up to this point, [to believe] that both political parties are dirty and can't be trusted, and so the tactics implicit in the Watergate bugging do not again have a great net impact on the political attitudes of the electorate. It is about the only issue the Democrats seem to be enjoying, and so they are pressing it hard, and perhaps eventually it will be damaging to the Republicans if there are further revelations of high-level involvement. Clark MacGregor has told us at the White House meeting that he understands indictments will be forthcoming in the near future.

October 5, 1972
I have been home regularly on the weekends, and I find that my own campaign is more interesting than I thought it would be. My Democratic opponent is a lively and articulate fellow who does not regard himself as a sacrificial lamb and who is taking his function seriously, apparently campaigning full time, although

13. This is the first mention of Watergate in the journal.

with very little in the way of campaign financing, and showing up frequently at meetings where he cannot be expected to make many points but only to call attention to himself. I do not have any feeling that I am in trouble, but I do expect that he will cut into the plurality I would otherwise get.

Frustration with the president and his relations with Republicans in Congress grows constantly among my colleagues. The president avoids with great care any possible indication that he would like a Republican Congress, continuing to raise money in obscene amounts for the overkill he will doubtless demonstrate toward the end of the campaign, and effectively foreclosing any possible money-raising for congressional candidates. We have had several recent White House meetings and find him in a relaxed mood, thinking very politically, and anxious to chat about any political stars in the wind. There is no congressional input as far as I can tell into his campaign.

At SOS breakfast yesterday morning, Jerry Ford expressed his frustration to Don Rumsfeld about his efforts to get through to Clark MacGregor, who resolutely refuses to return his calls. The upshot was a surging of morale all around the table, where other members of Congress, realizing that Jerry couldn't get through to Clark, no longer thought the dark thoughts they thought about their efforts to get through to Clark. In short, Clark's ego trip seems to be a lonely road which he does not share with anyone else. . . . I am convinced the president will reap bitter harvest in the next administration because of his refusal to consider Congress relevant in any way, not just ignoring it but ignoring it as a matter of policy.

October 16, 1972

I have been getting considerable lumps in the press and on the hustings for my part in revenue sharing, strange as it may seem.[14] I am personally convinced that there would be no revenue-sharing bill if I had not kept it alive during the difficult months of the summer of 1971. The House bill, with its urbanization formula, provided considerably better benefits for the Rochester area than the Senate bill, with its emphasis on per capita income. The compromise worked out by the conference committee was better than the Senate bill but worse than the House bill, and so Rochester, with its affluence, would end up with less money than originally expected on the basis of the House bill. City politicians, scrabbling up each other's backs in the political sweepstakes, are accusing each other

14. The State and Local Fiscal Assistance Act of 1972 was signed into law by President Nixon on October 20, 1972.

of having let Rochester down, and although none of the Republicans attacked me directly, it was obvious to the Democrats that I was the one who had failed the city, and so there have been comments from my opponent and from Democrats on the City Council to the effect that Barber Conable, who comes from the rural part of the district, has failed the city. My Democratic opponent even accused me of not caring enough to get on the conference committee, and I suppose lots of people who don't understand how such committees are appointed could feel that somehow I had been derelict. Thus, the bill which has been one of my major legislative accomplishments and certainly one of my most earnestly sought legislative goals, as it is being finally interpreted to the people of our area, is being used as a club by people who would be getting no money at all if it had not been for my persistent work in behalf of the president's initiative.

I feel at the year's end that it might be appropriate for me once again to go over the performance of members of the Ways and Means Committee, including my own performance there. I have done this at times in the past, and when I read back through my journal, I am aware that frequently I have made incorrect assessments of the character, industry, and effectiveness of my colleagues on the committee. Some of them are more active at some periods than they are at others, and frequently my first impressions have been proven wrong in the past.

First of all, my own performance has been somewhat spotty this year. As I have mentioned frequently in this journal, I have the impression that I am spread too thin and that this unfortunate condition has affected the quality of my work. Since the most important work I do is on the Ways and Means Committee, the quality of my work there has probably been more serious in its deterioration than has the quality of my work elsewhere. I am aware that great things are expected of me in my Ways and Means work. I have the reputation of being one of the most thoughtful members, and my infrequent participation is usually well received. Even after the difficulties I have had with him this spring, the chairman seems to defer to me and to call on me if I wish recognition more promptly than he does most other members in the course of an executive committee deliberation. When I take an unexpected position, I find I get more reaction from it than do other members who are frequently more erratic than I. Press people seem to prefer to talk to me over some of my colleagues about what is going on in the committee, although this may be more of a reflection of my candor than of my judgment or reputation. My colleagues outside the committee always express surprise to learn that I am not on the conferences, since they think of me as one of the leaders of the committee. This year, almost without exception, John Byrnes has asked me to speak on the floor about Ways and

Means bills that are coming up. This estimation of my work is, I think, more a reflection on my colleagues than a compliment to me. Neither my understanding nor my industry is in a class with the performance of John Byrnes. Even if I had sufficient seniority to be on a conference committee, I could not replace his contributions during the coming Congress, and those who expect it of me are bound to be disappointed.

The three Republicans who are ahead of me in seniority on the committee are all particularly erratic performers, and indeed, I do not think much of anything can be expected of either Collier or Broyhill. Collier was so personally piqued at not having been put on the conference committee on revenue sharing, due to his absence from the city on the day on which it was appointed, that he voted against revenue sharing as it emerged from the conference committee. This was a pretty irresponsible performance for a man who had been one of the six original sponsors on the committee. Broyhill's relationship to me continues to deteriorate as he finds it absolutely beyond his control to avoid needling me on every issue that comes up, as I have fairly consistently voted against all his "special projects" affecting the District of Columbia. He has really very little interest in the work of the Ways and Means Committee except as it can be turned to his own personal political advantage, and that resides entirely within his constituency.

Herman Schneebeli, who will be ranking [minority member] next year, is a well-intentioned man with an impulsive nature, a considerable lack of industry, and a tendency to think in broad generalities without understanding the precise points of the legislation which faces us. It is Herm's basic decency on which I pin my hopes for next year, because I can only anticipate great difficulties in holding our Republican side together and in making the constructive contributions to any consensus that comes out of a faltering committee. Since the announcement of John Byrnes's and Jack Betts's retirement, Herman has been more diligent in his attendance and appears to be trying harder to get on top of the committee's work, but I can only say that he has a long way to go.

Charlie Chamberlain, who is next junior to me, appears to give only a small part of his concentration to the Ways and Means Committee. He has a certain native shrewdness and a fairly consistent conservatism, but Charlie is not a man to withstand pressures very well. His district includes East Lansing, Michigan, where Michigan State is located, and the articulacy of the student population seems to be driving him up the wall in the course of the primary he has just been through and as he prepares for the general election. I do not believe that Charlie will stay in Congress much longer, having been here for a long time and being pretty well fed up with the pressures of congressional life to which he is not particularly equal.[15]

Jerry Pettis, the next Republican on the committee, is an interesting man, although I have never fully come to grips with him. An inventor of some success and a businessman of several careers prior to his coming to Congress, he is a millionaire and a man who demonstrates some balance in his thinking on social and economic issues, although his basic orientation still remains elusive to me. He seems to want to make common cause with me on many issues, and I suspect that I have rather more influence over him than I have on any other Republican member of the committee. There are some issues on which he has strong feelings and where I suspect nobody could influence him, but for the most part, he detaches himself emotionally from what we are considering and rarely expresses himself. He is diligent and, to the extent that I can understand him and come to grips with him, I have some confidence in him.[16]

Next comes John Duncan, a superb politician in his ability to identify with his district but an unknown quantity on legislation generally. Almost everything John has said on the committee so far has had its roots in the politics of Tennessee and of the city of Knoxville, where he used to be a very successful mayor. John is generally a quiet man with a phlegmatic manner, but some of the political stunts he pulls back in his district are flamboyant and ingenious. . . . I think he is personally very shrewd and that his politics will be of a very shrewd nature also, although the contributions he will make to the committee remain uncertain at this time. I think he will be a good team player and a man who has above-average understanding of the issues.

Last in seniority on the Republican side is Don Brotzman of Colorado. Brotzman has the air of a youthful enthusiast but has a very good and strong mind. I think he is capable of first-class work, and certainly his diligence has been above question during the past year.

Let us now go to the Democratic side of the committee. . . . There is no doubt that the chairman's general reputation suffered badly from his erratic performance during the preconvention period. His reputation, the reputation of the committee, and his reputation on the committee were all badly affected by the unreality and the irresponsibility of his political maneuvering during this time. But in a larger sense, there obviously is no alternative to Wilbur Mills in the Ways and Means Committee at the present time. He will dominate the committee with his

15. Chamberlain won a very close race in 1972 and did not run for reelection in 1974.
16. Pettis was killed in 1975 when a small plane he was piloting crashed.

mentality and his judgment to a much greater degree next year than he did when John Byrnes was a part of the committee. I suspect that he will find the burden almost insufferable, since he has relied on John much more than is generally realized. John has formed the consensus that the chairman has led. John's complete intellectual honesty, his diligence, and the degree of his experience and judgment have all been major committee assets that the chairman could use in the type of political leadership he has given to our legislative function. If, as I suspect, the political gambits of this spring represented an effort on the chairman's part to cap a long, distinguished, and anonymous legislative career, certainly he is thinking about retiring and his time on the committee is limited. Certainly John's retirement will hasten his retirement. Certainly the fragmenting of the committee's consensus as a result of the younger liberals coming on the committee during the past four years will make his job harder and hasten that retirement also.

I believe the chairman will have to bury the hatchet with me and will have to rely on me to help him with a committee consensus during the coming two years, and if he confirms this by his attitude early next year, I will have to subdue my natural political instincts and help him where I can. I must say parenthetically that it would be an incredible position for Herman Schneebeli to be chairman of the committee and for the chairman to become the ranking minority member, because of the unequal roles their abilities would force them to play.

The number-two man on the Democratic side is Al Ullman, and his case is an interesting one also. Al obviously is relishing the role of heir apparent. He has recently remarried after a divorce, has no Republican opposition this year, has allowed his hair to grow and to be styled to reflect the role of the youthful bridegroom, and has become, if possible, more earnest and more serious in his approach to legislative issues than he was previously. He is slow, methodical, and tremendously self-impressed. His mind is good, his instincts conservative, and his partisanship somewhat subdued. He would be a better chairman than most of the men on the other side, but I suspect that he would have a very difficult time handling some of the more brilliant members of the committee on the other side. His great friendship for our late lamented colleague John Watts of Kentucky leaves me to suspect that he may be somewhat venal. I have no idea what his financial condition may be, but I assume it is not good in the light of his recent divorce. I have seen some evidence of his accessibility to the special interests, and the fact that he has no Republican opponent this year in Oregon may indicate that he also is a dealer.

Al is a great guy for coming up with a constructive alternative, and I suspect that frequently the chairman uses him for trial balloons when something the chairman has proposed has not had the immediate acceptance he had hoped. Despite the reservations I have expressed, my feelings about Al Ullman are generally more positive than negative, and I am pleased that he is the one who is next in seniority to the chairman if the chairman's tenure in the Congress is coming to an end.

Jim Burke, the next in seniority, is something else. A shrewd Irish demagogue from Quincy, Massachusetts, Burke is a likable man who does everything on a personal basis and judges his colleagues entirely by whether or not they cooperate with him in his foibles. Jim's positions are articulate and partisan and frequently accompanied by the playing of violins. He is a passionate advocate. He talks too long, and on several occasions I have become impatient and pursued some ill-advised course, like moving the previous question, which brings from him a violent reaction of personal antagonism. He is unfair and devious on occasion and extremely accommodating on others. He wins over 80 percent of the vote in his district and probably persuades a fairly conservative constituency that he is conservative, while voting a traditionally liberal line except where something which is a particular legislative hobby of his comes up.

Loyal to the chairman, he can be persuaded to do anything the chairman really wants him to do, even when it is diametrically opposed to his announced position. The other day, he said to me after we had had some sort of a heated exchange, "Barber, the trouble with you is that you think this is all on the level." I shudder to think what would happen to our committee if he were to become the chairman, and I shudder even more about what would happen to me if he became the chairman. Despite his ultimate intellectual dishonesty, I expect that he is personally quite honest, wanting very little for himself but enjoying the manipulation of issues and whipsawing of conflicting politics. He talks about the "little fellow" a lot and seeks to identify everything he does with the little fellow, even his representation of substantial special interests.

After Jim comes Martha Griffiths, whose position I have not reassessed since earlier estimates I have written in this journal. She continues to be quite brilliant, erratic, unpredictable, extremely partisan, and very much caught up in a few legislative hobbies like equal rights for women and the castigation of welfare frauds. Martha is a strong advocate and an effective congresswoman. She seems extremely friendly to me, but I would not trust her because, above all else, she is partisan. I respect her abilities.

After Martha comes Phil Landrum. Phil has continuing trouble with his hearing and, I suppose, will not stay on the committee much longer.[17] He is a

17. Landrum served two more terms. He did not seek reelection in 1976.

man of moderate shrewdness and some personal charm when he wishes to be charming but has a short fuse and seems quite inflexible about many things. He works quite hard for the Democratic side of the committee and seems to be becoming increasingly conservative. I like Phil and think he is a man of some integrity but of comparatively limited ability.

Next comes Danny Rostenkowski, Mayor Daley's henchman on the committee. Danny is an extremely affable and agreeable man, part of the chairman's apparatus on the committee and quite disinterested in the legislative work of the committee. His political ambitions, reflected in his previously having been chairman of the Democratic Caucus, were set back by his unexpected defeat for caucus chairmanship by Olin Teague of Texas at the beginning of this Congress. Danny rarely shows up and then participates only minimally. He is quite popular in the Congress as a whole, and I have very little strong impression of his abilities, which may be considerably greater than his record would indicate.

Next is Dick Fulton, whom we may beat this fall but who probably will survive simply by virtue of the fact that he is on the Ways and Means Committee.[18] A handsome, vain man (whose wife recently committed suicide and who shortly thereafter remarried a very young girl), Dick Fulton is a southern moderate from Nashville, Tennessee, who shows very little interest in legislative work and who participates in committee work only on rare occasions.

Next is Billy Green of Philadelphia, whose ambitions in Philadelphia politics are inherited and frustrated by the success of [Frank] Rizzo, the mayor who defeated him in the primary.[19] He was supposedly marked for extinction by being redistricted into James Byrnes's district, but Billy campaigned vigorously, while Byrnes relied mainly on his organization, so Byrnes was defeated in the primary. Presumably, this makes Billy once again invulnerable. He considers himself a Kennedy in his charm, ability, and liberalism, but he has yet to demonstrate anything but the last in committee affairs. He rarely comes to meetings, and I would not consider him an effective member in anything except pressuring the chairman for modest special clauses in tax bills for the benefit of Philadelphia special interests. I would not judge him to be a man of any potential, and certainly his present effectiveness on the committee is marginal.

Next comes Omar Burleson of Texas, a man who gave up chairmanship of the House Administration Committee and twenty-two years of seniority to come

18. Fulton did indeed win reelection, and he later served a dozen years (1975–1987) as mayor of Nashville.

19. Green would succeed Rizzo as mayor of Philadelphia.

on Ways and Means. Omar is a very nice man, gentlemanly, and, as far as I am concerned, a comparatively passive member of the committee, despite his extreme conservatism and his tendency to vote against most committee bills. Dick Bolling [D-MO] has told me that Omar is the intellectual leader of the southern Democrats, an astounding assessment of his role in the light of my experience with him.

Next is Corman of California. Jim is a good friend of mine, although he despairs of my conservatism from time to time. A true liberal, an articulate man, and persistent in trying to achieve his goals, he more than anyone else has brought a new element into the committee in recent years, and he more than anyone else will eventually destroy the committee's consensus. He is emotional but controlled. He is quite independent of the traditional Democratic coalition pressures, but I suspect that he is very much dependent on the support of the far-out liberals of the California Democratic delegation. His partisanship leads him occasionally to overstatement—a very effective liberal.

Next is his close ally in most matters, Sam Gibbons of Florida. Sam has a certain rough integrity to him which overemphasizes his independence and is quite abrasive for his colleagues. He, like Corman, is determined and persistent on matters in which he believes, but unlike Corman, he is not politic in express-ing his viewpoint. I would have more confidence in Gibbons's independence of judgment than I would of Corman's, although he also is an extremely partisan man. They are an effective pair.

Next is Hugh Carey, one of the most effective people in our New York City del-egation in the Congress. Hugh is a decent man, capable of independent judgment except on matters Catholic, and usually showing a very high level of ability and understanding on the legislative issues which face the committee. He is the lead-ing spokesman of the Catholic Church in not only the committee but in Congress as a whole. He will be a solid performer on the committee in the years ahead.[20]

Joe Karth of Minnesota follows him. A former labor organizer, Joe had my complete respect as one of my subcommittee chairmen on the Science and As-tronautics Committee seven and eight years ago. He has a reputation of being something of a womanizer, but I believe him to be adequately diligent and a man of fairly strong character and ability. I expect Joe to emerge as the spokesman for the AFL-CIO at some point in the course of the next few years.

Last in seniority is Joe Waggonner of Louisiana, a fascinating case. Waggon-ner likes to be the spokesman for the southern bloc of ultraconservatives and

20. Carey was elected governor of New York in 1974.

shows all the characteristics of a southern country lawyer, constantly arguing on constitutional points and taking up a contentious and manipulative role. He loves to be referred to as a spokesman for his viewpoint and is frequently the man with whom the Republicans seeking southern votes make their first contact. I suspect also that the chairman will use him effectively when he wants to and that Joe is subject to some manipulation himself because of his absolute belief in his ability to manipulate other people. Liberal Democrats regard him with loathing, and Republicans regard him with some amusement, but I suspect Joe gets what he wants, in that he is able to maneuver himself into the middle of many coalition-type efforts.

It should be apparent by now that I have left out one of the people on the Democratic side that I would most like to leave out, and that is Charlie Vanik of Ohio. He continues to perform from his middle seniority position on the committee as one of the lowest grade and most incredible demagogues of the Congress. A man of considerable pretense. I do not believe that he has an honest bone in his body, and I am constantly dismayed to hear of his success in holding his suburban Cleveland constituency.

November 28, 1972

I wanted to talk to Jerry [Ford] about Ways and Means. He apparently had not thought about it at all, despite the terribly important two vacancies which have to be filled. I told him about [Bill] Steiger [R-WI] and found him uncertain and noncommittal about Steiger. I also talked to him about Ohio's seat, which I assume that state will try to claim because of the size of its delegation. . . . When I suggested Bud Brown as a possibility . . . his reaction to Bud was, "Barber, you are the only one on the committee who will stand up to Wilbur Mills. If Bud Brown were on the committee, you'd have a partner." I agreed and told him that I thought the great problem on Ways and Means on the Republican side was going to be quality and that Brown and Steiger would represent the kind of quality that would pay dividends for Republicans on Ways and Means for some years ahead.

All in all, it was a very pleasant and relaxed chat with Jerry which took about an hour and probably imposed on his time more than I had any right to do. I seem to have a close relationship with Jerry Ford, and I appreciate it. I don't have any illusions about his strength or his brilliance, but I find him a thoroughly decent man who is willing to listen to everybody and who is therefore everyone's slave. We could do a lot worse than to have a man of such basic decency in the leadership role for the Republicans in the House.

The Nixon administration and congressional Republicans grow ever more estranged as the shadow of Watergate lengthens. Herman Schneebeli, the new ranking Republican member of Ways and Means, is a source of vexation. Conable is embarrassed when *Congressional Quarterly* cites him as the member of Congress with the most pro-Nixon voting record. When Vice President Spiro Agnew resigns, Nixon selects Gerald Ford to replace him; Conable, though entertaining no illusions about Ford's capacities, is pleased. Conable ascends further into the House GOP leadership, over the opposition of a growing right wing. The year ends with forebodings of disaster.

The center cannot hold? Watergate, which Conable first suspected was a matter of stupidity and "petty criminality" rather than "grave moral turpitude," emphasized the gap between House Republicans and the White House. Wilbur Mills, the sun around which the lesser planets of Ways and Means revolved, became erratic, restive, and often absent. The House GOP lost its minority leader when Gerald Ford became vice president, and Conable's oft-expressed doubts about him gave way to qualified enthusiasm due to Ford's decency.

For all his pragmatism and impatience with true believers, Conable was at heart an idealist: sticking up for Ways and Means, he deplored that committee assignments were made on the basis of (gasp!) politics rather than ability.

At age fifty, the usual intimations of mortality encouraged introspection in the congressman. He seemed to be in something of a slough: although his voting record aligned with Nixon's preferences, he confessed to a feeling of "revulsion" when contemplating the president. He edged up the leadership ladder, but not without drawing his first real open opposition from the party's discontented right wing.

January 18, 1973

I have had a bitter time about the appointment of the two members to fill the vacancies created by the departure of John Byrnes and Jack Betts on Ways and Means. I worked actively to get Bud Brown interested, and after he became interested, it was all snuffed out by a mindless Ohio operation giving the vacancy to the senior member of the delegation who wanted it—namely, Don Clancy. I talked with Jerry Ford about this, saying that Clancy was number five on Armed Services, that he had not had a distinguished career on that committee, that we needed some stand-up people on Ways and Means, and that Clancy was not a stand-up type.[1] Jerry agreed with me but subsequently pretended to have mis-understood me and explained to me that Clancy had agreed with him in detail on voting out of the committee every bill the administration wanted this next year. Nothing could be farther from my objection to Clancy. . . . Jerry simply didn't want to stand up to Ohio when they decided they were going to be passing out an important legislative assignment without regard to ability.

[To fill] the second vacancy I was pushing for Bill Steiger, an extremely bright but somewhat controversial younger member who would be able to understand the issues of the committee and who would also be uncommitted in his relation-ships to the special interests. Jerry seemed to agree with me on this but accepted with complete equanimity [the] appointment of Bill Archer from Houston, ap-parently dictated by the oil interests operating through Les Arends. Les, of course, continues to control the Committee on Committees,[2] and as a result of Archer's appointment, I felt completely frustrated and determined to bring Les Arends's remarkable career here in the House to a close. I have taken some steps to try to start nudging him in the direction of retirement. If we get the chance to take a secret ballot vote on his ranking minority membership on the Armed Services Committee, I suspect that we can get some negative votes organized. The information I have been able to pick up of Les's plans indicates that he will probably retire at the end of this Congress in any event, but I want to be sure he understands that if he wants to quit while he is ahead, he had better do it fairly soon.[3] Incidentally, I have nothing against Bill Archer as an appointment to the Ways and Means Committee. He may be quite bright, although I understand he is a bullhead. My objection to him was simply the motivation back of his ap-pointment, which I consider offensive and unnecessary.

January 26, 1973

That Committee on Committees group would think that the function of Ways and Means was to protect the oil depletion allowance and to become a part of

1. Clancy's claim to fame was defeating future TV talk-show host Jerry Springer in Clan-cy's 1970 reelection race.

2. The Republican Committee on Committees consisted of one member from each state with Republican representation in the House. The Ways and Means Committee functioned as the Democratic Committee on Committees.

3. Arends did not run for reelection.

the Republican muscle in fund-raising. Someday we will start picking people to be good legislators and not to be reasons for giving money to the Republican Party, but I am afraid that day is still a long way off. I reacted with considerable bitterness and in discussing it with Bill Steiger expressed the strong opinion that Les Arends had to go and that Les Arends was the real leader of the Republican Party rather than Gerald Ford. Unfortunately, this view was extensively developed in a Novak[4] article which came out several days after I had a long lunch with him at the Capitol Hill Club, and so once again my image as a troublemaker, a blabber to the press, a disloyal part of the Republican establishment, and a sorehead loser has been assumed by all. The only one who got any amusement out of the Novak article (Bob scrupulously avoided mentioning me in it) was Bill Steiger, who, of course, was not terribly happy about the results in Ways and Means.

The result of my appearing on the cover of *Time*[5] with about nineteen other members of both houses of Congress as one of the active people in Congress has been that everybody wants to interview me now about every issue that comes up. I have enjoyed my anonymity since I came to the House of Representatives, and I still have hopes of recapturing it as it becomes apparent that I do not have the influence or viability which seem to be attributed to me now by the press and people in the White House who are desperately trying to pretend they have friends in the Congress somewhere. The *Time* reporter who wrote the story on me said that my "close ties to the White House" were described to him from the White House, rather than from anyone in Congress. If I have close ties to the White House, I can only imagine what it must be like to be remote from the White House.

March 26, 1973

Another development that seems to have been getting out of perspective is Watergate. It now seems apparent that there were incredible stupidities in this affair, going either to the top or very close to the top in the Republican Party. I do not find grave moral turpitude in the bugging of the Democrats, but I do find incredible stupidity and serious reflection on the judgment of those who thought this was the way to political success. The other day one of the figures[6] was given six to twenty years in jail and a $40,000 fine as his penalty for participating in this comic opera caper. A murderer would have scarcely received a more severe

4. Robert Novak, who wrote a syndicated column with partner Rowland Evans, Jr.
5. "A Cast of Characters for the 93rd Congress," *Time*, January 15, 1973.
6. G. Gordon Liddy.

penalty. Why Nixon does not give the quietus to it by meeting it head-on makes it clear that he finds it considerably more embarrassing than anything which has currently come to light would indicate that it should be. As a result, I can only assume the worst. Further disclosures will doubtless enhance the image of a man who considered himself safely entrenched in a position of power and hence above the law.

April 3, 1973

The Watergate affair continues to confound members of Congress, who can only assume from the White House's reluctance to make a clean breast of affairs and get it off the front pages of the paper that things are much worse than anything which has been previously disclosed. There is some interest in it back home, but not much. The attitude of the American people is one of cynicism about politicians generally, and apparently, one of the great tragedies of the Watergate affair is that it distracts us from more important matters which should have our attention at this time. Stupid conspirators who set out so obviously to get themselves caught, and for so little purpose, appear to be pawns of a big money game of small consequence.

Al Hunt of the *Wall Street Journal* is allegedly writing a profile of me for his paper. He has been writing it now for about three weeks and, when I ask him when he expects to be done, says only that he will not print it until he gets enough people to say unpleasant things about me so that it will be newsworthy. He confronted Herman and asked him if it was true that there was trouble between the two of us, and Herman went into a near state of panic, rushing over to talk with me about his answer, which . . . was that I was a fine, constructive congressman. I chastised Al about "stirring up trouble," and he said, "Listen, Congressman, I am not the first one who has asked that question." It appears I have a reputation for arrogance and there is much expected of me in the intellectual leadership of the committee, a posture I cannot claim.

April 17, 1973

Last Thursday Jerry Ford invited me and all the other members of the leadership to a joint House-Senate Republican leadership meeting in Hugh Scott's office. He acted as though such meetings were quite usual, but this is the first time, to my knowledge, we have had one. It turned out to be quite an unstructured and remarkable discussion of the difficulties that the members of Congress are having with the White House, and the decision was made, taken in great confidence, to ask for a meeting with the president in which we would have a chance to confront Ehrlichman and Haldeman about their lack of cooperativeness and their obvious feeling of irrelevance about the Congress. It is felt that such a confrontation with the president present would have a salubrious effect, although I remain quite skeptical.

The most remarkable thing about the meeting was that Spiro came and assumed a leadership role, saying, in effect, that while he had been assigned the role of liaison between the Congress and the White House, he simply could not crack the "two-man rule" that thwarts all opportunities for communication between the two institutions. This and the other things he said made it clear that he was casting his lot with the Congress, having given up on any chance of White House participation in the government. He obviously is looking for long-time plans rather than short-time allies, and I told Jack Edwards and Bob Michel [R-IL] on the way back from the meeting that it was quite apparent to me that Spiro was indeed a candidate for president and that this meeting had represented from him a historic decision, despite the long time remaining for Richard Nixon in the White House, to abandon his ties there in the interest of building a power base in the party. Now that he has apparently made this decision, it will be interesting to see if he follows it up and becomes a congressional spokesman of vigor or rather a querulous middleman complaining about the White House but not really attempting to lead.

Following this meeting, I am told the president assented to an audience and that everybody in the leadership is to be permitted the opportunity to ask one question or make one comment to the president, without restriction of any sort. It will be interesting to see if any candor develops, and I must consider my own comment or question before next Tuesday, when the meeting is supposed to come off. The fact is that I say pretty much what I want to at the meetings anyway and don't really feel as frustrated as some of the boys who have been sitting on their hands saying, "Yes, Mr. President," and failing to put in their own two cents at the regular meetings.

April 23, 1973

I am now in the middle of Easter recess in a mountain fortress in Tennessee, and since I have been neglecting the journal this spring, I feel it would be well to review the 93rd Congress to date, listing some of the major items impressing me at this point.

1. One of the overpowering disappointments has been the failure of Democratic leadership. We have long known Mike Mansfield would make a better college professor than [Senate] majority leader. In the 92nd Congress we all

knew Carl Albert would make a better anything else than Speaker. But there were brave words about the new Carl Albert early this year. The sad, unconfirmed death of Hale Boggs[7] gave him the chance to take unto himself a new majority leader who was not a legacy of the past. Tip O'Neill [MA] was the result, and for all his grubby Boston-Irish, Curley-machine background, he brought a more consistent liberalism to the upper ranks of the leadership than any who have been there during my tenure. At the same time, nobody could doubt his pragmatism.

The only major issue the Democrats have won is the obvious straight party-line vote to deny the minority a share, as is its right, in the investigative staffing on the committees. Three times in the past two weeks, we have even prevented the adoption of rules. The Democrats chose the first two veto issues for their popularity—vocational rehabilitation and rural water and sewers—and were resoundingly defeated (once even by the Senate Republicans!). With the president's influence definitely shrouded by the Watergate mystery, and Republicans more restive than ever about tying their future to his leadership, he nevertheless wins every test of wills by default.

2. This brings me to the second point about the 93rd Congress. It will be between the Republicans in the White House and the Republican leaders in Congress that the major confrontation takes place. Following the meeting in Hugh Scott's office two weeks ago, where Spiro Agnew placed himself in alliance with Congress against the White House (thus confirming his presidential ambitions), we have had one more meeting. This, in Les Arends's office, was held the Monday before recess to prepare an agendum for our confrontation with the president. . . . Those responsible for scheduling it at the White House had apparently become unnerved that it had to do with Watergate and refused to permit it unless the questions to be asked were submitted in advance—a singular lack of confidence and of communication! We drew up quite an innocuous series of questions about prior consultation, early warning on vetoes, advance notice of appointments, etc., and supposedly they were communicated to the White House, but nothing happened.

After the list had been prepared, I asked if no one was going to mention Watergate, saying that, as representatives of congressional Republicans, I was sure our leadership should at least express our concern about a political situation deteriorating to the point where it would reflect on all our political futures. Jerry

---

7. A small plane carrying Boggs, Representative Nick Begich (D-AK), and two others disappeared while flying from Anchorage to Juneau in October 1972. It was never found.

was ready for me, saying that my point was well taken but that if such a question was asked while we were all there, it would look too much like a confrontation and that a better alternative would be for him and Hugh Scott to express our common concerns privately to the president, *a trois*. I readily assented. I don't really want to know about Watergate. I have such a bad feeling about it, and I brought it up only out of a sense of duty to all those scared Republicans.

But the point implicit in all this maneuvering is that, far from improved relations coming from the 1972 election and our early victories in the 93rd Congress, the White House and its supporters in Congress are farther apart than ever. I can foresee, if things continue without improvement, that Republican leadership will be judged in the House not by its loyalty but by its independence of the White House.

The saddest aspect of this estrangement is that the president could have moved easily, without much investment of his precious time, and effectively to reduce it to one-quarter of its present frightening dimension at any time during his first administration. Congressmen are delicate flowers, responding instantly to the first warming rays of the sun to open their petals and show their best colors, but with too little sunlight over a long period of time, it is doubtful that they can be revived as fine specimens for the administration's garden, no matter what the president does as his sun sets.

3. If it is between the Republicans of [the] executive and legislative [branches] that the major confrontation is a-building, the Democrats of the Ways and Means Committee will have a confrontation of sorts, as well. In the 92nd Congress I used to enjoy saying that Wilbur and John were 80 percent of the committee, the rest of us 20 percent. I divided the 80 percent about 50 percent to Wilbur, 30 percent to John. I said that when John left, I was not sure Wilbur would remain 50 percent. He has not: to date, he has been 100 percent, treating the rest of us (and the press goes along with him) as though we were total irrelevancies, involving us in protruded and possibly pointless hearings on tax reform, while he lurks in his office in Kensett,[8] nursing a bad back which in no way disabled him from giving strategic interviews to "in" reporters or firing off headline-making press releases. . . . Most of the committee is perfectly satisfied to be an irrelevance—they have status without the burden of responsibility and can play their special-interest games with taxpayers who aren't quite sure whether we're serious or not and want special-interest reassurance.

Herman Schneebeli is comforted by Wilbur's nonconsultation. Despite his

8. Mills's Arkansas hometown.

hard work and his surface self-confidence, he is prepared to cooperate fully with whatever Wilbur decides and anxious not to have to make any decisions himself. He is a nice person, unsure of himself in a role he does not relish and serious about turning the Republican side of Ways and Means into a real democratic institution with collective decision the rule and not the exception. He shows wisdom in this, because he is in over his head and not intending to swim very long. I feel protective and defensive about Herman, whom I like, and yet I am bound to be a thorn in his side if I fulfill the role which must be taken by someone if the committee is to have any corporate existence and prepare itself for dealing with the vacuum following what I believe to be Wilbur's imminent departure.

I also have the feeling that I can be the committee's hair shirt much more easily than one of the Democrats. There are few bona fide and legitimate leaders among the House Democrats, and Wilbur is one of them. Some of the able Democrats on the committee can challenge the chairman only at some personal political peril, some incubus of disloyalty among noncommittee rank and file who do not know the extent of committee members' grievance against the chairman. But if I take the lead in challenging Wilbur's unilateral decisions and in trying to force the consultation to which we are entitled, I will be seen as carrying out the political role appropriate to my leadership position, and I have at least covert support (assuming my battleground is carefully chosen) from Pettis, Brotzman, probably Archer, Corman, Gibbons, probably Carey, possibly Waggonner, and possibly even Griffiths and Green. These are enough to challenge a one-man consensus and to reduce Wilbur's influence unless he accommodates in ways he is not willing to do now. I will cause grief in the staff and hurt myself in the short term, although in the long run it will be good for my position in the committee. Perhaps at my age and state of uncertainty I should not worry about the long run—but I'm convinced this type of low-silhouette thinking is what has sapped the vitality of the legislative branch.

4. Beyond my limited opportunities as a mischief-maker in Ways and Means, the 93rd Congress has brought me to some serious questioning of my future as a congressman. What do I want to do with my life, anyway? I can't drift much longer without a conscious decision. These things have made me ask that question:

a. The retirement of John Byrnes at age fifty-eight so that he would have time for a new beginning. John is a vital man, at the height of his powers, unwilling to stand longer in Wilbur's shadow, with financial pressure and a long history of minority frustration. He decided to practice law, something I doubt I would do.

b. I reached age fifty myself in November, an unexpected trauma when I realized that the time left to me does not stretch on indefinitely. Could I stay another ten years in this meat grinder? If I do, would I then be able to do any-thing but retire completely, lacking skills and the resilience of youth? My wife and I talked about this, and I more or less decided to stay in Congress through the election of 1976, thereafter deciding only on two years at a time.

c. Bill Steiger, a young man from Wisconsin whom I admire and have great hopes for, came to see me to get my views about whether he should stay in Congress. He must be about thirty-two,[9] quick, articulate, and thoughtful. He has been offered a job as head of the National Safety Council, which would be a raise in pay and a national forum. I suspect he was bitterly disappointed, as I was, when, for all the wrong reasons, Texas beat out Wisconsin for John Byrnes's seat on Ways and Means this January. I couldn't think of much of an answer to his "Why should I stay?" except to say that he had time, at his age—not a very reassuring answer for the impatience that goes with ability.

I can only muse, as I think of my own future in the House, that effectiveness is more a function of who leaves than of who stays. Our best people leave, frus-trated and dissatisfied, to go to greater political frustrations and dissatisfactions or to resign from political life. Those who are left pool their ignorance, choose unworthy leaders because no one really working remains, and fritter away their lives either sustaining and enhancing empty status or complaining about the mysterious decline of the effectiveness of Congress. The House could be a place of action and of national leadership. But I cannot look with any real hope to the future until people like Bill Steiger can find fulfillment not only in its opportuni-ties but also in its realities.

May 8, 1973
Watergate has absorbed our attention since the last entry, creating among Re-publicans, in particular, anger that the president has been so stupid as to create an environment in which petty criminality could become the norm for high places. The mail is still quite modest about it, but what we receive is an expres-sion of shame from thoughtful people, and I don't blame them. To me, it seems unlikely that President Nixon will be impeached unless further revelations tie him directly to the stupid affair, but I do not see how it can fail to poison not only his place in history but his influence during the remaining three and one-half years.

Having observed Nixon in action at so many leadership meetings, and his lively understanding of the things going on outside of that vacuum with which

9. Steiger was born May 15, 1938, and was about to turn thirty-five.

he surrounds himself, I find it hard to believe that he did not know more about Watergate . . . [than] what has come out so far. The whole thing is so sickening, so unnecessary.

June 5, 1973

This morning we had our long-awaited meeting without agendum with the president at the White House. I say it was without agendum, but in fact, we had a series of written questions or comments that we prepared some seven weeks ago when we first thought we were going to have this meeting and it was apparently forestalled by Ehrlichman or Haldeman or both. The questions did not have any relevance to Watergate but had considerable relevance to the relationship of the White House and the Congress. It is interesting to see how closely we watch the president now that we assume he is under great pressure on account of Watergate. He came into the room with his head down and his face red and a rather grim look on his face. Realizing he was in a company of friends, he began to open up and to act more relaxed after he had been in the room a little while. He fidgeted with his watch for the first half hour or so again and acted distracted throughout. . . . Watergate was not mentioned, except to the extent that he talked about the "show" going on in town and the extent to which it was distracting people from their work. None of the boys took him on directly, but there was considerable firmness in the positions expressed about defects in White House standard operating procedure with respect to legislation.

All in all, I expected more of the meeting than ultimately emerged, a not-infrequent condition. I got quite tense about it, feeling that it was terribly important to us to get through to the president the extent of the difficulty he now finds himself [in], but looking at him and sensing the tension of the group as we met with him, we all found it difficult to believe that he was not firmly aware of the extent to which his triumphs have turned to ashes in the squalid little affair known as Watergate.

July 19, 1973

We came back from the Fourth of July recess [to read a *Wall Street Journal*] pro-file done of me by Al Hunt[10] which was very largely favorable and made a point that I was a coming leader in the Ways and Means Committee and the man who was willing to stand up to Wilbur Mills. This article has created something of a

10. Albert R. Hunt, "Ways and Means' Unsung Mr. Conable," *Wall Street Journal*, July 9, 1973.

sensation among my colleagues, many of whom found it inexplicably favorable to me. It does not seem to affect my relations with the chairman, for which I am grateful.

We have been on the downhill slide of Watergate. The president has evoked the dismay and enmity of many of the Republican congressmen, who now pin all their hopes for any salvation for the Nixon administration on Mel Laird as the assistant president.[11]

Last night I went to the annual birthday party that the Lear Siegler Corp.[12] puts on for Jerry Ford. Jerry got quite drunk celebrating his sixtieth birthday and gave a rather mawkish performance in two rambly talks with the cake-cutting sandwiched in between. It would have been acutely embarrassing, except for the fact that there were mostly friends there and they seemed to be in a mood to forgive him his inebriety. His wife looked embarrassed.

July 31, 1973

We have been working on the trade bill, but in a desultory and sporadic way due to the absence of Wilbur Mills, now out for almost two and one-half weeks. We hear that he is in this or that hospital (usually the rumor is wrong). Yesterday we heard that there is really nothing wrong with his back but that high nervousness and shallow breathing resulted in muscle spasms for him. I do not doubt that the man is suffering real pain because he acts in a manner consistent with this when we see him around and when he finds it difficult to sit still for any particular period of time. We did note, however, that he had good enough health to go and spend over an hour with the president last Wednesday talking about trade, the economy, and other issues, some of which did not directly affect him or the committee.

I saw the president Thursday afternoon and thanked him for spending so much time with Wilbur. The president said that he felt it was a wise investment and mentioned that when one talks with Wilbur, one must be prepared to listen to a lot of stories. He said that Wilbur acted in pain and got up several times to leave but then thought of something else to say and came back. I repeated to the president what I had said the morning before at a leadership meeting at the White House: that we were terribly dependent on Wilbur's leadership to get the kind of trade bill with which we could all live and with authority adequate for

11. Laird had resigned as secretary of defense after Nixon's first term. In June 1973 he returned to the administration as counselor to the president for domestic affairs.

12. An aerospace-avionics company.

the president to make the negotiations necessary for our new relationships in trade. The president said to me, "Barber, when you think it is time for me to talk to Wilbur again, please let me know. I am glad to do this sort of thing and I do think it makes a difference with people like Wilbur Mills."

A few minutes later I was back at the Capitol being interviewed by Al Hunt of the *Wall Street Journal* about things that had been happening in the committee with respect to the trade bill. Al said that he had just previously interviewed Wilbur Mills about his conversation with the president. Wilbur said the president looked terrible, that he acted distracted, that he worried about whether the president was in full possession of his faculties, and that he had never seen a president in such desperate condition. The president had been barely coherent on a number of issues and had found it difficult to string thoughts together, something which Wilbur obviously feels he is himself very good at. The juxtaposition of the two versions of the meeting between these giants on the summit was a rather interesting contrast, and I am rather more inclined to believe the president's version than I am the chairman's.

Watergate groans on. A television set is kept in the Republican cloakroom, and the members watch with some fascination the vigorous, murky testimony given by the Haldemans and the Ehrlichmans about their great role in saving the nation.

September 21, 1973

An open White House to the contrary notwithstanding, I am increasingly distressed and depressed by the necessity of dealing with and following the presidential leadership of Richard Nixon. It was discovered by an analysis by *Congressional Quarterly* that, for the second year in a row, I achieved the highest support ratio of any member of either house with respect to presidential leadership.[13] I do not feel that I am in fact making any effort to respond to such leadership and have to conclude that my support is based generally on agreement with his policies, but I am sore tempted to vote against some things the president wants just to try to draw a different picture, not only for my constituency but also for myself. A year ago, those who were highest in support of the president were mostly liberal or moderate; this year, they were mostly conservative. In both cases I was number one, thus eliminating any possible excuse that my support

13. According to *Congressional Quarterly*, Conable voted with Nixon 86 percent of the time. "Nixon Support in Congress Hits Record Low in 1973," in *Impeachment and the U.S. Congress* (Washington, DC: Congressional Quarterly, 1974), 43.

is based on ideological conviction. Drawing such a picture of myself as a rubber stamp is very bad for my self-respect.

Last Wednesday night I went to supper with the "Good Guys,"[14] although the reason for my receiving an invitation from Sam Devine to attend this supper is not clear. I have been hearing rumors of considerable conservative activity by this group, and so I was anxious to see who they were and what they were doing. They have a steering committee which has hired some staffing and is preparing conservative papers and conservative positions on various legislative matters that come before us.

I must say that the supper I attended was quite unimpressive. To begin with, the speaker was Roy Ash, the director of OMB,[15] who is less impressive every time I see him. The group behaved for all the world like a small-town Kiwanis Club, throwing wet rolls at each other and demonstrating very little seriousness of purpose and some inebriety. I came away relieved and convinced that they were not sufficiently numerous or potent so that they could constitute a serious alternative to the current Republican leadership of the House. Most of them are the kind of people who make a religion out of laziness, saying no because it is the easiest thing to say, and rarely understanding what constitutes a truly conservative position as opposed to a reaction to other people's initiatives.

October 18, 1973

There has been a great deal that's happened since the last time I made a journal entry. . . . One of the most interesting things has been the nomination of Gerald Ford as vice president to succeed Spiro Agnew.[16] I was considerably involved in the event, and it will have a good deal of impact on not only my position in the leadership but my future service in the House. As soon as the resignation of Agnew was accepted (and it had not been expected—it came over the ticker, and many people on the floor chose not to believe it at first), immediate speculation about his successor buzzed around the floor. A number of us immediately concluded that Gerald Ford might be a good successor, and a boomlet was going for him within ten minutes of the time there was some confirmation of Agnew's resignation.

14. A dinner club of conservative Republican House members.

15. Office of Management and Budget.

16. Vice President Agnew resigned on October 10, 1973. On October 12 Nixon announced his nomination of Ford to the vice presidency. Ford was confirmed by the Senate on November 27 and by the House on December 6.

The remarkable speed with which several petitions, one by Jack Kemp of New York and the other by Dan Kuykendall of Tennessee, began to circulate indicated to me that if the president did not want Ford, he was likely to have some trouble with Congress over it, and so I immediately called Mel Laird at the White House and the congressional liaison boys there to tell them that it was essential that any nomination the president wanted to make should be made promptly if we were not to have very substantial organizing activity on behalf of Jerry. It came back to Kemp and Kuykendall promptly to stop circulating the petitions, but we called a special meeting of SOS, and the discussion there led me to believe that at a conference Jerry had called for the next morning, a major effort would be made by people who felt the Congress should dictate the appointment of the new vice president to put the conference officially on record in support of Ford. This I also dutifully reported to the White House, telling them that the only way in which such a draft could be avoided would be for Ford to make a clear statement that he was not interested. Bryce Harlow argued with me at some length about it, saying that he would get back to me before the following morning. I was unable to reach Mel Laird.

About eleven o'clock that night Mel called me at my home and talked for over twenty minutes, saying that he was convinced Jerry did not want it, that the way to influence this president was not to try to push on him, and a number of other things which sounded to me somewhat sour. I told him that if Jerry didn't want it, he certainly was creating an opposite impression, and Mel said, "Well, I'll call Jerry and get that straightened out right away." The next morning I asked Jerry if Mel had called, and he said yes, that he had called about 11:30 and had talked to him for half an hour. He did not volunteer what the upshot of the conversation had been.

The next morning we had our conference, and Ford explained the procedure the president wanted to use whereby each member would write him a letter which would be personally delivered in a sealed envelope to Ford's office and delivered by Ford before six o'clock that night to Rose Mary Woods[17] in the White House. There was considerable dissatisfaction with this procedure, which was designed to keep only the president informed of what the Congress really wanted on a secret ballot basis, and many of the members, myself included, described it as a charade and a clever ploy for them to keep not only Congress but the other Republican groups the president was polling from knowing the results of their poll. The procedure was carried through with Jerry Ford's support, and

17. Nixon's personal secretary.

the president went up to the mountaintop at his Catoctin retreat at Camp David, communed with the Lord, and came back with the nominee's name in his pocket the next morning. It was then announced that there would be a White House meeting for most of the senior Republicans and a few friendly Democrats at nine o'clock that Friday night at the White House.

I had a speaking engagement up in the district and had very little inclination to participate in what I thought was a massive demonstration of presidential bad taste. I talked to Jerry on the floor in the middle of the afternoon, saying that I was turned off; that just because bad taste was involved, I felt I did not wish to be part of it; and that I was telling him I was not accepting the White House invitation to come to the meeting, despite my being a member of the leadership, and I wanted him to know the reasons. Jerry said to me that he thought I might want to be there, that it might be a historic event, and that I would probably regret it if I did not go. I told him the only reason I could think of to go would be if he were to ask me to be there. He said, "I am asking you." I said, "Can I draw an inference from this, Jerry?" And he said, "No, you cannot, but I still think you want to be there." I canceled my speaking engagement and went.

The crowd was quite restive, but when the president announced that Jerry was to be the vice-presidential nominee, it was enthusiastically received, since the president had been careful to surround the announcement with particular friends of Jerry Ford. It became my line in talking with the press about this that it was the right appointment at this time and under these circumstances, and I believe that to be an accurate statement of what I truly felt. Gerald Ford is not a brilliant leader, and I have never had any illusions about his brilliance. I think, however, that the appointment was the only one that can have a fairly comfortable time in confirmation by the Congress, and I consider that tremendously important when we have been having so many confrontations. The singular thing about Gerald Ford's leadership is that it has not offended the Democrats, despite his partisanship, and that on both sides of the aisle he is considered a loyal, decent man doing his job as well as he can and working very hard at it. It is also remarkable how many people seem to be talking in terms of having a friend in the vice presidency; Gerald Ford has been so uniquely accessible to his colleagues in the Congress that virtually everyone thinks of him as a personal friend, and certainly this attribute is going to serve him in good stead not only in his relations with the Congress but in his relations with the public generally as an outward-reaching and direct and decent person.

Where do we in the House go from here? On Friday night I decided that I would support John Rhodes, assuming there would be a very substantial movement toward minority leadership, and although I had several indications from the younger fellows that I myself would be an appropriate candidate, it seemed like an unlikely role to me that I should be the Republican political leader of the House, and it seemed that my best contribution would be to try to avoid an ideological division over the choice of the man who was to be minority leader. I talked with Bill Steiger and asked him to report to a meeting of John Anderson's friends the next morning that I felt John should not run, that his candidacy would be divisive, and that I was going to support Rhodes. I called Rhodes's office twice the following morning, since I could not reach him, and told him more or less the same thing and that I would be happy to support Rhodes in any way he wished me to. The following Monday I went around and called on him and offered to tender my resignation as a member of the leadership and urge other members of the leadership to do so, so that the new minority leader could impose his own trend on the leadership. Rhodes asked me not to do this, saying that he would need John Anderson in the leadership, as well as others, and that he was afraid John Anderson would not be reelected as conference chairman if, in fact, everybody was forced to resign from the leadership and to be reelected.

December [no date] 1973

I expect to spend [Christmas recess] for the most part talking to service clubs and schools and in general moving around my district to demonstrate my ability to an increasingly skeptical electorate. Although I do not know any specific political problems which I have, it is quite obvious that incumbents are in trouble generally, and Republicans in particular, as the public reacts more and more to the Nixon administration's amorality. I find it hard to believe that a man with as much experience in politics and as obviously intelligent as Nixon is can have allowed himself to get in such deep trouble politically with not just specific elements of his constituency but with virtually everyone. The problem for Republican politicians generally has been one of polarization: half my mail blames me for not standing up for the presidency, which these people seem still to regard as an institution above criticism, while the other half scolds me for having failed to have in some individual way removed the president from office before this. So many people think of impeachment as something quite simple, involving simply the decision to dismiss a president as though he were an employee of the Congress, and since to many people in this district I *am* the Congress, therefore it is within my power to dismiss the president if I simply would not be so stubborn about my political loyalties.

The symbolism of Nixon's tendency to look at himself as a big shot has become increasingly damaging. He has, for instance, failed to take this into account in his frequent trips to luxurious places at some distance from Washington in which the taxpayers' money has been invested. . . . He has failed to take it into account in his defense of the Watergate matter, where he has relied on the advice of his lawyers as to what had to be proved and what did not have to be proved, rather than taking a very high level of disclosure and anticipatory explanation of his role to the American people before they demanded to know. In short, Nixon has been a singularly insensitive politician and as such has shown the capacity to snatch disaster from what could have been a very strong and progressive administration. I find it hard to think about him or to look at him without revulsion at this point, not because I consider him loathsome but because I consider him incredibly stupid as a leader. I doubt that he is much worse than any other president in historic times, and I doubt that he is even more amoral, but insensitive he is to a degree that makes everyone who has by force of circumstance been identified with him suspect and a potential political victim.

Since my last journal entry, I have had a real brush with the right wing. What it means for my political future in the House I do not know, but it was at first a tempest in a teapot and finally somewhat unpleasant as it emerged. I ran for the Policy job in the House[18] vacated by John Rhodes when he moved up to be minority leader on Gerald Ford's accession to the vice presidency. The selection of Rhodes was unanimous: the tactic of my own and several of the other leaders of the House who immediately rallied to John's support—rather than letting John Anderson and Sam Devine get into an ideological battle for it, and rather than rewarding Les Arends for many years in the second spot—proved to be a successful tactic, and Rhodes became, in his own words, "a voice of independence" as a new minority leader.

I found Sam Steiger [AZ] and several of the so-called Good Guys group headed by Sam Devine circulating a letter for the support of Del Clawson [CA] for the Policy job. I immediately decided I better make up my mind either to stay in the Research position or to announce myself for Policy. I was being pressed to run for Policy by John McCollister [NE], Lou Frey [FL], and a group of younger members who banded together in an informal activist study group for their own purposes, and their position was that while they were entitled to representation in the leadership, they could not get one of their number elected to the Policy job because of its distinction, while they could probably get one of

18. Chairman of the Republican Policy Committee.

their people in the Research job if that were to become vacant as a result of my going for Policy.

I felt as though I were being kicked upstairs to a certain extent, although I must confess that I was also convinced that I was not doing a good job in Research because it required more brainstorming than I had time to give it, and the Policy job was more structured and less demanding in terms of time, while having a greater prestige. I therefore decided quite quickly when I found that the job would otherwise go to a representative of the right-wing group that the Policy move was something I should try to do, and I immediately got out a letter to all Republican Conference members announcing my candidacy. I also had a meeting in my office of the younger group, from which I chose Jim Hastings to be my campaign manager and to which I added Jack Kemp, both because he was anxious to do something for me and because he has a closer identification with the ideological right wing, although he tends to vote rather more liberally than I do.

In the usual time-honored custom, we divided up the entire Republican Conference among this group of younger members, Jack taking a large number of the right wing and reporting enthusiastically that a number of them are "with me all the way." It later developed that many of them signed the letter for Del Clawson, and the other members of my campaign group were pretty sour on Jack before they got through, feeling that he had not in fact talked to any of them at all, or if he had, he had not reported accurately what they had told him. . . . Jack wanted to nominate me, and the other members of the group absolutely refused to permit him to do so, although I never told him the reasons why I didn't accept his kind offer. . . . The final result was 88 for me and 77 for Del, nowhere near as close as it appeared, since 13 of my supporters were at committee meetings instead of at the conference, while only three of Del's supporters stayed in committee meetings when the conference was being held.

During the first week, John Rousselot, a former [John] Birch Society member from California, asked me why I had joined the Council on Foreign Relations [CFR], an internationalist eastern establishment group which puts out a good journal that I wanted to read and before which I have debated issues like trade, which are part of my committee responsibility. I laughed at him and said that I didn't think it was a communist group, since David Rockefeller was the president, but he apparently took it very seriously, and several other members of Del's supporters asked me why I had associated with this "ultraliberal" group.

On Wednesday afternoon of the second week, the night before the vote and after the conference had already been delayed twice for unknown reasons, a letter alleged to have been addressed to me from a lady in Chicago attacked me for my membership in the CFR and expressed disappointment that I had moved out of the mainstream of the Republican Party. I had not received this letter, but a couple of my supporters had brought it to me, troubled and wanting to know what the CFR was. I must confess that I did not know myself immediately what it was, but my staff told me it was the Council on Foreign Relations and that this apparently was related to the Policy job campaign and to the right-wing antipathy for the Council on Foreign Relations. It appears that about a hundred copies of this letter were circulated to the more conservative members of the Republican Conference the afternoon before the election, and when I looked at it, I thought it looked phony. Nobody by the name signed to the letter lived at that address in Chicago, according to the Chicago phone book; the signature was scrawled in an illegible fashion; and I had not received the original at all, which led me to be very suspicious of it.

John McCollister immediately latched on to the envelopes in which it was being circulated, which appeared to be inside mail envelopes, and checked with the page organization, finding that Phil Crane was the only one who had sent out a general mailing that afternoon. The word got to Phil Crane through Jack Kemp that he was suspected. He came around and denied it, saying that he had sent out a mailing of a different sort, copies of which he showed me. I told him that I didn't care about it one way or another and that I regretted it had come to his attention that he was being accused of delivering this letter. I then decided that it was just a Birch Society trick coming in from outside of the Congress.

At the conference, Del Clawson and I sat in the back of the room together, chatting and having a pleasant time, since we were pretty good friends, and announcing to the group as a whole that we were taking a live pair and that we were not going to vote at all ourselves. After the voting began, Bill Steiger came back and said he regretted that Del had not repudiated the tactics used in his behalf. Del said he knew nothing about those tactics and assumed, as I did, that it had come from outside the Congress. Sam Steiger said that that was not the case, that John Conlan, an Arizona freshman, had lost his receptionist the day before and she had come to him saying she had resigned because she did not approve of this type of tactic. I told Sam to forget it, but he said he was going to look into it further and see if he couldn't get an affidavit from the girl for purposes of censuring Conlan for his tactics.

Then Evans and Novak got hold of it, and John Rhodes came to me on the floor at one point, saying that he was upset that the letter had come from a member of the Arizona delegation and that he hoped I would not forget it. I said

I felt I had already forgotten it, and that if anybody was to be upset about it, it should be the Arizona delegation. He said Sam was very upset and determined to pursue it further. I said he should not do anything on my account, that I wasn't mad at anybody, and he ruefully asserted that if he had been as active against Conlan during the primary the previous year, they wouldn't have that problem at this point. Conlan subsequently visited me and denied that he knew anything about it. I told him again I wasn't mad at anybody and that I assumed he was telling the truth if he said he knew nothing about it.[19]

The whole thing seemed to me like a tempest in a teapot and probably added up to more damage to Del than to me. I must say, however, that since the Evans and Novak article on it has been printed in the Rochester papers, I have had a great many calls to my Rochester office asking what kind of a subversive organization I had joined. It is very confusing to people in my district who consider me a conservative to find that I am not considered that conservative in the Congress as a whole and that somebody could run a whole campaign against me in the Republican Party for a Republican leadership post on the basis that I am not sufficiently conservative to be safe.

John Rhodes is setting up an elaborate minority leader staff and has indicated to me in no uncertain terms that he intends to be the sole liaison with the White House and to run a much more authoritarian leadership than Jerry Ford, with his insecurity and group decision penchant, ever did.

[Rhodes] bawled me out for resigning from the Research job after the vote had been taken but before it had been counted. I did this for an obvious reason: if I resigned after the vote was counted and I lost, it would look like sour grapes; if I announced that I was resigning as Research chairman before the vote was taken, I would lose some of the young members' support, [as they were] simply looking for a vacancy to put one of their members in, rather than really wanting to help me for Policy. Rhodes said, "Barber, you gave me a bad time there for a few minutes when I thought you might get beaten [and] that we might not have you in the leadership and that you would have left me with all those right-wingers and nobody to talk to." I told him that he had John Anderson to talk to, and he grimaced and said, "Yes, but how could you do that?" He doesn't like Anderson and apparently doesn't trust him, although he feels he needs a liberal in the leadership just as he needs Sam Devine in the leadership to keep the conservatives from attacking his leadership directly.

19. Conlan served one more term in the House before losing a primary race for a Senate seat to Sam Steiger in 1976. Steiger lost the general election to Democrat Dennis DeConcini.

I increasingly feel that my role in Congress is legislative rather than political. Ways and Means is not a good forum from which to move to top House leadership, since we have so little floor work, with our closed rule and our constant committee meetings. I also do not believe that I am good in a partisan role or effective in debate, and the top political leaders should have these qualities in particular. . . . As a matter of fact, after having been identified as a dangerous eastern liberal, I question whether I can get myself elected to anything else politically in the Republican Party in the House, since the center of gravity in the party quite obviously geographically and ideologically is to the right of me. It seems incredible to me that I should be considered anything but conservative, and yet I guess I am being unrealistic if I maintain that my reform-mindedness is simply part of the responsibility of a conservative. It looks to others more like an opting for change than like systems maintenance work.

Of course, I'm home now, not moving about very much, but talking with my neighbors about the affairs of government which I observe in the course of my job. There seems to be very little doubt but that people are deeply distressed by Nixon's leadership and by their image of the government itself. I am treated with considerable restraint by many of my neighbors, since they do not know how much I am involved myself but assume that I conform to the political pattern when I am in Washington. Nevertheless, dissatisfaction and distrust are obvious as far as the institution of government is concerned, regardless of what their attitude toward me personally may be. Nixon has virtually destroyed the confidence of the people in the institution of government, and he must be held accountable for this.

I am sure most of my colleagues will bring the same message home from vacation that is apparent to me: that Richard Nixon is a severe liability at this stage in his political career and in the light of the things he has done to express his view of the presidency. Many people seem to cherish the hope that he is going to resign, but in my view, this is doubtless wishful thinking and does not reflect the probable view of the president himself in the isolation he has constructed around him. I can see only a disastrous year ahead.

Minority leader John Rhodes talks to Conable about possible "contingency" plans should Nixon's impeachment become inevitable. A formidable election challenger emerges, her war chest overflowing with union money. The extent of Nixon's involvement in the Watergate cover-up, as well as his abuse of power, dismays and then enrages Conable. A friend, Gerald Ford, assumes the presidency and calls on Conable for advice. Betty Ford wants to kick him in the shins. He gets in hot water with both candidates he recommends for the vice presidency. Conable wins reelection, with help from a noted political scientist. Wilbur Mills falls apart.

This was Conable's annus horribilis. His sense of betrayal by Richard Nixon was profound: Nixon wrote to him after leaving office, but Conable refused to answer his letters. He took some solace in the accession of Gerald Ford, who struck just the right note during his first days in office.

The bottom fell out for Wilbur Mills, victim of his own alcoholism, bad judgment, and personal weakness. He forfeited his chairmanship of Ways and Means over a public affair with an ecdysiast. Conable refused to snicker.

The 1974 election was the only really competitive congressional race Conable ever ran as an incumbent. His opponent, Rochester vice mayor Midge Costanza, was feisty, charismatic, and well funded. Conable was outspent and outcampaigned, yet his rural constituency pulled him through.

January 25, 1974

I visited with John Rhodes the week before the recess was over, having come back here to keep Senator Proxmire honest during one day of hearings on the energy crisis. . . . John was in town at the same time also, and I sought the opportunity to talk with him to see what was happening. He opened the conversation at a very general level, talking about the president and the continuing downward cycle of Watergate-type revelations. He then asked me what I thought of the possibility of contingency plans in the event it was disclosed that Richard Nixon in fact was personally involved in the cover-up of Watergate affairs to the extent that he was in fact impeachable. I asked him if he knew anything that I didn't know about the president's involvement in these matters, and he said he did not, but he felt we could ill afford not to at least consider the possibility that further disclosures would compromise the president beyond redemption. I asked him what he then meant by contingency plans, and he said that he thought perhaps the Republican members of the House were the only coherent group which could call on the president to protect his place in history, the welfare of the country, and the survival of the Republican Party by resigning rather than facing an inevitable conviction on impeachment. I said to him that if he were asking me if I was willing to stand up and be counted among those who would go to the president and demand such a resignation, he could count on me. He said that was really all he was asking and that he did not know whether many of our colleagues would be willing to join in such a desperate venture if it were necessary. The whole thing was left quite vague, but I got the impression that he was testing me to find out if my willingness to stand up and be counted was sufficient so that he would be able to call on me when and if the time comes.

February 18, 1974

The White House meeting this morning indicated that the president is even farther from reality than I had thought previously. He spent the entire time talking about campaign reform—long, rambling reminiscences about his campaign with Kennedy and his campaign with Humphrey—very little in the way of pointed suggestions and a great deal in the way of discourse. It was distressing because we spent two and a half hours and got only halfway through our agenda, largely because of presidential interventions. At the end of the meeting I suggested to him that as much as possible be put through George Bush.[1] He immediately said that of course George had been consulted on all this stuff. George was present but had said very little. My only point was simply that I felt the Republican National Committee would have a good deal more credibility than the White House itself on the issue of campaign reform, but apparently very few people got that point.

March 11, 1974

Last Friday I went to another White House leadership meeting, this one better than the last but still demonstrating a garrulousness on the part of the president, which was disturbing. Among other things, he had Henry Kissinger brief us on Middle Eastern developments, which the secretary did with grace and his usual

1. Since January 1973, Bush had been chairman of the Republican National Committee.

high level of informativeness. The president interrupted him constantly and followed with long-winded monologues relating to his theories of foreign affairs, his personal experiences, and other, for the most part, irrelevancies which were apparently distressing to the secretary, although he kept himself under diplomatic control during the period.

April 16, 1974

The situation with respect to the presidency continues to deteriorate. We have been to several regular leadership meetings, at least two, since my last journal entry, and each has involved some small input by the members of the cabinet or the legislative leaders, followed by a long and embarrassing monologue by the president, drawing on his vast political experience and his reminiscences, similar to those one would expect from a man in deep trouble and trying to relive the moments of his glory. . . . The president never brings up Watergate and never refers to it, although that is the subject on everyone's mind.

I am hearing from a number of different sources, deliberately planted in all probability, rumors that the AFL-CIO will spend $50,000 in contesting my seat this year. . . . I find it hard to believe that organized labor will put any substantial sum of money into my race, since they have a finite amount of money with which to work in any event, unless a poll taken in June or July of this year indicates that I can in fact be beaten. My percentage of the vote in the last election was 68 percent, although I expect that to be down very substantially, since I am the [most consistent] supporter of Richard Nixon's administration in the statistics that have been prepared by *Congressional Quarterly.* I do not think it will be possible, unless I fall flat on my face sometime in the interim, for that plurality to be cut back to a minority. At last it is quite clear that almost the only issue in my campaign will be whether or not I am a puppet of that man in the White House, and I will have to be well prepared on every issue to indicate that I was not simply responding to his arm-twisting and cajolery when I have voted the way I did. I suppose no one will listen to my protestations anyway, and if my image is that of an intransigent Nixon supporter back home, it will be virtually impossible to explain away, and I will have to rely on hard-core Republican support for any possible eking out of survival.

This raises the obvious question about impeachment. I have been saying to all and sundry that I am virtually a member of a grand jury and that the impeachment process is one of indictment and that I should not commit myself in advance of knowing the factual basis reported by the Judiciary Committee for any report recommending impeachment. I think this is the appropriate posture to take, since our function is a constitutional one, but I must say that more and more of my colleagues seem to be talking about impeachment as though it were a political matter. In other words, they are being polled by network and newspaper types to find out if the votes are there and how they would vote on their present understanding of the facts. I fear that many of them will get backed into a corner long before any Judiciary Committee report is forthcoming and that the result will be a politicization of the process, which will satisfy no one that justice has been done or that the issues in Watergate have been resolved to anyone's satisfaction. I don't know how we can be so dumb.

May 9, 1974

I'm headed this morning for a White House leadership meeting, the first one we have had in a month.[2] [The] condition of things in the Congress is such that even though this meeting is about economics, a comparatively nonvolatile subject, the tension around the table will be considerable. The president is described as quite relaxed, but Congress certainly is not. Disclosure of the digest of the subpoenaed tapes, while it initially had a good reaction in the public because of the apparent movement toward full disclosure of the circumstances of the Watergate affair, in the long run has proved extremely damaging to the president through the somewhat squalid and extended conversations he had with his aides demonstrating very little moral concern about the relationship of the presidency and the crimes committed in its name. At SOS this past Tuesday night, there was almost a unanimous consensus that the president was a severe liability and that he should resign. At Wednesday Club[3] last night, this consensus bordered on the hysterical. I find the grave concerns about the president's viability cross ideological lines to a degree I would not have thought possible in view of the blind support the conservatives have given this not very conservative president over the past year.

Tuesday morning of this week, John Erlenborn, Jack Wydler [R-NY], and I were invited to the White House mess for breakfast with Al Haig and James St. Clair, the president's lawyer. Max Friedersdorf[4] and Bill Timmons[5] also were present, and we discussed things which were intended to give St. Clair the "feel" of the House of Representatives with respect to his client's position. We prob-

2. The House Judiciary Committee began impeachment hearings on this day.

3. A congressional study group of moderate and liberal Republicans.

4. Deputy assistant to the president for legislative affairs.

5. Assistant to the president for legislative affairs.

ably were more encouraging than we should have been, but we understood our mission to be one of tactic: how can the president be presented in the best possible light from the point of view of the House of Representatives from this time forward?

I wound up giving two strong items of advice: First, that the president go back to the business of leading the country and let his lawyers speak for him with respect to future tapes. It seemed to me that the president was cast too much in the role of the defendant and that if he went on the tube and talked further about what he was and was not going to do, it made it appear that he was actively conducting his own defense and that, in matters of strategy, this was not an appropriate posture for him to take. Second, I said it was inevitable that the attack would shift now that the president had been forced to take off his clothes and expose himself to the public through the digests of these conversations in the Oval Office about Watergate. I assumed that further demands would be made for other information which could extend the investigation indefinitely, and I urged them that if they were required to turn down additional subpoenas or demands for tapes, to do it in a way that would make clear they were not trying to hide the facts, only to prevent an indefinite extension of the investigation.

Thus, I suggested that they handle the matter like a game of roulette to a degree, in that they say, in effect, "No, we will not give you 141 additional tapes, but we have decided that we will let you choose from among 141 the five you want the most and we will give them to you without any reservation of editing rights or anything of the sort, making them public also at the same time, just to make clear to you that we are not trying to hide anything but only to prevent an indefinite extension of the investigation through the necessity of processing and analyzing such a large number as you have requested." Decision of what five tapes they wanted would then be up to the people doing the subpoenaing—making it clear that St. Clair and the president did not in any way intend to hold anything back that was really needed or wanted, but that they were unwilling indefinitely to extend the investigation. St. Clair showed a good deal of interest in my proposal and said that it was an intelligent suggestion and he would consider it seriously. That afternoon he turned down a request for additional tapes categorically and without any condition, thus preparing the whole matter for confrontation and in no way indicating the president's willingness to be forthcoming in any other way. Well, it was an interesting idea anyway.

It is interesting to note, as my wife pointed out to me, that the Republican Party is virtually unmentioned in all the extended discussions between Nixon and his aides following the discovery of the Watergate affair which has so demonstrated the moral shabbiness of him and his closest aides. They quite clearly thought neither of the country nor their political associates, nor of the party that brought him to power, but only of how they could in some way squash the investigation of their silly tactics.

Later the same morning:

The White House meeting turned out to be a routine meeting on the economy. . . . The president engaged in somewhat less protracted monologues than usual, and most of us got the chance to say something. The president seemed relaxed and did not refer to Watergate in any way. After the meeting. . . . I . . . pulled George Bush aside and said that I thought it was awfully important that the party assert its corporate identity. George said that he was extremely uptight, didn't know what the right thing to do was, would value my advice, etc. He indicated that he was considering resigning, and I told him that I thought this would be a serious mistake because of the necessity of the party having a clear identity in the event the president, as leader of the party, was further pulled down. Before we finished our discussion, Al Haig came along and said, "They're getting a little testy up on Capitol Hill, aren't they?" I confirmed that they were. From these various conversations, it is clear to me that everyone in the White House knows quite well that things are extremely bad on the Hill.

June 26, 1974

My last journal entry has probably been as difficult a one as I have had in Congress. Back of most of my tensions and concerns I have laid the real concerns about my possible defeat this fall by one of the Democrats now running against me in the Democratic primary. The apparent candidate who will succeed is Margaret "Midge" Costanza, the vice mayor of the city of Rochester, who ran well ahead of the ticket when the Democrats took over the City Council during the 1973 election. Midge is an articulate and very smooth former vice chairman of the Democratic Party in Monroe County and has no particular record, having been in office for only four or five months, on which she can appear vulnerable. She pretended not to want to run against me, feeling that she was vulnerable on account of her rapid movement from council to the national scene, but I understand that the rather elaborate drafting efforts made up by organized labor were, in fact, organized and orchestrated by the Democratic chairman, Mr. [Laurence] Kirwan, and a labor operative by the name of Flavin.[6]

6. Robert J. Flavin, president of Rochester's Local 1170, Communications Workers of America.

There is little doubt that organized labor is willing to make a major commitment to my defeat this year. They have been talking openly in the paper about spending $50,000 to unseat me, talking about my antilabor record, as evidenced by the fact that I have a zero COPE[7] rating this year, and [about] my unresponsiveness to the desires of the "little people." It seems remarkably arrogant of them that they would talk openly of raising $50,000 to defeat me when I have never spent as much as $25,000 on my own election campaign in the past. There is little doubt in my mind that if I were talking about spending such sums of money, it would elicit the usual comments from all sources about Republicans and money, Republicans and Watergate venality, etc. The particular means by which they are going to raise $50,000 is stated to be a Labor Day rally with raffles, and it appears that they are already trying to sell tickets to organized labor rank and file, some of whom have sent me anonymous letters saying they resent this kind of arm-twisting. I also very much doubt, since organized labor constitutes only 11 percent of the workforce in the 35th Congressional District, that they will be able to raise anything like $50,000, and the whole operation, therefore, appears to be nothing more than a cloak for the shifting of national money in from some other area.

Miss Costanza told one of my friends that after she had turned down labor's request that she run following a rally put together to try to draft her, they had raised the ante to $150,000, and she felt she could not turn it down on that basis. If that is so, which I doubt, there could be little doubt that COPE money will be coming in from outside.

Miss Costanza also has too strong an identification with the city of Rochester for her to generate any appeal which would be district-wide. I think she will be the toughest opponent I have ever had, and if she spends anything close to $50,000, it will be a most impressive campaign and one that will, quite obviously, cut substantially into my plurality.

This may be wishful thinking, but I am constrained to doubt such massive expenditures in an election district like mine when a finite amount of money is available even to organized labor and there are so many other congressional districts where massive investment would be more probably fruitful. I also find it difficult to believe that, despite my antilabor record of this year, the labor leaders in Washington actually feel that my influence is that negative for them on the Ways and Means Committee. Despite these doubts, I note that at least two other well-known Republican leaders from the House [Jack Edwards of

7. The AFL-CIO's Committee on Political Education.

Alabama and Al Quie of Minnesota] have had the figure of $50,000 surface in their own campaigns with respect to organized labor opposition.[8]

I was invited one evening to go on the *Sequoia* with ten other congressmen and to have a "pleasant evening" with the president himself. We went aboard the *Sequoia* at about 6:30 and were back at 8:30, having simply steamed out into the Potomac and done a quick circle rather than going upstream or downstream in any way.

I had never had the opportunity before to talk with the president informally in a group as small as ten people, and I used the opportunity to question him at some length about the Syrian-Israeli cease-fire which had been achieved that afternoon and about which the president was quite elated. As a matter of fact, he spent at least 85 percent of the time talking about that and about the problems of dealing with Arabs and Russians in the complicated foreign relations of our time. He seemed relaxed and conversational and did very little discussion of anything but the great triumphs of his foreign affairs policies. At one point, one of the impatient southern gentlemen in the coterie around him said, "Well, let's talk about domestic policy, Mr. President," and he turned to inflation for a while, thus giving me a chance to interrogate him some about the economy. I did a great deal of talking during the predinner period, and some of the others were feeling resentful of the extent to which I was monopolizing conversation about matters of substance. I found myself seated at the dinner table way down at the end, some distance from the solid core of loyalists who surrounded him, and could not hear all the conversation going on there.

At some point, Sonny Montgomery [D-MS] asked the president what we could do to help, and he responded that he felt it was very important that we not leave the country in the middle of an impeachment trial over a long period of time, since there was an absolute necessity for someone to have credibility in dealing with the very serious foreign affairs problems that confront us. It seemed to me remarkable that he did not discuss in this connection his guilt or his innocence, although he did say at one point, "If I thought I was guilty, I'd retire." The point is that, far from it being an arm-twisting operation or one which dealt with Watergate to any substantial degree, as the press insinuated it must have and as my constituents have accused subsequently, the evening was a comparatively relaxed and substantive evening greatly affected by the president's elation over the Syrian-Israeli cease-fire that very afternoon. I must say that it was a substantial mistake for me politically to have accepted the invitation and

8. Both Quie and Edwards were reelected.

gone out on the yacht, since it has been repeated a great deal in the press and on the radio since that time, the assumption being that this identifies me clearly as a man willing to engage in opulent support of the president at the taxpayers' expense when I should not be a party to "jury tampering."

Another example of internal problems within the Republican Party in the House came this past Friday morning, when a press report indicated that [Judiciary Committee chairman] Peter Rodino [D-NJ] had said, in advance of a presentation by James St. Clair of the president's side of the argument and in advance of any live witnesses before the committee, that all twenty-one Democrats had decided on impeachment and that five Republicans had to be won over if there was to be any chance of impeachment in the House. A group of the freshman Republicans in the House became very excited about this and insisted on the leadership confronting Rodino and getting some explanation.

We had a meeting in John Rhodes's absence (he was speaking out of town somewhere, although he showed up later in the day), and we more or less decided that Les Arends was the one to handle it, since he was the number-two man. Les then backed out, and as a result, Bill Young of Florida, [Skip] Bafalis of Florida, Larry Hogan [MD], and some others finally took it on the floor after Rodino had already retracted any statements attributed to him and, in a five-minute emotional speech to the House, declared that he had in no way made the statements attributed to him. Subsequently, an ABC commentator announced that he had been present at the meeting and could confirm what the *Los Angeles Times* had reported about Rodino's prejudicial statements, and it appeared that it was another example of serious error on the part of the Judiciary Committee that the matter had been handled as it had. I urged Les Arends to take on the issue on the floor during our meeting, feeling that John Anderson must not speak for the leadership on this, since he was already a questionable spokesman on the issue of impeachment as a result of his statements about resignation.[9]

As if the tensions within the leadership were not enough . . . it appears that there is increasing rank-and-file disenchantment with the Republican leadership as the impeachment pressures grow, that feeling based primarily on the comparatively low-key, low-silhouette, and indecisive type of leadership that Rhodes is giving. There is little doubt that Rhodes is a less outgoing leader than Jerry Ford was. He seems to expect us to follow him without making any clear effort to indicate to us in which direction he himself is moving, and although

9. In May 1974 Anderson had asked Nixon to "spare the nation one last agony" by resigning.

he keeps his own counsel to too great a degree, he nevertheless appears to have a higher standard of expectation of other members of the leadership than Jerry himself did. Anderson continues to demonstrate an insensitivity to rank-and-file attitudes which I think augurs ill for his continuance as chairman of the Republican Conference.

The Ways and Means Committee has been going through a very difficult period as well. . . . The chairman appears to be badly distracted and even more unpredictable than usual. He is frequently absent, at least on two occasions blaming it on the illness of his elderly mother but, to my knowledge, frequently maintaining his presence here in Washington, despite the fact that she is in a hospital back in Arkansas. He has been attacked in the press lately as a result of some of the disclosures about his campaign for the presidency and the extent to which it was financed by milk cooperatives and business lobbyists, but I have not detected any great concern on his part as a result of these attacks, and I suspect his distraction is more general than that. It is quite clear that he is having a good deal of trouble with the changing Democratic Party and with people in the House Democratic delegation who feel that he has too much power and that his leadership is somewhat passé.

I feel some affection for the chairman still, but in his present state, I wouldn't trust him as far as I could throw him. He is a very bright man and a man who has been extremely nice to me over the period of my tenure on the Ways and Means Committee. He even went on a television program of mine two weeks ago, saying that he wanted to note for the people of my district what fine service I had given to his committee and how much he valued the assistance I had given him, something that he would not do if he were really out of sorts with me. Nevertheless, the caliber of his leadership appears to have been declining ever since he sensed that great groundswell pressing him towards the presidency in 1972 and went through what was apparently for him an agonizing discovery that his role has been too anonymous in the House for him to develop any national constituency. I continue to wonder if he is not going to step out of this year's race at the last possible minute, putting a handpicked successor in to run for his seat after he had adequately flattened the Republican opposition he has.[10]

10. Despite the Fanne Foxe scandal, which is yet to come, Mills was reelected in November 1974 with 59 percent of the vote.

August [no date] 1974

Progress towards impeachment is apparent.[11] Tremendous tensions are developing within the Republican Party in the House as a result of this progress, and
it is to be expected that considerable assault will be made on leadership during
the period of time between now and the impeachment vote. I feel sorry for John
Rhodes, who walks a desperate tightrope between the obdurate loyalists on the
one hand and the inveterate haters on the other.

At least partly because I wanted to feel independent about impeachment (I
really have not made up my mind how I am going to vote at this point), I sought
the opportunity to talk with John Rhodes and to tell him that I did not expect
to run for Policy chair again. His response was unequivocal, in that he said he
wanted me to stay in the leadership. I told him that I was doing a lousy job as
Policy chairman, and he immediately rejoined that he had spent eight years in
that frustrating job and he was well aware that it was not the most satisfying opportunity in the world when one brings in a carefully drafted statement and the
tigers tear it in small bits before one's very eyes. He said he didn't care what I did
about Policy but he wanted my brain and my judgment in leadership meetings.
It was a flattering response, whether sincere or not, and I agreed to put off any
decision about a leadership role until after the election.

I also told him that I was interested in serving on the Budget Committee[12]
and received an equivocal answer there. . . . My sole claim to the Budget Committee is my emphasis on fiscal responsibility: I have been making speeches on
the floor of the House all this spring urging improvements in fiscal policy and
the kind of bipartisan effort that could indicate clearly to the American people
that we are going to try to get government spending under control, irrespective
of presidential impoundment and the kind of presidential leadership that may be
forthcoming if we ever get out from under the impeachment cloud.

The word seems to be getting around that I am in trouble in my district. I
think I may have generated a good deal of this word myself, but the result has
been that Jim Cannon, Governor Rockefeller's man now working with him on
the Commission on Critical Choices, came to see me yesterday to say that the
governor had heard from both Wilbur and Herman Schneebeli that I was in the

11. Between July 27 and 30, the House Judiciary Committee reported out three articles
of impeachment against Nixon: for obstruction of justice, misuse of power, and contempt of
Congress.

12. The House Budget Committee had been created by the Congressional Budget and
Impoundment Control Act of 1974.

midst of a very tough race and anything the governor could do to help me would be appreciated. The governor, of course, responded gallantly through his man Friday, but I was not in a position to suggest any tangible way in which he could help at this point. Expressions of goodwill come easy to the governor, and I do not have any doubt that he would follow them up with concrete acts of kindness or support if I were to find some way in which he could so do, since he must have decided long ago that I was a key person in relation to the New York delegation that may be considering nomination of a candidate for president in 1976. I do not mean this as cynically as it sounds, because I am sure the governor does feel some gratitude to me for my work on revenue sharing, but I think it would also be accurate to state that I am not sure that his covert assistance would be that much of an advantage to me in the 35th Congressional District at this time.

I do not doubt that I have a tough political race, the general election fight of my life, but I also do not doubt that I would have to be considered a strong front-runner in relation to Miss Costanza or her various opponents for the Democratic nomination. I expect a surly electorate, but the ones who are most surly will also be the ones least likely to go to my political opposition. I certainly am not about to push the panic button at this point, and if I have created that appearance with Herman and with the chairman, I think I had better consider ways in which I can avoid others outside the Congress getting that feeling as well, since panic is one of the least constructive postures I can have as I go into a tough political race.

September 1, 1974

The month of August was hard to believe, and the events of August seem very long ago. The reason they seem hard to believe, I suppose, is that they were unprecedented in the history of this country, and the reason they seem long ago now is because we have so determined not to look back but to face a more tranquil future during the short time left to us before the election period. I suppose, from a political view, President Nixon's resignation[13]—following shortly after the disclosures he made on that famous Monday when he acknowledged he had participated in the cover-up of the Watergate affair as quickly as four days after the event and that he had been misleading us in the interim—could not have created a more graceful exit and denouement for all the sweating congressmen who were uncertain what the right course of action was. The week before, we had finished up our work on tax reform and had sent the bill to the draftsmen and were working on health insurance. I told Chairman Mills that I was not

13. Nixon announced his resignation on August 8, 1974, and made it official the next day.

going to be available [during what turned out to be] the week of Nixon's resignation because I wanted to spend the time reading the evidence which was then
coming out in printed form from the Judiciary Committee. Mr. Mills looked
completely blank; apparently, it had not occurred to most of the Democrats present that they should read the evidence about Mr. Nixon.

I instructed my staff to pull out the evidence from Judiciary relating to abuse
of power, feeling that that was probably the most serious charge against Mr.
Nixon. I never considered the Watergate affair much more than a contrived
event of comparatively modest significance, but I was deeply troubled by allegations that the president used the IRS, FBI, and others to harass citizens whom
he considered to be political enemies of his. I was shocked when Harry Nicholas
presented me with six of the thirty-six books, saying these all related to presidential abuses of power. I took them home with me, struggled with them over
the weekend, and got one completely read. I had heard the transcripts were bad,
but I was not prepared, even then, for the tone of them, which was comparatively
low grade and immature, consisting of a number of discussions between President Nixon and H. R. Haldeman and John Dean about how they were going to
"get" this or that political enemy. It seemed like the sort of thing that would go
on in a college fraternity, and I would have felt much better if at one point or
another Haldeman had just said "yes, sir" to the president.

That Monday,[14] John Rhodes had promised to have a press conference and
announce how he was going to vote on the matter of impeachment. I don't know
why he felt this was necessary, and at the time, I remember thinking that perhaps
he was pulling some sort of a pressure tactic on the White House. I asked John
if he had made up his mind, and he said to me that he knew what he had to
do but was having trouble with his conscience in doing it. That is the closest I
ever came to finding out what his intentions were.[15] On Sunday, I was called by
press people at my home in Alexander and asked if I knew anything about what
was going on up at Camp David. I did not, and it appeared that the president
had summoned his speechwriters and was secluded at this traditional spot of
seclusion. I also learned that John Rhodes had called off his press conference for
Monday, claiming that he had laryngitis.

14. August 5, 1974.
15. J. Brian Smith, Rhodes's former press secretary and biographer, says that Rhodes had
prepared a speech announcing that he would not vote for impeachment, but on Sunday, August 4, Al Haig persuaded him to postpone his statement. J. Brian Smith, *John Rhodes: Man
of the House* (Phoenix, AZ: Primer, 2005), 137.

On Monday, the day was normal up until about quarter to four, when John Rhodes called me and said that the president was ready to drop another shoe, that it consisted of a tape showing his involvement from the start and substantial misleading of the Republican members of the Judiciary Committee who had stood up for him and voted against impeachment. He said that it sounded as though the president had had the course. He said that he was letting me know because I was the only member of the leadership he cared about and that I might want to protect myself. He told me at that time St. Clair was meeting with the ten Judiciary Committee members who had supported the president and that a statement would be available over on the floor in a little while, with the president expected to release this tape at 4:15.

I rushed over to the floor and found Joe Bartlett,[16] who got me a copy of the statement. I had read it about halfway through when I saw the Republican members of the Judiciary Committee filing into the back of the chamber looking gray and unhappy. Sam Donaldson of ABC rapped on the door of the lobby and asked me if I knew anything that I could make a statement about. I said I did and followed him to the television studio, where I stated before all three network television cameras that as far as I was concerned, I had found the "smoking gun," that the president had lied to us, and that I felt sad and angry that I had put my trust in a man who was not worthy of that trust. I said that as far as I was concerned, the only issue remaining was the orderly transition of power from Richard Nixon to Gerald Ford. This phrase was later picked up on by Chuck Wiggins [R-CA], who put out a statement about an hour and a half later that he was changing his mind about impeachment. By the following morning, all the members of the Judiciary Committee who had voted for the president announced that they were changing their vote.

I reacted with such anger before the television cameras that I could not remember exactly what I had said afterwards and was somewhat chagrined that I had not been more artful in denunciations of the president. I received quite a bit of hate mail about this later on by people who had not yet absorbed the extent of the president's confession. Since I made this statement before the release was really completely out, it got wide currency throughout the country, and I was grateful thereafter that I had been one of the early ones to tip over, since it was immediately apparent that not just the ten members of the Judiciary Committee who had previously been for the president but most of the members of the House were fed up and that the president had no base of support remaining in

16. Clerk to the Republican minority of the House.

the Congress. When the anger had subsided, a great feeling of relief seeped in on me that I was not going to have to vote on the basis of inconclusive evidence, either to support or impeach the president. It would have been a most unhappy necessity, and I was dreading the two weeks before the beginning of the impeachment debate in the House, during which time I would have had to read those thirty-six books of evidence, squalid as they were, and try to find in them some basis on which I could comply with my constitutional responsibility and still survive politically. It was quite clear from the start that the president could not survive politically, once he had made the disclosures he made on Monday.

On Thursday night, when he was expected to resign, I was at the Moiseyev Ballet with my daughter Anne and heard his speech during the intermission. The affect of the audience was not at all jubilant or regretful; people just seemed numb. There were, of course, a few who jumped up and clapped and a few others who told them to keep quiet. I left the Moiseyev early and went to NBC and taped a statement about Gerald Ford's probable economic policy with Charles Schultz of the Brookings Institute. It was never used. The night before, I had been on television with Martin Agronsky[17] and Senator Lloyd Bentsen [D] of Texas, supposedly also to discuss economics, although at that point, Martin was interested only in putting Richard Nixon in jail and we never got to talk about economics until twenty-four minutes of a thirty-minute program had expired. I lost my temper with Martin on the program and urged him, as a member of the press, to temper justice with mercy, saying that the press had a great victory in bringing Nixon down and that it would not improve the image of the country if we then treated him like a common criminal. Martin Agronsky subsequently called me twice the following week, talking with me over the phone at some length, apparently trying to make me feel better about his attitudes. I heard that after he left the television program on which I appeared, he showed up at a dinner with a number of other Democratic members of Congress and his opening line at the dinner was, "It took twenty-seven years, but we finally got the son of a bitch."

I was not asked to go to any of the farewell parties for Richard Nixon at the White House. I understand there were mostly southern Democrats there.

I did go to the Ford inaugural and was thrilled at the delicacy and tact of his inaugural statement. Going through the line subsequently, shaking the new president's hand, I said to him, "Let us all help you, Mr. President." I gave Betty Ford a hug and she pushed me away, saying again that she should kick me in the

17. *Martin Agronsky's Evening Edition.*

shins. She had reacted similarly when Jerry was appointed vice president. Apparently, she still thinks I had a good deal to do with his appointment. We had business on the floor that Friday, and I left to go up home sometime after five o'clock. I never arrived until 2:30 a.m. and was quite tired. Because I had asked all the "boys" to meet me at coffee the following morning at Batavia,[18] I thought I had better go up and so got up at seven o'clock that Saturday morning. The reason I had asked them to meet me was that NBC was going to send a camera crew to photograph me around my district, and I was amused at the thought of having my old cronies on national television. Of course, Friday afternoon NBC called to say that since the focus was shifting away from Congress, now that it had been decided there was not going to be any impeachment, they no longer intended to do the profile of me the following Sunday night, [which had been] based on the assumption that I was going to be a key vote on impeachment.

I had a fairly tough day, meeting with a number of people and speaking briefly at a luncheon with Frank Horton and Senator Charles Percy in Rochester, then coming back to Alexander to prepare for a Cornell Club picnic at which 250 people showed up and picnicked in our backyard. In the middle of the picnic, I was called to the phone and found that the new president was asking me to come and meet with him the next day, Sunday, at 2:30 p.m. to discuss the vice presidency and to get my views about who it should be. I discussed this with the guests of the picnic in an impromptu speech and found a general atmosphere of relief and of acceptance, with no clear choice for the vice presidency among these friendly college graduates who were picnicking at my house.

I got up at 4:30 a.m. and drove all the way back to Washington, arriving exhausted and having only a little time to go to my office and type out a short note of general advice for the new president, in case I didn't get to talk to him about various public relations things I thought he should do to solidify his position with the Congress. In this letter I also told him of the members I felt were influential in the House, as a result of changes or developments since he had left the House. I went in the West Wing. I was taken into the congressional liaison office, where Mel Laird and Bryce Harlow were sitting. Mel was making notes on program matters. I expressed the opinion that in the president's State of the Union address, which he was giving to the joint session of the Congress the Monday night following, he should talk about tax reform. Mel took the attitude

18. For years, Conable met with his Batavia buddies for Saturday morning coffee at Genesee Hardware.

that Ways and Means should be more interested in health insurance, so we got into quite an argument about it. . . . When the president gave his speech, it was clear that Mel had won out over me on this particular issue.

I was taken into the president's Oval Office then by Max Friedersdorf. I found myself alone with the president, whom I called "Jerry" three times in the course of the conversation. We were photographed together, and then I asked him why he hadn't met with the seven or eight leaders of Congress he had decided to talk to all at once. He said he didn't want us exerting too much influence on each other and wanted our frank appraisals of the various people involved, something he knew would not be forthcoming if others were there to quote us. He showed some impatience when I asked him what kind of vice president he wanted to have, saying that he had brought me in to tell him what kind he should have, that I knew him better than he knew himself, and that he wanted me to be completely open in expressing what I thought would be the best addition to an administration of which he was the president. We talked mostly about Nelson Rockefeller, George Bush, and Melvin Laird, but he then ran a number of names by me, getting my reaction to them and taking notes. We also talked about a wide range of subjects, including my wife's activities in the women's movement, Martha Griffiths and Edith Green [D-OR] as potential appointees to his administration, and matters affecting leadership of the House. It was a relaxed and direct conversation, and I look back on it with considerable pleasure. Leaving the West Wing of the White House, a whole mob of television and radio reporters taped my comments in avid detail.

Subsequently, I had an unhappy time about the recommendations for the vice president. The announcement was to be made the following Tuesday. I had been interviewed a great deal and had talked indiscriminately about both George Bush and Nelson Rockefeller. On Monday, I was called by Dick Rosenbaum, the Republican chairman of New York State, and told that George Hinman, Rockefeller's confidant, was very upset that I was pushing George Bush so hard. I, of course, denied that I was pushing George Bush any harder than Rockefeller, saying that either one would be an acceptable vice president but that they would reflect quite different wishes on the part of the president for his administration. It wasn't an hour later that Jerry Pettis, who tried to organize support for George, said to me that George was quite personally hurt that, after having sat next to him for four years on the Ways and Means Committee, I was pushing Nelson Rockefeller so hard. I appear to have offended both sides and convinced them that I was for the other, which demonstrates the worst of possible worlds.

When Rockefeller was announced as the new vice president, I was perfectly well satisfied, although the reaction in my district was bad. I took it as evidence that Ford wanted strong people rather than sycophants around him. Two days later, Rocky called on me in my office as a courtesy call, and we had a polite conversation in which I stated that I thought he would have good credibility as a budget-cutter, expressing confidence that he would be tough enough to do what was expected of him in this respect, as compared with someone like Ronald Reagan, who had not had the opportunity to demonstrate the human concerns that Rockefeller had showed as governor of New York.

December 1, 1974

This fall has been a maelstrom of difficulty, controversy, and unhappiness. I shall start by describing the personal campaign which I had for reelection to my sixth term in the Congress. It was obvious from the time that Margaret (Midge) Costanza allowed herself to be drafted by organized labor that I was in some trouble in this year's election, at least relative to the cakewalks I have had in other years. Miss Costanza ran ahead of the Democratic ticket when the Democrats took over City Hall last year. Her name recognition in my district was very high. She was a good "gut" politician, using the stiletto and a ready wit, as well as some occasionally offensive masculine language to endear herself with the coarser elements of the population, while hiring for herself a campaign manager of some grace, professionalism, and elegance.

This campaign manager, Peter Regenstreif of the University of Rochester's Political Science Department, had some experience as a professional pollster and . . . proved to be a virtual Pygmalion, polishing Midge, filling her head full of slogans, running issue polls, and adapting her debating techniques to my weak spots. During the campaign, she wrapped President Nixon around my neck so frequently that I rarely got the luxury of substantive discussion, spending most of my time on the defensive and frequently further eroding my position by trying to describe complexities while she went right to the kind of simplicity the electorate craves. When the New York legislature set the primary for September rather than its usual June date, they not only demolished Malcolm Wilson as governor[19] but also damaged me, since Midge had a primary contest in which she spent upwards of $15,000, thus adding to her already established name recognition and giving her a momentum leading into the general election.

---

19. Wilson was defeated by Conable's Democratic Ways and Means Committee colleague Hugh Carey.

In September, while my main preoccupation was the inflation summit[20] and I was also returning from time to time to an embattled Ways and Means Committee, I began to get bad vibes from the district, in the way of reports from friends that Midge was appearing everywhere at coffeehouses and in parades, campaigning as much outside of Monroe County as inside it, and that I had better try to spend more time in reestablishing my own presence in the home district. During this period also, my friend Dick Fenno[21] of the University of Rochester's Political Science Department called me and warned me that I should abandon all Washington activity, come home, and save myself, inasmuch as he had a high opinion of Regenstreif's abilities to disrupt my own image and to advance his client's. As a result of these warnings, I found myself extremely anxious to get home early in October and, in fact, adjourned about a week and a half before the House did. This has not been my custom in the past, but my attendance record was already badly marred by attendance at the inflation pre-summit and summit meetings, and so [I] felt, since survival was the issue, entirely justified in neglecting my legislative job.

I had trouble getting started. I had always before run an amateurish campaign, based entirely on a modest volunteer corps which supported me as I did low-key, cookbook campaigning in the shopping centers of the suburbs of Rochester. When I arrived home with already prepared television spots of a low-key, name-recognition type but with no other real plan for the campaign, and with my one-man professional staff of Tom Benton, I was greeted by polls run by the county Republican committee showing me in the western half of Monroe County to be 10 percentage points behind. These polls were suspect, but they were warning enough to launch me into a much more active and professional type of campaign than I had previously had. My campaign manager was John Riedman, an effective insurance agent businessman who had no identification with the Monroe County Republican Committee (a group that seemed to be in shambles) and who I knew was politically sophisticated enough to tell me the truth and to understand the nature of my political difficulties. Riedman took virtually a full month off from his work and performed yeoman services of an occasionally impolitic but usually effective nature. I asked Shirley Blackmore, who was then working for me part-time in the Federal Office Building in Rochester, to take a leave of absence

20. The White House–convened Summit on Inflation was held on September 28–29 at the Washington Hilton.

21. Author of the classic political science work *Home Style: House Members in Their Districts* (1978).

without pay and serve as organizer of a volunteer corps, something she did with a selflessness which leaves me deeply in her debt. We opened two campaign headquarters, one in Greece and one in Henrietta, and proceeded to put together a large number of volunteers who did calling and addressing work for me.

We received information that Midge was planning campaign expenditures in the neighborhood of $75,000, following her achievement of the designation of our district as a target area by the AFL-CIO. How she got this done when my previous margin was 68 percent is something of a mystery to me; the answer may be suggested by the following tactic: Gerald Ford pardoned Richard Nixon on a Sunday morning. That afternoon, Peter Regenstreif ran a telephone poll for the entire district, reflecting the trauma which followed the announcement of the pardon. The next morning, Regenstreif and Costanza headed for Washington with the results of the poll in hand and apparently talked with labor officials at COPE, that day securing additional commitment on the basis of erosion of my strength by virtue of my Republican identification.

I had to make a decision about my own campaign financing. Since 1967, I have followed a practice of not accepting more than $50 from any source. I was reluctant to give this up, but it was quite apparent that the maximum I had ever raised under this kind of a campaign contribution restriction, $23,000, was inadequate to match the money Midge was planning to spend following labor commitments made to her. That these labor contributions were going to be forthcoming seemed apparent from the fact that, in an early campaign report, she acknowledged receipt of as much as $23,000 from labor unions. I decided not to give up the $50 ceiling but to go to a special fund-raising event—a cocktail party for which we sold tickets for $35 each, $25 of that amount of money representing profit. I believe we raised somewhere around $10,000 from this special event. I received additional amounts of money over what I had previously had committed to me by the professional Republican organizations such as the state committee, the Congressional Campaign Committee, and the Republican National Committee. Although I do not know the exact amount of these contributions, I think it must have been about $8,500.

The interesting thing about the remainder of my campaign financing was that the money virtually poured in from all over the country because of the widespread publicity given to the fact that I was in trouble for the first time since my original election. Although I had only one letter sent out by my usual solicitor, Ralph Olcott[22] of Batavia, and that to people who had been receiving my

22. A local banker.

newsletter for a year or more, the money poured in from all over the country as a result of completely unofficial and unsolicited [fund-]raising until I appeared to have raised somewhere in the neighborhood of $60,000, obviously more than $50,000 of it in contributions of $50 or less. This proved to be a very bad way to plan a campaign because the campaign contribution limitations make it impossible to predict how much money was going to be available. The dynamics of it, though, proved to be quite helpful: as much as $8,000 additional was committed the last week because of unexpected receipts, thus providing me with the equivalent of a television and radio blitz, which I had not anticipated but which was an obvious use of money which would otherwise have remained unused at the end of the campaign.[23]

I found my opponent to have quite a different dynamic because, as it became apparent toward the end, I was closing the gap on her. She apparently found her money drying up, with the result that she appears to have peaked two or three weeks before the election, while I was still moving up toward the end. It was characteristic of this election that there was a large number of undecided votes. For this reason, I felt that newspaper polls showing me behind as recently as a week before the election were unreliable, inasmuch as they failed to take into consideration the large number of truculent Republicans, robbed of their self-respect by Watergate, who were unwilling to admit to pollsters that they were Republicans, but many of whom were dragged kicking and screaming to the polls [and] reverted to pattern and supported people against whom they had no specific grievance.

I also had problems with my television and radio media advertising. Tom Benton, overworked by the large amount of writing he was having to do (and he did it very well), hived off the radio ads to the Darcy ad agency of Dick Tobias, these ads being comparatively bland name-recognition-type ads. When I finally heard them and my television ads, in conjunction with the tough issues-oriented attacks Midge was perpetrating on me, I decided that we had to change the whole format. Because of difficulty reaching Dick Tobias the weekend I made this decision, I talked at some length with Fred Eckert,[24] the controversial state senator from Greece who is himself a public relations man and who had been extremely helpful to me by [making] strong positive statements in my behalf ev-

23. Costanza outspent Conable, $125,000 to $76,000. James S. Fleming, *Window on Congress: A Congressional Biography of Barber B. Conable Jr.* (Rochester, NY: University of Rochester Press, 2004), 195.

24. Eckert was elected in 1984 to succeed Conable.

erywhere we were speaking to Republicans. Eckert suggested the kind of counterpunching campaign which I felt was necessary and moved with great dispatch
and considerable effectiveness to get together the kind of ads I was asking for.
Among other things, I supplanted the two television ads I had been using, which
were of a technically inferior nature and had virtually no wallop at all, by two ads
in which I looked directly at the camera and appeared to be fighting back against
the Democrats and in strong support of my own record. We changed the radio
ads that were being used several times in order to take advantage of opportunities for denial of misrepresentations of my record by Midge's ads, and the entire
result of this counterpunching campaign was a considerable improvement in
the morale of my own troops and considerably more interest in the campaign
from the point of view of the controversy that was being acknowledged by me
and my supporters.

From the television and radio media, let us shift our attention to the print
media. The Gannett papers[25] proved to be the biggest liability of the campaign,
not because their endorsement is usually the kiss of death but because, in this
case, their endorsement was left-handed, lauding Midge for her contributions to
the political scene and backing me only because of my incumbency, a fact which
was a negative factor in almost anyone's campaign this year. On the news pages
they insisted upon reporting not any substantive issue or fact about my service
during my past ten years but the image created by the campaigners. This was
summed up by the statement that Midge was warm and approachable, while
I was reserved and embattled. Harry and I had a meeting with the Gannett
people after the election to ask them why they had taken this course during the
campaign, but they were unwilling to acknowledge that there was in any way a
restraint in their enthusiasm for my candidacy and felt that their coverage of the
campaign had been completely justified. Needless to say, I got very good press
elsewhere, in keeping with the image I have generally of being a responsible and
hardworking legislator.

[Midge] was quite confident at the end that she had won, and I was by no
means certain that she had not. The vote, however, showed me with a total
percentage of over 56 percent, while she had only about 40 percent. A tough
Conservative opponent, confident of his ability to drag votes from a dangerous
liberal like me, wound up with only about 5,000 votes, thus, I hope, spelling the
demise of the Conservative Party as a factor in at least congressional elections
in our area. I had sought the Conservative nomination this year but had been

25. The *Rochester Times-Union* and *Democrat and Chronicle*.

defeated in the primary by my identification with Nelson Rockefeller and by a very modest Conservative vote at the time of the primary. I doubt that I shall seek the Conservative nomination again, having been repudiated by rank-and-file Conservative voters in the primary and thus being completely justified in not wanting to get involved in such penny-ante difficulties in the future.

The election as a whole was a disaster for the Republicans[26] but quite atypical of Republican disasters. Usually in an anti-Republican election tide, we lose our moderates because they are the ones from the marginal districts, the ones who have had to compromise conservative ideology with some acknowledgment of the real political world. These people seem to have survived well in the 1974 congressional elections, while the right wing, or the most conservative Republicans from the normally safe Republican districts, were devastated by their personal identification with Richard Nixon, whose program they never have supported very well. Of the seventy claimed members of the Steering Committee, the conservative study group in the House, thirty were defeated in this election, while four of their six officers were unexpectedly defeated.

The result has been an unexpected movement of the Republican remnant in the House toward the left, thus virtually eliminating the possibility of any Policy Committee opposition to me, the dangerous eastern liberal, similar to what happened when Del Clawson ran against me the last time. It probably also means that the resulting Republican Party in the House will be able to cooperate with Gerald Ford better than otherwise would have been the case, assuming that he does develop some degree of leadership during the next two years.

I am hearing now via the grapevine that the Democrats probably will try to put twenty or twenty-one members on the Ways and Means Committee (an addition of seven or eight Democrats, counting those who retired as vacancies) while leaving the Republicans at ten, necessitating the appointment of four additional Republicans. In this way, they can stack the committee through the caucus with seven or eight young liberal Democrats who will completely fracture the endangered consensus which has been so typical of committee deliberations over the years that I have been on the committee. This doubtless will sufficiently reduce Wilbur's control of the committee as a consensus committee, so that they will then feel it unnecessary to replace him as committee chairman.

This desire to reduce Wilbur's power predates the squalid "Tidal Basin" affair, in which Wilbur was found drunken in a darkened car with a nightclub

---

26. The number of Republicans in the House fell from 192 in the 93rd Congress (1973–1975) to 144 in the 94th Congress (1975–1977).

entertainer[27] who subsequently jumped in the Tidal Basin and had to be pulled out by the police. This snickering affair has had a great deal of attention in the press but doubtless is not basic to the problems of stature which Wilbur has in the Congress, an institution much more inclined to ignore such personal peccadilloes than the public at large or the press.

I wrote a long letter to Gerald Ford about two weeks ago criticizing him for his trip to Japan, Korea, and Vladivostok[28] and urging him, without further delay, to try to establish the character and personality of the Ford administration, rather than permitting the public to continue to think that the apparatus has taken him over and that he is letting holdovers from the Nixon administration establish the goals of his own administration. Increasing doubts are arising as to whether or not Gerald Ford can administer the government. I want very much to help him and to see him succeed, but the impression he has created so far is that of a nice man struggling manfully in the deep water far over his head. It doesn't look like a happy two years unless he can somehow capture the initiative that goes with leadership, and that is all the country expects of him, but there is little doubt that they cannot expect any less of him.

December 5, 1974

Bob Michel was easily elected whip, the interesting thing about his selection being the margin. He received over 70 votes, while Jerry Pettis received 38 and John Erlenborn 22. I voted for Erlenborn, as a matter of personal friendship, but was surprised that he did not run ahead of Jerry Pettis, also a personal friend of mine and apparently the recipient of Wednesday Club votes as well as the votes of the substantial part of the large California delegation. Erlenborn is a man of the first quality: he appears to be cool and aloof, although that is not my experience of him, and his membership on the Education and Labor Committee must have been considered the substantial liability in his quest for the whip job. Also, he does not fit the image of the team man who would be willing to spend a substantial part of his time on the floor, rallying troops and submerging his own views in the collective. I was disappointed that he did badly, although I did not expect him to win, since Michel so fully fits the general impression of what would make a good whip. Michel is a fine man, and I will have no trouble working with him.

27. Fanne Foxe, a stripper known as the "Argentine Firecracker."

28. The trip, which included a discussion of arms control with Leonid Brezhnev, general secretary of the Central Committee of the Communist Party of the Soviet Union, was taken in late November 1974.

John Anderson easily withstood the competition he received from Chuck Wiggins, winning by more than 30 votes in retention of his chairmanship of the conference. I regret that this particular election was not closer also, because Anderson is such an individualist in the leadership that he cannot help but feel the margin of his win was an endorsement of a posture which has been quite uncomfortable for other members of the leadership.

The major news story this week has been the death wish of Wilbur Mills. The weekend before the organizing caucuses to which I have referred, Wilbur showed up in Boston and appeared on the stage with his striptease friend, Fanne Foxe, apparently giving full sanction to the public airing of a relationship which came close to being his downfall during his election campaign. His behavior was not typical, nor was it designed to advance his career in Congress. The result was that the seventy-five new Democratic members of the House had very little on which to judge Wilbur's utility as part of the House power structure, and he played into the hands of those who were anxious to make an assault on that structure and bring about major change in the way in which the House operates. On Tuesday, I saw him on the floor but did not go over to talk to him, and after he had had apparently fairly normal discussions with a number of my colleagues, he suddenly disappeared and turned into the hospital, claiming that he suffered from exhaustion and was not well. The decision to drop him from the chairmanship of Ways and Means has apparently been made, and early in the week the non-unrelated decisions to increase the size of the Ways and Means Committee and to strip away its political powers were made by the Democratic Caucus.[29]

We Republicans standing on the sidelines and watching the . . . Democratic Party undergo such massive change have a sense of foreboding about it, because it will dramatically change the major characters who are making decisions for the House as a whole. It is quite clear to us at this point that Wayne Hays [OH] and Phil Burton [CA][30] will be running as weak a man as Carl Albert, rather than the old-line committee chairmen whose techniques and weaknesses we all know so well. Burton and Hays are aggrandizers. They have an instinct for power, and Burton at least has a strong ideological bent which will doubtless give a bias to the legislative thrusts being directed by the caucus during the 94th Congress. If this is so, it is likely to enhance the right-wing reaction that will set in in 1976 and . . . is not more in the interests of the country than the

29. The Democrats divested Ways and Means of its role as the party's Committee on Committees.

30. The new chairman of the House Democratic Caucus.

left-wing bias that Mr. Burton will direct. I am quite confident in predicting that if Mr. Hays has as free a hand as he is likely to get in dealing with Phil Burton, eventually there will be serious scandals emerging from Hays's direction of the House Administration Committee and the Democrats' Congressional Campaign Committee, since regardless of the man's relationship to any specific incident or decision, his whole personality reeks of corruption.

There is very little doubt that the Ways and Means Committee is going to be a whole new ball game. To begin with, if Wilbur is not the chairman, we are faced by the probability that subcommittee function will be real rather than nominal. In fact, with the decision having been made to increase the size of the committee to thirty-seven members, it would be impossible for us to continue to sit en banc or to go through the kinds of protracted questioning at hearings held by the full committee, which we have done in the past. Enough change is implicit in the number of new members that will make up the committee hereafter. A quick calculation indicates that one less than half the committee, eighteen out of thirty-seven, will be newly appointed this year. I am not sure the great pressure on the committee from the Democratic Caucus to legislate with dispatch items that my committee has been playing with now for three or four years will not result in a refusal to go through the educational period which should be followed for any committee dealing with technical subjects as Ways and Means does. The result is probably going to be some very bad legislation, prepared with a broad brush and in a great hurry.

December 11, 1974
Following a committee meeting which discussed the exemption of the savings account interest, the members of the committee were asked to stay for a private discussion with Joe Waggonner of his visit to Chairman Mills at Bethesda Naval Hospital yesterday morning. Waggonner, swelled up with the self-importance of his self-appointed mission, told us at great length and in an emotional way of his confrontation with the chairman, who was apparently heavily sedated but agreeable and expressing relief at the suggestion that he not serve as chairman of the Ways and Means Committee. It has been quite clear that the Democrats intended to strip him of this role, and so in order to save his face, Waggonner and some of his other friends felt it important that he request of the Speaker that he not be considered for this role on account of his health. The chairman was also urged, and further acquiesced in the decision, that he not make further requests as to the future of his service in the House until his medical situation has been further clarified. I understand that he is being tested for everything

in the world, that he has been getting a great deal of rest, and that he has put on seven pounds since his hospitalization last week, this latter fact indicating that he probably has been living out of a bottle and has been subject not only to exhaustion and alcoholism but malnourishment.

There seems to have been some veering of public attitude towards sympathy for the chairman at this point, and I must say that I have found myself quite turned off by the large number of shabby jokes going around about his involvement with the stripper. I cannot help but feel that the chairman's long service to the country should dominate his reputation, despite his later personal difficulties, the cause for which we still do not know. I sent some flowers from my wife and me to his hospital room the other day, feeling that he was entitled to a few more expressions of friendship than he has been getting from among his former colleagues. I hope he will retire from Congress, because I do not see how he could enjoy the role of a spear-holder in the rear rank in the Ways and Means Committee, given his vanity, his long service as chairman, and the tremendous retirement pension awaiting him when he does retire.

President Ford's meetings with congressional leaders are stimulating, freewheeling, and a welcome contrast to the stilted style of Nixon's, but Conable worries that the new president's legislative skills as a compromiser are weakening him as an executive. The politics of energy dominates Ways and Means, into which a bitter partisanship has seeped. The old "comfortable consensus" is gone. The young Democrats—the Watergate babies swept in by the 1974 landslide—do not impress Conable. He labors, with minimal success, to convince GOP leaders to make the corruption or arrogance of Democrats such as Wayne Hays and Phil Burton a political issue. With New York City facing, or claiming to face, possible bankruptcy, Conable urges the president to take a hard line.

The new chairman of Ways and Means, Al Ullman, and the wave of liberal young Democrats altered the committee in ways that were displeasing to Conable. Ullman was nowhere near as formidable as Wilbur Mills at the peak of his powers, in Conable's estimation, and the badly outnumbered (25–12) GOP was an afterthought in committee deliberations, seldom consulted by the majority.

Yet he was heartened by the addition of two new committee colleagues, Bill Steiger and Bill Frenzel, who were bright and inventive and just the kind of whip-smart younger comrades he had missed in the past. The Young Turk was now a mentor.

Balancing his social liberalism, as evinced by his staunch support of the Equal Rights Amendment, was Conable's behind-closed-doors advocacy of a strong fiscal conservatism. He reluctantly embraced a more partisan role, which he believed had been forced on him by Democratic high-handedness. Yet his distaste for the emergent Republican Right deepened. He feared a polarized politics of the future "in which it would be liberals against conservatives, and the inclusiveness of the old party situation, where American democracy benefited from dialogue within the parties more than the confrontation between them," would vanish.

January 22, 1975
The day began with another White House leadership meeting—this time, at a breakfast in the family dining room, which I had never seen before, including

all the members of the House Republican leadership, the Senate Republican leadership, and some selected economic advisers of the president. The president was expressing his determination with respect to his economic and energy program and gave a very earnest talk to us about his need for our support as well as his plans for trying to enlist public support. There was no dearth of suggestions from those present, and once again I marveled that the atmosphere in the Ford presidency is so open and so forthcoming, in contrast to the Nixon administration, where people tended to hang back when the president asked for comments and suggestions.

I sat next to Secretary of the Treasury [William] Simon, who has been receiving a good deal of support, including some from the president himself, following a long campaign—the sources of which are not clear—to unseat him or at least to indicate that he is in trouble and thus to undercut his strength as an adviser to the president. At one point, Bill Simon asked me quietly to raise the question of the size of the deficit and to make a point about stressing the necessity for keeping expenditures under control, the very point for which he has been fingered as disapproving of the president's policies. I did as he requested but did it rather poorly.

Today, following the meeting at the White House, Ways and Means had its organizing meeting. It was impressive to see the thirty-seven members of the new committee spread around a table which used to be considerably smaller. It was also impressive to see all these new reformers, not only so identified because of their subservience to the Democratic Caucus but because of their being, for the most part, younger members who think entirely in terms of changing the old status quo—it was impressive to see them all voting unanimously to close the meeting so that we could discuss an increase of our staff and budget by six times what it was last year and further voting to continue proxy voting on the committee, since they deem it in their interest to continue it.

I used this journal to describe to Bob Woodward—of the Woodward and Bernstein team that invented Watergate at the *Washington Post*—the contemporary condition of Congress during the collapse of the Nixon administration.[1] He was very interested in the fact that I kept a journal—although it was erratic—during the period of Watergate, and I excerpted and read him a number of relevant portions from the year 1974. The request he made of me that he be permitted to read the journal I denied, however, because I had so much other stuff in there that was sensitive in nature. Although I would let Dick Fenno

1. Conable's journal was a source for Woodward and Bernstein's *The Final Days* (1976).

of the University of Rochester read the journal, it is my intention to give it to Cornell University and to put a limitation on its use to prevent any quoting until I am dead.

February 4, 1975
The committee has been meeting in late sessions this week and is struggling manfully to discipline itself to the point of bringing out a simple tax rebate bill. It is interesting to watch the impact of change on the Ways and Means Committee. Al Ullman is an insecure chairman at this point, dealing with a committee half of which is new and the actions and conclusions of which cannot be predicted with any degree of certainty. He is unable to deliver on any promises made, but he appears intent on killing himself with public appearances, TV guest interviews, and a continual basking in the public's eye. I have told the president at meetings at the White House that he must not compromise with Al, since Al does not have the capacity to deliver, although he may have it later on after his leadership has been tested and proved.

I have found the new formula of leadership breakfasts in the family dining room far superior to the procedures of the Nixon administration because they turn out to be considerably less formal than the meetings around the cabinet table. There is real give-and-take, and it seems to be invited by a president who doesn't stand on his dignity and who is used to the members present yammering back and forth with him in a less dignified forum. At that last breakfast, late last week, I sat at the table with Nelson Rockefeller and found him as lively and vital as usual. He had a pocketful of rubber angleworms from his seven-year-old son's birthday party (the boy is a fisherman, apparently) and was having some fun pulling them out and showing people what his concept was of the CIA investigations over which he has already been instructed to preside.[2]

Nelson has apparently refused to serve as coordinator of the Domestic Council unless he can have his own staffing. Either Rumsfeld or someone else placed on a fairly high level in the White House is reluctant to have a Rockefeller staffing, feeling that a Ford staffing should be available for such a vital institution as the Domestic Council. I personally think that Nelson is dead right not to be willing to go into a job of that sort without having his own staffing, since he is used to having a high degree of loyalty and people with whom he can work closely. . . . In our meetings he has kept a very low silhouette, in one case mak-

---

2. Vice President Rockefeller chaired the Commission on CIA Activities within the United States, which issued its report in June 1975.

ing a sycophantic talk about the thrill he was having working with our brilliant president, and in the other two meetings speaking only once, although he spoke forcefully and sensibly. I take it his ducks are not in line yet and that he is not inclined to be pushy until he knows more of the lay of the land on the federal scene. He said to me that it seemed to be a never-never land to him compared to the comparatively simple state government.

I hear that Wilbur [Mills] has now left Bethesda Hospital and gone to a sanitarium to complete the drying-out process. He will be there until the first of March, when he expects to come back to full duty in the House. Those who have seen him—and they include Bill Simon, who described his conversation to me—say that Wilbur appears to be sharp as a tack, interested in what's going on, quite well informed about developments, and apparently looking forward to rehabilitating his reputation as a constructive member of the House. I think he underestimates the frustrations to which he is going to be subject as the former center of all eyes and now a man in limbo in familiar territory.

March 25, 1975

The condition in Ways and Means continues to be quite complicated and uncertain. Al Ullman is vigorously and assertively taking the leadership of the committee, but those liberals in the center of the committee seniority challenge him on almost every occasion. For instance, the other day, as we were struggling with the periphery of Al's energy bill, I wandered over to the Democratic side and had a most illuminating conversation with Sam Gibbons and Joe Karth, two of the strongest members of the committee, who told me in no uncertain terms that "if my president wants his energy bill, he can have it." By this, they apparently meant that they were unwilling to support Al's version, the central feature of which is a high gasoline tax. Al continues to speak very confidently about his progress with his own energy bill, but there appears to be very serious doubt that a majority of the majority party on the committee, even, will support something requiring as unpleasant an act as the imposition of a gasoline tax on the traveling American public. I reported my conversation with Gibbons and Karth to the White House in some detail and felt some confirmation of the advice that I had been giving them for some time—namely, that they should be cautious about compromising with a chairman who may not be in a position to deliver on his compromise.

I also have had a number of close and extended conversations with Frank Zarb, the energy czar, whom I have urged to have the president do all he can to build Al up. I feel that Al is a responsible element in the Democratic Party and that it is better for the president to try and encourage him than to engage in the participatory democracy which is the earmark of [Democratic] Caucus rule. I have urged Zarb to have the president talk publicly about what a tough negotiator Al Ullman is, so as to help his credibility with a caucus that views all leadership with suspicion. I don't know whether the president will do any of this or not, but it would be advisable in my view, since his expression of satisfaction at the cooperation Al is giving would doubtless sour Al's leadership in the view of the rank-and-file caucus members. I like Al Ullman and find his views generally sympathetic, but I do not expect to be a particularly relevant part of the committee for the next two years. He obviously makes his decisions in consultation with the Democrats and staff only, and sometimes I wonder about the Democrats. His leadership cannot include the kind of consensus approach that a secure and established leader like Wilbur made almost a matter of faith. I suppose I can find some relevance to the process through my ability and my willingness to interpret the committee to the White House, because even a corporal's guard (such as we Republicans are in the House) assumes some significance when the power of the presidency is added.

Speaking of the relationship between the parties, I participated in a fascinating supper last Wednesday night at Vice President Rockefeller's Foxhall home. It appears that Phil Burton had suggested that Rocky would do well to establish some liaison with a caucus group and that Rocky felt he should not do so without the presence of some Republicans from Congress also. As a result, Rocky, Jim Cannon, and Dick Dunham[3] served as hosts at a quiet and elegant supper which included Phil Burton, Don Fraser,[4] Abner Mikva, Tom Foley, Al Quie, Bob Michel, John Anderson, and [myself]. Phil Burton put on one of his sterling performances, roaring from time to time that if we didn't play ball with him, he would crush us like a peanut, ringing the vice president's handbell to summon more wine, and then claiming that there was nobody on the Democratic side who could speak for the Democrats because of the extent to which the caucus itself was not a homogeneous group.

If there was any particular message that emerged with greater clarity from the Burton rumblings than any other, it was that Republicans should not feel that they can deal with the Speaker and Tip O'Neill, and that these people were permitted to stay in the leadership only by sufferance of the mob. Burton seemed to display some animus toward me on occasion, but I suppose it was nothing un-

3. Rockefeller aide and deputy director of the White House Domestic Council.
4. A member of Minnesota's Democratic-Farmer-Labor Party.

usual, since he displays animus toward almost everyone at one point or another. Jim Cannon called me the next day to compare notes on whether or not the performance was a bona fide one and what message was to be derived therefrom. He expressed disappointment with Don Fraser, whom Burton constantly referred to as the "great dialectician" of the caucus, and to express his amazement that Tom Foley was such an intellectual and articulate fellow. In short, the supper party was one of those cryptic occasions when the message of the evening was somewhat obscured by the rhetoric.

President Gerald Ford continues to be closely in contact with the Republicans in Congress. His disposition remains cheerful and his manner open. Following the completion of the tax bill, in greatly augmented dimension, by the Senate, the conference was immediately set, and on this past Sunday he asked Herm Schneebeli and me to come to the residence in the White House to discuss with him and Bill Simon and Don Rumsfeld the strategy for the conference. I arrived early with Herm and was taken to the second floor, where Betty Ford was sitting in a housecoat, obviously under some sedation and yet hospitable in her greeting to us. She said she had just had a massage and that "the doctor tells me my bumps are down."[5] My wife was with me, since we were going to a supper party at the Alibi Club thereafter, and I had left [her] to study for a final exam at George Washington in the Diplomatic Drawing Room.[6] Betty sent down while we were talking to the president and had my wife join her, and my wife got a rare view of what it is like to live on the second floor of the White House. She said there was an air of considerable impermanence in the Fords' living quarters and that it was "creepy" to have help constantly moving in and out while the inhabitants lived as simple lives as they would have anywhere else. Betty appeared to be quite ill to my wife, although she chatted and was friendly and outgoing. My wife was disturbed by her appearance and felt she could not talk to her about much of anything serious, despite their shared interest in the cause of women.

April 16, 1975

I am alarmed at the increasing resentment of the president's leadership and the reported increasing strength of Ronald Reagan at the grass roots. At SOS tonight, we found almost the same story from all over the country. The president

5. Mrs. Ford had undergone a mastectomy in September 1974.

6. Mrs. Conable earned a master's degree in women's studies from George Washington University in 1976.

seems to be unaware of the extent of his problem with the conservatives, and I have tried to warn almost everyone at the White House about this.

I have my own troubles with the right wing. In Budget Committee last week, after we had performed many individual acts of extravagance in overestimating revenues and adding splendid spending programs to the package over the dead bodies of all the Republicans in the committee, the Republicans voted as a bloc to reject the aggregate reporting setting forth the arithmetic conclusion of all our individual extravagance. To our horror, enough liberal Democrats were unwilling to face up to the consequences of their cumulative spending intentions to vote against the bill and to defeat the report. The Republicans immediately caucused to decide that we had two options: (1) To acquiesce in the demise of the Budget Committee by its own hand, since we were unable to agree on a final report. (2) An alternative would be for the Democrats to go back and sweep more of their intentions under the rug in order to get the budget down to a figure so phony that the credibility of the committee would have been demolished, if not the committee itself. We thought neither prospect was potentially rewarding, and so [Al] Cederberg and I announced that we would change our votes in order to get a $73 billion deficit report to the floor of the House, where at least we could debate the fiscal consequences of our acts, and if the House wanted to kill the Budget Committee on the basis of that frightening deficit figure, so be it.

When we had announced this intention, reserving our right to vote against the budget report on the floor, and the report had been saved, the *Wall Street Journal* wrote an editorial attacking Cederberg and me as men of prudence but not of principle, saying that [it] wished somebody would stand up for principle around here. It was a patently unfair editorial, and my friend Al Hunt, the reporter who had reported this action in the *Wall Street Journal* story originally, wrote an angry letter to the editor about their not having read his explanation of our motives in having changed our votes.

Nevertheless, the Republican Study Group,[7] which has a newsletter of its own which it sends to its mailing list, reproduced the article in full, apparently for no reason but to make an attack on Cederberg and me as again people unwilling to stand up for principle and thus typical lily-livered liberals. I am not surprised that they attacked me, because I am falling into the position of a traditional target of the right wing, but certainly there is no more staunch and effective conservative than Al Cederberg, and I find myself wondering con-

---

7. A conservative caucus of House Republicans.

stantly what the right wing is headed for if they single out (for scolding to their membership) a person like him.

April 29, 1975

The subject of [Tuesday morning's White House] meeting, or at least the central subject on the agenda, was the energy tax proposal, and I found the president generally more complimentary to the cooperation of Al Ullman than I felt was justified. As he continued to talk about what a good job Al was doing in trying to bring the members of the caucus into line with his own program, I interrupted at one point and said, "Wait a minute, Mr. President, let me understand. Are you urging us to support this Mickey Mouse proposal my committee is coming up with?" The president flushed, put his head down, and said no, that he wasn't necessarily asking us to vote for anything that wasn't acceptable. I then pressed him as to what was acceptable in his view, saying that many of us in the House were concerned about his possibly accepting a gasoline tax as a central idea in his program and repeating to him, as I have before, that his own program is far preferable to the Democratic program and that he mustn't allow Al Ullman or anyone else to force him into pushing a compromise on which they couldn't deliver.[8]

I find myself embarrassed to be one of the few people in the leadership group who concerns himself about the president's image as a man who is weak and unable to take a strong posture relative to a Congress that is carving on his gizzard constantly. I seem to be emerging as a hard-liner, a man who is constantly advising the president to go beyond what he himself is willing to do. It seems to me that his legislative background and training push him toward compromise, when his image would be much better enhanced by the appearance of willingness to stand up and fight for what he believes in. . . . I don't think there is any doubt that the members of Congress still admire and like this man, but we increasingly lose confidence in his ability to be a strong leader, and that is what we want more than anything else, since our destinies are so closely tied to him and we are not in any way advanced by identifying ourselves with a man who winds up looking like a eunuch on every issue.

It would be an interesting study to see how differently motivated a president is from a member of Congress. Gerald Ford would be a good subject for that study because he was always loyal, direct, and hard-hitting, well prepared

8. Ford's energy package combined price decontrols with measures to reduce consumption; Ullman floated a forty-cents-per-gallon gasoline tax, to be phased in at ten cents per year over four years.

and comparatively disciplined to compromise. Now his training as a member of Congress seems to have prepared him for the role of a compromising president. Of course, a president has to look at all issues differently, since "the buck stops there" in the White House, and since the president has very little power to influence the members of Congress in the direction of his initial program positions. He has to live with a hostile and very large majority in the other party, and his own party (his loyal troops) is virtually incapable of influencing the legislative matters about which he has to make a final decision. There seems to be little doubt that he is a different man as president than he was able to be as our minority leader, and in the final analysis, I suppose I shall be tolerant of him while fighting to encourage him to take a harder line.

Last week we had a presidential leadership meeting of the usual routine sort in the Cabinet Room, and it proved to be one of the most stimulating and satisfactory exchanges we've ever had with the president in my memory. A large number of people were present, and we talked about Vietnam, the energy policy, and the Budget Committee. The president really invites vigorous exchanges, participates in them himself, and thus carries on his tradition of wanting a good collective input before he makes up his mind about matters of policy and strategy. This was his pattern when he was minority leader, and he appears to continue it as president. He is clearly capable of making up his own mind—I have never thought him indecisive—but he is extremely careful to be sure that he has not forgotten anything by encouraging colleagues he trusts to poke and pull and push all kinds of diverse brainstorming thoughts at him during the process.

I continue to be very discouraged about my role in the Congress. The Republicans are such a small group that I have very little opportunity to affect the course of events. I continue to be quoted and to be a somewhat controversial figure, but my life seems to be more in the press than in the institution itself. It is tough to be irrelevant and to be excluded from the moment of decision. I would find consolation in the hope that someday the Republicans will be in the majority in the House, but that goal seems to be receding farther and farther away, thanks to the splendid leadership of Richard Nixon and the increasingly minority-oriented views of our congressional Republicans, and I doubt whether I am strong enough to nourish myself indefinitely on the thin soup of such an attenuated hope. I suppose the existence of the president—the added interest he can give to my job through my associations with him and my opportunities to have some input into White House decision making—is the only possible hope of relevance as our government is buffeted with problems which I would like to try to help solve. If I thought Gerald Ford was not going to run for the presidency in 1976, or that it was beyond the realm of possibility for him to be elected, I think I would seriously question whether I should try to stay another two years. As it is, I shall conduct myself with the expectation that he is going to be a candidate and that thus there is some chance of having a modest relation to the uncertain processes of democracy in our declining country.

May 7, 1975

Yesterday the Trade Subcommittee started holding hearings on the admission of Romania to nondiscriminatory tariff and credit relationships with the United States. This has been something the Romanians have dearly desired for a long time, and many of us had the feeling that it was Romania's due, because of her independent posture between the East and West and her willingness to serve as an intermediary in relation to such sensitive points as Israel and Vietnam. The Romanians are, of course, somewhat Stalinist in their internal affairs, sensitive to the concerns of the communist world over their independent foreign policy posture. Thus, I suppose we should have anticipated that when we started these hearings, people would come forward from their positions of antagonism to Romanian internal affairs and to the police-state atmosphere of any communist country, but we were unprepared for the outpouring of frustrations yesterday morning and the strong opposition of Jewish groups. There is some irony in this latter opposition, because Israel considers Romania to be one of the better communist countries and trades with her extensively. This doesn't keep American Jews from opposing normal trade relations with the United States, since they feel that pressure from the United States is one of the only things that can improve emigration policies within the communist world. There are some hard-liners on the subcommittee, like Duncan and Archer, who don't want to see any trade with a communist nation which doesn't confess its sins, pay off all the bonds issued by the previous monarchy, and promise hereafter to be a perfect democracy.

Bill Green, the chairman of the subcommittee, did a stupid thing in asking people who are having bad immigration problems for members of their family, etc., with Romania to come forward and tell us all about it. If he, then, lets them do this, as far as the subcommittee is concerned, we will have thousands of recitals of the woe so typical of those wishing to get out of communist countries, which, by their nature, have to have barbed wire at the borders or they would lose all their intellectuals, people of independent mind, and those who dislike the force implicit in a communist state.[9]

9. Romania was granted most-favored-nation status in 1975, the first communist nation of eastern Europe to be so designated.

I continue to worry about the Ford presidency, as any normal Republican would. It is apparent that the strong people in the administration are rapidly becoming targets, as issues like Vietnam and Watergate fade into the background and the sharks of the press yearn for more blood in the water. The obvious targets are Kissinger, Simon, and Rockefeller; they have all been taking their lumps lately. Those who are weak in any government can dedicate their weakness to tranquility, while those who become standouts in any way invariably have the focus of hostility placed on them. Simon and Kissinger I recently sent half a gallon of maple syrup each, with an accompanying letter indicating that I hoped they would stay in government despite the barbs that were stuck into them constantly, telling each that I thought it was a compliment to him that he was considered such an appropriate target.

Dr. Kissinger has, of course, been bloodied by the failure of his recent shuttle diplomacy, since it is the obligation of a strong man always to succeed, and no one human being can ever live up to that obligation. Also, some of the simplistic minds in Congress feel that foreign policy should be transacted on immutable principles, or that the policy is otherwise to be condemned as amoral. It does not seem possible to such a simplistic mind, for instance, that the use of military aid as an instrument of international diplomacy could be in any circumstance an appropriate device, or that military aid is quite a different thing in respect to Saudi Arabia than it is in respect to Turkey or to Southeast Asia. So, when Henry Kissinger goes out into the world and improvises, apparently taking a different approach with respect to one country than he does with respect to another, he instantly is condemned as amoral by simple minds of the Congress and of the press who believe that international affairs are to be boiled down to a simple formula and based on rigid principles as open and as democratically accessible as those by which we govern our own country internally.

May 14, 1975

A few days ago the Ways and Means Committee completed action on the energy tax bill.[10] . . . The central idea is a gasoline tax, something which the president committed himself against and which the Republican members have been consistently opposed to. The last day, as we were working on the clean bill, to which there is every right of amendment, it appeared that there were two measures that the oil-state Democrats wanted as conditions for their voting the bill out of the committee.

10. The committee reported the bill by a 19–16 vote, with all twelve Republicans in opposition.

The first had to do with elimination of a government purchasing authority, which they viewed as a possible step toward nationalization of the oil industry. The Republicans throughout the putting together of this measure opposed this, and so we voted solidly with the oil-state Democrats on this issue, and the government purchasing authority was taken out of the bill. The second, I had been informed, was an amendment by Jake Pickle [D-TX] to make the triggering-in of the gasoline tax at an additional twenty cents a gallon beyond the three cents imposed initially subject to congressional veto, when the president finds that gasoline consumption has increased over a 1973-based period.

When Jake proposed this amendment, I reacted violently and emotionally, calling it shabby politics and pointing out that if the Democrats accepted this amendment, they would, in effect, be requiring the president to report to the Congress that a gasoline tax of large dimension was required under the terms of the bill, then letting Congress save the people from such a presidential determination by vetoing the central conservation measure of the bill. My reaction elicited an equally vigorous counterreaction, and when the vote was taken, only nine voted for Jake's amendment. I felt somewhat sheepish, but I am convinced that the strength of my reaction scared some of the Democrats off. Then Joe Karth attacked me for my partisanship, saying that if there was any shabby politics it was involved in the elimination of the federal purchasing authority, which I had voted for. I apologized to Joe publicly for not being privy to the deals the majority makes on such things and pointed out that I consistently voted against such things. Then Jake Pickle chose to be personally offended that I had accused him of shabby politics, saying to everyone's amazement that his amendment was not a clandestine one but one that had been cleared with the leadership and that he would bring it up on the floor of the House because he thought it would "strengthen" the bill to make the gasoline tax subject to congressional veto. So apparently, the amendment was a serious proposal, and I think on the floor of the House that it will be very difficult for congressmen to oppose, inasmuch as the gasoline tax is the most controversial feature of the bill.

This outburst on my part and the elicited responses caused me to think some about my own role on the committee, where I am clearly the Republican spokesman and the one who does the political work for the committee, and also caused me to muse on the increasing partisanship and polarization of the committee under Al Ullman's leadership. I apologized to the other Republicans at a minority meeting to consider minority views the following day, saying that I regretted having overreacted as I did to Pickle's amendment. Most of the Republicans, as long as they were not the ones involved, expressed great approval of my vigor and my alleged eloquence, and it appears that most of them are quite satisfied to be involved in partisan reaction. My relations with Al Ullman are personally pleasant, but I find that I am no longer the admired and judicious member of the committee, but increasingly viewed by the Democrats as a man to be watched closely and a man who plays more a political role than the legislative role which has usually been assigned me.

Wilbur Mills is back. He looked great when he first came back and appeared to have lost a good deal of weight, which he denied, and to be relaxed and confident. He did not want to involve himself in the tail end of the energy tax bill, saying privately to Herman Schneebeli that he thought it was a foolish bill and that he did not want to undercut Al Ullman, inasmuch as Al had committed himself to it so fully. Thus, every time a vote came up as he sat in committee, he would absent himself rather than participate. If he continues this practice, it will be a matter of comment eventually, and I can only assume that he is going to take some interest in the tax reform later on, which will involve his taking a stand regardless of Al's correctness or incorrectness. By yesterday, Wilbur looked very tired and nervous again, and I asked him if he was feeling all right. His response was, "Barber, I am having a tough time."

Charls Walker, the former undersecretary of the treasury who is now a consultant in Washington, came to my office yesterday with some people he was trying to aid as a lobbyist and, in a mood which could be interpreted in many ways, asked me what I knew about the boomlet going for me as secretary of the treasury. I expressed surprise at this, saying that I expect Bill Simon to stay, and he agreed, saying that he thought Simon had no intention of leaving. I asked him what he meant then by associating me with the job. He said he meant nothing but that he had been hearing all over town that I was going to be the next secretary of the treasury. As I think about this—something I did not take seriously at the time—I suppose he was simply flattering me, as a lobbyist would. I worry somewhat about it, because I have felt that Simon was a target by many forces in the administration and that they may have assumed that I could be used as a stalking horse to erode Simon's tenure. I think they overestimate my popularity in the Congress, and certainly they overestimate my ability to serve in any administrative post. If I can find out who is doing it, I will try to squelch the talk because I do consider Bill Simon one of the strong men in the cabinet and I can only be harmed by this kind of malicious speculation.

May 15, 1975

It is embarrassing to me to be number-two man to [Herman Schneebeli] as ranking minority member and to find other people relying on my judgment rather than on Herman's. I like Herman and generally agree with his conclusions, while being reluctant to follow his mode of operation. The White House is apparently coming to the conclusion that I am the one to be talked with about these things, and indeed, the legislative liaison people usually talk to me before they talk to Herman, so that I find myself frequently in a delicate condition requiring tact and supportive gestures on my part. Fortunately, Herman, nice guy that he is, is not sensitive and does not feel that I am upstaging him, because otherwise, my life would be miserable to be walking a tightrope between him and the White House.

The other personality on the committee with whom my relations are tense is Bill Archer of Houston, Texas. Bill is one of the most brilliant men in the Congress, with a finely honed intellect and an absolutely uncompromising conservative ideology. He is a man of strength and stubbornness who obviously considers me a compromiser, and [he is] a political thinker who, while he respects my political judgments, nevertheless feels unclean every time he comes into contact with a mind so willing to seek accommodation with things he himself considers dishonest and unnecessarily amorally nonideological. I have some difficulty with him also because of his absolute preoccupation with the problems of the oil industry, with which he is not only thoroughly familiar but able to deal with in the most remarkable detail and with the most complete understanding. Since we have been dealing with the problems of the oil industry over the past year, this has meant that protection of this industry has been almost as firm a part of his ideology as his uncompromising conservatism. I admire Bill Archer's abilities and find him a most attractive person. . . . I suspect our relationship will improve as we get to know each other better because we are both relatively strong people, and whether he is willing to acknowledge it or not, he needs my type on the committee just as much as any intellectually honest organization needs his type as well.

The other man on the committee with whom I have an almost constant state of tension is Joe Karth of Minnesota. Joe is unduly sensitive, and anything looking like criticism evokes an emotional response from him. He is a man of strength of intellect, of persistence, and of independence of judgment. . . . I suspect we are much closer together on most issues than our tension would indicate, and there is an element of respect present on each side, but I find myself regretting that I cannot be closer to Joe Karth and cannot find in him a little more tolerance of my position than he appears to demonstrate. If I were to choose somebody on the other side with whom I would rather be allied than anyone else, it would be Joe Karth, I believe, since he is, in my view, one of the most effective members of Congress. I expect the tension between us, however, to be a continuing thing rather than one which will be allayed by further contact.

In view of the great activity we have had in the Ways and Means Committee this year so far, it is not too early to assess the relative capacities of my new colleagues on this committee. On the Republican side, we seem to have a generally good group, with Steiger and Frenzel standouts, of course. Herm Schneebeli calls them his "terriers." They are enough to worry anybody with whom they disagree, highly intelligent and quick to express themselves on a very high level on almost any subject.

[Guy] Vander Jagt [MI] is quite solid, although not a very active participant. Jim Martin [NC] is also a solid fellow, although his follow-through and persistence have yet to be demonstrated. Skip Bafalis and Bill Ketchum, the man from California who succeeded Jerry Pettis, are both very political and very conservative but well above average in intelligence. The only one with whom I do not feel completely comfortable is Phil Crane of Illinois, who seems to be quite disengaged and whose motivations and performance are unpredictable. Phil is a member of the elite right-wing group in the House, a Ph.D. in history and a man of obvious intelligence, but a man also inclined constantly to ride legislative hobbyhorses of one sort or another. For instance, he has spent a great deal of his time the past year encouraging the ownership of gold, which he considers to be one of the more basic American rights and which he apparently was willing to bargain all else away to achieve as a legal right for the gold lovers of this country.

On the Democratic side, there are some obvious standouts and some obvious washouts. Otis Pike [NY] is a man I have always liked, and although he sometimes is too smart for his own good, his independence of mind will make him a valuable member of the committee, just as his sense of humor always enlivens the environment. [Richard] Vander Veen of Michigan is, I think, a fairly average man who works hard at his job and tries hard, but I do not expect him to be a standout performer or a man of very great independence of thought. Jake Pickle is next junior to him, and Jake is a popular Texan who is quite capable of a partisan role and less conservative than his posture. Henry Helstoski is a washout, every bit as bad and as useless as his advance billing. This is not unusual for a member from New Jersey. Charlie Rangel [NY] I believe to be a man of some quality, although he is obviously liberal and not a man whose independence of thought would make him in any way unpredictable in his liberalism. I think he will be a survivor on the committee and probably will be an adequate performer. Bill Cotter of Connecticut, a man whose alleged contacts with the insurance industry brought him into the Ways and Means Committee, seems pretty routine to me, although there may be more to him than immediately appears to the eye.

The next man on the Democratic side, Pete Stark of California, is, I believe, a bummer. A wealthy man of aristocratic bearing, he obviously considers himself extremely bright, although in his case, I think he could be more easily identified with the old saying "a little knowledge is a dangerous thing." He used to be a banker, sold his bank interest to the Arabs, and then, as a member of Congress, sponsored legislation to prohibit such transactions. He occasionally makes a great point of some small technical business thing, intending thereby to prove his great expertise in the commercial world but in fact creating the appearance of being a rather poorly informed nitpicker who does not have a consistent philosophy but only a liberal posture.

The man next junior to him is Jim Jones of Tulsa, Oklahoma, oil oriented, who is, however, a man of ability and who is forced by his conservative constituency to take positions of conservatism when it is not important. I think he will be a traditional, team-playing Democrat for the most part, but I expect he will also be a fairly consistent and above-average performer. The next man is Andy Jacobs of Indiana, a man of no serious purpose, as far as I can tell, and a flamboyant, swinging liberal who I would not count on in any respect. He is obviously very bright, but I don't believe it does much good.

Next to him is Abner Mikva of Illinois, a strong man, a true liberal, and potentially one of the leaders of the liberal group in the Congress. He is an archenemy of Mayor Daley and has been earmarked for extinction by Daley's redistricting plan in the newly and totally Democratic Illinois, but I would be surprised if Abner would not prove to be a survivor.[11] Martha Keys, next junior to him, is an attractive girl, the sister-in-law of Gary Hart, the new senator from Colorado who once managed George McGovern's campaign. The appearance she creates so far is that of being a very ingenuous liberal who wants to do the right thing but doesn't understand a great deal about how to do it. I think she is a nice person, and I suspect she has basic intellectual ability, but I also suspect that she is [too] inexperienced to have been thrown into the Ways and Means Committee and put in a position where, as a freshman Democrat, she is expected to perform miracles in that role.

11. Mikva survived a series of nail-biting races before President Jimmy Carter nominated him for a federal judgeship in 1979.

The junior member of the committee on the Democratic side is Joe Fisher [VA], the man who beat Joel Broyhill. Joe Fisher is a judicious, thoughtful man with a Ph.D. in economics, no less, who considers himself, despite a sound grooming in economics, to be a captive of the left wing and a man who must survive by going along with the caucus. It is interesting that Al Ullman has chosen him to be his "coordinator," despite his position as the junior member of the committee, which indicates Al considers him a valuable adviser and a possible bridge to a caucus that must be a very severe problem for Al's leadership.

Tonight I have been out on the *Sequoia* with a congressional group hosted by Frank Zarb, the administrator of the FEA,[12] and Rogers Morton, secretary of commerce. It was a comparatively undistinguished group, the only interesting figure from my point of view being John Glenn [D], the former astronaut who is now a senator from Ohio. He seems to me a somewhat solemn and undemonstrative fellow, and I would have thought of him as not very bright if I had not spent some time with him, Zarb, and Morton on the little secluded poop deck of the *Sequoia*, talking about the coming crunch on natural gas, about which Glenn is apparently very much concerned, as it affects Ohio. I had forgotten that he is a scientist, as most of the astronauts were, and I found his information and interest in the scientific aspects of gas exploration quite reassuring about his intelligence.

I find some antagonism between him and Mr. and Mrs. Clarence ["Bud"] Brown, Jr., who were also present on the trip, incidentally. Brown has been at the last two White House meetings and has almost foreclosed all other conversation by his volubility. Lou Frey leaned over to me in the middle of the last meeting, while Bud was holding forth at particularly exasperating length on some subject of energy expertise (he is a member of the Commerce Subcommittee on Energy), and Lou said to me that if Brown came to the next energy meeting, he was going to skip it. I have some insight finally on why as bright a man as Bud Brown is unpopular with the other members: [it is] because of his tendency to talk too much. I have always found Bud an attractive guy because of his intelligence, but apparently, his tendency to fairly egotistical discourse is his own worst enemy as far as his colleagues are concerned.

June 19, 1975

This afternoon we finally completed the energy bill after a very long period on the floor marked by intense exchanges of partisan denunciation and somewhat desultory substantive debate. I am ashamed of my committee's performance on

12. Federal Energy Administration.

this bill and am not all that pleased with my own role. As I see it, the committee was instructed to bring out an energy bill by the Democratic leadership. Either as a result of his instructions or of his understanding of the political expectations of the Democratic Caucus, Al Ullman felt he could not accept any part of the president's energy proposals, and so, the president having staked out the central position, Al had to put together a hodgepodge of peripheral measures and call it a policy. The president had been much more politically realistic; he had not felt the craven collective would pass a gasoline tax measure and so had taken unpopular steps of his own farther up the chain of oil production and refinement in which the Congress had only to acquiesce. Al made the central conservation measure in his proposal a gasoline tax; it was stripped out on the floor. The result was a measure which the Democrats now claim to be an energy policy but which certainly is no more than a shell.[13]

The Ways and Means Committee has achieved a partisanship I never would have thought possible during the other eight years of my service on this committee. Riding back from the floor last night with Charlie Vanik, he described himself as "ticked off" at us Republicans for our partisanship. James Burke has been incredibly partisan, so much so, in fact, that even the Democrats have become apologetic about his performance, constantly calling for more cooperation on the part of the Republicans and claiming that we are obstructing every effort at constructive activity. Burke is more than a caricature. He is an abysmal bore, and I have got to the point where Herman Schneebeli and I are organizing the Republicans to get up and walk out one of these times when he starts on his partisan kick again. Yesterday afternoon he insisted on holding hearings of the Social Security Subcommittee during the debate on the floor of the House of the final measures in the energy reform bill. He noted the absence of any Republicans and claimed that we were unwilling to take part in trying, as he was, "courageously" to correct the fiscal imbalances in the Social Security system.

Archer, Steiger, and I are members of this subcommittee, and we felt that we were needed on the floor for the energy debate. Burke sent word that he would give us fifteen minutes to get to the subcommittee and thereafter would express his dissatisfaction with the cooperation he was getting from the Republicans. We refused to come, and I went to the press gallery to explain to the members

13. The House-passed bill was not approved by the Senate. Rather, the Energy Policy and Conservation Act of 1975, signed by President Ford on December 22, 1975, bore little resemblance to either the Ullman plan or the president's original proposal. It did not include a gasoline tax hike.

of the press what was happening and that I thought Burke was simply trying to pressure us to leave the floor because we were effectively countering the energy bill. Of course, the effectiveness of our work was illustrated by the fact that it passed by a comfortable margin ultimately over our objections,[14] but the whole episode reflects the political partisanship which has become a constant matter of maneuver and expression on a Ways and Means Committee which used to enjoy a comfortable consensus in a different Congress.

I continue to be concerned about my relations with Herm Schneebeli, although Herm is a gentleman and seems to have very little jealousy about the extent to which I have become the Republican spokesman of the committee. Yesterday afternoon I was the one who was asked by the networks to go and explain the Republican position on the energy bill immediately after its passage. This morning I am the one quoted on the front page of the *Washington Post*. I have been quoted in three of the past four *Time* magazines. I seem to handle the key amendments and motions on the floor rather than the ranking minority member himself. I worry about Herman's feeling that I am upstaging him, and yet he seems to show no resentment and in fact to be glad that I am willing to accept the responsibility I do. I feel increasing affection for him personally, and I think I must make more effort to see that his feelings are not damaged by my vocal expressions of legislative interest and of the Republican point of view. He is a good guy.

July 12, 1975

Yesterday, as I was leaving the floor of the House, Wilbur Mills, sitting in the lobby, asked me to sit down next to him and talk for a few minutes. I launched into a lively discussion with him right away, saying that I heard he was not feeling well again and that I was sorry to hear it and hoped he would be able to return to full activities soon. He said that he felt pretty good physically but that emotionally he wasn't as good as he had been, and he had talked to a new doctor who had gone over all his records at Bethesda. This doctor told him, he said, that he must not return to full duty for another six months at least. I said, "Mr. Chairman, we need you, we need a constructive force on the committee again, such as you can offer. We need you on tax reform in particular."

He said, "Barber, I have every intention of sitting right with the committee and actively participating in any markup of a tax reform bill, but I guess I have got to take it easy until then." Then he told me how concerned he was about Al

14. The bill was approved by the House on June 19, 1975, by a vote of 291–130.

Ullman's bitterness toward Gerald Ford. He said he felt that Ullman felt that Ford was playing politics with him, was not being supportive, and was pulling the rug out from under him whenever he got the chance. I told Mills how silly this was when there are only twelve out of thirty-seven of the committee who are Republicans and explained to the chairman that during the energy proposal, Ullman had not consulted with us at all and yet considered us partisan when we didn't give him support when he needed it. I also told him that I had actively participated in a meeting at the White House in which the president had offered to try to help work out a compromise on energy, which was rejected by the Democrats, including Ullman. Mills then said he was awfully disappointed with the way things were going and that he didn't like to see so much politics in the committee. He said, "Of course, I have to be awfully careful not to appear to undercut Al Ullman myself." He also said he had been invited down to the White House a couple of times to talk with the president but felt he could not or should not do so in view of the delicacy of his relationship to Al. He also expressed dismay at how little the new members knew about anything and how assertive they were.

I have no idea why Wilbur Mills would have had a conversation like this with me, but I suspect that it does not relate to his intentions on the committee but simply to an effort to recapture some of his old friendships. It may be that he is planning to leave the House because of the impossibility of his position on a committee which has been taken over by someone else and by changed circumstances. Certainly, I do not take his report of another doctor telling him that he could not be active for another six months very seriously, although that might be the sort of thing he would hold out as a reason for resigning from the House. I suspect he is beginning to realize that he made a mistake in not taking a clean break at the time of his greatest embarrassment and that he is, at this stage, not inclined to want to reassert any degree of authority on the committee, since it is evidently beyond his control.

July 22, 1975

Bill Frenzel showed up this morning with his arm in a sling, and Lou Frey appears to limp badly. This is the result of the usual carnage of the Republican-Democratic baseball game, an institution that has long since ceased to amuse me. Once a year each team fields some of its "younger" members in connection with a major league baseball game (this year in Baltimore) to demonstrate the relative machismo of the parties. Republicans have always won before, since I have been in Congress, thereafter losing the elections. This year, thanks to the infusion of a lot of vigorous, young, useless Democrats, the Republicans lost. I think everyone loses at such a display of juvenility, and it is my conviction that one of these days, one of these overly competitive, over-the-hill, overfed congressmen is going to be seriously hurt trying to prove something he shouldn't be wasting his time trying to prove. The people of this country may very well ask if this was what they sent their representatives to Washington to do, and were I to be given the chance, I would do everything I could to end not only the suffering but even the temptation.

September 27, 1975

I am increasingly convinced that the American people must be given very explicit and not very high-level reasons for voting for Republicans in Congress if we are ever to achieve any near parity with the Democrats here. In fact, the Democrats are most vulnerable on the issues of the emoluments of office, congressional aggrandizement, extravagance, and refusal to be straightforward about things. I am trying to develop some enthusiasm among the other leaders for the Policy Committee or some similar institution taking on the "Imperial Congress" and, in particular, Wayne Hays[15] and developing a Republican puritanical phalanx here which will exploit the issues of increased salaries, massive expenditure of the public money for reelection purposes, etc. I find my incumbent Republican friends are probably the wrong ones to talk to about this, since many of them quite enjoy having more money to run their offices than they have ever had before, without the responsibility of having to vote for it. This is, I think, a Democratic Achilles' heel, but unless the Republicans are willing to exploit it, we will go on appearing to acquiesce and thus be tarred with the same brush as the Democrats as far as the public is concerned. It seems to me that the less than 20 percent acceptance of Congress in the public is something that we should try to exploit, to make more specific, and [to] use as a major reason for sending Republicans to Congress rather than continuing to let the people think that we are part of the leadership here just as we are in the White House.

October 21, 1975

I am appalled about the extent to which various people with special problems about the tax laws seem to be depending on me to get them changed. My reputation apparently is such that everyone wants me to handle their business, and I am increasingly doing things I do not enjoy simply because people are depend-

15. Tyrannical chairman of the Committee on House Administration.

ing on me to do them. It is much more fun to talk about general tax principles than it is to secure special favors for people, and I am afraid I will get the reputation of being a special-interest operator on the committee unless I blow some of these assignments so badly that disenchantment sets in. It is very difficult to say no to friends or others who come in with obvious technical problems and who nevertheless are dealing with issues not of general interest.

As one might expect, I am relying more and more on Steiger and Frenzel to get support and do my little ploys in Ways and Means. They are both ideologically uncommitted, extremely bright, adroit arguers, and inclined to friendship with me, while some of the others resent my dominance. There has been some difficulty with Herman lately. He blew his cork at Al Hunt of the *Wall Street Journal*, who had referred to me several times as the Ways and Means Committee's most influential Republican. Herman apparently didn't blame me for this characterization but told Al that it was extremely embarrassing to him with his constituents and that he resented the constant characterization of me as in fact the leader of the committee.

Herman is a bright fellow, sometimes too quick in his decision making, but not without flashes of insight, and if lame, lame only in a strategic sense rather than [in] his grasp of the subject matter in which we are dealing. He's currently engaging in an old error of his: assuming that Wilbur Mills can be a powerful and friendly ally. This able former chairman continues to sit around and feel sorry for himself as a result of his personal embarrassments over the Fanne Foxe incident. The White House called him down to consult with the president last week during the recess, and he was telling Herman how anxious he was to be of assistance and to serve on a conference on the tax bill, still a long ways off, and an environment of maneuver in which Mills traditionally cannot be trusted. I am sure he would be a more effective conferee than Charles Vanik, who plays his own games and tends to be a loner, even in conference discussions. But I am also sure that in Mills's condition, he is even less trustworthy than usual in terms of seeking allies for a Republican cause. I agree with Herman fully, however, that it would be very much in Mills's interests, and probably the country's interests, to get him back working on the committee rather than feeling sorry for himself, and so I myself have been urging him to take hold and give us the benefit of his judgment and his experience in matters that he understands better than any of the rest of us.

Today Hugh Carey came to see me and sat chatting with me for about half an hour about the problems in New York City.[16] He looked thinner than I remem-

16. Throughout 1975, the City of New York was in danger of declaring bankruptcy. On

bered him, professed himself to be "numb" about the problems he was having as governor of New York. We had a pleasant chat and were not in serious disagreement, although I explained to him, and he seemed to understand, the strong negative feelings about New York City at this point in the Congress. I told him, accurately, that I'd had a meeting with John Rhodes yesterday to discuss Policy Committee matters in the Republican Party and that we had jointly agreed that it was not time to take up the issue of New York City as a policy issue, since we both felt that the prevailing view would be extremely negative and that it was doubtless a potential embarrassment for the Republicans if we put out the kind of statement we could find agreement on now—rigidly negative—and later found out that it really was necessary for us to do something to tide the city over if we were not to have serious danger of the infection spreading.

I think Bill Simon and the president have been unnecessarily rigid in their refusal to consider New York's problem one in which the federal government can play a constructive role. They apparently are gambling on the city's willingness to do what it has to do to get its house in order and [are] therefore assuming that the situation will not change sufficiently so that the federal government could do more than lend the city deeper in the hole.

November 19, 1975

I have just come from a fund-raising reception for John Rhodes. I had a very interesting conversation with Mel Laird, who was there and in a very ebullient mood. His comment to me was, "Goddamn it, Barber, I have just read your letter to the president. I have just checked the telephone register down there and find that you never even tried to call him about the stuff you were complaining about. It isn't fair to him for you to write letters like that if you aren't even willing to pick up the phone and talk to the president." I explained that I felt it was an intrusion on the president for a person like me to pick up the phone and talk to him, and he said that he would assure me that anytime I picked up the phone and asked to talk to the president, the president would be glad to talk to me.

What this is all about is a feeling that has been festering in me for some time that the president was not doing well politically. I wrote him a letter to this effect, saying that he must stay home more in the White House, trying to become a statesman on domestic matters rather than traveling all over the world in cer-

---

October 29, 1975, President Ford said that he would veto any congressional measure providing for a "bailout" of the city. The next day's headline in the *New York Daily News*—"Ford to City: Drop Dead"—was a classic.

emonials and engaging in fund-raising exercises for the Republican Party. I also told him that he was out of touch with the members of his party in the House of Representatives, quoting Al Quie to that effect, and saying that he must increase his informal contact with the rank-and-file party members, involving them in his campaign if he wanted their help during the ensuing election. I also said that if he caved on both energy and New York City, it would badly damage his credibility with the members of his party in the House, and that he could not afford to have the image he was developing of not being firm on any principle. Having had this conversation with Mel Laird, I was very grateful that the president was at the same reception and I had the chance to go up and tell him how pleased I was with his statement about New York City, in which he did not lay down a series of conditions for federal aid to be given to the city. There is a considerable story to tell about this also.

Yesterday was a particularly difficult day for me, since I started out the morning at nine o'clock in New York City talking to a convention of corporate financial officers; then moving to the Lou Harris seminar for multinational corporations, where I talked about international tax and trade concerns just before Henry Kissinger; then speaking at a luncheon for the NAM[17] in a nearby ritzy club. The morning was punctuated by phone calls from my Washington office telling me that Perry Duryea, the leader of the Republicans in the assembly in New York, had heard the president was about to make a statement in which he laid down conditions, including the raising of taxes in New York State, for the granting of any federal aid or federal bailout through guarantee of New York City.

[I] placed a call trying to get through to a number of different people in the White House, [then] finally dictated a message to Max Friedersdorf's secretary, since it appeared that all the important people with whom I could establish contact were in a meeting with the president about New York City. The message I gave was that under no circumstances must the president give Hugh Carey the excuse for a tax increase on New Yorkers generally, so that the Carey tax package would become the Ford tax package. I repeated the old axiom that Republican leaders don't advocate the taxing of Republicans to bail out Democrats and expressed in the strongest possible terms my hope that the president would not fall into the booby traps that Carey was laying for him as a man who was unnecessarily involved in the dispute as to whether or not taxes should be raised in New York State or the state's expenditures should be cut, as Warren

17. National Association of Manufacturers.

Anderson, the leader of the Republicans in the Senate, was advocating. In short, I urged the president to tell Carey to get his ducks in line, and if he then came back and showed they were in line, the federal government would then provide any reasonable and short-time tiding-over assistance that was appropriate assistance to the city.

Within an hour, I was called back from New York City to Washington to attend a meeting at the White House, which the president had decided was necessary, in which all the Republican congressmen in the New York delegation, plus the two New York senators, attended and argued before the president the various strategies that were possible for him and what their political implications were. I took a very strong position at this, also, and was appalled to find that a number of our New York delegation, including such people as Frank Horton, Don Mitchell, probably Bill Walsh, Ben Gilman, Norm Lent, and Ham Fish, were in active support of the banking and currency bill,[18] which has been outdated now for a week while Carey carried on his negotiations with the White House, and has been changed four times in the past four days. These members were somewhat appalled to find how hard-line the rest of us, and particularly Hastings, Wydler, and I, were about the difficulties the president would get into if he softened perceptibly on the NYC issue.

The president appeared genuinely not to have made up his mind on this and was earnestly seeking guidance from us, which everyone was quite anxious and willing to give. He said he would issue a statement sometime today, which he finally did at noon, going right down the line with us hard-liners and saying absolutely nothing about preconditions to federal aid, which Carey could then describe as . . . converting the Carey tax package into a Ford tax package. I was relieved, and I told him at the reception for John Rhodes tonight that I was very pleased with the understanding he had shown of our intricate politics.

November 23, 1975

The day of the president's statement, I did not mention that the minute it was received, the Democratic leadership announced that under no circumstances, in view of the president's attitude, would it be possible to achieve a consensus on NYC and that they were therefore pulling off all legislation until after the recess. Since included among the legislation was a bill changing the bankruptcy laws in order to preserve local services in the event of a NYC default, many of us immediately assumed that the governor, in consultation with the Democratic leaders,

---

18. This provided for $7 billion in long- and short-term loans to New York City.

[had] decided there was no imminent danger of default and therefore, much of the crisis talk had been carefully designed to encourage the federal government to step in and make unnecessary [any] tough decisions by the local leaders in the New York City area.

The more I see of this, the more skeptical I become about the dimension of the crisis and the more I am convinced that leaders like Carey and [Mayor Abe] Beame are trying to institutionalize the old dance that NYC leaders have gone through for years of trying to transfer the blame for tough decisions to the federal government. I wrote a newsletter just before I left in which I lamented the fact that there was virtually no legislation to talk about in my usual immaculate way and that I had to take the risk of discussing issues of high political content in a letter which is supposed to be nonpolitical. I think this is going to be my condition for the next year, and my posture will appear much more partisan than it has in previous elections. I was described in an Evans and Novak article which came out this weekend as having a very high-profile political role in respect to NYC. Even my wife is extremely nervous about this, telling me that the American people are fed up with partisan politics of a Republican-Democrat type and that, up until this time, I have appeared, at least in her eyes, as something special rather than as another one of those old honky-type politicians.

While I am convinced that it would be advantageous for me politically to keep a low profile and to go along with developments in Congress as though I was completely nonpartisan, I do not see much point in continuing the vapid role that has kept Republicans as a small minority [of] low-risk participants in congressional affairs. I would just as soon gamble by drawing issues more clearly—by posturing, if you will—if the alternative is for things to continue as they have been. It fascinates me that people, including my wife, will blame me for a partisan role [when] what I am trying to do in issues like the New York City issue is to protect a comparatively innocent president from the booby traps partisan people are setting for him in order to make it appear that he is the one requiring unpleasant conditions [for] New York City aid. I suppose the bearers of bad tidings get no applause for statesmanship from either side, and I am sure the president somewhat resents the showiness and insistence of my position that he not fall into Hugh Carey's trap.[19]

Now that I am home and moving around in a comparatively slack schedule, so that I can have extended conversations with friends, I find . . . that many

19. On December 9, 1975, President Ford signed the New York City Seasonal Financing Act of 1975, which authorized the secretary of the treasury to loan the city up to $2.3 billion.

people up here find Ronald Reagan not only extremely attractive but much more interesting than President Ford. My position on Ronald Reagan has been as follows: Yes, he is attractive and says a lot of things that need to be said. Barry Goldwater played the same role. I recall with some anxiety what it was like to run on a national ticket headed by Barry Goldwater, and so I am from Missouri when it comes to acceptance of Ronald Reagan as the top man on the ticket, at least to such time that he can prove that he has a broader base of support than Barry Goldwater had.

December 30, 1975

I found myself late in December being interviewed by Henry Hubbard of *Newsweek*, who asked me why I had abandoned the moderation for which I had acquired a reputation in my dealings with the White House. I told him that I felt the president, in trying to "work things out," had arrived at a point in the image the American people have of him of appearing not to stand for anything. I said that he had reached the stage where he had to take political risks in framing issues sharply, realizing that the risks might backfire, or he might emerge initially as the pleasant historical figure who held the world together between Nixon and the next elected president. I told Hubbard that there was a caretaker aspect to Ford's presidency which would make it difficult for the American people to take him seriously when he asked for a mandate for the next four years.

Hubbard is a liberal Democrat. I asked him what he thought would happen to the Republican Party if it did not make a good showing with respect to the presidency in 1976, and he acknowledged that it might mark the end of the Republican Party as we have known it. I asked him then what he wanted to see emerge from a bad case of suicide on the part of the Republicans, and he said he thought a two-party system would somehow go on, perhaps not with the same labels. I told him it was my impression that if the Republicans died as a historic force, a new and polarized political scene would emerge in which it would be liberals against conservatives, and the inclusiveness of the old party situation, where American democracy benefited from dialogue within the parties more than the confrontation between them, would be gone. In its place, zigzag government would emerge. I said to him that I thought the press would have some responsibility for the end result of such an ideological split, and while I realized [the constant confrontation] would make for "better press," . . . the country would in no way benefit, and I asked him to consider this as he participated in efforts to knock Ford out of the box so that they would have the splendid target of Ronald Reagan to demolish during the election campaign.

Incidentally, Henry Hubbard reported his interview with me in one sentence: "Ford appeared to be a caretaker and was simply a pleasant hiatus between Nixon and the next elected president." I am sure the White House won't like that quote.

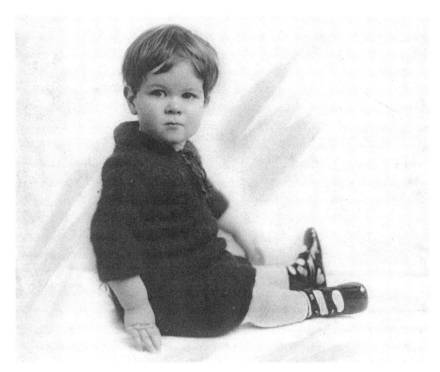

Barber Conable, pre–Ways and Means. (Courtesy of Conable family)

An undergraduate at Cornell University. (Courtesy of Conable family)

During his first campaign for public office, Barber and Charlotte pose in front of "Benjamin Bump," their durable campaign trailer. Daughter Anne recalls spending several summers crisscrossing western New York in that trailer, blowing up "Conable of Course" helium balloons at carnivals and county fairs. (Courtesy of Conable family)

BARBER B. CONABLE, Jr.

Republican Candidate

FOR

STATE SENATE

53rd Senatorial District

ALLEGANY CO.	ORLEANS CO.
GENESEE CO.	WYOMING CO.
LIVINGSTON CO.	

P.O. BOX 155   ALEXANDER, N. Y.

Campaign card from Conable's 1962 state senate campaign. Note his five-county rural district. (Courtesy of Conable family)

Swimming against the tide: Conable was elected to the House in 1964, in the teeth of LBJ's landslide. (Courtesy of Conable family)

Changing of the guard: Conable (right) in 1964 with the man he would soon replace, Congressman Harold Ostertag, who was retiring. (Courtesy of Conable family)

Such a photogenic young congressional family! The Conables in 1965. (Courtesy of Conable family)

Freshman congressman Conable (left) of the House Science and Astronautics Committee with astronaut Neil Armstrong at the Kennedy Space Center, 1965. (Courtesy of Conable family)

Conable interviews an expansive Senator Everett Dirksen on his television show, which was beamed back to the district. (Courtesy of Conable family)

Vox populi: Conable stands next to a stack of returned constituent surveys. (Courtesy of Conable family)

CONGRESS

The voters of the 37th Congressional District can be proud of the thoughtful and responsible representation they have in Congress through Barber B. Conable. Congressman Conable is a staunch advocate of election law reform to control exhorbitant spending by candidates. He supports the complete overhaul of the federal tax structure to eliminate unfair provisions. He has sponsored legislation for a study of ways to eliminate wasteful overlapping of federal programs. He has urged creation of a Congressional Committee on Urban Affairs to handle the great volume of vital legislation affecting our cities. As a member of the Ways & Means Committee, he helped win the fight to improve Social Security benefits while maintaining the sound insurance character of the System. In addition, he provides the kind of personal representation that eases the problems of our citizens in their dealings with the federal government.

Conferring with William McC. Martin, Federal Reserve Board Chairman.

Hearing views of constituents on a local problem.

Making a point at a Ways & Means Committee Hearing.

Interviewing FBI Official on the Crime Report.

With Rochester Editor Howard Coles (C) at Frederick Douglass commemorative stamp ceremony.

Presenting an award to a farm youth.

Congressman Conable and family on a week-end tour of the Capitol grounds in Washington.

Campaign literature, circa 1968. (Courtesy of Conable family)

A friend in the White House: Conable (right) with Gerald Ford in the Oval Office on August 11, 1974, two days into Ford's presidency. (Courtesy of Conable family)

Cruising to reelection, October 1976. (Courtesy of Conable family)

Conable (center) chats with Carter's secretary of the treasury, Michael Blumenthal (right), as Representative Jim Broyhill looks on. (Courtesy of Conable family)

Conable often worried that he was loquacious. (Courtesy of Conable family)

Greeting the new president and vice president in the Oval Office, January 1981. (Courtesy of Conable family)

A pensive Conable. (Courtesy of Conable family)

Conable in his office at the Cannon House Office Building. (Courtesy of Conable family)

Conable (left) has breakfast with Vice President George H. W. Bush in November 1982, a dozen years after they served together on the House Ways and Means Committee. (Courtesy of Conable family)

Conable at his beloved Wooton patent desk in his final year in office. (Courtesy of Common Cause)

To Barber Conable
   With best wishes   Ronald Reagan

President Ronald Reagan shakes hands with his World Bank president appointee,
February 28, 1986. (Courtesy of Conable family)

Conable's doodles, drawn during tedious committee meetings, were collected by connoisseurs of congressional art, including Ronald Reagan. (Courtesy of Conable family)

Conable returns to Cornell University, 1998. (Courtesy of Conable family)

Within mooing distance of the Schmieder cows: Barber and Charlotte's bench in the Alexander Village Cemetery. (Photo by Lucine Kauffman)

Conable views a Ford victory over Ronald Reagan in the race for the Republican presidential nomination as crucial to the maintenance of a functioning two-party system. Sam Gibbons, a Democratic colleague on Ways and Means whom Conable has heretofore regarded as bright but obnoxious, becomes a close ally. The corruption of Ohio Democrat Wayne Hays sullies the institution's already tarnished reputation. Conable marvels at the irrelevance of Vice President Rockefeller. The Republican convention that nominates Ford illumines the ideological fractures within the party. At home, Conable's chief opponent is the Conservative Party, which he regards with a reciprocated enmity. Conable is heartened by the quality of the Republicans on Ways and Means, despite their being outnumbered, and for once, he ends the year on an upbeat note.

Conable's dislike grew for an insurgent Republican Right, embodied in the candidacy of Ronald Reagan. His references to Reagan and his supporters over the next five years displayed a grimacing suspicion bordering on contempt, although his attitude softened when he saw Reagan up close as president.

For once, Conable's policy preferences clouded his political judgment. He dismissed Reagan as a political force, predicting that "Ronald Reagan at the head of the ticket will be a disaster for the Republican Party." Reagan, he said, had a narrow appeal to zealots, and Reagan supporters at the 1976 Republican National Convention reminded Conable of the crowd at Nuremberg.

Conable demonstrated his concern for the Ways and Means Committee by trying to talk labor Democrat Joe Karth, whom he admired, out of retirement. He also admitted to voting for Daniel Patrick Moynihan, the newly elected Democratic senator from New York, with whom he would have a relationship that vacillated between vexing and comradely. When Moynihan was good, he was very, very good, but when he was bad, he was a "traditional jowl-shaking party hack."

January 29, 1976

One of the most interesting developments [over the Christmas recess] centered around Vice President Rockefeller. I took Dave Broder[1] out to lunch, since he is

1. National political correspondent for the *Washington Post*.

a journalist whom I admire and whom I believe to be a valuable source of information and advice. We had a wide-ranging talk, and I expressed to him, among other things, my dismay that Nelson Rockefeller was not proving to be a more constructive force for the Ford administration. He told me that Rockefeller not only was surly and resentful of being dropped off the ticket, he was actually bad-mouthing the president.[2]

I subsequently had lunch with Jim Cannon, Rockefeller's prime assistant and currently the staff head of the Domestic Council. I told Cannon that I understood Nelson was bad-mouthing the president and I wanted to understand what Nelson's motivations were, saying that the perception on the Hill was that Nelson was interested himself in the presidency and would make a pitch for it if Reagan were able to knock Ford out of the race. He told me what I personally believe myself: that such an ambition on Nelson's part would be foolish, in that the Republican Party would never give him the nomination over Reagan if Ford were to be knocked out of the race by Reagan's strength. He also stated categorically that Nelson was not bad-mouthing the president and that I must be misinformed. I told him that I thought David Broder was a responsible reporter and that I had learned this from him. He expressed dismay and changed the subject.

Two days later, David Broder called me from New Hampshire, saying that he had just hung up the phone from talking to a furious vice president who denied bad-mouthing Ford and castigated him for spreading such rumors. I apologized to Dave for any embarrassment I had caused him, because he apparently was angry with me for having involved him in such a confrontation. I told him that his reputation was such that I felt the mentioning of his name would attract Nelson's attention, and I thought this was a very important thing to do at a time when Nelson was obviously going to get himself in serious trouble unless his attention were attracted. I subsequently wrote a letter of apology to Dave Broder and received a gracious acknowledgment, and every time I have seen Nelson Rockefeller since then, he has denied to me that he was bad-mouthing the president and has tried to explain to me when it happened. I have simply said to Nelson that I was grateful we were not reading about it in the paper and he had gotten it straightened out with Dave Broder. It was interesting to me that Nelson Rockefeller's reaction was one of direct and positive confrontation with the source of this unhappy intelligence.

2. In October 1975 Ford asked Rockefeller to publicly withdraw from consideration as Ford's running mate in 1976. In early November, Rockefeller grudgingly complied.

February 26, 1976

The big news this week has been the New Hampshire primary. . . . [Ford] won by the narrowest of margins,[3] but the general feeling in the House following his win is that it was psychologically a big boost to his campaign and that Reagan is definitely going to be on the defensive in Florida and virtually out of the race if he does not win there.[4] . . . I am convinced the Republican Party will not survive as a national party if it is led into this election by a candidate who appeals to a very narrow ideological segment, and that American democracy will not continue as we have known it if we do not have two inclusive national parties with at least a potential of majority control, rather than the ideological fragments characteristic of some of the other developed nations of the world. Thus, I see Ford's leadership not only as vitally necessary to my own survival as an effective member of the House but a necessary ingredient in the continuance of the two-party system as we have known it.

May 6, 1976

I would like now to talk about the Ways and Means Committee, which continues to be a microcosm of the Congress as a whole, exhibiting all the same problems of leadership and participatory democracy that the House has now locked itself into for the duration of the 94th Congress.

Joe Karth, the man who has seemed to me time and again to be the most centrally located and one of the most effective figures on the committee, has announced his retirement. John Meagher[5] told me two months ago that Karth was seriously considering retirement. This upset me a great deal, and I immediately called Joe to ask if I could talk to him. I went over to his office and had a very tense and somewhat emotional discussion with him about the possibility. I said to him that I understood he was considering retirement and that I didn't want his comment on it because I hoped it wasn't so; that I had come for the sole purpose of urging him not to do it, saying that if he thought he was frustrated, he should consider what it must be like to be for ten years on the minority on the Ways and Means Committee; that I considered him one of the most effective members of the committee and that he should be aware of the fact that when he takes a position on an issue, it makes a difference; that while he and I had

3. 50 percent to 48 percent.

4. Ford won Florida, but Reagan rebounded with a victory two weeks later in North Carolina and competed throughout the primaries and into the convention.

5. Minority counsel and staff director of the Ways and Means Committee.

differed on many substantive issues and that there had been times of personal tenseness between us, I respected him fully and would feel the committee much diminished by his departure.

He thanked me and said that if he had to make up his mind at that point, he doubtless would announce his retirement because he was frustrated. I pressed him on why he should feel that way, and he referred to a bill relating to Investors Diversified Services, which was a special-interest matter he had tried to push in the committee three or four weeks before, seeking a special tax concession for this very large investment trust, when his colleagues had not supported him (I remember that I was one of those who had not). He said that if he couldn't accomplish anything with a bill like that, he certainly had very little influence on the committee and would be just as well playing golf somewhere. I was not in the position to argue with him a great deal about that because I knew it was important to him and yet I had voted against him, but I repeated my message and left the room fairly quickly, feeling deeply distressed and somewhat emotional to see a man who had apparently made up his mind and who, by all rights, should consider himself on the pinnacle of success as the member of an effective part of the Congress. About three weeks later he announced his retirement, as expected, after eighteen years.

I find myself drifting into increasing relationship with Sam Gibbons of Florida. Sam is an abrasive man who irritates many of the members on the committee by his outspokenness and his apparent unpredictability, but I think of him as an honest man without particular partisan bias and with the courage and honesty to take positions damaging to him if he is intellectually satisfied that they are the right positions. I think he is sometimes impulsive, sometimes almost capricious, but I trust his motives completely and admire his independence. Once again, we do not vote alike on many things, although we seem to share the same general philosophy on matters of trade, where he is particularly outspoken.

Ways and Means is doing virtually nothing at this point, although we may be bringing out a few routine bills prepared by subcommittees and relating mostly to housekeeping. Herman [Schneebeli] has been asking me to handle more and more of these bills on the floor, and it is apparent he considers himself in a "tapering off" condition as he prepares for his own retirement at the end of this year. We have been having a fascinating time with the projected reform of the estate tax. This has not been changed in any major way since 1942, and the farm bloc from the Midwest has decided it is time to push on raising the exemption from $60,000 to something close to $200,000. I started out in discussion of this matter by taking the attitude that the farm bloc was unreasonable in asking a

Congress as liberally oriented as this to give almost half the revenue of the estate tax away to those people with estates of over $100,000. I found I was casting myself in the role of the heavy, since most of my liberal Democratic friends, and particularly those in upstate New York, had promised their local farmers they would raise the exemption to $200,000, confident that the Ways and Means Committee would never permit such a bill to emerge and give them a chance to vote on it.

Thus, although I had told Al Ullman originally that I would be glad to co-sponsor, in the interests of bipartisanship, a "balanced" bill that made modest improvements in the estate tax, I subsequently went to him and told him that the political situation in upstate New York was resulting in my looking like the enemy to my Farm Bureau and others as I tried to talk sense to them about what the Congress was likely to do. I told him that I had decided I was going to give my liberal Democrats the chance to vote for a $200,000 exemption to see if they were willing to be honest about it. In other words, I came to the conclusion that the condition was 1,000 percent political and that I would force the Democrats to either bog the bill down in intricacies and kill it in that way or put their money where their mouth was. I was not myself going to be the restraining element and the responsible member who damaged the farmers' hopes. I do not usually behave this way, but I was angry at bright, liberal freshman [New York] Demo-crats like [John] LaFalce and [Matt] McHugh, who were obviously playing the special-interest game with the farmers, in reliance on people like me being responsible and saving them from themselves.[6]

May 26, 1976

Wayne Hays, the tyrant of the House, has been suffering a terrible embarrass-ment lately after disclosures by the *Washington Post* that he had hired a woman to be his mistress and put her on the committee staff.[7] I would believe almost anything of Wayne Hays, but it had not occurred to me that he would achieve that level of arrogance, and I am surprised to find that most of my colleagues believe everything that is said about him in the papers. He made an emotional speech to the House yesterday in which he acknowledged an illicit relationship with the woman, saying that he had lied primarily because he had wanted to

6. The exemption was increased to $120,000 for 1977 decedents.

7. Twenty-seven-year-old Elizabeth Ray said she was paid $14,000 annually for two years to serve as a clerk to Hays, despite the fact that she could not type, file, or answer the phone—or so she claimed.

defend his new marriage against slander and calumny. I signed a letter to the Ethics Committee asking that his conduct be investigated, but I must acknowledge that it was not a courageous act, despite Wayne's reputation of being a buzz saw, because before the letter was sent, he had requested such an investigation on his own.

Bill Archer tonight came to me and stirred me up on a subject I have been interested in before: how to take advantage of Democratic malfeasance and scandal in the conduct of Congress so as to encourage the election of Republicans to Congress by people who intend to hook congressional elections on the coattails of presidential candidates or otherwise simply to return incumbents to office. Before the last election, I went to John Rhodes and suggested that a task force be put together to document and to accuse the Democrats of many sleazy practices we all know they engage in as part of the arrogance of their safe control of the House of Representatives. John immediately became defensive, fearing that such a campaign might embroil some Republicans and backfire on us, since we do not control the sources of information. I took the position that if there were Republicans who were abusing their position here, our party could do well to expose them as well as the Democrats, and that it was my feeling that probably the Democrats were far worse than the Republicans in any allowance abuse or personal scandal.

Archer told me I should try to interest Bob Michel in this campaign, asking if he didn't think it would be a good idea to put together a task force to gather the documentation necessary so that we would not appear to be making wild and unsubstantiated charges. Bob acted quite uncertain about it, but this is something I would go with some joy to do, confident that I am myself invulnerable because of my puritanical practices, and feeling that it is important to purge the House of its seamy side at a time when Wayne Hays's peccadillos have so attracted attention to unhappy generalizations about politicians in general and a congressman in particular. I find the clublike aspects of our institution quite distressing and doubt that there will be any vigorous movement toward cleaning house. I have always thought the Republicans could exploit this situation, if only they had the courage to do it and the willingness to let the chips fall where they may.

There is a remarkable amount of bicentennial activity going on up home, and [it] will be pretty gravely foreclosing my weekends between now and the middle of the summer. One of the least satisfactory aspects of the job of the congressman is the amount of time he has to spend away from his family and making himself accessible to his constituency. I have from time to time had all kinds of resolutions to change this unsatisfactory pattern of a part of my life, but some old friend from back home will call up and say, "We've got an event, Barber, that we really need you at." Then my having attended that will become an excuse for going to something else the same weekend, and before you know it, the weekend is so full that I am leaving on Friday and coming back Sunday night unrefreshed and lonely, pulled seventeen ways by the pressure of importunate constituents hoping to get an "important" official to come to their modest community undertaking. I do not believe members of Congress should legislate in a vacuum, but the way I have been living recently is ridiculous, and I must say that I might as well be in a vacuum for all the meaningful conversations and exchanges I get with the people that surround my hectic schedule. Everything seems to be name recognition rather than real accessibility or a real exchange of ideas, and while I am sure name recognition is the stuff of which political survival is built, I am not sure that political survival is worth it under these circumstances. In the Emersonian sense, there is not much point in being a successful politician if you are not a successful human being.

June 10, 1976

Things are bad in Congress, with low morale, a lot of backbiting, and a great deal of dispute about how to handle the affair of Wayne Hays. We are aware that nobody is talking about anything else out across the countryside, and Republicans in particular are upset that nothing is being done to capitalize on the absolute mess the Democrats have made, with their arrogance, of the image of the Congress. John Rhodes tends to take the soft line, apparently afraid that someone will take away his limousine if he gets unpleasant and tries to act political, and that, of course, does not help the image of the Republican leadership with the rank-and-file Republicans of the House.

We hear nothing from the White House. We have had no leadership meetings for a month now, as Gerald Ford has done his one-man stand around the country trying to shake hands with every American as an offset to Ronald Reagan's disciplined organization and the hard line of the zealots. A handful of uncommitted delegates will decide the outcome of the convention, and I persist in the belief that the best way to deal with them would be to turn loose a lot of Republican congressmen on them to express their self-interest, their desire for survival, and their conviction that Ronald Reagan at the head of the ticket will be a disaster for the Republican Party, second only in dimension to that which started our downward slide in 1964. The question remains: how far can you slide before you come to the end of the chute?

June 24, 1976

Yesterday was a White House meeting, the first one since early in May. Many of us have been anxious to have such a meeting, feeling that the president's campaign continues to falter through disorganization. He spent most of the meeting talking about busing,[8] a subject that he continues to approach as though he were a congressman from Michigan rather than the president of the United States. Proposals are modest enough: a Justice Department study showing ways in which the court's determination that busing is necessary in de facto cases (as opposed to cases of wrongdoing) can be limited constitutionally; a second proposal for a council made up of constructive citizens from communities that have handled the busing situation well. But he acts as though he continues to believe that this issue is one of the overriding issues in American public life and one that he must deal with or be considered a failure as president. In fact, there is great skepticism out in the public about whether anyone can deal with a constitutional issue of this nature in any way that will change things in communities where racial patterns have become distorted to the point that the school systems have become involved. For this reason, at an appropriate time, I made a rather sour speech saying that I hoped the president would not put too many political chips on a subject which I did not feel could redound much to his benefit and might actually wind up making him look like an impotent president rather than a leader.

Later in the day, at a New York delegation meeting, I had a chance for a private conversation with Nelson Rockefeller, at which time he told me that I was right on the issue and right about the possible political [dis]advantages to Ford in his continuing to let it dominate his political utterances, but that he was afraid Ford would continue to treat this subject as he does most others about which he has wrapped his stubborn streak. One has the sense of watching a nice but misguided child make political mistakes unchided. The idea that this activist former governor, brought into the Ford administration to provide experience, administrative ability, and recruiting services, could have become as complete a spectator as he seems to have become is one to bemuse the historians of the future.

July 31, 1976

[The] most dramatic recent political development was the announcement early this week by Ronald Reagan that, if nominated, he would choose as his running mate [Senator] Richard Schweiker of Pennsylvania. This affair is one that defies

8. Federal court-ordered busing of schoolchildren for the stated purpose of achieving racial balance in public schools.

comprehension. It is apparent that Reagan did not check Schweiker out or that he had much more obscure motives than anyone can define a man like Reagan having. Schweiker has very little respect in either the conservative or the liberal camp: the conservatives hate him because he is the most liberal Republican senator, far surpassing Clifford Case [NJ], Edward Brooke [MA], and Jacob Javits [NY] in his opposition to his own party's position and having a COPE rating of 100 percent, while [Walter] Mondale [D-MN] has only 95 percent. The liberals consider him a formula politician, a man who shops around for support and does not truly believe in the positions he espouses in voting in the Senate.

When the announcement came and was confirmed by a Schweiker press conference—indicating, without a doubt, what a true prostitute he is, as well as Reagan—many of our true believers in the House of Representatives were slinking around with their tails between their legs, caught completely off guard because they had not been consulted at all before the announcement, and shaking their heads in disbelief. We Ford supporters held virtually a full-day celebration in the lounge off the floor of the House, savoring the dimensions of the Reagan disaster, marveling that the press was underplaying it as much as it was, and speculating about the motivation.

That night I went to a state dinner at the White House for the Australian ambassador and found the president feeling pretty cocky. He told me that he had written a scenario for the campaign so far, including the Reagan announcement, and that I should have more faith that things were going to turn out all right. I suspect that he was just as surprised and delighted as I was by this turn of events.

The beginning of this week, an episode involving Frank Horton came to light which has caused me some embarrassment and worry. Frank, a week previously, returning from some sort of celebration with two women ([neither] his wife) in the car, went through a radar trap on the Thruway in the town of Stafford, New York, at a speed of 78 miles per hour. When the troopers tried to stop him, he made them chase him for six miles at speeds of up to 105 miles per hour, finally stopping, conducting himself in such a way that they were sure he was drunk, and then being taken into custody for two hours, after which he took a Breathalyzer test showing a very high degree of alcohol in the blood.

Frank told me nothing about this episode but reported to his two Republican county chairmen, saying at the time he wanted to have a press conference and disclose the double life his wife had forced him into. They talked him out of this, and Ron Starkweather[9] immediately consulted with me. I told him to have

9. Monroe County Republican chairman.

Frank plead guilty to drunk driving, to take his punishment, and to try to get that episode behind him before the election. Frank has not been inclined to do this and did not consult me until a week later, after it was apparent the newspapers were on to the episode, at which time I repeated the advice. He showed some intent of stringing it out and trying to delay the trial until after the election and to further stimulate interest in who his unknown woman companion was at the time of the episode. For a man knowledgeable about public relations, he seems to be handling this about as badly as he could, although I doubt, in the long run, that it will hurt him that much at the polls. He is bitter about what he thinks is a railroading by the state troopers but around the House seems to be inclined to want to make a joke of it, since there is not much else he can do. I find some of my constituents are confusing him and me and think I am the one charged with drunk driving. Of course, I have no intention of getting dragged into it anyway, either putting pressure on in Frank's behalf or in any way trying to explain his behavior away, except to say, quite truthfully, that I am somewhat mystified because I have never seen Frank Horton take a drink before. Perhaps this affair will bring to a head his relations with his wife, which have been in bad shape for a long time.[10]

August 23, 1976

The past two weeks have been spent at the Republican National Convention in Kansas City. I was appointed one of the vice chairmen of the Platform Committee, in charge of the plank relating to economics and agriculture. . . . It was remarkable that we wound up with even a vaguely literate document, because we found the Reagan people contentious and anxious to argue about almost everything.

In fact, it wasn't Reagan people who were causing the trouble but Helms people. Ronald Reagan, like the president, put scant stock in a platform he could not control. Among his followers, however, there were many affected by [Senator] Jesse Helms [NC], who wanted a very tough and very specific campaign document, either to have some input into the president's campaign, if the president was to be successful with respect to the nomination, or to cast Senator Schweiker in brass, since he had agreed, despite his liberal record, to be bound by the platform.

And so we spent several nights until the early-morning hours in the trenches,

---

10. Horton was fined $200 and given an eleven-day jail sentence, of which he served less than a week. He and his wife later divorced.

slugging out word by word economic and agricultural planks that were quite conservative and scarcely literate, put together by a committee in an atmosphere of ranklement and bearing more the marks of battle than the impress of thought. There proved to be very little controversial in our piece, which was more than could be said of some other subcommittee documents.

The major platform battles proved to be federal aid to education and foreign affairs. Federal aid to education had been recommended for termination by Congressman David Treen of Louisiana. . . . In a very tense series of speeches in which most of the members of Congress participated as loathsome liberals, we tried to discuss the pragmatics of termination of a program like impacted aid, which could be translated directly into school tax rates in a number of communities. And only after I discovered that Dave Treen had no intention of terminating impacted aid, although his resolution did not make this clear, were we able to throw sufficient confusion into the discussion to get a compromise worked out between Treen and [Bob] Dole.

Dole, incidentally, equivocated throughout as a member of my platform subcommittee and apparently was anxious to play ball with both sides. Finally, the Treen amendment was set aside and a study substituted for it, but not before Anderson, Conable, and [Silvio] Conte [MA] had done themselves a great deal of damage as political prostitutes in the eyes of those earnest people from the boondocks who felt that federal aid to education in any form was anathema.

The fight on the foreign policy plank was, of course, [an] undisguised assault on détente, on Kissinger, on those who wish to give away the Panama Canal, etc., and was conducted with ill humor and very little thoughtfulness. It went on at some length, but there is not much point in recounting its gory details.

[We] also had a fight on ERA and the abortion plank, which, while it did not expressly support a constitutional amendment for the prohibition of abortion, nonetheless supported the efforts of those who sought such a "right-to-life" constitutional amendment.[11] I voted with the minority against this plank and with the scant majority that supported ERA. The ERA, incidentally, was the only issue on which the Ford people intervened actively, their feeling being that the president was fully committed to ERA, and as such, it must be preserved in the platform.

As for the convention itself, it was not an intellectual exercise. The devotion

11. The platform stated: "The Republican Party favors a continuance of the public dialogue on abortion and supports the efforts of those who seek enactment of a constitutional amendment to restore protection of the right to life for unborn children."

of the Reaganites was frightening and to me raised echoes of Nuremberg. The din was overpowering. A rules fight, in which the Reaganites attempted to force the president to disclose his vice-presidential nominee in advance of his own nomination, was the tense turning point, and once it was demonstrated that Ford had the votes, I lost interest in participation and spent much of the time in the galleries with my wife, marveling at the hubbub below. I had the worst seat in the house, two seats directly behind the vice president, and Rocky appeared relaxed and outgoing so that the aisle was constantly clogged with newsmen and others interviewing him and blocking the view, drowning the speeches, and clawing those of us who sat near Rockefeller in order to try to get closer to the great man. The famous telephone incident took place directly in front, and Rocky handled it well, pretending the whole thing was a joke, even after it had taken a vicious turn by the intrusion of a Utah delegate who smashed his telephone to pieces.[12]

At the end of the convention, the president gave an acceptance speech which was as good as any speech I have ever heard him give and [was] generally accepted as such. We left there dispirited by all that had transpired up until the acceptance speech, but feeling a thrill of hope as the din died down. The president had given us the necessary upbeat for the end of an exhausting and not very satisfying political exercise.

October 10, 1976

My attendance record wound up below 90 percent for the second Congress in a row, unsatisfactory by my own standards and probably the subject of some political commentary during the ensuing political campaign. I must say that the quality of my participation has declined in later years, along with its quantity. I find that as I become absorbed in the work of my committee, I am less patient with the obligation to find out the details of what I am voting on among the complex legislation that came from other committees. Through the years of experience in the House, I have come to have confidence in a handful of people representing most of the major committees and to base my vote more on their judgment than my own knowledge of the details of the legislation. This is a cop-out of sorts, I suppose, and my conscience bothers me when I find myself saying, "I am voting for this measure because Al Quie seems to feel strongly about it" or because "I un-

12. Rockefeller and a North Carolina Reagan supporter got into a tussle over a "Reagan Country" sign, and a Utah delegate retaliated by ripping out the New York delegation's telephone.

derstand Bill Frenzel has looked into it carefully and has had a part in formulating the final result." It certainly is true that a small number of people have a disproportionately large influence on the outcome of controversial legislation because of the respect with which their judgment is held. I am sure I am not an exception in this respect, and in fact, I suspect that I still have a better understanding of most of the legislation that has to be voted on than the average member of Congress. I am terribly distressed, for instance, to find fellow New Yorkers—people like Bill Walsh, Don Mitchell, Ham Fish, or Norm Lent, otherwise decent people— casting their votes almost entirely on the basis of the appeal they think the label of the bill will have to special-interest groups in their districts.

The presidential campaign goes badly. I have uneasy feelings about the final outcome. Gerald Ford, a man in whom I have been forced to place my confidence because there is no one else available, is proving to have the feet of clay we have always acknowledged him to have but hoped would not show. He is a decent, earnest, well-intentioned man in over his head and swimming in a school of sharks who seem increasingly lethal as he thrashes around in the water. Jimmy Carter himself is the shark with the sharpest teeth and the most insatiable appetite; my misgivings about him are not in any way diminished by his conduct in the campaign to date. One yearns for him to overstep the bounds of decency in some illuminating way that will suddenly give a turn to the campaign in favor of Ford, but one fears that Carter is too smart, and managed by too many intelligent people, to permit that illuminating moment. If he is elected and the Republicans do not pick up substantial strength in the House, I cannot conceive of circumstances combining during the next two years in such a way that I would want to stay to face the electorate once more in 1978. I feel jaded and ineffective, and the toll of the life I lead on my personal values and my family's peace of mind is beginning to tell.

I have an uneasy feeling about my own race this year, in that I find it very difficult to get emotionally involved in any way. Mike Macaluso, a small businessman who runs a collision business in the city of Rochester and who has made any name he has through picketing X-rated movies and supporting the right-to-life movement, insists on identifying me as a liberal and on putting more substantive stress on his Conservative Party endorsement than his Democratic endorsement. I find the Democratic leaders are considerably less enthusiastic about his candidacy and assume that, although there is little interest in the race . . . , I will eventually get somewhere around 60 percent of the vote.[13]

13. Conable received 64 percent of the vote.

December 1, 1976

The campaign period, the election, and the postelection period have not been times to gladden one's heart. . . . I debated [Macaluso] several times, and three themes emerged: (1) that I have persistently voted for high deficits, thus robbing the American people of their savings via inflation; (2) that, for some reason probably related to my lack of patriotism or understanding, I am anxious to turn the Panama Canal over to a Marxist government; (3) that I have been persistent in efforts to give special trade concessions to the Soviet Union so that American technology and resources can be diverted into aiding [the Soviets] with their destructive military buildup. As I said at one point during the campaign, "I am used to having my judgment questioned, but not my honesty or my patriotism." I thought he was simply mistaken about me early in the campaign and tried to explain my record in the earlier debates. In a debate on public television, however, he "zapped" me in a way which led me to believe that he was not amenable to reason or explanation, so in subsequent appearances, limited in number, I took him on more directly and more vigorously. The Democratic officials of our area all told me they were voting for me.

His success in receiving the Conservative endorsement as well as the Democratic led me to believe that the Conservative Party really wants to defeat me and has made me feel somewhat bitter about their use of the word "conservative." With the demise of Senator Buckley, who was defeated by Daniel Patrick Moynihan, perhaps the Conservative Party of New York will peacefully go out of existence. They came into being as [an] organized reaction to Javits and Rockefeller, and the departure of these two estimable liberals from the New York scene will doubtless give them little reason for cohesion hereafter.

My relations with Buckley during the campaign were tense, although they were also very modest. I was angry that the Conservative Party endorsed my Democratic opponent, and so I was determined not to be active in Buckley's support in any event. He asked me, when he announced his candidacy for reelection, to stand on the platform with him in New York City at the time of his announcement. I refused to do so, saying that I would agree only if he would agree to back President Ford. Since he was not prepared to do this, I therefore did not stand up with him. Subsequently, he was asked if he was going to endorse me. He replied that the way such things worked was that I must ask him for his endorsement, and he would doubtless confer it. I did not ask him. Some of my Republican county chairmen told him when he came through that I was a popular politician in the area and that he needed me a good deal more than I needed him. Thus, when reporters in Rochester asked him if he would support the Conservative-endorsed Macaluso or the Republican-endorsed Conable, he did not hesitate but said that he considered me a national asset and that he would support me.

Although there was no quid pro quo for this statement on his part, I decided that it would be expedient for me to at least appear with him on the platform, and so I introduced him from the rear of the train when he whistle-stopped through Batavia, New York. The burden of my remarks in introducing him was that he was a man of sufficient personal integrity not to have been corrupted by the Washington scene and that he was the same low-key, unassuming fellow he had been when we sent him to Washington six years before. I had declined, however, to introduce him from the rear of the train when he went through Rochester, preferring to limit my apparent support of him only to my hometown of Batavia. I must say that he did well in his debates with Moynihan, who, for all his creative and lively spirit, appeared on the campaign trail to be a traditional jowl-shaking party hack rather than a man of grace and an intellectual figure. Buckley kept his dignity and returned Moynihan's cheap shots with composure. On the basis of the debates, I would have voted for Buckley, but knowing the two men and their potential from other parts of their records, I finally, quietly and without telling anyone, voted for Moynihan, as did most of the members of my family. I look forward to working with him, having some confidence that he will be the same creative type of person in the difficult environment of the Senate that he was in some of his earlier incarnations.

It seemed improbable that the president had much chance of winning when the campaign began, but as he surged in the polls, despite a pedestrian and inarticulate performance in the debates, I got caught up in the drama and dynamics to the point where I thought he had a good chance. I leaned on his staff very hard to get him to Rochester, feeling that it would be a considerable boost for us in our area if he were to come through. He came in a drenching rain to the Rochester airport a few days before the election, acting like a man possessed, performing the presidential candidate's role to the hilt, and evoking a crowd response of warmth and support that would have gotten any politician's heart.[14]

Election night was a strange combination of personal sadness that my friend had come so close yet had lost; of anxiety as to the uncertainty a Carter administration, based on so little commitment, would bring to at least the early part of the next four years; and relief that I would no longer have to struggle in the mixed role of supporting a minority president in a hostile congressional

14. Ford won Monroe County but lost New York State.

atmosphere. It really has not been a very happy or comfortable time, even after the demise of Richard Nixon, for Republicans in the Congress. Opposition, constructive or destructive, comes more naturally to a minority in Congress, and I am not sure after all these years that it also doesn't come more naturally to Republicans under any circumstance. It occurs to me that Jimmy Carter, regardless of his personal intentions, will be subject to sufficient liberal pressure from his primary constituency and from the Democratic coalition in Congress so that he will inflict more government on the American people during the coming few years, thus bringing about a reaction at the polls in 1978 and 1980 which will be the greatest Republican opportunity since 1966. I am determined, if this predictable reaction actually comes to full flower, to see that it is not simply reactionary: that the Republicans are sufficiently organized and adequately reflective of their constituency so that a broadly based group of candidates will be brought to power in 1978 rather than screaming right-wingers anxious only to denounce and destroy. Since the quiet middle-class folk, those who abhor politics, who pride themselves on splitting their ticket, but who make up the bulk of the natural Republican constituency, have retreated into their caves to lick their wounds following Richard Nixon's betrayal of them, they will have to be carefully nurtured and coaxed forth if we are not to have the heirs of the 1978 reaction be only that ideological fragment who seems to become the caretakers during periods of Republican disaster.

December 13, 1976

The old Republican leadership met with Jimmy Carter during his last visit to Washington and had an interesting if indeterminate exchange with him. He is reported by the press to have announced his intention to meet with the Republicans as well as the Democrats and to have been warned against it by Tip O'Neill, who described us as "the enemy." Nonetheless, he gave about an hour one afternoon in the east front room under the front stairs to meeting with those members of the old Republican leadership who were around, including five or six from the House and three or four from the Senate.

The whole meeting was very general in tone. [It] opened with remarks of his in which he said, among other things, that he "wanted our advice, needed our support, would welcome our criticism." In rejoinder, John Rhodes made a statement for the assembled Republicans to the effect that we intended to support him when he was right and that it was entirely possible that he would get more support from the Republicans than he would from some elements of his own party. [Carter] then reminisced about his period as governor of Georgia, during which he received almost always Republican support but rarely the support of his own party in the Georgia legislature. I assume there were about three Republicans in the Georgia legislature, and they had little to lose from supporting him.

A number of individuals had courses of action to urge on him, John Anderson, for instance, telling him that he should take a strong and early look at the organization of the Congress since he would be hard put to reorganize the executive branch unless the reorganization of the Congress was concurrently pressed. [Carter] then said the one substantive thing of our discussion: that his expectation was that he would reorganize the executive branch in cooperation with the Congress over a period of time and easy steps, rather than being the kind of president who would spring a total plan on the Congress without plenty of prior consultation. I got the impression that he had very little concrete in mind but that he was beginning to face the realities of accomplishment and to be aware that he was going to have to deal with a difficult Congress and a lot of vested interests, even in his primary campaign goal of reorganization of the government.

After the meeting was over, I introduced myself to him and he immediately identified me as a man he had campaigned against and told me how delightful he felt Midge Costanza was both as an ally and as a person. He did not mention any job pending for her. My general impression of him was that he is an attractive and articulate man, very self-confident about his abilities and his capacity to control the events affecting the presidency, but with comparatively modest understanding of the complexity of the goals he has set for himself.

For three weeks I have quietly tried to help Dick Schulze of Pennsylvania and Bill Gradison of Ohio in their efforts and desires to take the vacancies on the Ways and Means minority left by the defeated Don Clancy and the retirement of Herman Schneebeli. In each case, there were three possible candidates from those states for the Ways and Means slots, and it is my understanding the Committee on Committees has settled on these two. They are of sufficiently high quality, particularly Gradison, so that I have the feeling the Ways and Means minority is going to be an oasis blooming in the desert. We now have a number of highly qualified and intelligent members, diverse in their views, but unusually high in ability and articulacy. We have been so successful in attracting strong people, as a matter of fact, that I am afraid we may have created a vacuum in the Republican Party in some other important committees. For me, though, it will be not only a pleasure but a challenge to lead such a highly qualified group of congressmen in such a vital area of congressional jurisdiction. This and other developments have led me to feel that I may have greater reason for enthusiasm about my own role during the next two years than I have had for some time.

The Republican Party organized this past week. . . . There was no challenge to John Rhodes, Bob Michel, or John Anderson. Since I am required by the rules of the party to make a choice between continuing in the elected leadership or moving to the ranking minority membership of Ways and Means, I did not seek reelection as Policy chairman, thus opening up the race between Lou Frey and Del Clawson, the man who challenged me three years ago when I was first elected Policy chairman. I seconded Lou's nomination both since he is a friend of mine and because he is also a nonideologue, despite a conservative voting record. I also find him bright, attractive, and one of the future leaders of the Republican Party. Del Clawson defeated him by a vote of 71 to 63. I know this is upsetting to John Rhodes, who had privately expressed to me the opinion [that] Del Clawson was probably too negative to be a good Policy chairman, and I watched John carefully to see that he moved surreptitiously to talk with Bob Michel after the results of the Policy chairman election had been announced.

The next vote up was on the choice of the person to fill Lou's place as Research chairman. The contestants for that race were Marjorie Holt [MD], currently chairman of the Republican Study Group, and Frenzel. I had no formal part in this race, but I was strongly for Frenzel, fearing that Marjorie's election as well as Del Clawson's would be taken as a sign the Republican Party was leaning sharply to the right. Apparently, John Rhodes's surreptitious conversation with Bob Michel had to do with the same fear, because after seconding speeches had been made for Frenzel, Bob Michel rose and in a very strongly worded speech supported Frenzel, saying that he wanted the leadership to be representative of the Republican Party. It is my assessment that this speech probably changed as many as fifteen fuzzy votes from Marjorie Holt, who is personally popular, to Frenzel. The result was that Frenzel won by a comfortably wide margin and will become the Research chairman. He will be excellent in that role. I have a very strong feeling of friendship for Frenzel, who has been supportive in every sense since he came on the Ways and Means Committee. He is extremely bright, accurate, and articulate to a degree that few members of the Congress can claim.

Conable is at first pleasantly surprised by Jimmy Carter, especially his adroit use of symbolism and public relations, but he soon sours on the new president, seeing him as excessively political and a perpetual candidate surrounded by mediocre yes-men. His old challenger Midge Costanza arrives in the White House from Rochester and roils the waters. Eyes roll at President Carter's proposal for a $50-per-person tax rebate. Conable's service on the Budget Committee is profoundly unsatisfying. The Carter energy program, which the president has compared to the "moral equivalent of war," passes the House, but its languid legislative journey reveals weaknesses in the president's style.

Conable the moralist, the self-described "old fud" (though he was only fifty-four years old), regretted the careerist ethos he detected in younger members of Congress. Given his strict limits on campaign contributions, his practice of paying for the printing of his own newsletters, and his donation of speech-making honoraria, he was beginning to feel like a man who just wasn't made for these times.

Lamenting the breakdown of the Strategic Arms Limitation Talks (SALT), Conable once again exhibited his foreign policy realist streak, as he had done earlier with his defense of Nixon's détente with the Soviet Union and opening to China, his support of most-favored-nation status for Romania, and his respect for Henry Kissinger. Obviously, he was no longer the youthful pacifist at Cornell, but neither was he comfortable with what he believed to be a bankrupting arms race and the Reagan Right's Manichean view of the world.

February 18, 1977

The 95th Congress is off to what seems to me to be a uniquely slow start. The whole purpose of our organizing in December, which we do now as a matter of law, is to get many of the preliminaries out of the way that would permit us to spend the first two months of a new Congress actually working on committee work and getting something into the pipelines for full floor consideration. Untoward deliberation and many personnel disputes among the Democrats frustrated this design, and we are still finding the one or two sparse bills available for consideration during the week unaccountably and unexpectedly eliminated, leaving us sometimes without any real substantive legislation to consider during the entire legislative week, even though it is now after the middle of February. We do not have recesses—or, as they are now called, "home work periods"—in any greater degree than we had in earlier Congresses, but just the same amount of time in Washington without any legislative activity of any sort. A certain amount of this is due to the newness of the Democratic leadership in both houses, I suppose, but I have nonetheless been disappointed in the lack of decisiveness of the [Tip] O'Neill [MA]–[Jim] Wright [TX]–[John] Brademas [IN] leadership. In my opinion, they constitute the strongest potential of Democratic leaders for the House since I have been in Congress, in touch with all elements of the Democratic Party and tough, articulate partisans. They should be nothing if not decisive.

In contrast to the poor performance on the part of the new Democratic leaders of the Congress, it seems to me that Jimmy Carter has been doing very well so far. Of course, he has not been called upon to do much more than set the tone of his administration and try to establish the pattern of its outward appearances. A great president is going to be determined by his ability to organize the country to deal with the nation's needs, and by the reaction of him and his team to the inevitable crises that occur in the modern world, both internally and externally. Nonetheless, his public relations are superb, and he has seen with a clear eye of an outsider many possibilities for symbolic acts and expressions that will have a special meaning to the American people. . . . I do not believe he has any fixed idea of how to run the country, nor does he have any program measures that are either carefully thought out or historically crystallized. This may be his greatest weakness—his tendency to want to wing it on everything that comes up—but of course, many of us who have been dealing with traditional Democratic politics for some time are just as glad that he is not locked into the pattern, as an insider would have been.

Except for the meeting with the House Republican leadership early in December and the initial reception he held at the White House two days after his inauguration, I have not had the chance to meet the president or to work with him. When I went to the postinaugural reception at the White House, all he could think of to say to me was, "Well, I won Rochester anyway, didn't I?" I affirmed that he did, not telling him about Monroe County, and that was the extent of the conversation. I don't expect that I will have much chance to develop a meaningful relationship, nor am I yearning for one, since my role will now be almost entirely congressional. At this stage, however, giving the devil his due, I think he is doing very well, and I hope he continues it.

The Ways and Means Committee has been plunged into consideration of the Carter economic package.[1] This package will be in markup later today, and the advent of substantive decision in the committee is one of the reasons why I am finally starting this journal entry after a long gray period. . . . A substantial part of this package has gone to Ways and Means, since it involves $50 rebates to almost everyone and a few sops to business in the form of [an] increased investment tax credit and a new jobs credit proposal which has been rejected by virtually everyone.

It is apparent that the pay raise is going to go through and that the majority party people, who clearly have the responsibility for that, are going to try to impose an ethics code as a condition, hoping to buy public favor in this way. Ethics codes are usually disasters for people like me, who take them seriously and hew to the line on the requirements. They have very little effect on the rascals. The current Democratic majority in the Congress seems to feel that almost any outrageous burglary can be committed in the name of ethics, judging from the way they performed after the Wayne Hays affair, at which time they pooled all our allowances and, in effect, doubled their economic value to us, and judging from a proposal now floating around which would require people to give up their office slush-fund accounts in return for an additional $5,000 allowance. This latter proposal is equivalent to paying everybody $5,000 to be good: perhaps acceptable Skinner psychology, but questionable public ethics. In the meantime, we have agreed to put some money into a Korean investigation, which probably is money wasted, since the Korean scandals reach into the high levels of the Democratic Party, and I cannot believe the investigation will be a serious one for this reason.[2] At least I shall be very surprised and very reassured if anything ever comes of the Korean investigation beyond the possible indictment of a few of the expendable mediocrities already in public notice, like poor Bob Leggett of California.[3]

1. The package comprised tax cuts for individuals and businesses, government-subsidized employment, and a $50-per-person tax rebate.

2. The Korean equivalent of the CIA was suspected of passing money through an intermediary to as many as thirty members of Congress in exchange for their support of a stronger military relationship between South Korea and the United States. Only one member of Congress, Representative Richard Hanna (D-CA), served prison time for his role in the "Koreagate" scandal.

3. Leggett was never indicted for his role in Koreagate. He retired at the end of this Congress.

February 19, 1977

Right on schedule, we completed the work on the tax part of the president's stimulus package in Ways and Means Thursday night. We did not even have to stay late, and I arrived in time to do the Brookings seminar speech before 8:00 p.m. Thursday was a long day, however, particularly for me, [and I] did not perform well because I did not have a clear idea of what I wanted to do, nor did I feel terribly emotionally involved in the subject matter of the stimulus package. As a matter of fact, the same thing could be said about almost every member of the committee. The typical Republican, I used too long a word to be readily understood by the television audience as I described the work of the committee outside the door of the hearing room and before the cameras Thursday night. The word I used was "lassitude." I would have done better to have called the whole performance "ho-hum."

The proposal which drew the lightning, if anything can be said to have done that, was the so-called rebate plan. It was not in fact a tax rebate, since we eliminated that class of taxpayers making over $25,000, after a small phaseout above that level, and since a very substantial part of the money to be sent out goes to people who are not taxpayers but rather Social Security recipients, black lung recipients, SSI[4] recipients, [and] recipients of aid to families with dependent children.

I discovered a number of Democrats not only lukewarm about passing out so much money in such a questionable way but some actually against it, notably Charles Vanik and Sam Gibbons. Nobody expressed any great optimism about the impact on the economy of such a "shoveling of money out of airplanes," as I described it during the hearings. A number of different Republicans on the committee made motions against different aspects of the president's program, and on final passage, eight, including myself, voted against reporting the bill to the House floor, but our major effort was against the rebate itself. Al Ullman apparently was very nervous about this and sent John Martin[5] around to talk to all the individual Democrats about the great concern of the president and the chairman for passage of the rebate part of the plan. As a result, when it appeared that the vote was going to be extremely close, he was able to persuade both Vanik and Gibbons to shift their votes. I had an understanding with Skip Bafalis of Florida—who has 650,000 constituents, 400,000 of whom are drawing Social Security—to vote with us if we needed his vote. But it was apparent that even

4. Supplemental security income.
5. Chief counsel and staff director of Ways and Means.

with his voting with us, we were going to lose by one vote. I told him to go ahead and vote the way he wanted, and so he supported the rebate when the roll call finally came. We lost by three votes, thanks to the shift by Vanik and Gibbons. That probably was the high-water mark of opposition to the rebate; once on the House floor, most Democrats will shrug their shoulders and decide to support their new leader, however unenthusiastic they may be about the substance of his proposal. The Senate has no record of opposition to uneconomic giveaways.

February 23, 1977

We continue to have a sticky time with the proposed ethics code. The Obey Commission[6] has followed the usual practice of non sequiturs, reporting a $5,000 increase in district office allowance as a condition for the termination of office slush funds. This seems to characterize the Democrats generally in the area of congressional reform: every time a scandal is disclosed, they dip further into the public treasury for usually irrelevant new additions to our allowances, the theory apparently being that if we are made sufficiently opulent by salary increases and increased allowances, we will no longer be tempted to do anything crooked. I cannot quarrel much with the provision that puts a 15 percent limitation on the amount of outside income that can be earned in relationship to the salary we are receiving. This will hurt the lawyers and the orators, while exceptions are made for farmers and the owners of small family businesses. In view of the size of the salary and the pressure of congressional business, outside earned income should not be the issue it once was. The only misgivings I have . . . [are] that once again we are putting the emphasis on election to Congress of people with unearned income, who are in no way cramped by limitations on the money that can be earned by the impecunious but vigorous younger people.

Another singular provision of the Obey report prohibits the sending out of newsletters under the frank if the printing is not paid for by the public. In other words, anyone like me who puts his own money into the newsletter will be prohibited from using the frank on it, hereafter forcing me to do it at the taxpayers' expense. Crooks will still be crooks, while people who lean over backward to observe strong personal ethical codes and to subsidize their service with their personal resources, where possible, will be further harassed in the future.

My old opponent Midge Costanza[7] continues to get considerable press attention as she shoots off her face in the same manner she used to around City Hall

6. Named for Representative David Obey (D-WI).

7. Assistant to the president for public liaison.

in Rochester. I thought it was evidence of inexperience and foolishness, at first, and that she would be cut down to size very quickly by the sophisticated Washington press corps and the jungle that usually obtains inside the White House. Now I am not sure that Midge is not playing it brilliantly: she may very well be making an issue of herself, knowing that she can never survive as a sheep; taking a high-silhouette position in attacking Hamilton Jordan[8] and others in the White House openly; and relying on the protections of Jimmy Carter himself rather than on the tender mercies of her colleagues. I do not have any doubt that, as a meek and quiet sheep, she would quickly be led to the slaughter, if only by those who coveted the proximity of her office to the Oval Office. We will see if she can carry it off.[9]

Incidentally, my own relations with Midge seem to be on the upswing. She has told members of the press corps that she feels I am a fine man and probably that she was justified in running against me only because I belonged in the cabinet rather than in the Congress. I have heard this routine before and so do not take it very seriously, but it is taken by others as evidence of her goodwill to me. I did call her last week at a critical juncture to urge her to tell the president that he should rely more on Republicans if he wants to undercut Jack Brooks[10] [D-TX] in seeking the reorganization powers [that] Jack has so far indicated he wants to frustrate. Shortly thereafter (although I do not believe it was as a result of my call), Carter did have a number of Republicans down to the White House and secured their support for the reorganization procedures that he has wanted ever since he indicated his first priority would be the reorganization of the executive branch of the government.

March 19, 1977

It seems that most of the meetings that are going on at the White House are not with the president himself, as they used to be with Ford and even with Nixon, but with staffers who do the talking and indicate their innocence of congressional ways, then at some point in the meeting step back to allow the president himself to make his usual generous and gracious remarks, only to depart a few minutes after his arrival. Congressmen and particularly senators are finding their

8. Presidential adviser and later chief of staff.

9. For a pre-postmortem on Costanza's White House tenure written just before her resignation, see Judy Bachrach, "The View from the Ground Floor," *Washington Post*, July 26, 1978.

10. Chairman of the House Government Operations Committee.

noses out of joint as a result of what they think is a very casual massaging by the president himself, and they constantly express dark doubts that he doesn't understand the issues and doesn't wish to become involved in them to any degree of dialogue. In the meantime, Carter continues to talk to the American people in a most effective public relations way, going to Massachusetts to spend the night with an ordinary family, attending town meetings, having open lines to the American public in which a few people are allowed to ask questions out of many millions who try. And the results of all this personal activity on his part are beginning to show up in dramatic increases in his popularity at the polls.

In the work of the Ways and Means Committee, so far, I have been more than satisfied with the thoughtfulness and industry of Bill Gradison. Dick Schulze, on the other hand, appears to be something of a grandstander, and unpredictable to boot. My relations with Frenzel continue to improve, and I find him my closest ally on the committee on almost all matters. My relations with Steiger continue tense because he is so explosively and almost belligerently independent and unpredictable, sometimes taking very conservative stands and other times taking stands which surprise even the Democrats.

I find myself resisting strenuously efforts to put all possible congressional-related expenditures on the backs of the taxpayers, as this weekend the Wednesday Study Club [met] in Fredericksburg, [and] most of my colleagues put in vouchers for their hotel and meal costs, something that I probably will refuse to do simply because I don't like the feel of it.

Well, so it goes, as rules and regulations change, the old fuds like me find themselves resenting and resisting the new morality which makes service in Congress more a career and less an expression of citizen responsibility. I suppose eventually I'll adjust, but with me, it will take longer than for some of these bright-eyed young people with their highly developed moral sense who think of morality in terms of special interests rather than in terms of the public they are supposed to serve, not exploit.

April 1, 1977

Ways and Means continues to do very little. I have spent most of the past two weeks in Budget Committee, a locus generally unfamiliar to me and considerably less satisfying than Ways and Means Committee work when we have something to do. There are a number of reasons why Budget is not satisfying. First, my Republican colleagues view it with as little interest as I do. It is partly because Del Latta of Ohio, the ranking minority member, is essentially a lazy, negative fellow with no intention of spending a lot of time in complicated or constructive work. He is almost a prototype of the leather-lunged honker, occasionally working himself up to a frenzy of denunciation and negative enthusiasm, and the rest of the time performing as little as possible. Jim Broyhill [NC], the number-two man, is a decent fellow, capable of constructive action but very little interested in it and quite involved elsewhere. I am the number-three man, having moved up dramatically since I was put on the committee two years ago. Next junior to me is Marjorie Holt, a nice but average sort of girl, very interested in military affairs because of her constituency in suburban Washington, identifying with our Republican right wing, although she herself is pragmatic about matters affecting her constituency.

The committee as a whole is considerably less effective than it was when Brock Adams [D-WA], the new secretary of transportation, was the chairman. Bob Giaimo of Connecticut, the new chairman, is a man of reasonable ability, while Brock was highly competent, clearly committed to the development of the budget process, and highly regarded by his colleagues in the Congress. Many of the Democratic members of the committee do not belong there under any definition of the Budget Committee's role. Jim Wright, the new majority leader, is an active member, given to making his studied and perfervid orations in behalf of the Democratic leadership and seeming to me more posture than position most of the time.

Bob Leggett of California, the man with the remarkable personal life, as disclosed by the *Washington Post*,[11] and the mark of extinction on him to the extent the Republican Party can put it there, brings his expertise from the Armed Services Committee for the apparent purpose of reducing the military budget, and despite his apparent intelligence, [he does] not giv[e] very high priority to the work of the Budget Committee. Parren Mitchell is there also, an intense and bright black from Baltimore who is anathema to most of my Republican colleagues (I suspect primarily because he is black) but is more effective than he is credited in behalf of such questionable activities as public-service employment and other government jobs programs of liberal hue.

One of the most effective junior Democrats is Butler Derrick [SC], a southerner without, apparently, ideological bias and [with] a willingness not only to think for himself but to work hard on the Budget Committee's affairs. Another recent arrival who does a great deal of talking but with undemonstrated ef-

11. Leggett maintained two families and also had an affair with Suzi Park Thomson, a central figure in the Koreagate scandal. Richard Pearson, "Ex-Rep. Robert Leggett Dies," *Washington Post*, August 17, 1997.

fectiveness is a man by the name of [Jim] Mattox, from Texas, who replaced Alan Steelman from the Dallas area. Liz Holtzman is pretty good, given her prejudices and her unvarnished liberalism. I expect Norman Mineta [CA] will be a valuable member on the liberal side, although he has done very little so far. I find myself drawn more and more to pleasant regards for Otis Pike, one of the ultimate pragmatists and a man of grace and wit, even if he is only occasionally effective.

We have some conceptual problems on the Budget Committee. First is the obvious fact that none of us takes much interest in any committee on which we can serve for a maximum of only four years. This rule, part of the Budget Reform Act, [was] designed to prevent the creation of a power elite which could come into effective conflict with the old-line power elites of Ways and Means and Appropriations. Fortunately, nothing incapable of becoming a power elite can attract the attention of high-quality people in a bunch of power-mongers like the House of Representatives. As if this structural problem were not sufficient, the requirement that five members of Ways and Means and five members of Appropriations serve on the Budget Committee ensures serious gaps in the participation of the committee, since these two front-line committees meet constantly. When there is a choice between a Ways and Means Committee meeting of general importance and a Budget Committee meeting, I always choose the Ways and Means meeting. I know people will be counting on my judgment and experience there. I never will have a chance to give judgment and experience in Budget.

My wife has just finished her book,[12] I hope for the last time, and should get it off to the printer. Dealing with the myths of equal education for women at Cornell, I believe it will be a credit for her and to her industry. If I ever had any temptation to write a book, the tyranny of this effort over her time and her energy is enough by itself to dissuade me. She has worked long into the night, day after day revising, rewriting, correcting, checking, editing, and letter writing. I can see that it takes a special type of person to be able to undergo the self-discipline that is involved in such a protracted writing effort. I can dash off a 700-word news column in less than an hour, or a 1,300-word newsletter in less than two hours, but I am confident after watching my wife that it would fall apart very quickly if I tried to write as much as the average chapter in the normal American book.

12. Charlotte Williams Conable, *Women at Cornell: The Myth of Equal Education* (Ithaca, NY: Cornell University Press, 1977).

I was recently very distressed by the failure of SALT,[13] . . . which came quickly after the meeting of Secretary [of State Cyrus] Vance with Brezhnev and Gromyko in Moscow. It seems as though the long struggle of nine years to find modest ways in which to loose world tensions, the prodigious efforts of Henry Kissinger, of Nixon, and of Ford, have been reversed and destroyed by two months of open-mouthed diplomacy on Carter's part. Some of my Republican friends are exulting in the demise of SALT, but I feel that SALT represented the best alternative to an absolutely bankrupting arms race with the Russians. I'll expect Carter to move toward the Chinese following this failure and to use other obvious direct and confrontational strong-arm methods on the Russians, at the same time his party in Congress insists on cutting back on defense spending.

I cannot quarrel with his position on human rights—Ford probably made a mistake in not being willing to talk with Solzhenitsyn[14]—but it seems to me that our posture on the side of virtue and superficial moralization with respect to the internal affairs of other countries should be subordinate to our willingness to accept the responsibilities of diplomacy and world leadership. I am not sure. What may appear to be only the amateur hour now may in fact prove to be an important new direction and emphasis in American foreign policy. Carter appears to be extremely bright, and it may be that he thinks a good deal more than he is given credit for. The Russians may just be testing the new boy on the block, as bullies always do. Until these possibilities become more apparent, I think we can be pardoned if we worry a little about slipping back into the environment of confrontation which used to characterize the Cold War. We are not as strong as we used to be during the Cold War, whether or not we have military parity with the Russians, nor are the American people willing to accept these simplistic [word missing] of military power. And all our economy needs at this point is a massive new commitment to military spending in an atmosphere of crisis to destroy the market environment forever.

May 7, 1977

Chairman Ullman shows little anxiety about any initiating role, preferring to hang back and to wait for administration initiatives. The reason for this is rooted

13. Strategic Arms Limitation Talks.

14. In mid-1975 President Ford refused to meet with exiled Russian Nobel Prize–winning writer and dissident Aleksandr Solzhenitsyn because it might endanger the policy of détente with the Soviet Union.

in the (to him) unseemly demise of the $50 rebate.[15] He was the man who led that fight for the president on the floor of the House of Representatives. To my knowledge, the president has not yet talked to him about the possibility of the rebate being withdrawn. His reasons for withdrawing the rebate are uncertain, although they were justified on many points.

First, the proposal had been prematurely made. If Jimmy Carter had waited three days for the economic statistics of December 1976 before he announced the stimulus program, he doubtless would not have gone ahead with it, since the government figures showed the very substantial upthrust in the economy and decline in unemployment during December. The intervening months had confirmed and accelerated this trend. Next, on political grounds, the rebate was not a proposal which caught fire with the public. The public apathy with the mailman's delivering a $50 check out of all the tax monies paid was rampant. Sensing this public apathy at every stage, the Congress passed the rebate by the narrowest of margins. Last, the Senate apparently had the rebate in trouble when it came to final passage after protracted and pointless deliberation on it. Howard Baker [TN], who came to Rochester to speak for me at a Republican fund-raiser, told me during the dinner and before his excellent and well-delivered speech that he and Bob Byrd [D-WV] had sat down and compared whip checks on the rebate vote, learning from cross-referencing that they had forty-nine Senate votes solidly against the rebate and as many as ten leaning against it. Byrd asked Baker if he was determined to try and defeat this proposal, which was the centerpiece of the Carter economic stimulus program, and Baker told him his intentions were ironclad. The next day Carter unexpectedly withdrew the rebate, saying, "I have changed my mind" about it. He never consulted Ullman and apparently felt he owed no obligation to Ullman, despite Ullman's earnest service in behalf of the proposal in the House.

While I don't believe Al Ullman was hurt by his stand in favor of the rebate in the House at the behest of his president, this vacillation on Carter's part, combined with the fact that Al has already been up and down the difficult issue of the gasoline tax, has made him very cautious in predicting any success for Carter's comprehensive and tax-centered energy program.[16] We will begin hearings on the energy program on May 16, with the timetable calling for its completion by the Ways and Means Committee before the Fourth of July recess.

15. In April, President Carter abandoned the rebate idea, saying that in light of changed economic circumstances, it was no longer necessary.

16. Announced by the president in a televised speech on April 18, 1977.

I am skeptical that it will move that fast, since the president's program is not only incomplete, dealing only with the conservation side of the energy equation, but it is also bound to be politically unpopular in its efforts to change the lifestyle of Americans, whose lifestyle has to them been a matter of unrestrained joy up to this time. The rebate episode, the unpopularity of a retail tax on gasoline, and Carter's vacillation on this and other issues up to this point lead us to wonder if, in his energy program, he has not included a number of bargaining positions, cheerful in the expectation that Congress will jettison them and enact only the popular parts of his proposal.

May 22, 1977

Ways and Means began, on Monday morning of this past week, the hearings on the energy program.[17] Hearings are never a place on which to base an assumption of what the committee attitudes are, because of the tendency to posture on the part of those who are only asking questions rather than supplying answers. Nevertheless, it was a matter of general surprise and, I suspect, some consternation in administration circles that the Democrats appeared to give the Carter energy proposals as tough a time as the Republicans did. I wrote a very tough statement at the outset of the hearings, receiving the characterization of a "broadside" from Al Ullman, but the mood of the hearings was as specifically negative as my statement had been, even for those who should be engaging in presumptions in favor of the leader's work.

The witness who made the worst impression of all those appearing was James Schlesinger,[18] a pedantic and dogmatic man who had a tendency to preach rather than to explain. I found his performance unattractive. I feel some sympathy for [Secretary of the Treasury] Mike Blumenthal, who carried a great deal of the burden of the denunciations, since he was the leadoff witness, inasmuch as he apparently had very little to do with the putting together of the package and thus found himself exposed without an opportunity to accept any responsibility for the end result.

[Carter] continues to have very little contact with the Congress, to apparently vacillate on the major issues, and to be unaware of how complicated they are, requiring more persistence than he seems willing to invest to get anything started. His is an odd performance in the presidency so far, almost casual in his

17. Five House committees dealt with various aspects of the administration's energy bill, with Ways and Means considering the energy taxes therein.

18. Carter's "energy czar" and later the first US secretary of energy.

relationship to government and apparently caring only about the public relations opportunity of the presidency.

June 3, 1977

This morning, all the members of the Ways and Means Committee were invited to the White House for a discussion of the energy program with President Carter. It was announced as a breakfast meeting, but when we arrived in the State Dining Room, we found only sweet rolls, orange juice, and coffee, all to be eaten standing up. The president allowed us about ten minutes for that and then called us over to an unadorned table, where he sat between Al Ullman and me and proceeded to open a general discussion of energy. He talked for about half an hour, holding a card on which a few key words were written down but obviously relying on his remarkable memory and detailed statistical grasp of the energy problem. Mike Blumenthal and Jim Schlesinger were both there but were not called on to say anything, the president doing all the talking until he opened it up for questions. Questions were all over the map, respectful but some of them quite firm in their opposition, and he fielded them with grace and wit. It was clearly a virtuoso performance.

When he finished his formal presentation, he asked Al Ullman to speak, and Al gave quite a point-by-point analysis of where the president was going to have problems with the program. The president then looked at me, although he said nothing, but obviously was expecting me to respond also. I thanked him for his hospitality and said that we welcomed his tender of partnership, and all that implied, and complimented him on his ability to speak to the American people. Then I said that that ability would have to be more pointed than simply a description of the need, because we congressmen were confused about letters from constituents who said, "Support the president's energy program, but don't let the price of gasoline get any higher." He laughed at that. I then said that he shouldn't be upset that we debate his program at some length because we were the only branch of government that could do such things, inasmuch as when he came down with a recommendation, everybody in the executive branch had to march to the same drum thereafter. He laughed at that also, because Al Ullman had made a point of telling him how Brock Adams had contradicted his plan for rebate. In short, in my response I said as little as I could, realizing that the Republicans present were waiting for me to give away the store or to signal that I was willing to support more than they were willing to have me commit myself to.

After about an hour, the president said he had to go to another appointment and left Schlesinger to answer questions. The group thinned out very quickly after that, since Schlesinger has the reputation of being the "Man from Dogma" and since he does not wield presidential influence or graceful rhetoric.

June 18, 1977

During the past two weeks, we have been working on the energy tax proposal. It has been a difficult operation, tense and foreclosing of all other effort. The cost in terms of my temper, my relations to my family, my day-to-day obligations, and even in terms of my self-respect has been quite high. I mention the self-respect because I never go into an activity of this sort without feeling that I could be more effective than the bottom line proves me to be. I have had rather more cooperation with Al Ullman than I ever had on any single measure during the 94th Congress.

There has been a cost in terms of backlash among the Republicans. I feel in some cases that I should have stonewalled a little more than I was willing to do. The Republicans seem generally to break down on issues of cooperation around pretty close to a fifty-fifty basis, with Steiger, Frenzel, and Gradison more willing to cooperate than others, but some others are coming along on individual issues and items on which they do not feel strongly. The noncooperators are almost always Bafalis and Ketchum; on the pure energy issues, Archer and, by proxy, Crane. Crane continues to be a problem by his nonparticipation, wasting his intelligence in some other form or simply coming and doing very little to use his brains on the subject at hand. . . . Jim Martin, an extremely bright man with a Ph.D. in chemistry from North Carolina, has come into his own on this bill to some extent, since his knowledge of industrial processes has permitted him to pinpoint problems with the administration bill, a proposal obviously put together by amateurs.

The first couple of days, nothing was accomplished except the elimination of the gasoline tax as a possibility and the elimination of the rebate on small, fuel-efficient cars. . . . Another interesting aspect of this measure has been the development of the "gas-guzzler" tax. Although we eliminated the rebate on fuel-efficient cars, fearing it would appear that we were taxing American cars to subsidize the importation of efficient foreign autos, at the time this part of the measure was brought up, I was reluctant to see it killed completely because we had, until then, only dealt with the gasoline tax and the rebates. I encouraged Al Ullman to meet with the auto industry, and [I] attended the meeting, telling the auto people they ought to get something with which they could live, rather than play Russian roulette with whether or not they had one more vote than necessary to kill the measure completely. I told them that the gas-guzzler tax was a terrible idea and that unless we were able to come up with a better form of tax than the

Carter administration had proposed, they might very well find themselves in a position in which the government was helping General Motors at the expense of Chrysler and Ford, putting a dimension of economic pressure on them that they would not be able to live with. The auto industry took this effort on my part with bad grace, and so did some of my Republican colleagues, who thought we should have moved to kill it and to embarrass Carter by, at that point, appearing to destroy every portion of his energy recommendations. We held a meeting of the minority in my office shortly thereafter and gave them a chance to blow off, but by then, they had cooled down at least to some degree.

Tuesday night of this past week, with great reluctance, I went to the fund-raising dinner for the New York State Republican Committee in New York City. This year they were honoring Nelson Rockefeller for his past service, and a great deal of arm-twisting was done by Dick Rosenbaum and Jack Wydler of our congressional delegation to get the Republicans of Congress to come. We all sat in a group at a table right in front of the speaker's dais in a location which should have been the best in the house at the Waldorf but which proved to be the worst, since all the earnest Republicans in New York State leaned in our mashed potatoes, kicked our chairs out from under us, clawed and scratched their way through us in order to shake hands with Gerald Ford, Nelson Rockefeller, Henry Kissinger, Bill Brock, Howard Baker, and the other attendant Republican dignitaries.

Ford was sitting directly in front of me and proved [to be] in a friendly and chatty mood. His speech was the usual earnest and inarticulate expression of Republican outrage which he seems to make constantly nowadays. I find it difficult to take anyone who plays as much golf as he does very seriously as a force for the future. The only person all evening who spoke well was that empty oilcan Malcolm Wilson,[19] who introduced Nelson with the full flower of his oratory. I have not been to this dinner for at least six years, and it will be all right with me if I don't get to go for another six. Incidentally, Jack Kemp was fiercely disappointed that the members of Congress were not individually introduced after the effort he had made to get there. He doesn't seem to realize how irrelevant congressmen are to state politics.

July 16, 1977

June was about the toughest month I have had since I have been in Congress. Ways and Means, operating on a very tight schedule, ran from 9:30 to 5:30 every

---

19. The former lieutenant governor (and briefly governor) of New York, defeated by Governor Hugh Carey in 1974.

weekday of the month, with an abbreviated noon hour. It was not unpleasant, but it was exhausting, and when the Fourth of July recess came, I spent three or four days mostly looking at the ceiling and recharging my batteries. I do not remember ever having been so tired. Although it was not unpleasant, it was somewhat tense, with the decisions coming in fast succession. The Republicans did not try to obstruct or to extend the discussion and, on many issues, voted all over the map rather than trying to have a unified position. I was relaxed with Al Ullman, who seemed to appreciate it, telling him when we had votes for his position and when we did not, rather than leaving him guessing. He got pretty much what he wanted, and although the newspapers early in the month stated that we were "ravaging" the Carter proposal, the president got pretty close to what he wanted as well.

Twice during the month, the Ways and Means Committee went down to call on the president at "breakfast," a euphemism for stale sweet rolls, a small glass of orange juice, and stand-up coffee. At both meetings with the president, Republicans asked him why he was not in favor of production incentives to try to get more oil and gas. The first meeting bore his responding by denouncing the oil companies and saying that they were getting rich and had no reason to need any further incentives. It was a populist diatribe, surprising for its vehemence and somewhat cowing to the listeners. After we had dropped out the gas tax and the rebate for fuel-efficient cars, watering down also the gas-guzzler tax, Jody Powell[20] gave an analysis of the president's attitude, which [was] that he felt we had all sold out to the special interests. It was an intemperate overreaction.

Because the response among the committee was one of injured innocence and resentment of presidential vehemence, shortly thereafter Carter invited us back and, at that point, very much lowered his silhouette and his voice. His response this time to our questions about production incentives was that he felt that twenty years from now, the oil we had not taken out of the ground as a result of a crash program at this point would probably be one of our greatest national assets. It was an argument which had not surfaced before and, of course, could be used by Saudi Arabia as complete justification for keeping more of [its] oil in the ground by raising the price. The shift of position and this questionable argument left us feeling even more than before that he is a strange man, unpredictable and not always forethought[ful] about his positions.

At both these meetings, Carter paid tribute to me, saying that the Republicans had cooperated very well in trying to achieve an energy policy. Since that

20. White House press secretary.

is not necessarily the case, I tended to think this was a smart trick to try to reduce my credibility with my Republican followers, who invariably looked at me
flinty-eyed and squinty-eyed to hear that I was cooperating with the president,
and one could almost hear them wondering to themselves if I was making deals
on the side or behind their backs.[21]

October 23, 1977

Since the last journal entry [September 26], we have had a sense in Congress
of the Carter administration falling apart. Certainly, the partisanship of his opposition is so judging events in the interim, reflecting increasing partisanship
addressed to Carter himself and less to the Democrats in Congress. The public
acts vaguely uneasy but still continues to hope great things for the president,
whom it obviously likes and wishes to see succeed. His attention focuses first on
one issue and then on another, seeing nothing through to fruition and leaving
the general impression that while he is thinking of something else, nothing gets
done on the next-to-last item to which he addressed his attention. This impression arises from the general assessment that Jimmy Carter himself is the only
decision maker in his administration and that he has brought into the White
House a team sufficiently inexperienced, young, and lacking in judgment so that
nothing can progress without his personal attention. As this idea gets increasing
currency in the country, uneasiness mounts, and just in the past month or so, it
has been apparent that the president himself is aware of the deficiencies in his
follow-through and the depth of his team. So he is struggling harder to create
new spectaculars for the distraction of those disappointed. This weekend, he is
off on a trip around the United States with the usual public relations overtones
and with disturbing echoes of his earlier stridency in the denouncing of the
special interests who are fighting his energy program.

The energy conference is moving very slowly, with the House members reflecting the pro-Carter bias they displayed when the larger ad hoc committee[22]
was rushing his program through the House. The Senate, of course, is always
difficult in conferences of this sort, particularly when the issue has been debated
at such length in the Senate that all those dignified and egotistical senators
have had the chance to get themselves completely committed to the point of

---

21. The Carter energy package, as modified—and including the gas-guzzler tax—was
approved by the House on August 5, 1977, by a vote of 244–177. Conable was one of 127
Republicans voting nay. Thirteen Republicans voted aye.

22. The House Ad Hoc Committee on Energy, created April 21, 1977.

view prevailing in their legislation. I think it will be a long conference and one in which there will be a lot of noisy recrimination from such emotional types as John Dingell [D-MI], Bud Brown, etc.[23]

Although I was disappointed not to be on the conference in the first place, I am dismayed that John Rhodes felt he could not appoint me but did appoint two other ranking members, Frank Horton and John Wydler, neither of whom had more involvement in the issue than the van-pooling proposal, which was not a part of either bill as they went to conference. John [Rhodes] is ostentatiously friendly to me in his personal relations but obviously considers me a competitor or a threat or something, which leaves him deviously, perhaps almost subconsciously, trying to cut me out of action that normally would be automatic, considering the positions I hold. A number of my colleagues have expressed surprise to me that I was not on the energy conference, but I guess I should be grateful.

23. The conferees were unable to reach agreement before the December recess, so an energy bill was not enacted until November 1978.

Conable urges Jack Kemp to run for governor of New York but finds that the Buffalo congressman is curiously risk-averse. Conable courts unpopularity with his Republican colleagues by taking leadership of the exiguous GOP bloc in favor of federal financing of congressional campaigns. Social Security taxes, capital gains taxes, income taxes: Ways and Means is busy. Conable issues his lengthiest assessment of his committee colleagues, the bad and the beautiful alike. Conable talks up the long-shot presidential candidacy of his old Ways and Means friend George Bush.

Conable did not hoist the banner of public financing of congressional campaigns without misgivings. He was innately skeptical of new federal programs and expenditures, and he acknowledged the argument that statutory limits on campaign spending disadvantaged challengers, who typically lack the name recognition of incumbents. But his loathing of big money in politics overrode these reservations, and he found himself making common cause with Common Cause.

Conable's latest evaluations of his Ways and Means colleagues found him in a generous mood. He was effusive about his favorite liberal Democrats—Abner Mikva, Jim Corman, and Otis Pike—and even called Jim Burke and Charles Vanik, whom he had detested for years and considered cheap demagogues, "likable."

February 11, 1978

The second session of the 95th Congress has now been under way for more than a month, and although I personally have been very busy, I cannot say that the tempo of activity indicates urgency on the part of the leadership. Clearly, the president has lowered his sights when looking at legislative targets for 1978: his perception as an incumbent is considerably more complicated than his perception used to be as a candidate, when, like my old opponent Midge [Costanza], he thought the solution to all problems was to have someone in a position of authority who would care that problems be solved. He appears to be no more effective as a problem solver now than he was shortly after his inauguration, largely because he has stubbornly refused to change his mode of operation. Other presidents have made the classic mistake of isolating themselves in the company of their previous campaign staff, young people without judgment, experience, or anything to qualify them for office but their enthusiasm for the chief. Other presidents, except Richard Nixon, usually discovered after a time that they could not run the presidency in such an artificial vacuum, that they needed to have some people of judgment who could screen out the issues not requiring their decision and could prepare them for the use of pure judgments with respect to those issues that did require their decision. Carter's White House staff seems to be telling him that he need not concern himself about the skepticism of the press or the concern of the citizens.

If he were not so bright, if he were not a speed-reader, if he were not willing to work from 5:30 in the morning until after midnight every night, he would quickly have realized that one cannot conduct the presidency alone. His very virtues prolong his isolation. Nevertheless, in due course, the White House will have clearly established a pattern during his administration of being a place of caprice, bottleneck, and unpredictability. On the basis of his public relations predilections, it is also likely to become and to remain a place apart from the government, where someone not of the government judges the rest of us for our failings. In this respect, Carter seems intent on preserving the image of the outsider, despite the fact that he has now for a year been an incumbent on the most inside job in the world. He still shows no signs of interest in persuading rather than judging, and he clearly continues to view Washington as a mess for which he has no responsibility.

I have yet to have visit my office a single member of the White House legislative liaison staff. Mike Blumenthal has called on me twice, each time coming alone and spending as much as an hour, talking in general ways and probing for an understanding of the Ways and Means Committee and the other institutions in which I serve in the Congress. He is an attractive man, somewhat aloof and ascetic, but the implication of his remarks to me is that he has as much trouble getting through to the only man who can set policy for the Carter administration as I would have were I to try to make that contact myself. Because of Blumenthal's quality, this in itself is an indictment of Carter's concept of the presidency.

I have recently been urging Jack Kemp to run for governor. He wants to run statewide so badly he can taste it. He is politically ambitious and frustrated by the patient ways of the House. I have consulted with a number of people about this, John Sears[1] and Fred Eckert included, and have concluded that Jack has a

1. Republican political strategist who managed Ronald Reagan's 1976 campaign.

better chance of winning the governorship than either [Perry] Duryea or [Warren] Anderson.[2] Ironically, one of the best reasons Jack is a favorite candidate is that he is not known. An attractive and articulate man, he has ties to the Conservative Party and a conservative image far beyond his voting record, which would give him a ready-made constituency in suburban New York City. I will leave open the question of whether he would be a better governor if elected than Anderson or Duryea, mercifully declining judgment on that point until later.

At this time, I am using him with the expectation I have that Henry Kissinger might be interested in the senatorial nomination in 1980. Jack would like to run to replace Javits, but it is possible that Kissinger would want that seat and would have an inside track in getting it because of his strong Jewish support in New York City. Everything Kissinger has done is consistent with his wanting to keep open an option of this sort after he has written his books and made his money. If Jack thinks the senatorial job will not fall in his lap in 1980, he is more likely to run for governor in 1978. Unfortunately, Jack suffers from the usual political syndrome in that he wants to be president of the United States without taking any risks on the way. Thus, at this point, he is quite uncertain whether to run or not, and I know that a number of people are pushing him to make a decision he hates to make because it involves him in a no-retreat position and may result in the loss of his House seat without his achievement of statewide office.

I find it almost amusing, and I probably am not adequately sympathetic, to find a man so ambitious and yet so unwilling to take the chances which are always involved in great stakes. Perhaps he is more realistic about his chances than I am, and in fairness to him, I am probably not adequately concerned for his own welfare and his being badly wounded by an unnecessary misstep. As of right now, I would judge him rather less likely to run than to stay in the House for another two years, hoping that something will drop in his lap at the end of that period of time. He is not a very effective member of Congress in the meantime, rarely attending meetings of the Appropriations Committee and spending more time in promotion and personal advancement than he is in legislative work. I have noticed that strong politicians with good futures normally are not very good members of Congress.

March 19, 1978
The tension of this past month has been quite debilitating for me. It seems as though I no sooner get one period of controversy behind me but some new dif-

2. Republican majority leader of the New York state senate.

ficulty springs up in which I have become if not the central figure [then] one of the more involved ones in the Congress.

The issue on which I seem to be having the most trouble is something that I probably should not be involved in at all—public financing of elections. The federal election law requires some amendment and extension. The Democrats have chosen this occasion to sharply curtail the amount of money that a political party can give to its candidates. This has a potentially devastating effect on Republicans, who raise their money in mailed fund-raisers in small contributions from a large number of contributors. The Republicans have a very large campaign chest on hand for the 1978 elections. The Democrats have now decided, since they do not, that they will so sharply curtail party contributions that a substantial part of the Republican war chest would remain in the bank account because it could not be legally spent. This has not only caused exasperation but fierce cries of outrage from the Republicans, who have been engaging in floor harassing tactics in an effort to call the president's attention to the partisanship of the Democrats.

In this environment, Common Cause has decided to make a major push to get public financing, and the environment could not be worse. I am committed to public financing and have emerged as the Republican spokesman on the issue, leading a quavering group, a quivering and vacillating group, of comparatively weak Republicans of moderate liberal view in an effort to provide a little bipartisanship for the issue. Although there are only about twenty in number, the Common Cause people feel that we represent the balance of power, and so whatever we do has become terribly important. We are weak reeds to lean upon.

Because I am identified as the leader of this group, I am currently very unpopular among conservatives in the Republican Party and viewed as a traitor by the leadership. I sincerely believe that the leaders are wrong about the anti-Republican bias in public financing, because Republicans will have many more challengers than incumbents running for Congress in the foreseeable future, and challengers must rely on small contributions compared to incumbents. Public financing, which provides matching grants for small contributions from the public treasury, clearly is to the advantage of challengers, but it is incumbents in the Republican Party who are setting policy for the party, and since they have been through a very difficult time in which they had to spend large amounts of money, they resent anything which seems to favor the small contributors incumbents are in a position to scorn. I'm afraid, quite apart from the party interest I have in seeing public financing advance despite the majority opposition of my party, that I would appear to be a hypocrite if, following my own campaign practices, I did not try to put everything I could in the law to favor the small contributor.

March 25, 1978

During the past two weeks, a great deal of my time and even more of my stomach lining has been invested in the issue of the public financing of congressional campaigns. I think I will take the time to discuss what happened in some detail. The cast of characters includes Dave Cohen and Fred Wertheimer of Common Cause; John Rhodes and Guy Vander Jagt of the Republican leadership; myself and Dave Stockman [MI] of the apostate group of Republicans; Frank Thompson [D-NJ], chairman of the House Administration Committee; Abner Mikva, chairman of the DSG;[3] and, lurking somewhere in the background, John Brademas, the Democratic whip.

The leadership of the public financing issue on the Republican side has been in the hands of John Anderson, and the basic vehicle now being proposed is an extension of the old Anderson-Udall bill which I have cosponsored in the past. John, however, during the period of this journal entry, has been deeply involved in a primary contest testing his survival in the face of heavy right-wing contributions to a fundamentalist minister trying to wrest the nomination from him.[4] For that reason, Cohen and Wertheimer called on me and asked me if I would take a leading role in trying to organize the small group of Republicans who were alleged to support public financing. I demonstrated some reluctance, but after an appropriate mixture of pressure and persuasion, I finally was brought to the point where I did not object too much when Cohen announced in a speech in Rochester that my support of public financing was not only assured but my role a significant one.

Republican leaders in the Senate had already threatened a filibuster of sufficient dimension so that the Senate had clearly rejected public financing for this Congress. This development in the Senate was accomplished by a flannel tactic of attaching public financing monies to primary elections as well as general elections, thus securing the eternal enmity of the southerners, and so the proposal before us in the House was designed to avoid this pitfall and applied only to general elections. Thus there were two very significant limitations on the public financing bill we were considering—no primary money and no public financing for senatorial candidates.

For reasons not clear to me, but probably tactical, the public financing measure had been pulled out of the Federal Election Commission Extension Amendments in the course of the hearings on the measure in the House Ad-

---

3. Democratic Study Group.

4. Anderson won the primary by a margin of 58 percent to 42 percent.

ministration Committee. The Republican Party, through its able Congressional Campaign Committee chairman Guy Vander Jagt, had heretofore raised very large sums of money for the 1978 war chest, accomplishing this largely through a mail campaign quite different from the tactics used by the Democrats. The Republicans had large amounts of small contributions already in hand, while the Democrats were, as usual, relying on labor support to finance their candidates. Thus the Federal Election Commission Extension Amendments were pending as the bill was being made ready to report to the floor, sharply limit[ing] the amount of money which a party could give to its candidates. Had the partisan tactics of the Democrats succeeded, a very large part of the Republican war chest would still have remained in the Republican bank accounts after the election was over, because it could not have been legally given to our candidates in the proportion intended.

When it was clear that this was the strategy of Thompson and Brademas, Republican outrage knew no bounds, and the party members started displays of parliamentary tantrums on the floor of the House, which led a number of rank-and-file Democrats to believe that Thompson and Brademas had overreached themselves. At that point, I made several statements to the papers to the effect that the Democrats were, perhaps deliberately, "poisoning the well" on public financing, which it was anticipated would be offered as an amendment to the Federal Election Commission Extension Act.

The strategy of the majority of the Republicans under the Republican leadership which emerged was to try to defeat the rule, since it was known that there were sixty or seventy southerners who did not wish to consider public financing and so would vote against taking up the bill at all. We had several meetings of a group of eight or nine Republicans, the stronger of those who supported public financing, and decided that we would not vote for the rule ourselves unless assurances were given by Thompson that he would put the Republican Party back in a position similar to the one it is now in with respect to contributions from party to individual candidates. It seemed to us that we clearly were being disloyal if we supported a rule which . . . did not in any way vary the extremely restrictive contribution rules. The whole issue was to go to the Rules Committee on Monday of this past week and to hit the floor on Tuesday.

On Saturday afternoon Thompson announced that he had capitulated on the issue of contribution and expenditure limits for parties. Monday morning Vander Jagt contacted me and said that Thompson had left out an essential ingredient if the party was to have the chance to contribute to its candidates as it had before: it seems that the Federal Election Commission had been permitting us to transfer authorized aggregate contribution amounts from state parties and the National Committee to the Congressional Campaign Committee, so that a maximum of $22,500 could be given to each individual candidate. If this transferability was prohibited, only a maximum of $10,000 could be given, and since our practice was to raise all our money in the Congressional Campaign Committee and to transfer authorizations from the other two political entities, Thompson had cleverly appeared to capitulate without addressing the issue of transferability and thus had, in effect, overridden the Federal Election Commission regulation.

After another meeting of our group, of which Dave Stockman was quickly emerging as the brightest and best informed, not excepting me, we decided at 11:00 that morning that we would not support the rule unless Thompson would put in the record his assurance that transferability would still be permitted. I looked up Thompson on the floor, sat down with him, and told him this, immediately finding him unwilling to commit himself on the issue of transferability "until I've talked to my boys," apparently meaning Brademas and some of the other more partisan members of the House Administration Committee. In the meantime, Mikva—who had been giving me assurances that his entire Democratic Study Group would support not only the removal of party contribution limitations that were in the bill as it emerged from House Administration but also would support us on the issue of transferability—had gotten up a letter signed by approximately one hundred Democrats saying that they would not follow Thompson's leadership on the restrictions. Mikva and Thompson had heated words about the issue of whether or not Thompson would give way on transferability. Mikva finally told me that Thompson would and that he would put in the record his statement to that effect that night, so that before we voted on the rule the next day, we would know where we stood.

With that assurance, I went to the Rules Committee, where the cosponsor of the public financing amendment, Tom Foley of Washington, was testifying in favor of public financing. While I was waiting to testify, Dick Bolling of the Rules Committee gestured to me and took me into the next room to ask me about the public financing bill. I sketched its outlines to him, and he said, "It appears to me that it's not ready; I'm going to see the Speaker." He came back later and told me, "I don't think it's ready, but the Speaker wants it." During the questioning of Foley on public financing, someone asked him if he had any Republican support for the idea. I rose and said I was prepared with a small group of Republicans to support the rule on the assurance that Chairman Thompson was going to put in the record his statement that full transferability was to be permitted the party, in addition to a removal of the contribution and expenditure limitations. I was immediately sent a note signed by David Cohen, who was in the audience, saying that he was informed that Thompson had "had to" change his mind about putting transferability in the record, but that Mikva would do it. I immediately walked out of the Rules Committee and did not testify.

Because of the uncertainty then of what the Democrats were going to put in the record, we waited until the next morning. Thompson did not mention transferability. I talked with Dave Stockman early in the morning, and we decided we had better not support the rule because there was at least ambivalence on the Democratic side, with the leadership apparently determined to limit use of the Republican war fund by denying any transferability of authorization from state and national party organs that would normally be permitted to contribute but had not raised any money for that purpose. I then went to a Republican conference which had been called as a closed meeting and was well attended, apparently for lynch purposes, but which clapped and cheered when I announced that our apostate Republicans were not going to vote for the rule. . . . I stated, however, that most of us would support public financing if the rule passed.

The rule lost by about eleven votes,[5] and not a single Republican defected. Common Cause people immediately blasted not us for defeating the rule but Brademas and Thompson for their partisanship and their unwillingness to give the assurances that would have saved the rule. The Republicans felt better about us than they will the next time it comes up. I immediately got about twenty Republicans to cosponsor the public financing bill again as a demonstration that we will support public financing and think our party is wrong on this issue. . . . I am convinced that public financing will come, but probably not until after we have a big enough scandal so that public outcry will require it.

May 20, 1978

Sometime in March or early April the Democratic Caucus held a specific meeting and, by a more than two-to-one margin, instructed the Democratic members of the Ways and Means Committee in general terms to roll back Social Security taxes. There was a good deal of discussion of this issue, and Abner Mikva and I and Bill Steiger had quite a few conversations trying to establish the manner of rolling back Social Security taxes. Steiger and I were most interested in rolling back increases in the wage base, since that has considerable effect on the dynamic and growth of the system, since it affects capital formation more than

5. The vote was 209–198.

anything else, since it is difficult to compensate for through the income tax, and since it reduces our capacity to finance future cost-of-living increases in benefits. Mikva, a traditional liberal, was more anxious to roll back the rate, which would affect all people, although he acknowledged that it would not improve the long-term soundness of the system if the rate was rolled back.

When the Ways and Means Committee finally met on this issue two weeks ago, during the hiatus in consideration of income tax cuts, we went through a day of elaborate motions and countermotions trying to adopt some method of rolling back taxes that would have majority support. One after another, the alternatives, most of them having to do with the diversion of a part of the disability trust fund, were defeated. Finally, the last motion of the day involved Sam Gibbons offering what had been, in effect, my motion to recommit, less the coverage of federal employees. By the time the chairman was ready to vote (he is traditionally the last vote cast by the committee), the vote stood at 18–18. He thought for a substantial period of time, I think almost a full minute, and then cast his vote in favor of my proposal. Sam Gibbons and I went before the TV cameras outside the door and claimed a great victory for the people and a substantial rollback of Social Security taxes, the increases in which would have been cut in half as of next January 1.

The staff had been instructed to draft up the proposal made, which they did, and four days later, we met to vote the bill out of committee. At that point, Al Ullman announced he had changed his position, and since, in the intervening period, the majority and the president had announced a reduction in the size of the income tax cut, Bafalis and Frenzel on our side of the Ways and Means Committee also changed their vote. . . . I argued privately with both of them, urging them not to change their position because it seemed to me that the Republicans had a major issue in the failure to roll back Social Security taxes and that the decision of Frenzel and Bafalis was robbing us of that issue, since it left only three Republican members voting for the rollback. I was able to persuade John Duncan to change his vote, which had previously been against the rollback, so that we finally got four, but I don't think we are in a position to be holier than thou relative to the major increase that now will take effect next January. This increase raises the wage base to $22,900 and the rate to 6.13 percent. It will fall on the American people like a thunderclap at that time, because it represents a much greater increase in Social Security taxes than we had the first of this year. I intend to campaign on it a good deal this fall.

Now let us look at income taxes. The president's income tax proposals at the beginning of this year were very substantially reduced from his original expecta-

tions. . . . After several weeks of public hearings, the committee started marking up the bill. The first item involved the elimination of deductions for state
gasoline tax paid, for state sales tax paid, [and] for state personal property taxes
paid and a consolidation of casualty and medical losses, thus reducing the size
of that deduction. By a fairly narrow vote, myself voting in the affirmative, the
committee decided to eliminate the deduction for state gasoline taxes, which
has some energy policy overtones to it and which I have supported at least twice
in the past when efforts were made unsuccessfully to eliminate the deduction.
The other deductions, however, we voted against eliminating, then mov[ed] to
reconsider and stat[ed], as Republicans (all twelve had voted against the elimination), that we were going to hold these items hostage until we saw what tax
cuts were proposed. It was my statement at the time that since these deductions
were generally of value to the middle-class home-owning taxpayers who are the
only ones continuing to itemize their deductions, we were not going to use the
simplification involved in the elimination of the deduction to contribute further
to redistributive economics. . . . It was left in that way, the assumption being that
we would come back to discuss it further.

Then up came the issue of the amendment which Joe Fisher and I cosponsored and were pushing to permit charitable deductions to be offset against
taxes, despite the claiming of the standard deduction. Our purpose in proposing
this amendment was to open a dialogue upon the impact on charitable contributions of the constant growth of the standard deduction, currently available
to 75 percent of the taxpayers and available to 84 percent of them if President
Carter's tax reforms go through as proposed. It is our position that we were
so narrowing the area of tax incentives for charitable contributions that charitable contributions were beginning to look like loopholes and were narrowing
the base of philanthropy in the United States and affecting not only charitable
policy but the very pluralism of our society. I will say frankly that I did not expect
my amendment to pass, but it developed such support in the committee that it
passed by a comfortable margin and caused great consternation in the administration, since it was an antisimplification amendment extending the size and
scope of the short-form reform.

At this point in the deliberations, we began to hear of an amendment initiated by Bill Steiger, I think at the behest of the lobbyist Charlie Walker, to return
capital gains rates of taxation to the pre-1969 level. I cosponsored this amendment once I learned of it, and a poll indicated that twenty-two members of the
thirty-seven-man committee were willing to support it. At this stage, Al Ullman
suggested that our deliberations be suspended until we could put together some

kind of package that would have majority support, telling me personally that if the Steiger amendment passed, a proposal by Charlie Vanik to abort the whole tax bill, with the exception of the $9 billion in temporary tax cuts to be made permanent, would carry in the committee and that it would be a big blow to the prestige of the committee. I agreed to the suspension because I also feared the Vanik amendment might carry if the members of the committee perceived that our munificences were getting out of control, and I felt that the Vanik amendment would put the most members in an untenable position. The House itself would be in an untenable position if the Vanik amendment carried. We would be sending only a $9 billion extension of temporary tax cuts to the Senate. The Senate would then pass a tax reform bill, and we would go to conference on a major tax bill for which there was no House version. I was convinced, and I so told Al Ullman, that if this scenario occurred, the result would be that he would be stricken of his chairmanship because of the failure of the House to have any input of significance on a bill.

The president has once again changed his mind about the size of the tax cut … [saying] that he would reduce the tax cut to $20 billion net from $25 billion net. … I have done a series of one-minutes this past week, deploring this decision on the part of the president and majority party and urging the president to hold firm on his original tax cut proposal. The effect of his failure to cut taxes by at least $25 billion will be to have a gradual increase in the real rate of taxation, rather than continuing the rough indexing that Congress has been doing since 1963. The normal rate of total federal taxation as a percentage of the gross national product is about 18.6 percent, and in our press conferences, we Republicans are attempting to show that the extrapolation along current lines of expenditure and taxation would not balance the budget below a 24 or 25 percent rate of taxation, clearly excessive in any historical sense. In this sense, Jack Kemp is right: the Republican Party will promote its own cause much more effectively by talking about the level of taxation than by talking with major emphasis on cutting government expenditures, all of which have their adherents.

Jack, incidentally, said to me the other day on the floor, "I'm getting to be a cult figure myself!" Jack has always been extremely competitive with me and was resentful of a recent *New York Times* article which described me as having achieved cult status.[6] If I have achieved cult status, I have achieved nowhere near the attention Jack has with his vigorous and charismatic advocacy of major

6. Edward C. Burks, "Republicans Turning to Conable as Their Spokesman in Congress," *New York Times*, January 21, 1978.

tax cuts. Jack is almost monomaniacal on this issue, missing no opportunity to repeat the slogans of the Kemp-Roth bill[7] and the passion of production-side economics. He is an attractive man, brighter than the average, and ambitious to the point of boredom. He does not wear well on people who have to listen to him quite a bit, but the first impression he creates is tremendous, and I have been, until recently, urging him to run for governor, feeling that he would have a good chance against Carey, in contrast to Perry Duryea, the old Rockefeller lieutenant who for years has been shepherding Rockefeller tax increases through the legislature. Jack wants to be president but doesn't wish to take any risks en route. I wish him well, but I expect he's going to be pretty hard to take during the many opportunities he'll find to expound about the Laffer curve,[8] the virtues of tax cuts, [and] his abhorrence of Keynesian economics (although he comes out about the same place as Lord Keynes did) and his exhortations to the Republicans to stand for something positive, like what he's advocating. The mood of the country is such that he may very well be able to sell his particular variety of snake oil, and certainly I will help him, in the sense that I do not like to see the Carter administration opting for higher and higher taxes rather than dealing directly with all those vested special interests that want extension and expansion of government programs.

May 28, 1978

It seems to me that this might be a good time for me to review the membership of the Ways and Means Committee and record my personal impressions. . . . Inherent in everything I have been saying about the chairman is my dismay at his apparent inability to control the committee. Al is a methodical man and a decent man. He is not quick, but he cares sufficiently about doing a good job and he struggles to understand the issues and to be prepared for the decisions that have to be made. He seems to have much more staff and to rely on them more extensively than Wilbur Mills did. People are always asking me to compare or contrast his leadership with that of Wilbur, and I usually demur on the grounds that the situation of the two chairmen is completely different because of the changes in the Congress itself and the committee in particular since Wilbur stepped down. Al is scarcely more direct than Wilbur, although when cornered

---

7. Sponsored by Kemp and Senator William Roth (R-DE), the bill proposed to cut marginal tax rates by 10 percent a year for three consecutive years.

8. Economist Arthur Laffer's famous graph plotting the relationship between tax rates and tax revenue.

he will state unequivocally what his position is. He does not have the subtleness of mind nor the strategic adroitness of Wilbur Mills, nor does he understand the motivations of the members of the committee, the real basis for Wilbur's success as a legislative leader over the years.

Al also permits himself to get flustered, either by committee staff slurping around behind his chair and giving him conflicting advice because he has never drawn them together or clearly assigned lines of communication with them, or because of members on his side who seem to enjoy putting him in an ideological crossruff. Sometimes I feel sorry for him when a lot of people are pressing him with advice at the same time, because it is not his nature to sort out conflicting threads of thought easily. He continues to think of me as a disruptive partisan, a posture I am sometimes driven to by the pressures on my own side and his unwillingness to accommodate them in any way. Generally speaking, I not only like Al but am somewhat defensive about his troubles with the committee, and frequently I find myself trying to work out some way to accommodate him, even though it will damage my image in the eyes of some of the Republicans at the end of the line like Bafalis and Ketchum, who enjoy nothing so much as a good fight.

The number-two man on the committee is Jim Burke of Quincy, Massachusetts, who has already announced his retirement.[9] Jim has had very severe heart problems, resulting from uncontrolled diabetes, and the loss of a leg after a lesion of several years standing on his heel failed to heal. Jim has accommodated very well to a motorized wheelchair and has found himself enjoying the Social Security fight (he is chairman of the Social Security Subcommittee) this year as not only the classic type of struggle he is good at but also the last battle of his career. He has frequently referred to his Social Security speeches as his "last hurrah." He has long supported the AFL-CIO's bill that would put a third of the money going into the Social Security Trust Fund from the general treasury, a third from the employer, and a third from the employee. He is undismayed by the fact that a third of the benefits each year would amount to $35 billion or thereabouts. He frequently plays fast and loose with the facts in his passionate advocacy of the bill but doesn't seem to resent at all people like me taking him up and sternly correcting him in discovered misrepresentations. A thoroughly likable demagogue, Jim Burke is also a party man, and no matter what he is saying, he will give his vote to Al Ullman unless he is firmly locked into a contrary position. He loves to say things like, "I may be a liberal, but I am not one of those

9. Burke, who did not run for reelection, died in 1983.

flaky Democrats." Another quote that typifies his complete cynicism in the face of opportunities for gamesmanship is, "Barber, don't get so excited. You act as if you think this is all on the level."

Dan Rostenkowski, the number-three Democrat, is more of a voice on the committee than he was several years ago. As long as Mayor Daley was alive, he was clearly the mayor's man, representing him above all others in the Illinois delegation. His interests were more the politics of Cook County than the politics of Washington. . . . Following the mayor's death, he decided to involve himself in the fight for the majority leader at the beginning of this Congress and helped put together the coalition that defeated Phil Burton for majority leader and elected Jim Wright by one vote. In return, he was chosen deputy whip and now seems to represent the leadership as much as Al Ullman does in the deliberations of the Ways and Means Committee. Danny talks a very conservative game and grumbles a lot about extravagance and all-out social welfare programs. He votes entirely as his party wishes him, and I have cautioned Republicans not to rely on Danny's vote going where his mouth is. . . . Rostenkowski rarely attends committee meetings except when critical votes are held, at which time he is a devoted party man and unquestioning in his support of leadership strategies.

The number-four man is Charles Vanik of Cleveland, a demagogic and erratic liberal more interested in the headline than in consistency or in truth. Charlie is a likable man, gregarious and outspoken, and a man of some ability. . . . He has shown some willingness to apply himself to trade issues, although the minute his provincial interests get in the way, he chucks his interests in the world scene in order to advance the domestic demagogy. His wife is a lively and attractive lady who has known most of the people on the committee, and I understand that she is dying of cancer,[10] which bespeaks a little restraint in our relations with Charlie at this point. But nevertheless, I would say there are very few on the committee who would follow Charlie's lead in a big fight or depend on his vote in any matter of substance.

The next man on the committee is Jim Corman of California. Jim is one of the ablest members of the majority side. He is also one of the leaders of the Democratic Party. He is chairman of the Democratic Congressional Campaign Committee and is respected not only for his intellect but for his sharp and cogent tongue. He becomes emotionally involved in issues from the point of view of a man of the far left but does not allow himself to be trapped in ideology to the extent that some people of his ideological views would. He is a consistent

10. Vanik's wife survived the congressman, who died in 2007.

liberal, pressing for the cause of the moment with not only effectiveness but a multipronged approach which is not above dealing with conservatives to get his way. He seems to feel that accomplishment requires a good deal of bargaining, and as chairman of the Welfare Subcommittee, he has proved more than the equal for Guy Vander Jagt, our ranking minority member and a man so preoccupied with the political side of his job that he frequently falls into traps set for him by Corman.

I shall probably not get the order of my colleagues on the Democratic side in terms of seniority, but somewhere near Corman is Sam Gibbons of Tampa, Florida. Sam is an abrasive and sometimes overbearing man of intemperate language and attitudes, but I count him as one of my best friends in the committee. He is an honest man. He is capable of independence of thought and initiative in action. He is afraid of nothing. His views are balanced and not unduly party oriented. He is dependable in his stubbornness. I like him, even when he is being unpleasant.

Joe Waggonner of Louisiana has also announced his retirement. His departure from the committee will mark an end of an era, since Joe has been consistently the most conservative member of the committee in his relationship to business interests. He obviously views himself as representing business and is not only amenable to the lobbyists in almost every type of issue but obviously proud of his role in this respect. A shrewd lawyer, Joe is an expert on parliamentary procedure in the southerners' eyes. . . . It is difficult to understand why Joe Waggonner is retiring from Congress, although when I asked him, he said it was "stomach trouble—I have just had a bellyful." Joe was fingered by the *Washington Post* two years ago for having solicited a policewoman, thinking she was a prostitute, a charge which he promptly denied, and it is my understanding from some of his friends that he has remained bitter over the incident ever since.

Otis Pike, one of the next in seniority, is also retiring. Otis is a man of grace and looks, light on his feet as only a Democrat representing one of the most Republican districts in the state of New York could be, and spectacular in his articulacy and persuasiveness. Since he has announced his retirement, which he saw fit to relate primarily to the ethics code's ban on outside income, he has been voting not only a conservative but almost a curmudgeonly line, reflecting more the views of his district and less the views of the Democratic Party than any other time since he came to Congress. Like Sam Stratton [D] of the Schenectady area, Otis Pike has been adroit at creating an image contrary to the basic thrust of his voting record, both for purposes of survival and because he enjoys the game of politics and plays it very well.

Charlie Rangel of Harlem comes next, and he is, I think, an underestimated quantity on the committee. . . . I find him attractive and I enjoy talking with him. He is a special-interest legislator in the sense that he can be reached on issues which do not directly affect his racial prejudices, and people who leave him out of the Ways and Means Committee's equation because he is black make a serious mistake. I would certainly put him a notch above most of the New York City representatives . . . in ability, personality, and, probably, honesty.

We now go to Fortney (Pete) Stark. Better yet, let us pass him by. He is a wealthy flake.

Next is Jimmy Jones of Oklahoma. I have underestimated Jimmy Jones in the past. A moderate conservative with some ties to the oil industry and a former member of the Johnson White House staff, he was found guilty of a misdemeanor because of his involvement with the milk cooperative lobby. He is a rather unimpressive-looking man and not a flashy performer. Nevertheless, Jimmy is willing to take responsibility and to initiate efforts at compromise and harmonization that have resulted in compromise where none was apparently possible. He has a good mind and is capable of independent thought and action. He grows on you the longer you know him, and I suspect his influence on the committee will continue to grow also.

Bill Cotter . . . creates the appearance of not being very bright, but he is an active member of the committee and a man who breaks with the party line on matters about which he is capable of feeling strongly. He worries about his vote. I suspect he even wants to do the right thing. The only issues on which he is not capable of independence are those affecting the insurance industry, since he comes from Connecticut and has close ties to the insurance industry. This is not only his Achilles' heel, but it is the handle by which lobbyists take hold of him.

Andy Jacobs of Indiana is next, if he can be placed anywhere. Unpredictable to the point of capriciousness, Andy would rather make a bon mot than he would any common sense. He has a broken period of service as a result of a defeat at the polls in the middle of his career, and perhaps that has made him want to make occasional conservative gestures, most of which seem ludicrous but which he apparently takes very seriously. Andy has a good mind and is perfectly capable of thorough understanding, but nobody depends on him, and his flights of fancy sometimes cause exasperation among the members who find him difficult to take seriously.

Next comes Abner Mikva of Illinois, one of the real leaders of the committee. Abner is a man of sparkling ability, a very pleasing personality, and an ideological purity which seems to engender much more hostility than is due him. Unlike

Corman, Mikva, when defeated, shrugs his shoulders and returns cheerfully to do battle in another opportunity. He is the chairman this year of the Democratic Study Group, the liberal core of the Democratic Party, and I am sure he is effective in this role. Every year we hear that Abner is due to be defeated at the polls because he represents the wealthy and conservative Evanston area of suburban Chicago, having been redistricted by Mayor Daley . . . but it is difficult for me to believe that he could be beaten by anyone in view of his persuasiveness and his attractive personality. A most impressive man, and as my conservative colleagues say, he is so effective he must be terribly dangerous.

Next is Martha Keys of Kansas, Andy Jacobs's wife. Following a Ways and Means Committee romance, we saw her ditching her college professor husband and children and saw him picking up a very attractive wife-colleague after at least one unhappy marriage. Martha is an attractive and earnest girl, liberal and emotionally involved in many causes, predictably controversial in her conservative home state, and doubtless a good deal more predictable and consistent than her husband. She is as serious as Andy is a wisecracker. A pleasing personality, but one occasionally questions how thoroughly she understands many of the issues to which she addresses her occasionally fervent oratory.

Next is Bill Ford of Memphis, Tennessee. A black ward politician from the Memphis machine, Ford has had some bad publicity about his handling of accounts and his cutting corners on official duties. He is not a man whom anybody knows very well, and he seems quite inclined to give Al Ullman his proxy whenever anything tough comes up. He occasionally casts an unpredictable vote for reasons which remain obscure, but for the most part, I would call him one of the most traditional Democrats on the committee.

Bill Brodhead of Detroit is next. He is hard to classify, being a somewhat insecure-appearing liberal who is closely identified with the auto industry through his UAW[11] connections. He asks quite a few questions but with not any great depth.

Next comes Ed Jenkins of Georgia. Ed is a conservative—a man who frequently votes with the Republicans and a man capable of dogged and carefully thought out conservative positions.

Next comes Dick Gephardt of St. Louis, Missouri. Gephardt is a handsome man with considerable intellectual ability. He has made an impressive beginning on the committee. . . . I have been telling people who come to see me about issues subject to active lobbying that they could not talk to a better man for influ-

---

11. The United Automobile Workers union.

ence in the front row than Dick Gephardt, feeling that I want to identify him as a comer, encourage him, and involve him as much as he is willing to be involved. I suspect he is quite liberal, that he is capable of independent postures, and doubtless his constituency is a fairly conservative one. A comer, a man to watch.

The second most junior Democrat is Jim Guy Tucker of Arkansas, now holding the seat once held by Wilbur Mills. A flashy and handsome, ambitious young man, Jim Guy (that is what he likes to be called) is already deeply involved in the senatorial race, in which he seems to be running second to the governor. . . . Another man of obvious ability, doubtless his ambition will either catapult him into early prominence or destroy him. He is not one to play the waiting game of the Ways and Means Committee, and we may never see him again after this senatorial race, although I suspect he will be running for some office or other all the rest of his life.[12]

Now I suppose we must do the same for the Republicans that we have done for the Democrats.

The number-two man on the committee is John Duncan of Knoxville, Tennessee, my classmate and a longtime local politician of the eastern Tennessee scene. John demonstrates native shrewdness and apparently enjoys the manipulative and political opportunities of the Congress.

Next comes Bill Archer of Houston. Bill is a constant disappointment to me, in that he uses his ideological purity as a conservative as an excuse to cop out on issue after issue. He has one of the finest minds in the Congress in terms of his abilities and his understanding and education. He does not like responsibility, and he constantly rationalizes reasons not to exercise his vote in a constructive way.

Next comes Guy Vander Jagt of Michigan. Guy is politically ambitious and, I believe, will be the next minority leader of the House.[13] He spends most of his time raising money for candidates. He is a very effective conservative speaker and shows a lamentable tendency toward making deals either with interest groups or with the opposition. He does comparatively little Ways and Means Committee work, but what he does shows him to be a man of understanding and ability. He is not a force on the committee, but likely he will become a force in the Congress as a conservative leader. There is an uneasy edge to our relationship, but I think we respect each other on most matters. He

---

12. Tucker lost the 1978 Senate primary to David Pryor. He later succeeded Bill Clinton as governor of Arkansas.

13. He was not.

is currently very upset with my espousal of public financing of congressional election campaigns.

Next comes Bill Steiger, one of the workhorses of the committee and a man of sparkling ability. He is one of my good friends, although considerably brighter and frequently impatient with my slow and plodding ways. He has a tendency towards stubborn defense of unpredictable and I think occasionally very wrong-headed positions. Not very popular in the House, his problems are based in his excessive brilliance, which, relative to the rest of the Republicans, is not a hard position to achieve. I feel defensive about Steiger and view him and his wife with considerable affection if occasional exasperation. I wish we had a few more problems like him.

Next comes Phil Crane, the darling of the right wing. Phil almost never comes to the committee, and when he does show up, I am tempted to introduce him as a new member. As the head of the American Conservative Union, he is constantly moving around the country collecting handsome honoraria (he is a very hand-some fellow himself) and evidently running for president.[14] He and Jack Kemp are bound to come into collision among the candidates on the far right. As far as the Ways and Means Committee is concerned, he is a waste of time.

Next comes Bill Frenzel of Minnesota, one of the brightest men in Congress and one of my best friends. He is bright, articulate, and strong. He has occasion-ally shown, like Steiger, a tendency toward being a smarty, but one can forgive a man who consistently makes as fine a contribution as he does with every issue with which he becomes involved. Frenzel is first class.

Next comes Jim Martin of North Carolina, a former chemistry professor at Davidson College with a Ph.D. from Princeton. . . . He involves himself in sub-stantive issues in the Ways and Means Committee only occasionally, but then demonstrates a doggedness and an understanding that leave one feeling that he is one of the good performers on the Republican side. He is sometimes not as much of a team man as I would wish, given his ability and intelligence.[15]

Next comes Skip Bafalis, a wealthy, natty coal dealer from the Palm Beach area of Florida. Skip is very political and usually more interested in the politics of an issue than the issue itself. He considers himself something of a strate-gist and is frequently critical of me because of my tendency to want to work something out rather than leave the Democrats and the nation in a bad hole.

14. Crane, dogged by scandalous stories about his sexual adventures, was one of the first GOP hopefuls to drop out of the 1980 presidential race.

15. Martin later served two terms as governor of North Carolina.

He is quick and positive and rarely placid. . . . I suspect that Skip will not stay in Congress long, as he will be exasperated with the effectiveness of his leaders generally, and so convinced that he is part of a party of dolts.[16]

Next comes Bill Ketchum of California, the ultimate political exhibition-ist. An extremely bright man, Bill Ketchum cannot resist the temptation to preen himself in public and congratulate himself on seeing everything a little bit clearer and a little bit differently from his colleagues. He knows a great deal about welfare, having served in the California legislature under circumstances which involved him with the issue, but after demonstrating his great knowledge on an issue of this sort, he finds some way of detaching himself from the mob and not participating in the solution. He takes great joy in attacking his own party leadership, and he and Bafalis are natural allies at the end of the Republican line on the Ways and Means Committee in criticizing my ineptitude. Ketchum loves to make speeches as a self-acknowledged expert in almost any subject that occurs to Congress as a fit subject for legislation. He is hard to take and hard to cooperate with. If he were to mellow some, he could be an outstanding legislator.

The junior member on the Republican side is Will Gradison of Cincinnati. Gradison is one of my special friends, although I am sometimes disappointed in his desire for publicity and his avoidance of team responsibilities on an occa-sional issue. Another man who is capable of independence and initiating work of a high quality. . . . I suspect he also has some political ambitions, since he was so intent on seeking a congressional seat in the first place that he split off with his wife over his desire to run for Congress.[17] . . . I think he is Jewish, but his voting record would make one believe that he is Catholic, and I am surprised at how socially conservative he votes, in view of the very reasonable views he seems to have about many issues. All in all, a very attractive man, and one whose presence on the committee brightens my relationships there.

With all this talent, it is surprising to me that the Ways and Means Com-mittee is in such disarray at this stage in its life. During the 94th Congress I expected such disarray because political accountability was being imposed on a committee that before had a life of its own. Now all the new members have had time to become familiar with the issues, to take hold of them in constructive ways, and to get used to working together. That we are not working together but seem to be flying off in every direction at once I am afraid is an indictment of the leadership of Al Ullman to some degree.

16. Bafalis skipped out after two more terms.
17. Gradison served in Congress until resigning in 1993.

June 25, 1978

We have now been more than two months without resuming our Ways and Means tax markup. I do not fully understand what has happened to frustrate this important piece of legislation, but to the extent I can reconstruct the events, I will try to do so.

Increasingly, it is apparent that the Steiger amendment, which would roll back the tax on long-term capital gains to the rate (including the minimum tax) which was effective before the 1969 Tax Reform Act, was the real reason for the administration and the chairman to decide that our tentative decision making had gone on long enough. The majority of the committee supported Steiger, reflecting frustration about capital formation, the level of taxes, the speed of the economy, and the increasing conservatism of the younger Democrats. That ubiquitous "super-lobbyist" Charls Walker apparently drew on his shrewdness [and] put together a package which he thought would sell and would provide an adequate conservative vehicle for the sentiments of the committee. He took it to his friend Joe Waggonner, who took it to Al Ullman. Ullman thought it looked pretty conservative and sat on it.

Five weeks went by while the chairman negotiated with the liberal members of the committee and found no ten of them able to agree with anything. Finally, Walker, frustrated that Waggonner had not achieved anything, talked to Jim Jones, the moderate conservative from Tulsa, Oklahoma. Jim, rather than talking to Democrats, went and talked with Steiger. Steiger and he made a few little changes in the package, and then Steiger came to me. I called a meeting of the minority, and although there was grumbling and the usual reaction to Steiger's initiatives, which leave some of his less bright colleagues in the minority jealous, the conclusion of our meeting was that I thought the package could be sold to the Republican minority and so advised Jones and Ullman. Ullman then began to feel that a deal was possible and, at about the seven-week level of the hiatus, started actively pushing the Jones package with the Democrats, saying that he did not wish to bring about as a solution anything which a majority of the Democrats could not support. The liberals, who were unable to agree on anything positive, now agreed that they could oppose the Jones package, which not only contained the despicable Steiger amendment relative to capital gains but also provided for major tax relief for taxpayers [earning] between $15,000 and $50,000. Ullman, who has had a low silhouette in the whole affair and never initiated any discussions himself, then subsided and did nothing, while one by one enough conservatives flaked off, deciding this was the best they could do, until he had close to the thirteen Democrats he needed to have a majority of the majority party on the committee.

Enter Mike Blumenthal, Charlie Schultz,[18] and Stu Eisenstadt.[19] They have the lowest possible opinion of the Jones package, not personally but because the president has a low opinion of it, and they started discussing his intention to veto anything that had a provision vaguely reminiscent of the Steiger amendment. . . . This past Thursday, Al Ullman called me to say that a proposed meeting to try to resolve the whole affair . . . had been called off, that he washed his hands of the whole affair for the time being. He said that he had told Secretary Blumenthal that if the secretary wanted to put together a better package, he could go ahead and do it. He said to me, "Barber, you and I know they're not going to get anything better from their point of view than the Jones package, and I have told the secretary that if he has not accomplished anything by July 15, I will resume control and we will pass the Jones package." He said that, in his view, one of the biggest dangers was that Roth-Kemp, the 30 percent tax cut phased in 10 percent a year, had a good chance of passing on the floor because he thought at least seventy Democrats would vote for it and the Republicans would vote solidly for it. I had previously counseled with him and urged him to see to it that any bill taken to the floor be taken subject to a rule which would make Roth-Kemp in order, for Jack to have his day in the sun pushing his own amendment as an allowed amendment early in the amending process. [I told] . . . Al that if he left it for a motion to recommit at the last stage of the enactment, many liberals might vote for it to destroy the bill. Ullman is perhaps overreacting to the publicity Jack Kemp has received on this proposal following the enactment of Proposition 13,[20] since the Kemp-Roth bill is considered the federal equivalent of Proposition 13 by many people.

Speaking of Kemp-Roth, Jack Kemp is having the great joy of being a "cult figure" in his own right now. As attractive as Jack is, and as recognizable a figure as any major league quarterback is bound to be, he is much in demand as a speaker all over the country and is receiving a great deal of attention in the press. He relishes it because he has an ego much bigger than a football, and his promoters' zeal, his single-mindedness about tax cuts, and his obvious national ambitions have made him something of a butt of the jokes of his colleagues. That doesn't bother Jack, as long as he is getting the public attention and press that he currently is.

18. Chairman of the Council of Economic Advisers.

19. Carter's domestic policy adviser.

20. A property-tax limitation approved by California voters in 1978.

July 9, 1978

The last week before the July 4 recess, as expected, was, in the tradition of pre-recess weeks, a particularly unfruitful one. The weekend before, in Bakersfield, California, Bill Ketchum of my committee played tennis all morning, ate a large lunch, [and] played tennis all afternoon. At 6:20 he took a cold shower and dropped dead. He knew he had a bad heart condition as the result of a recent examination and had been told to take it easy. Recently, he took off thirty pounds. In his usual uncompromising way, though, Ketchum refused to give way to any degree to the forces around him and with[in] him, and so was spared a decline that would have been intolerable to him.

On Tuesday, two air force planeloads of congressmen went to Bakersfield, a very long round-trip for a half-hour service in the small Episcopal church to which he belonged. His wife, a spirited lady whom I do not know well, said to me only, "That damn Ketchum—wouldn't you know he'd leave me like this. I was supposed to die first."

On the plane, and because I had been urging prompt action, the California Republican delegation met and presented me with John Rousselot as Ketchum's replacement on the Ways and Means Committee. As soon as I heard of Ketchum's death, I had tried to call Pete McCloskey [CA], who was attending a whaling convention in London. I finally got through to him a day later. I was not in when he returned my call, but he learned from my office that Ketchum had died and immediately indicated his intention to try to get on the Ways and Means Committee, saying that he would stay in Congress if he could get such an assignment. He apparently had been considering retiring. He became more determined after another day and started actively lobbying for the position, but of course, by then, the decision had already been made by Bob Wilson [CA], who hates McCloskey as an antimilitary type, that he would use his considerable influence with the California delegation in behalf of anyone else. Thus, we move from a man of passion and prejudice, an intellectually honest and extremely capricious smart aleck like Ketchum, to a jolly, hardworking, and completely uncompromising right-winger like Rousselot. I respect John Rousselot, but I cannot work with him.

July 29, 1978

Despite cries of anguish from the liberals, [Al Ullman] did exactly what he said he would do, first having gone through an elaborate series of discussions with me and others to try to persuade us to keep the package intact by voting against expected "sweetening" amendments by the liberals, including even the possible offering of Kemp-Roth as a way of weighting down the package.

At first, the measure moved quite well, with the discipline of the group keeping any interesting amendments from being added. On Wednesday, Bill Archer, despite urgings from us not to do it, insisted on offering an amendment which would prospectively strip out all inflation after 1980 from the base of capital assets before determining how much capital gain there would be. Most of us felt that this was a good proposal but feared that if it passed, a number of people would then feel that the Jones package was so weighted down that we would have to move to substitute a more austere measure.

Four Republicans who would normally have supported Archer voted against it, but Stark, Vanik, Mikva, Gephardt, and other liberals voted for it, and it passed, owing its success entirely to liberals antagonistic to it who were trying to freight the bill with impossible burdens. The chairman called a meeting in his office of the people who had been working together trying to maintain the Jones package and announced that he would take the Archer proposal to the floor with the package if we could hold everything else, announcing with some satisfaction that he intended to embarrass the liberals by making them live with what they had wrought.

The other amendment which caused some problems was the so-called Fisher-Conable amendment, which would permit charitable deductions by those claiming the standard deduction. This proposal had been advanced to offset the proposed elimination of a number of deductions in the original Carter package, which would have the effect of raising the number of people claiming the standard deduction to 84 percent of the taxpayers. Since we had knocked Carter's reforms out of the box, I had lost some enthusiasm for the measure, but it was very popular with the charities, and I felt I had to offer it since it had been tentatively adopted during the early deliberations before our three-and-a-half-month hiatus. Enough people switched their votes so that the measure was defeated. I'm well satisfied. The issue remains alive, my support for it remains unsullied, [but] it's not as badly needed as I thought it would be, or as it will be at some time in the future, when the political pressures are apparent all around. The only regret I have is that some good people were damaged by what they felt was a responsible vote against the measure.

At the end of the consideration of the bill, the liberals presented a series of comprehensive but poorly thought out and virtually unarticulated alternatives to the Jones package. It was incredible that neither they nor the administration had really focused on a serious alternative, feeling somehow that Al would not have the guts to bring up the Jones package as long as they continued to oppose it. Al told me that it was vital he get thirteen Democratic votes for the Jones package, because Tip had told him that he would not support him in the caucus on any kind of a modified rule if less than a majority of Democrats voted for whatever bill he brought out. He was able to get the thirteen by casting the thirteenth vote himself, and so thought that he had insured some leadership support for the measure. Danny Rostenkowski, however, voted against the bill. More on this later.

It was almost 9:30 on Thursday night when we completed the measure, but at my urgings, Al continued immediately to consider the rule to recommend to the Rules Committee for consideration of the measure. John Meagher listed four possible amendments which would give broad range of choice to the rank-and-file membership of the House: (1) the Vanik-Pickle amendment to extend temporary tax cuts of $9 billion and do nothing more; (2) the Fisher package, generally conceded to be the last gasp of the administration on the issue and being a somewhat more liberal Jones package; (3) the Corman package, an obviously thrown together last-minute effort to create a more liberal package than the Fisher package; (4) the Kemp-Roth proposal as it applied to individual income tax. A fairly high decibel rating was achieved as far as Kemp-Roth was concerned because the measure itself had not been offered during committee deliberations, that being part of my understanding with Chairman Ullman and he feeling quite strongly that, in any event, the measure would have to be offered on the floor in order to get Republicans to vote for the rule. After a certain amount of breast-beating by the Democrats of both ideological hues on this issue, however, we were able to get it made in order as a Ways and Means recommendation by a fairly narrow vote.

The next morning, Al Ullman was summoned into the Speaker's office and berated for having abandoned his Democrats in the interest of getting a tax bill. It was indicated that Danny Rostenkowski would lead the fight against the measure. The Speaker expressed himself in no uncertain terms that the Kemp-Roth bill was not going to be made in order by the Rules Committee, no matter what Ways and Means recommended. The general assessment was made that this is the opening gun of Dan Rostenkowski's campaign to unseat Al Ullman as chairman of the Ways and Means Committee during the 96th Congress, with the tacit approval of the Speaker. I have reported these developments to John Rhodes and find him quite relaxed about the possibility of our not getting the right to offer Kemp-Roth on the floor during consideration of the bill, since he can use the motion to recommit for the same purpose, give Jack a more modest rhetorical run at the mark, and score whatever political points are to be made about the Republican desire to cut taxes more than the Democrats.

Last weekend Bob Michel of Illinois, the Republican whip, was jumped by muggers as he came home late one night and was badly beaten around the face and head. He spent several days in the hospital and came back looking very badly damaged, although I guess he is going to be all right. He had a press conference in which he mentioned that about a month ago I had a similar experience, although I was not done physical harm, and as a result, we have had a lot of reporters trying to find out about my episode, which never made the Washington papers. They seem intent on trying to make a big deal out of it, asking me questions like the degree to which I had changed my lifestyle since I was held up and whether or not I regret having come to Washington. I have been elusive and tended to downgrade the whole experience in my conversations with the press because I find the posture of a victim quite undignified and don't wish to extend my conversations about it. I must say that my constituents all seem to be aware of it, from the [*Rochester*] *Times-Union* story that was somewhat lurid in its detail, and one would think that I had done nothing of any significance down here in recent years except to get held up.

Gerald Ford is sounding more like a potential candidate than he has previously. I regret this. Ronald Reagan sounds like a candidate also, and indeed, Phil Crane and Jack Kemp do as well. Opportunities for us are so great that I find it hard to believe that we are capable of booting the chance to recapture the White House in 1980. We will have to work very hard at it, but we appear to be determined. When asked who I would like to see as a candidate for president, I am mentioning George Bush's name, but so far, he has caught on only like tame fire. I am going to Maine to spend two days with him just before our August recess begins, presumably to give him advice about issues and tactics. I like and respect George, although he insists on acting like less of a heavyweight than he is, and I would love to see him moving forward in name recognition and public esteem. Goodness knows we need a new face, an attractive face, a younger candidate, and a cleaner slate of issues than the old boys can bring us.

August 13, 1978

This past week has been the week of the tax bill. Having completed our report, we were scheduled for the Rules Committee on Tuesday. Interest in the bill ran high, and it was announced that there were at least thirty witnesses who wished to testify before the Rules Committee. Last Friday, Mike Blumenthal announced a new administration bill, which was to be called the Fisher-Corman bill and which he alleged was a melding of the two amendments offered as substitutes by Fisher and Corman, the Corman version being more liberal, but neither one being particularly friendly to capital gains or to the middle class in the type of tax reduction that was given. I did not see the sixteen charts that Treasury prepared to accompany the bill, which the Republicans determined early would be designated the "Blumenthal bill" rather than Fisher-Corman. On Monday, however, Jack Wydler asked me if I had any objection to Mike Blumenthal coming to the New York delegation luncheon to be held at its monthly time the following day. I had some misgivings about this because it was also the same day that we were going to the Rules Committee, but I told Jack that I had no objection, provided I could be recognized to say something after Blumenthal was through.

[The] Rules Committee did not take up the tax bill as the first thing on Tuesday morning, taking a small matter first, and Al Ullman was not there when the deliberations of the tax bill began. The result was that they recognized Jim Burke, who had gotten out of the hospital, where he was fighting to save his second leg from the depredations of sugar diabetes, for his usual speech about one-third, one-third, one-third or the saga of the lost jobs, which the statistics do not disclose but which Jim Burke is convinced are destroying America because of the level of Social Security taxes. Following him, Al Ullman was recognized and gave his usual long and plodding testimony about committee action, confirming a letter he had written to the Rules Committee asking for a rule which would correspond with the agreement in Ways and Means. The Rules Committee, in atypical fashion, did not have a proposed rule prepared, and as a result, shortly after the committee started, John Anderson made a point of order that he didn't know what rule was being considered. At that point, a rule was rushed up from the parliamentarian's office, which included a number of blanks and which obviously left room for hanky-panky. . . . Tip O'Neill was quoted on Monday at a press conference as saying that he didn't know what was in the Blumenthal bill and hadn't the faintest idea whether it ought to be considered by the Rules Committee or not. Evidently, he still had not made up his mind when the time came for the Rules Committee deliberations to begin.

I spent most of [Wednesday] in the Rules Committee and had my usual voluble and excited testimony. (For some reason, when I get in the Rules Committee, I find myself expanding and achieving a degree of articulacy that I rarely achieve in any other forum. It is perhaps because the small, informal setting of the Rules Committee brings out the conversationalist in me.) It appeared at that point that Tip wanted the Gephardt amendment made in order, providing a credit against income tax where Social Security tax is paid—an untried and untested scheme—as well as the Blumenthal amendment. It also appeared that he had decided that they would not try to block off Roth-Kemp but would force us to use it as a motion to recommit. I asked the Republicans on the Rules Committee to try to get extra time for the Roth-Kemp motion to recommit and was surprised when the rule finally came out to find that they had actually got a total of a full hour of debate on what normally gets only five minutes on each side. It was decided the bill would be taken up the next morning, Thursday morning, under only two hours of debate rather than the four the Ways and Means Committee had requested, and that it would be completed that day before the House was to go back to any other subject. I announced myself as satisfied with the rule and called John Rhodes, who was out on the hustings speaking for Republican candidates, to get his blessing as well. Jack Kemp announced himself as satisfied at that point; however, an abruptly called Republican conference the next morning found Jack arriving in a surly mood and announcing that he expected to vote against the rule. I put my finger on his chest and said, "Jack, if you screw up the rule and we get in trouble on it, it'll be your doing alone." I immediately reported to John Rhodes and got as many people as I could, including John Rousselot and other right-wingers, to push on him to support the rule, since it appeared to me that the probable assault on the rule would be made by Dick Gephardt and some young liberals disappointed that the Social Security credit bill had not been made in order by a vote of 8–7 in the Rules Committee.

We then went on to the debate. It was a tense one, as you might imagine, and had more interest than the usual floor debate. The time for amendments was closely regulated, and we completed the work by 8:00. I anticipated three close votes: (1) on the Archer amendment, which provided for a screening out after 1980 of inflation before the figuring of capital gains subject to taxation; (2) [on] the Blumenthal amendment, which we understood Kemp had decided to support without our strength at his command; and (3) [on] the Roth-Kemp motion to recommit. As it turned out, none of them were cliff-hangers, with both the Blumenthal amendment and Roth-Kemp being rejected by comfortable margins and the Archer amendment being retained by a somewhat less comfortable margin. I got most emotionally involved in the Blumenthal amendment, where I charged on the floor that there had been almost hysterical lobbying in its behalf, while referring to Blumenthal's appearance before the New York delegation luncheon the day before, and inferred that if there were a Republican presidency, we would hear talk of not only the imperial presidency but improper executive lobbying. Unfortunately, this part of my speech was taped and broadcast around the country, so I imagine I am in bad odor with Mike Blumenthal at this point.

Ullman hung in there doggedly and expressed surprise that the Republicans had been completely aboveboard and square with him on all deals made. I might say the same for him. I wrote him a note the next morning, saying, in effect, "Dear Al: It was a pleasure working with you on this one; we ought to try it again sometime."[21] I saw him the next morning also and found him walking on cloud nine, having bucked the president, the Speaker, the secretary of the treasury, and the liberal majority of his party, and having been not only successful but successful to a degree that must have enhanced his prestige and given the lie to some of the unpleasant things said about his lack of leadership earlier during our impasse in Ways and Means.

November 8, 1978

I have just been [re]elected by an apparent vote of somewhere around 70 percent.[22] I'm surprised at the margin of my victory because I would have expected this year to receive about 60 percent, inasmuch as I had an opponent who was livelier than usual. . . . Francis Repicci is the Democratic leader of my home county of Genesee, a rural county which does not loom large in my district. He has also served as an election commissioner and took his role as a candidate seriously.

Mr. Repicci's major point, made repeatedly in advertisements and in the four debates which we had, was that I am a national congressman and do not care enough about the district to lobby actively for its benefit. He promised to do differently if elected, abjuring a national role, which he would not have for some time in any event, and engaging in conspicuous public anguish about lost jobs, state disadvantages, the need for more federal money for a declining economy, etc. I kept my response to this type of attack as dignified as I could, rather than taking him on directly for the inconsistencies and inaccuracies in his position, saying simply that my district was not disadvantaged by the good reputation I have in Washington. Frank assumes I have a good reputation in Washington, and he could not deny that, since the point he made was based on my assumed national stature.

As I look back at the month of October, it seems to have been born in disorder and exhausted itself in drudgery. . . . The tax bill itself was a sad affair. The day before we went to conference, the secretary of the treasury called on me by himself, saying that he came to take my temperature and to let me take his temperature. He then proceeded to assure me solemnly that "this president is capable of vetoing the bill if he doesn't get what he wants." My rejoinder was,

21. The House approved the Revenue Act of 1978 on August 10 by a vote of 362–49.
22. Conable's share of the vote was 72.5 percent.

"Mike, the president may be crazy, but he isn't nuts," then going on to say that he had no choice but to accept whatever bill we sent him. He assured me again solemnly that if the cuts went too far, if major capital gains reductions were included, or if the tuition tax credit proposal were included, as some were then suggesting, the president would certainly veto it. I said that I thought he might believe what he was telling me, but I didn't believe it. Because of the tax increase that would result if the president vetoed the bill, and because it was almost certain that we would not send him a second bill remedying any dissatisfaction he might have with the first version, I was convinced that the president would have to take whatever we sent him.

The first skirmish came before we went to conference at all and was entirely satisfactory. It was to be the classic case of winning a battle and losing the war. The Senate, in a fit of whimsy, had adopted something called the [Sam] Nunn [D-GA] amendment, a provision which required additional 5 percent tax cuts in successive years up to five years, provided the rate of government expenditure did not exceed a certain percent of the gross national product, provided the deficit declined and the budget was balanced by 1981, and provided certain other modest conditions were met, including the president's determination that it was not destructive of the national interest to permit such automatic tax cuts to take effect. This was the kind of provision that I had been looking for, and it had the great advantage of Democratic sponsorship in the Senate, and so I immediately enlisted John Rhodes and some of the Senate leadership in a press conference to proclaim that we were going to move to instruct the conferees to accept this Senate amendment. The press conference went satisfactorily, except that [Senator] Bill Roth showed up with a box under his arm which, at the appropriate moment, he pulled out, opened, and showed that it contained cigars, which he then passed out among the press, saying that this was the "son of Kemp-Roth" and that we had won the Kemp-Roth battle. He permitted himself to be photographed with a cigar in his mouth while the rest of us in the press conference stood behind him uneasily eyeing the cigars, and this ridiculous picture went across the land, reflecting the gimmickry of the Republican approach and making us all uneasy about the image we were projecting. The next day, however, the House supported us by a two-to-one margin, since many people had opposed Kemp-Roth up to that point simply because it did not deal with the issue of restraining the growth of government and government expenditures. The seven Democrats who were to make up the conferees for the House, however, all voted against the Nunn amendment.

The conference began slowly, and because of the shortness of time, the Senate and the House started caucusing separately, sending staff members shuttling back and forth to comment on the things which one house or the other would or would not accept in the other's position. I began to be very uneasy about this course because it seemed to be subverting the intention of having an open conference, and I was afraid the staff members were funneling this information through Treasury representatives who were then giving the White House greater say in the communication process than it should have had. I don't know whether this was true or not. As time went on and the pressure built, it was apparent that [Senate Finance Committee chairman] Russell Long was not in his usual affable mood, as the "sugar bill," something that affected his constituency directly, occupied more of his attention than it should have. The sugar bill ultimately failed, much to his sorrow, and probably the distraction it provided him from the work of the tax bill was one of the reasons the conference did not seem to flow smoothly at any point.

The leaders, Ullman and Long, seemed to feel that if we met together to any substantial degree, someone would make a speech, the time schedule would slip, and we would wind up not being able to meet the scheduled adjournment. The result was not only damaging to dialogue but left us frequently misunderstanding the position of the other house, since the members were not able to express their views directly and only the conclusions were transmitted. I vow that I will never again participate in a conference which is not held openly and with the confrontation of the parties possible in the forum before the press and the public. Certainly this procedure nullified the salubrious effects of open conferences, something which I thought had been fully decided earlier.

Various issues were dealt with in one way or another, with the result that we had a good final solution of the capital gains reduction and minimum tax quandary . . . but without anything of the Nunn amendment. It seems that most of the members of the conference thought of that as pretty much a public relations gimmick, destructive of the orderly processes of representative government because it involved a formula tax cut rather than something which would be of political value to succeeding Congresses. When it was quickly abandoned by the House conferees despite the two-to-one passage by the Senate and two-to-one instruction of the conferees by the House, I vowed that I would take the matter to the floor on a motion to recommit, the papers coming to the House for first consideration, in view of the procedure as it had evolved up to that point. Russell Long, not happy with the Nunn amendment, apparently agreed with Ullman in private that, because of the pressure of events in the House, the Senate would take the papers back and consider the conference report first, thus leaving me without a conference committee to which the report could be recommitted, since the Senate would have discharged the conference by first passage of the conference report. This was an unusual procedure, but lacking the votes, I was helpless to do anything about it, and I had to abandon my effort to recommit. A serious effort thus wound up looking quixotic, and something about which I could have been considerably more enthusiastic than I ever was about Kemp-Roth sank without a ripple because of the lateness of the hour, the pressure of events, and the deviousness of the Democratic leaders.

The president apparently realized the error of his ways, although he was evidently upset over the reduction in capital gains tax which was included in this measure. The bill was held by the staff of the Joint Committee on Internal Revenue Taxation for more than a week after it had been finally passed by both houses of the Congress, leading me to wonder if some scheme had not been worked up between the leaders and the White House to permit the president to veto the tax bill shortly after the election. I raised this possibility in at least one speech during the campaign, suspecting that the president was keeping his options open in the event that a dramatic step like the vetoing of a major tax-cut bill were required by a deteriorating condition of the dollar abroad. He finally signed the bill, despite promptings by Senator Kennedy to follow through with this original vetoing intent, on election night itself, taking it to Camp David for this purpose, presumably signing it behind a bush up there and then returning to the White House to watch the election returns, confident there would be no publicity about his about-face in signing the bill because the election news would eclipse all else.

For the last three days, I have been in a bad depression because it was apparent to me that the Republicans were not going to pick up any substantial number of seats and thus that the 96th Congress was likely to be a repeat of the 95th.[23] I am sick of being in the minority and of having no prospect of being able to influence the course of events directly, without the deviousness that a minority member must have to get his opinions registered in any effective way on the laws of the land.

23. The 95th Congress had 292 Democrats and 143 Republicans; the split in the 96th Congress was 278 Democrats, 157 Republicans.

Conable frowns on the idea of a constitutional amendment requiring a balanced budget—at least at first. He is really down on Jimmy Carter. With Oklahoma Democrat Jim Jones, Conable takes up the treatment of depreciation under the tax law, which they will see through to success. He defends his previous legislative progeny—revenue sharing—from fierce attacks. Conable's frustration at being in the perpetual minority party grows. He agrees to serve as chairman of the steering committee for presidential candidate George H. W. Bush, expressing the hope that, although Bush has little chance of success, at least he might improve the quality of the debate. As the year ends, the outlook for the campaign brightens.

Richard Bolling, the famously choleric and erudite Missouri Democrat and chairman of the House Rules Committee, became another of Conable's special legislative friends, despite their often antithetical viewpoints. Like the others he was particularly fond of—Bill Frenzel, Bill Steiger, Abner Mikva, and Jim Corman—Bolling possessed a sharp intellect and was perhaps not as clubbable as the typical successful politician.

With revenue sharing on the ropes, Conable mounted a defense thereof on philosophical grounds. As was the case at revenue sharing's creation, Conable was dismayed by the widespread lack of interest in or understanding of the principle of decentralism. He expatiated on the devolution of power and influence entailed by revenue sharing and praised it as a restorative centrifugal program, but he was unable to impart this conceptualization to many of his colleagues.

February 19, 1979

It's time I started the journal for 1979 and began again to record activities of a new Congress. Despite all the preliminaries which are now so elaborately institutionalized, each Congress seems to start more slowly than the last, with nothing at all other than the organizing activities transpiring on the floor for the first two months.

As for Ways and Means, we do not seem to be afflicted with any major sense of urgency, any more than the Congress as a whole. Henson Moore [LA] was appointed by the Republicans to fill the vacancy created by the death of my dear friend Bill Steiger.[1] I still find it hard to believe that Steiger is gone, such a vital

1. Steiger died of a heart attack on December 4, 1978.

man he was, and his loss will so increase my burden by removing one of the most important elements of creativity and ferment in the entire committee. Henson Moore will doubtless be about as good a replacement as we could find, accepting keen responsibility and expressing the special interests of the Louisiana area with intelligence and conservatism.

Two weekends ago I attended the Tidewater Conference at Easton on the Eastern Shore of Maryland, at which a number of Republican functionaries met to consider five resolutions of current interest and to explore the areas of agreement within the Republican Party on these issues. . . . It was an interesting combination of discussion, heavy eating, and good fellowship around the piano after supper and well into the evening. As a matter of fact, my mellow bellowing of a large number of songs caused some commentary in *Roll Call*, the newspaper of Capitol Hill, afterwards, although, being a morning person, I did not stay up and celebrate anywhere near as long as most of my colleagues.

We got into some trouble discussing a constitutional amendment for the limitation of expenses of the federal government or for the imposition of a balanced budget constitutionally. John Rhodes and I took a fairly strong position against such a constitutional amendment, creating consternation among younger members of the party, a large number of which have already cosponsored such a balanced budget amendment. I was reported by Dave Broder, an active observer at the conference, to have said that I oppose such an amendment, in that I did not want to see every nitpicking amendment to come along included in the Constitution. My position was not that I opposed a balanced budget amendment as nitpicking but that I opposed a constitutional convention for the consideration of such an amendment, since the calling of a constitutional [convention] by resolution of the states would reopen the entire Constitution and make possible the adoption of many other amendments in addition to the balanced budget amendment, such as an abortion amendment, a busing amendment, etc.

Because of the reports coming out of Easton, and because of subsequent agitation of the issue by the press, John Rhodes and I are under some pressure and some disapprobation from many rank-and-file Republicans at this point. I heard John Rhodes at an SOS meeting, after being berated by Paul Trible of Virginia, say to Paul, "Young man, when you've been around as long as I have, you'll find that it is not good politics not to be right." Trible had told him that maybe his position was a logical one, but it wasn't good politics for him to be advocating it openly.

The unexpected death of Nelson Rockefeller[2] also found me going to New

2. On January 26, 1979.

York City on Air Force One to attend his funeral service. It was the first invitation from the president I have had to do anything out of the ordinary, and I was somewhat surprised to be singled out to fly on his plane. Our two senators went along, Jim Hanley [D-NY] and his wife, Sam Stratton and his wife, John Rhodes (who couldn't go at the last minute because of food poisoning), and Mrs. Lloyd [Beryl] Bentsen, who sat with me and spent most of the time putting on her lips and otherwise adjusting her makeup. Several cabinet officials were also on board, and the president and Mrs. Carter, who stayed up front most of the time but did at least walk back through the plane and chat with us individually briefly on the way up. The food was the worst I have ever had on a presidential excursion, be it Air Force One or *Sequoia*, and I have found it hard to believe that President Carter could so damage every aspect of White House operations that even the food on Air Force One was no longer edible.

March 19, 1979

Since my last journal entry, we have had our usual troubles with the debt ceiling. Poor planning resulted in that being the first substantive issue to come up in the 96th Congress, and so, of course, all the newly elected conservatives felt they had to vote against it the first time around. Predictably, it went down by twenty votes; then, predictably, Ways and Means cut $6 billion out of the increase in the debt ceiling, [and] then, predictably, it passed. I voted against both increases in the debt ceiling but announced on every possible occasion that I would sell my vote for any improvements on the procedures. Nobody appears to be interested in improving the procedures, and so I shall continue to vote against debt ceiling increases. I have a good deal of fun at the Rules Committee when these things come up because earnest Al [Ullman] doggedly repeats the same arguments, while I go in and wing it . . . speaking with a frankness that beguiles the Rules Committee usually, which Chairman Bolling does not know how to handle.

My relations with Dick Bolling involve mutual respect and a good deal of gingerliness. He is a man of fine intellectual equipment, too long excluded from the councils of power, and altogether too arrogant to be popular with his less intellectual colleagues, whose ignorance he suffers with some difficulty. I find him an attractive personality, but of course, he is a strong partisan . . . one of the most effective partisans in the House. It is a sad thing that a man of his ability has not been used by his party for the heavy lifting of which he is capable. Lucky for us Republicans.

Jimmy Jones and I have decided to engage in a new "Steiger-type" initiative relative to the business community. We are going to try to generate broad and extensive business support for change in the character of our depreciation laws. . . . Competitively, we are at a severe disadvantage in selling the products of our technology abroad because of the capital costs which are involved. Not only are interest rates high in this country, but most of the rest of the developed world permits very rapid write-off of capital investment, which helps reduce the static costs involved in such sales. The American tax philosophy with respect to depreciation is that a machine or other capital asset must be depreciated over the length of its useful life, while even a "decadent" country like Great Britain will permit an asset to be written off in the year in which the investment is made, as though it were a business expense rather than a capital investment. It is our plan to try to push a change which will completely eliminate the concept of useful life, going instead to an arbitrary shorter write-off of something like ten years for buildings, five years for heavy equipment, three years for light equipment, and one year for that type of investment which is mandated by government for reasons of pollution control or safety. The revenue loss from such a change would be very substantial in the first year, which may require some compromising of the length of time over which the write-off is permitted, but I shall not be disappointed if we can simply get away from the useful life type of depreciation and go to an arbitrary and shorter mode.

Jimmy and I held a meeting with a number of Hill business representatives, springing the idea on them, asking them if they thought the business community could coalesce behind such a proposal well in advance of the expected 1980 tax bill, and asking for some feedback during the next two weeks so that we could make any adjustments they thought appropriate before we held a press conference and started seeking cosponsors. Not surprisingly, most of the business representatives seemed to favor the idea, although there is some concern about the size of the revenue loss, and we are trying to get ballpark figures from the Joint Committee on Taxation as quickly as possible before we find ourselves in an embarrassing understatement of revenue loss. It may turn into quite a campaign, if we can adjust the figures so that the proposal appears to be reasonable, because it is so obvious we are not going to get any other type of capital formation tax legislation during the Carter administration.

April 16, 1979

[There] was a sense at the outset of our Budget [Committee] markup that this was going to be a little different this year, with Dave Broder doing a special article in the *Washington Post* to the effect that I was going to be the key Republican strategist and would have to decide if we were going to take the Republicans out again from any constructive participation in the Budget Committee, the decision to be made on the basis of the size of the deals Bob Giaimo would offer me to get Republican votes for cutbacks that otherwise would have to be forgone as he was forced to deal with his liberals. Not much happened to bear out this prognostication. Giaimo and I were more relaxed with each other, and I generally voted a very conservative line, opposing almost all efforts to put money back into the president's budget and even agreeing to compromise the issue of defense, where conservatives are supposed to rally 'round and vote more money because of a concern over Russia.

If there was one subject on which sparks flew, it was revenue sharing, and there, I was the liberal. The decision was made by the Democratic caucus of the Budget Committee to eliminate the share of the states under revenue sharing, even though this is the last year of revenue sharing and the whole item should be reviewed late this year or early next. I moved to put the money back in and made a philosophical speech about decentralization and about the desirability of continuing revenue sharing and [suggested that] if it was necessary to cut back on any aid to the states and communities, to cut money out of the categorical grants instead.

It was surprising to see how few people have a philosophical interest in revenue sharing. Bob Giaimo made a vehement talk against revenue sharing, saying it was a waste of money, that the states were all in surplus, that they were pushing us to balance our budget, but any effort to merely phase it out would meet with his undying enmity as well as any effort to put it back in, since "it's a snake and it's got to be killed quickly." I accused him, as a member of the Appropriations Committee, of always having opposed revenue sharing because no power went with it, in that it relied on principles of democracy rather than central bureaucratic administration to arrive at an equitable distribution of money. When the time came to have a roll call vote on the issue, only Bill Frenzel and I would raise our hands to the positive, some of the urban Democrats who had been supporting my position apparently folding under the chairman's negative rhetoric. . . . I hope the governors will mount a strong lobbying campaign on behalf of revenue sharing, one of the few real accomplishments in which I feel I have had a significant part since I came to the Congress.

H.R. 1, the public financing measure of this Congress, chugs along with my nominal support. I am of two minds about it, hating to get into the tremendous federal bureaucracy which will have to administer any such law, to the sorrow of all candidates for office and probably [contributing] to the decision not to run of many otherwise potentially strong candidates. The [special-]interest money that goes into our current manner of financing elections really frightens me, however, and I am convinced that nothing can do more damage to the credibility of representative government than for the public to find out how much money people are spending and what its sources are. Fright, then, causes me to support public financing, while almost everything else about the measure would cause me to oppose it. I would look like a hypocrite if I did not support it, with my long-standing practice of not accepting more than $50 from any source and with my great emphasis on the importance of small contributions, the influence of which would be doubled under the public financing law's matching grant program. Also, the major proponents of the measure, John Anderson, Mo Udall, and Tom Foley, have accommodated me in raising the maximum . . . that can be paid in election campaigning so that the part of the proposal which tends to favor incumbency (with its built-in name recognition) will be less objectionable to the members of my party. I get no credit for this, nor are many Republicans patient with my advocacy of public financing; indeed, most of them seem to be considerably more strident in their denunciation of my "having taken leave of my senses." Particularly sharp on this score are two members of my committee: Guy Vander Jagt, the fund-raiser for the Republicans, and Bill Frenzel, the ideological leader of the opposition to public financing.

June 15, 1979

I had a difficult personal relationship to the budget process. I was determined to try to work to keep the deficit as low as possible, through cooperation with Giaimo, if necessary, and through a more moderate fiscal course than the one I have espoused in earlier years. It was my hope that we could cut the president's deficit of $29 billion in half, thus making possible the balancing of the budget next year, assuming a fairly decent level of economic activity. A Republican proposal that I worked hard on and supported strongly to reduce the deficit to $15 billion did not do well, even the Rousselot "balanced budget" amendment with forced figures and very little staffing getting more votes than the Republican alternative.

A refusal to vote for the Rousselot amendment, consistent with my actions in other years, brought my name to a list of "Republican fumblers" in a *Wall Street Journal* editorial which never asked the question whether the amendment was a responsible or carefully thought out proposal, but only whether Republicans should play the game of posturing a balanced budget with or without reality behind it. Ralph Regula [OH] and Marjorie Holt were not enthusiastic about the Republican alternative, and as two credible members on the Republican side of the Budget Committee, they pushed instead a $19 billion deficit character-ized primarily by more spending money for defense, Marjorie's pet posture. The Joe Fisher alternative to cut a small percentage out of the budget did pass, and the final figure was somewhere around $23 billion of deficit. I voted against this, feeling it was still too high, but immediately went across the aisle, saw Bob Giaimo, and said, "Bob, I would like to help you during the conference and will do what I can to preserve the House figures, since I expect them to be better than the Senate's."

He expressed satisfaction, but it wasn't until the following afternoon that I asked Harry Nicholas, my administrative assistant, to check up and find out when the conference was beginning. To my surprise, I discovered that I had not been appointed a conferee by Del Latta, the slots going instead to junior members who could be assumed to follow his leadership to a greater degree than I. I don't know whether he had learned of my conversation with Giaimo and deliberately left me off for that reason. The figure that came back from the conference, close to $23 billion, was achieved simply by restating economic assumptions rather than by maintaining the House cuts. Nonetheless, the liberals all voted against the conference report, feeling that there should be $350 million more in education and/or CETA[3] and $350 million less in defense. The result was the conference report was struck down. I then was assigned to the conference committee, Del Latta deciding that he didn't want to have anything further to do with it; and yet we never met, the issue being thrashed out among the Democrats without Republican help. In opposing the final result—to wit, $350 million more for education without any reduction in defense—I called this a majority solution to a majority problem. . . . In retrospect, I feel quite irrelevant to the work of the Budget Committee and I am discouraged that I did not have greater effect or at least better comprehension of what was happening at the time it was happening.

We have begun to be aware, some of the Ways and Means Committee, of what a destructive force also the five freshman Democrats are on the committee. These men—[James] Shannon [MA], [Frank] Guarini [NJ], Wyche Fowler [GA], [Cecil] Heftel [HI], and [Tom] Downey [NY]—appear to know very little about tax law, but they have a strong sense of cohesion and a thrust to the left which cannot be ignored because of their numbers. If they were bright, like Mikva or Corman, or somewhat sounder in their ideology, I would feel much better about them. It is my impression that Downey is the ringleader of the

3. The Comprehensive Employment and Training Act, a public jobs program signed into law by President Nixon.

group, being the brightest, and that he will give Al a very tough time over the short-term future because of his aggressiveness and his strong leftish tendencies.

We are now working on the windfall profits tax. This promises to be a debacle every bit as distressing as any I have observed since I have been on the Ways and Means Committee. The president is his own worst enemy on this issue. One day, he engages in strident populist rhetoric denouncing the oil companies for their special-interest rip-offs. The next day, he querulously asks why the American people won't submit to decontrol, fearing rip-offs, when that's the only course left open to us. His inconsistency would appear funny if it weren't such an obstacle to a rational consideration of a very sensitive area. I continue to support the idea of a windfall profits tax (something the oil companies don't like), with a plowback (something they mistrust) and decontrol (the only thing they really want). I have told Al that I would support the president's position if it is necessary for him to get Republican votes to keep people like the fearsome five in front from changing the whole exercise from one related to energy policy into a punitive raid on the oil companies.

Imagine my chagrin—after my feeling that we had worked out a probable area of cooperation, minority and majority—to find in the *Washington Post* a story that indicated a Democratic caucus of the Ways and Means Committee members had taken place and that Al had got agreement on some way of converting the president's proposal into something much more punitive than incentive producing. At the beginning of the markups, following the reading of the article, I unloaded on Al, saying that he wasn't going to get any Republican votes if he decided the issue in Democratic caucus and asked for our assistance only after the agreed Democratic solution had failed. . . . I really am fed up with being in the minority and much frustrated by the difficulty with which I or any of my colleagues achieve a reasonable degree of input into legislation which is critical for our constituents.

It appears that John Rhodes is expecting to retire at the end of this term. A modest article to this effect has already appeared in the paper, and John did not deny it to me when I talked to him about the article. He asked me if I wanted to be minority leader, saying that I would be a fine one, but acted relieved when I said I was not in the least bit interested and that I would probably want to support Bob Michel for the position. Since John Anderson has announced that he will withdraw from the chairmanship of the conference following his announcement for the presidency, there has been a good deal of maneuvering among the Republicans for the expected filling of vacancies. I talked to Rhodes and asked him who he wanted me to support for the leadership, saying to him that I thought the critical issue was one of support.

My attitude on this has been strongly affected by developments within the leadership: Bud Shuster [PA] has defied Rhodes on the issue of a constitutional amendment for a balanced budget and has demanded, after securing the support of others in the leadership, that Rhodes change on this issue. Shuster is an ambitious, hard-driving, inflexible, and (to me) unattractive man. He is well organized but pedestrian. He has a large ego and is ambitious for things across the horizon which I do not fully understand. He is an ideologue. The other day, he put out a five-page statement on tax policy in which the words "Kemp-Roth" appeared a large number of times, apparently in an effort to help his friend Jack Kemp achieve goals I do not fully understand either. I called John Rhodes and told him that I did not take kindly to such a statement on tax policy without consultation with the minority members of the Ways and Means Committee. Rhodes came to the Policy [Committee] meeting and unloaded unmercifully on Bud Shuster, apparently reflecting his animus at Bud's end run on the constitutional amendment for a balanced budget. I felt that I had provoked a confrontation and felt apologetic with Rhodes about it, but Rhodes apparently dislikes Shuster so intensely that he was happy for the chance to unload.

The Bush campaign proceeds. George got a good psychological boost from Iowa, where 2,800 Republican leaders attending their annual fund-raiser voted 39 percent for him, 25 percent for Ronald Reagan, 13 percent for Howard Baker, and 11 percent for John Connally. There was considerable surprise that George did so well, but George has been telling me all along that he was heavily organized in Iowa as in New Hampshire and that his hopes lay in doing well in those early primary states. He shows nowhere near the rank-and-file support, but certainly his candidacy must be taken more seriously in view of this support among Republican professionals. I am the chairman of George's steering committee, having felt I could be proud of anything I could do for George, regardless of his chances, while I felt quite uncertain about getting on the bandwagon of either John Connally or Ronald Reagan. Both of these people have contacted me and obviously are interested in my support, but presumably both of them would understand my committing to one who has as modest expectancy as George has in view of his standing in the polls, particularly when that candidate also sat next to me for four years in the Ways and Means Committee.

I will do a little speaking for George but do not expect to have a frantically active role in his campaign, and evidently, he is perfectly happy to have me simply lend my prestige as steering committee chairman, a conclusion on his part that he probably has nobody of any real prestige willing to support him at this point. I like George and have confidence in him personally, and thus I am perfectly willing to reflect a personal lack of ambition by supporting a candidacy which nobody in the media seems to take very seriously at this point. . . . I shall be satisfied if he conducts himself with dignity and makes his contribution to the dialogue of the Republican electoral campaign.

Last weekend, I took Marian Wallace, Linda McLaughlin, and Wendy Lechner up to the district for the first time. These three ladies have worked for me for a combined total of at least twenty years, and it seemed to me that I could quite wisely invest the cost of such a trip [so they could see] the people and the institutions they have been working for all this time. We had a simply great weekend, nostalgic for me and enlightening for them, and came back better friends than ever.

August 5, 1979

It has been almost two months since I did a journal entry, and I am at a loss to identify any real achievements during this two-month period. . . . The most singular occurrence of the period has been the presidential reelection gambit involving his ten days at Camp David, followed by his ruthless extirpation of the independent and intelligent spirits in his cabinet.[4] This performance by the Carter White House has had heads shaking on Capitol Hill, and the urge to disassociate among Democrats is almost complete. Such a review and revision of executive branch personnel would be quite normal for a two-term presidency at the end of the first term, but to do it after the third year of the first term, risking the major paralyses which would result in the affected departments of the government, is to gamble not just with one's political future but with the effectiveness of the government at the time of the need of maximum problem solving: the last year of a four-year term, when all the complex and difficult issues which have been accumulated during the previous three years must be dealt with, if they are to be dealt with at all. President Carter believes in polls: he is in trouble in every poll worthy of the name, and he evidently feels that he has very little to lose from taking major risks in efforts to attract the attention of the public and persuade them that he is a vigorous and forceful leader.

4. On July 17, 1979, at President Carter's prompting, the twelve members of his cabinet tendered their resignations. He accepted the resignations of five: Transportation Secretary Brock Adams; Attorney General Griffin Bell; Treasury Secretary Michael Blumenthal; Health, Education, and Welfare (HEW) Secretary Joseph Califano; and Energy Secretary James Schlesinger. Housing and Urban Development (HUD) Secretary Patricia Roberts Harris left HUD to take Califano's place at HEW.

Following the departure of Blumenthal, Califano, Schlesinger, et al., he has embarked on a major new campaign strategy which will take him to many parts of the country and detach him from the Washington he describes as an island. It is as though he had suddenly discovered that Senator [Ted] Kennedy [D-MA] is real and realized that the time left for him to recapture the presidency is only from now until January instead of from now until Republicans have nominated their candidate. He continues to sink in the polls, but of course, a president of the United States, however unpopular and however much he concerns the people, still draws crowds when he moves about the country, and that is evidently his design. It is hard to believe he will be an effective administrator during the year ahead or that he will be able to lead the Congress in any semblance of responsible leadership. I am more distressed with him than I have been during his term so far, since I have been convinced until this time that he would eventually learn the responsibilities of incumbency and accept the obligation of running the country. I now think he is comfortable only in the role of the candidate, that he will preserve the image of the outsider to the extent that he can do so until he leaves office. Truly anyone who thinks the reorganization of the government begins with the upgrading of Hamilton Jordan[5] has a strange idea of his governmental responsibilities.

October 22, 1979

I am coming back from a glorious weekend in the district, and I am dictating this on the airplane. Indian summer is at its fullest, if a warm spell so early in the fall can be considered Indian summer. The colors of the countryside are enough to make your spirit sing, and the bright blue October weather is the finest period in western New York.

I continue to have a disturbing time with Al Ullman. We have started a number of initiatives, many of which have either petered out or resulted in questionable bills by narrow margins, leaving in doubt any action on them by the Senate or, in some cases, even by the Rules Committee. Other matters have been started but have not been acted on by the committee . . . , leaving them in limbo. As a result, during the past two weeks, I have made elaborate preparations and gone over to meet with Al privately in his inner office, saying that I was disturbed by our incapacity to face up to the issues we had previously identified, and asking what his plans were for the rest of the year. He surprised me by saying that there were reasons for every position he has taken in temporization, and told me that,

5. Jordan was named chief of staff during the shake-up.

beginning November 5, he hopes to start general hearings on his proposal for all types of business tax relief to be financed by a 10 percent value-added tax. It appears that he has prepared legislation, which he expects will have the effect of opening the entire tax law, and that this will be the subject of the hearings, thus occupying us with "busy work" for the entire month of November, assuming that we are going to be meeting during this period while the Senate debates the SALT treaty.

I am appalled by this suggestion, which appears to me to have very little potential for constructive results, but I have held a meeting of the minority members of the Ways and Means Committee to consider the manner in which we should organize testimony to achieve the various things we want to achieve. This meeting had little interest among the minority members, but I suspect that adequate witnesses will come forward anyway to support such initiatives as the Capital Cost Recovery Act (the Jones-Conable bill) and other matters which Al refuses to look at except as plums to be bought by the value-added tax. Incidentally, on the value-added tax, I find very little general support or, indeed, anything short of outright hostility among the Democrats on the committee or among the Democrats in the House generally. I think he is misjudging very badly the mood of the Congress, assuming that the desire to give tax relief will carry with it eventual acceptance of a regressive and unpleasant tax burdened with major administrative complexities. I cannot believe that Russell Long is infatuated with this ill-advised project and assume that he is going along with Al only for devious strategic reasons of his own.

George [H. W. Bush] remains tense in his public utterances, and his views remain sufficiently compromised to be without any attention-compelling vigor. John Connally, on the other hand, obviously realizes his candidacy is in trouble and has taken a high-silhouette position on issues like the Middle East and Chappaquiddick, preferring to go down swinging rather than end his campaign with a whimper or a modest showing against the entrenched power of Reagan. Reagan seems like a plate of warmed-over hash,[6] without the fervor in his support that was present in 1976 and without, as yet, even an official candidacy.

November 21, 1979

Hopes for an early adjournment of the Congress have, as they always do, evaporated, and it now appears likely that we will be here until sleigh bells ring.

---

6. He used the same phrase to describe Richard Nixon in his journal entry of July 19, 1968.

I have surprised some people by saying that I thought a value-added tax might be inevitable eventually but that I was going to drag my heels all the way to enactment, since I didn't like the tax and thought it was inappropriate, except for those who have already given up on the income tax. I'm not willing to give up on a progressive tax based on ability to pay. . . . It's put me in a position where I appear to be niggardly in my desires for tax preferences, even though tax preferences reduce taxes and therefore should have the support of a conservative, but I do not want to erode the income tax base to the point where a value-added tax becomes inevitable. This, and the state of the economy, may eventually make the decision for us, but I am unwilling to make it voluntarily and to rush into regressive taxation before I have to.

December 31, 1979

Looking back over the past two months is a discouragement: I don't know what accomplishment I expected, but it has been increasingly apparent that the 96th Congress, unless it changes dramatically, will have little to characterize it or to give its members pride in their service. The illusion of an early adjournment was as hollow as most such mirages. Chrysler and the windfall profits tax were the two pieces of "must" legislation which kept us until the weekend before Christmas.

Chrysler surprised me—I never believed, and remained convinced until the end, that Congress would bail out this giant, troubled enterprise, feeling that the prospect of success was too uncertain and the precedent too troubling.[7] The labor implications bothered me also: the UAW settlement increased workers' benefits by $1.3 billion just before the application for a $1.5 billion bailout, convincing me that the net improvement of the company as a result of the guarantees was not a strong argument for the additional, unguaranteed financing on which the guarantees were conditional.

I am not sure on what rationale the large majority of my colleagues who supported the bailout acted. Chrysler made a shameless special-interest pitch to Congress, listing all the Chrysler money which goes directly or through sub-contracts into each congressman's district. Chrysler dealers, the real losers in the event of a bankruptcy, thronged Capitol Hill and were the toughest group for a naysayer like me to talk to because I quite sympathized with them and couldn't

---

7. Congress authorized the Treasury to guarantee up to $1.5 billion in bank loans to the financially distressed Chrysler Corporation. The House approved the conference committee report on December 21, 1979, by a vote of 241–124, with Conable voting in the negative.

blame them for Chrysler's mistakes. I am afraid the president and Congress, in the final analysis, decided the issue on sympathy, hoping to fend off the tough decision until after the 1980 election, when it will be back with a vengeance $1.5 billion later. Who knows what other companies will be there, hat in hand, at that time to press similar appeals?

The windfall profits tax has not been as great a disappointment as Chrysler, but I don't think it's going to be easy to resolve. After much greater travail than anyone expected, the Senate finally passed an increase much greater in scope (because of the inclusion of many billions of dollars' worth of tax credits for energy conservation and some nongermane matters which will prove trouble-some) than the comparatively simple tax measure passed by the House last June.

The conferees met for the first time a couple of days before everybody wanted to quit for Christmas, and both Al and Russell made it apparent from the start that all they wanted was some "breakthrough accomplishment" to announce before departure, rather than a completed conference. The obvious target was a compromise on the amount of money to be raised by the tax over its ten-year duration, and we quickly, with only one or two dissents, settled on the remark-able sum of $227.3 billion (give or take $100 billion). This in itself is remarkable: the country assumes the windfall profits tax is part of an energy policy for the nation, while the president and a majority of the conferees see it primarily as a vehicle for raising a large sum of money for the Treasury.

This has been a bad year for me in terms of my peace of mind and a comfort-able relationship to my job. . . . If I were to decide at this point, I would retire at the end of this term, but I shall deliberately delay the decision until March or April and then try to be as objective as possible, regardless of the pressures of the moment. One big plus for me this year is an increasing sense of closeness and unity with my staff: Harry and Linda have been great, providing the support I needed and shielding me from unnecessary distractions and pressures. I have complete confidence in their abilities, their loyalty, and their discretion. I largely deal with the rest of the staff through them, and it is my belief that the rest of the staff is far above the average in ability and industry.

Maybe next year will be better. If so, I will likely owe it to George Bush. When I agreed to go on George's steering committee, later becoming its chair-man, I thought I was making a decision to stay out of the 1980 campaign, with Connally, if anyone, being the logical challenger to Reagan. I am today coming back from a weekend at George's house in Houston, where we spent nine hours of two days in disciplined and informative discussions for George's benefit of a series of domestic and foreign issues. George showed confidence and singleness of purpose—a thoroughly mature and concentrating candidate—and I felt good about the way his campaign is unfolding. He may do better than expected, despite his current low standing in the polls, and Iowa will be the first indication. Reagan has decided to avoid the Iowa debate, and Connally actually seems to be slipping. I have never doubted George's capacity—only the public's perception—and Reagan's long lead may evaporate in the heat of a pressure cooker George seems better designed to withstand.

George Bush has momentum—for a while, at least. Conable actively campaigns against a Reagan-Ford ticket at the Republican convention. He casts a disapproving eye on the younger Republicans who advocate tax cuts unaccompanied by commensurate spending cuts. Relations with his neighbor Jack Kemp grow tenser. Election Day predictions demonstrate that Conable is no Nostradamus. The Democrats stack the deck in Ways and Means; Conable is furious.

This is the only presidential election in which Conable was significantly involved. He was:

- *chairman of George Bush's steering committee;*
- *an instrument of Bush's timely departure from the primary race against Ronald Reagan, which may have helped bump Bush into the vice-presidential slot—a nomination Bush had "no hope at all" of achieving, according to a preconvention Conable;*
- *a vocal raiser of Cain over the prospect of a "collective presidency" consisting of Reagan and old friend Gerald Ford; and*
- *an occasional traveling companion for candidate Bush.*

Conable addressed the value of his errant predictions in a discussion of the importance of contemporaneous as opposed to retrospective accounts: "One tends to rearrange one's memory of such events after the fact, and frequently one is wrong on one's predictions, one of the most interesting after-the-fact values of a journal. It is through our errors, through our misplaced expectations, that we learn not to despair before the reason for despairing is known."

February 12, 1980
I begin a new year after a disturbing delay but nonetheless with full determination that the journal must somehow reclaim its priority as contemporary comment rather than as sporadic and partial review. I am sure that this has been one of the few unique contributions of my service in Congress. Although I readily

acknowledge that it may never prove useful to anybody, it clearly is something of my own nobody else could have written.

The legislative activity preempting my time since the seventeenth of January has been the still-unresolved windfall profits tax conference. . . . This past Thursday night, in some sort of macho performance I never understood, [Russell] Long and [Al] Ullman dared each other to keep on working until after midnight, ricocheting back and forth through the many credits for fuel conservation which the Senate added to the bill. Ostensibly, it was an effort to complete the conference, but too much remained to be done, too many key people were missing, and so much was unprepared that from the start it was obvious that we could make only partial and tentative decisions. I was angry, but I was also frustrated because my own contributions have not been numerous or good. While I occasionally rise to rhetorical fervor, usually I doodle in truculent silence. I have little expert to add to energy legislation. Possibly Al and Russell pressed last Thursday in an effort to expiate the sins of the Congress, since the ABSCAM scandal[1] has been all over the newspapers all week, and some accomplishment would offer needed diversion.

One of the biggest unresolved issues in the windfall conference is the disposition of the proceeds of the tax. We Republicans and a group of conservative Democrats led by Sam Gibbons would like to see the bulk of it returned to the people in income tax cuts. Ullman resists that but has no clear alternative and has so far created the appearance of wanting to give in to the Senate, with [its] exotic, impractical tax credits, since that's the easiest way to harmony. I have never seen him less effective, more distracted, less in control of his own committee members. Perhaps it's the opposition developing at home in the form of a bright young Republican millionaire who is exploiting Oregon's resistance to the VAT [value-added tax] or any other form of sales tax. He starts all his negotiations with Russell Long in a way that foredooms the House position, to the consternation of the House conferees as a whole. Yet he shows signs of wanting to run again, starting a major fund-raising campaign which I am sure will ultimately put the arm on every lobbyist in the world.

George Bush has momentum! Iowa was a great boost,[2] separating him from the pack and making him the focal point of an anti-Reagan feeling which is

1. An FBI undercover operation that resulted in the convictions of six US representatives and one US senator.

2. Bush won the Iowa caucuses with 31.6 percent of the vote. Reagan finished second with 29.5 percent.

much greater than expected. . . . Reagan looks old, whether or not he's vigorous, and people are looking for strength, experience, and vigor in a leader, not persistent candidacy. We now have twenty-eight members of Congress on George's national steering committee, an interesting commentary on his ability to reach out and to sustain loyalty when he left Congress in 1970, while John Anderson, with one announced congressional supporter, has been chairman of the Republican Conference since 1969, with the strong defense of many of those of us now supporting Bush. I have no day-to-day contact with George (indeed, my duty as national chairman of the steering committee is not burdensome or even clearly defined), but my colleagues all assume that if he wins, I will be in his government. We have no understanding, nor do I have the administrative experience to do anything complicated, so we'll worry about that later. In the meantime, I tell those interested that I can't think of anything I can do this year that is more important than helping George, and I mean it.

John Rhodes has done a strange thing: he has announced that he will run for Congress again, and for Speaker, but if not elected by a majority of the House, he will then not serve as minority leader in the next Congress. This has set off, a year in advance, a scramble for Republican leadership positions from top to bottom. The two candidates for minority leader are Bob Michel and Guy Vander Jagt.

Vander Jagt is a brilliant orator (three or four major speeches a year, long and carefully rehearsed), smooth and clever. He has raised massive sums of money for the Republican Party in general and many grateful incumbents in particular, and I suspect he will win. I suspect him of being a dealer, judging from his performance as ranking member of my Ways and Means Public Welfare Subcommittee. I don't believe he could be expected to be a diligent floor leader of the minority. That's the reason I'm for Michel—a direct, hardworking, and matter-of-fact team leader as Republican whip under John Rhodes. I have always thought Rhodes was the right leader for us, but he has constantly disappointed me for his absence from the floor on anything but the most dramatic issues. The minority leader should be a *floor* leader, as Jerry Ford made it, rather than a man who spends most of his time in his office talking to lobbyists. I mustn't overstate my disappointment in John in this respect, but it is a matter of nagging discontent among the members, and the way to correct it is to choose the right successor.

March 21, 1980
Although the Senate continues to delay its final enactment of the conference report on the windfall profits tax, the House at least has it behind us. Completion

of the conference report by the conferees ended with a whimper and not with a bang, the proceedings having been protracted beyond all reason, and neither side feeling much enthusiasm in the result. Of the Republican House conferees, only I signed the conference report. . . . Thus I was left somewhat exposed on the issue, . . . a man somewhat suspect by my colleagues as having once again waffled or turned liberal while my tougher colleagues remained resolute.

I found an initially hostile Policy Committee, headed by hard-liner Bud Shuster, when I went to explain the bill as finally compromised in conference. Nobody took me on personally, but people like Jim Collins of Texas and Ed Forsyth of New Jersey (Ed was having a fund-raiser the next week) got up and berated the bill as a fraud on consumers, a devastating blow to the oil industry, and a measure antithetical to all good Republican principles. My position was not that it was a good bill but that there were a great many political booby traps in voting against it. The Teeter polling organization had demonstrated quite conclusively that the only institution less popular than government was the oil industry. I did not think, for that reason, that the Republican Party should take a position against the bill. I also pointed out that the bill had as one of its saving graces a requirement that 60 percent of the proceeds of the tax be earmarked for income tax cuts, a strong point in the Republican platform of recent years, and a twist in the windfall profits tax that made it considerably more palatable.

By the time the Policy Committee meeting was over, it had been decided that—as usual, on motion of John Erlenborn—the Policy Committee would not take a position until after a Republican conference in which a straw poll would be taken to see how many Republicans tended to go along with our oil-state brethren in their emotional antipathy, despite the facts. Of course, when the conference was called and we went through the whole exercise again—my dispassionate explanation followed by the emotional attacks of the oil-state representatives—the great bulk of the people in the room favored the Republican Party's not taking a position in opposition to the measure. But indeed, a very substantial minority of Republicans wound up voting for the bill, which passed by a comfortable margin.[3] I offered an olive branch to the oil-state Republicans by voting for an Archer motion to recommit the conference report (after it was apparent that the motion was going to lose), which would have reinstated the independent exemption, a grab for exemption from the tax by those producing companies that had a volume of less than a thousand barrels a day. (I am not

3. The House approved the conference report of the Crude Oil Windfall Profit Tax Act of 1980 on March 13 by a vote of 302–107.

proud of that vote but deemed it politic to show that I was not completely hostile to the oil industry.)

The distraction I have had during this period has been the absolute collapse of the Bush campaign, following the stubbing of his toe during the New Hampshire campaign.[4] . . . Thereafter John Anderson emerged as the darling of the press, the courageous candidate who took high-silhouette positions and therefore was "a candidate of substance," while George's tendency to try to balance his positions in ways he could live with as president [left] most people feeling that he was a "politics as usual" candidate. George was even sandbagged by claims that he belonged to the Trilateral Commission, a right-wing smear which is typical of Reagan people, although not necessarily of Reagan himself. That John Anderson was also a member of the Trilateral Commission apparently made no particular difference with respect to his candidacy, but it was considered damning for George. Anderson was not running in the South at all, never having pretended to be a national candidate, but of course, George was badly clobbered by Reagan there.

John's righteousness is showing through, and I continue to believe that George would wear better in a general election campaign than John would, despite John's high-level articulacy. Clearly, if the two of them go all the way to the convention and divide the anti-Reagan vote, they are assuring a Reagan victory. Last night, rather than staying in Washington for a protracted Budget Committee session, I came to Buffalo to appear for George Bush at a meeting of an uncommitted slate of delegates which was being wooed by Mrs. Anderson and Congressman Bill Green [R-NY], one of the few members of Congress actually backing John. It was a dispiriting event, since the constraint on me as a result of my friendship with the Andersons led me to a dispassionate recital of George's qualifications, while both Green and Mrs. Anderson made emotional appeals on behalf of "the candidate of courage." Jack Kemp, incidentally, was angry at me for attending such an event, saying that I was working against him and the Erie County committee, which he has tried to foreclose for Reagan. Behind this effort Jack feels his prestige is totally staked. Jack is as egotistical as John Anderson: as a matter of fact, congressional egos seem disproportionate to the importance of this crazy job, and there are no two larger congressional egos anywhere than those of John Anderson and Jack Kemp.

I would cheerfully leave this place and either go to a new job, presumably at a

4. Reagan won 50 percent of the vote in the New Hampshire primary. Bush, with 23 percent, was a distant second.

much higher pay, or return to the tranquility of my home in Alexander. My wife, however, is hostile to the idea, feeling that she has earned her day in the sun and that the work she is doing at George Washington University is a chance to be useful after long years of immobilization by children and household chores.[5] While I am sympathetic to her viewpoint, under no circumstances will I stay in Washington as a former congressman. There are too many of the spooks around here intruding on the work of the Congress, lobbying and otherwise peddling influence or trying to remain in a nostalgic posture with respect to an institution to which they no longer belong.

Since it appears unlikely that my wife and I will be able to resolve our differences about the relative virtues of living in Washington, I have been thinking more positively about running for another term, after several months of intense belief that I would not run again. I have no particular desire to serve under another Carter administration or under the administration of a Ronald Reagan either, for that matter. While I see virtually no likelihood that the Republicans will take over the House, or the Senate either, I am frustrated after sixteen years of minority status. I think it unlikely that my prestige and reputation will ever be higher than they are at this point.

It seems incredible to me that Jimmy Carter is apparently to have easy sledding during this political campaign. I cannot look at him without loathing at this point, because of the disasters he has brought upon the country, both economic and international in nature, and because of his apparent immunity to consequences. I have never known a more political president, and that includes Richard Nixon, whose political posturing made him such a disliked individual before he got through. Lyndon Johnson may have been political, but he wasn't the kind of hypocrite Carter is. Even Eisenhower had more ability than Carter.

June 3, 1980

George Bush is licking his wounds in Houston, preparing to go for a three-week period to Kennebunkport and then to slip out to the Republican convention with a quiet, unaccompanied presence and no hope at all of either a presidential or a vice-presidential nomination. I had a somewhat unhappy role in helping him get out of the race. He had concentrated heavily on Michigan, with the help of Governor [William] Milliken and Loret Ruppe,[6] and had had a command-

5. Charlotte Conable was public-policy project coordinator for the Women's Studies Program at George Washington University.

6. She would serve as director of the Peace Corps under Ronald Reagan.

ing victory there, beating Reagan by almost two to one. He proceeded to New Jersey and started tooling up for a major effort in Ohio. The networks, however, played the Michigan success down, saying instead that Reagan appeared to have now enough delegates to get him a first-ballot victory. George was crushed and asked his major supporters to have a meeting here in Washington to consider what they should do. They met in Dean Burch's[7] office, where Jim Baker stated that there was not enough money to go into California. California had been a hopeful place, since the polls there appeared to be even better at the outset than the Texas polls, where George came close to pulling off an upset. However, the cost of waging a full campaign in Reagan's home state would be close to a million dollars, and so Baker and David Keene[8] quietly started canceling the office space and media contracts which would have been necessary if they were going to make the push in California. When this information leaked out, it was assumed that everything was over.

[Later] Jim Baker called and asked if he could have a meeting of George's congressional supporters at my office the following afternoon. Twenty-two showed up, and several others called in to say that they would have come except for their having to catch planes back home for their weekend engagements. Baker and Keene made very little bones about the problems facing George, pointing out that he would have to borrow $400,000 to go into Ohio and an additional $300,000 to go into New Jersey. The prospects were for a win in New Jersey and a possible win in Ohio, despite the opposition of Governor Rhodes. A clear consensus of those at the meeting (Jim Leach [R-IA] to the contrary notwithstanding) was in favor of George's pulling out, the members feeling that he could close on a victory in Michigan, that he should not spend the rest of his life paying off a campaign debt, and that victories in Ohio and New Jersey would not help George but would cast him in the role of a spoiler by proving that Reagan was weak in those states. While they were here, George called from New Jersey and expressed surprise that Baker and Keene were meeting with us. He talked to Baker at some length, and Baker whispered to me afterwards that George appeared not to know of the California cancellation. Communication problems apparently were substantial.

Within fifteen minutes of the time the meeting broke up, Dave Broder called me and asked pointed questions about the meeting. Harry heard my end of the

7. Former chairman of the Republican National Committee (1964–1965) and the Federal Communications Commission (1969–1974).

8. National political director of the Bush campaign.

conversation and felt that I had been indiscreet and talked too much about what went on at the meeting, and he was correct, as later events showed. A *Washington Post* reporter went up to George in New Jersey and said that I had expressed a strong opinion that George should get out of the race. George was described as shaken by this information, saying that he would take such a statement by me seriously and that he would have to look into it. Millicent Fenwick [R-NJ] called me and told me about this, since one of her staffers had overheard the conversation between George and the reporter. I called Dave Broder back, told him that consensus was too strong a word for what had happened here, and stressed to him that all the congressmen in attendance had said that it was George's decision and that whatever George decided to do, they would continue to back him. Other press calls led me to try to cool it also, but the next day, the *Washington Post* reported the whole thing in great detail, and I felt that I should call George and talk to him at some length about it. He was cool but not unfriendly and said they were trying to decide what to do that weekend. Once again, he indicated communications problems within his campaign. He announced two days later that he was not going to campaign actively [any] further and that he had sent a telegram to Ronald Reagan congratulating him and offering his support.

I have since had another long call from him, this time less cool and actually including George's opinion that the meeting in my office had been helpful in explaining to his supporters in New Jersey and Ohio why he had to get out of the race. I am somewhat confused about the sequence of events, since I did not seek the meeting at my office, since Broder appeared to know about it, and since Baker and Keene did not appear at all upset over leaks, if that was what precipitated the whole affair. It may be that they felt they needed to use whatever they could on George to try to extricate him from a race which would have put him seriously in debt if he persisted in a cause which had already been lost.

The Oregon primary was a surprise for everyone, with . . . Al Ullman getting only 55 percent of the vote against a nonentity. Rostenkowski sat next to me on the floor a couple of days later and said that he was scared to death because knowledgeable people were telling him that Al had no chance of winning in Oregon this fall. I told Danny his concerns were premature. As a matter of fact, I doubt they are concerns at all, but premature exultation that he is going to be chairman of the committee next year.

July 18, 1980

This is a special report on the 1980 Republican convention. I approached this convention with great trepidation and thought that I would go and participate as little as possible, spending most of my time on social events, of which there were a plethora, judging from the invitations that poured in before the convention was assembled. . . . A week before the convention, I was called by Bob Michel and asked to be an assistant floor leader, sharing the duties for the Northeast with Bob Walker, the Reagan leader in Pennsylvania. About the same time, I was also asked by Dean Burch to introduce George Bush when he was scheduled to speak, immediately before the roll call of the states on the presidential nomination. George was given eight and one-half minutes, and I was given a minute and a half, indicating that the powers that be at the convention were anxious not to have us make policy.

I did comparatively little interview work on the floor and looked a little silly in the red hat I had to wear to identify me as a floor functionary of the whip organization.

On Tuesday, the New York delegation met to see if they wished to do anything about the platform or about the vice presidency. It developed that we were pretty closely split down the middle on the platform, with the New York City people mostly right-to-life and far right while the upstaters were the more moderate element of the party. As to the vice presidency, the Kemp people started out pushing for a vote to support Kemp. I had the feeling that the majority of delegates supported Bush, although I in no way tested that. I did arise at a critical moment and say that I was a Bush person, [but] despite that, I did not wish to see Jack Kemp hurt because I thought he had a real chance for the vice presidency in view of his close relationship to Reagan. I urged that the delegation not take a vote, which was bound to show a very substantial anti-Kemp vote in the delegation of his home state, which I said would hurt him badly and unnecessarily. . . . Many of the Kemp people came up and thanked me afterwards, and my remarks were loudly applauded by most of the delegates. As a result, we never tested the sentiment for vice president in the New York delegation.

On the floor, Jack's operatives acted as though they thought it were a convention of the Junior Chamber of Commerce, trying to whip up enthusiasm and passing out a lot of expensive placards calling for a ticket of Reagan and Kemp. The American Conservative Union[9] had rallies and receptions on Kemp's behalf. It was apparent that he was the most active campaigner for the vice presidency. I talked to Dean Burch, George Bush's political adviser, about trying to do something for George, and he consistently took the position that George did

---

9. A conservative advocacy group then best known for its annual ratings of members of Congress.

not want to embarrass Governor Reagan or to put pressure on him in any way through this type of activity. Finally, about an hour before I was to introduce George to speak immediately prior to the roll call of the states for the presidential nomination, I called Dean Burch and said that Massachusetts, Michigan, Pennsylvania, and the District of Columbia had all had placards printed up in George's behalf at their own expense and that the New Yorkers were very restive not to be doing anything themselves. Burch said that the states were doing it on their own, that George still did not wish such a show, but that if I wanted to protect myself, he didn't care, as long as anything that was done was not attributed to him or George. I then went and got some placards from the District of Columbia and from the Pennsylvania group and saw that the New Yorkers were adequately prepared at the time I came to introduce George.

Wednesday evening came, and we had some rumbles of negotiations between Ford or his representatives and Reagan over the vice presidency. I did not take them seriously until I arrived back of the podium prepared to introduce George. George was extremely glum and said to me, "Barber, I have just seen an interview of Gerald Ford by Walter Cronkite which was absolutely impossible to believe and poorly done by Ford but which indicated that he thinks he's going to be the vice-presidential nominee and has virtually worked out the conditions for acceptance." I said to George I could not believe it was true, that Jerry Ford was getting in bad trouble because there could be only one president, and that a collective presidency would not be good politics in the long run because it would not lead to good government. George said he agreed with me but that he was afraid it was already done. I said to him that he should not give up and went off in search of someone who could tell me more about it.

I found Bill Brock, and Bill reacted quite strongly to my protests at what was happening, saying that it would be a great ticket and that it was 99 percent sure that Ford was going to be the vice-presidential nominee, since Reagan had virtually accepted his conditions. When I went glumly back to George and confirmed his worst fears, he said to me that it wasn't the end of the world, that there would be other opportunities, that he was disappointed, that Gerald Ford was making a bad mistake but that we had to go ahead and perform our roles nonetheless. He then sat glumly in the back of the room looking at his speech while I stared in a depressed way at a Guy Vander Jagt keynote address which was falling far short of my expectancy. It went on for forty minutes, giving us quite a bit of time to share each other's gloom. By the time I introduced George (and it was a short, positive introduction which got a good reaction), Walter Cronkite and others were so caught up in the Ford negotiations that it was not carried on television, a matter of considerable disappointment, since it was the only chance I had for nationwide coverage.

I left the podium and went down and looked up Bob Griffin, who I knew would be in contact with Jerry Ford. I told Bob that I thought Jerry was demeaning himself, using the specific word, and saying that he would wind up very much embarrassed and forcing Reagan to repudiate any condition he accepted. I said that I blamed Jerry for the negotiations, since he had been president and should know better than to think that the presidency could be shared between two people. Bob tucked his head down, red in the face, and resented my comments, since he obviously was very enthusiastic about the possibility of Ford being on the ticket.

The same thing was true in the New York delegation, where people were calling it a dream ticket and predicting that the Republicans would carry both houses of Congress with Ford on it. I took the position that it would be a good ticket until about September 1, when, for failure of Jerry Ford to clear his speeches with Ronald Reagan's staff, the whole matter would fall not only into dispute but into considerable confusion as the press tried to find out which man was really running the campaign. When Griffin made it clear he was not going to talk to Ford to carry my viewpoint to him, I sought out Herb Kaplow and gave NBC an interview, [saying] that I thought there was very serious trouble connected with the euphorically received negotiations, regardless of what others were saying. A number of people in our delegation were upset that I was trying to throw a wet blanket on the affair.

As we completed the nomination of Reagan . . . a confused-looking political functionary of Reagan's with a walkie-talkie looked around and said to me, "My God, Reagan is going to be here in three minutes and is going to announce Bush." I said, "You mean Ford," and he responded, "No, Bush." I went to Bob Walker, and Walker did the same double take I did, finally confirming it by another walkie-talkie, since the phone lines were jammed up and we couldn't get through to the trailer in that way. There was disbelief everywhere. Reagan did show up and announce Bush, explaining that there simply hadn't been time to work out the Ford deal, that there were problems with it, and that he was grateful to President Ford for his willingness to consider it.

After giving some closing interviews and winding up that session of the convention, I stopped in at the Pontchartrain Hotel, where George Bush was staying. I was with Chuck Gengrich, a part-time reporter from Buffalo, and had no idea whether I could see George or not. It was at least 12:30, but I went to the nineteenth floor, where George and Barbara were staying, and as Chuck and I got out of the elevator, we saw Barbara threading her way through the crowded anteroom, trying to get back to her living quarters. She grabbed me by the hand and shortly thereafter grabbed [Representative] Joel Pritchard [R-WA] by the hand, since he was among the well-wishers, and pulled the two of us into the bedroom where she and George were staying. I asked if Gengrich could come in, too, first making him put his tape recorder outside the door. George and Barbara were very informally dressed and were having drinks and eating popcorn, look-ing quite confused but happy. I asked George when he had heard from Reagan, and he said a little more than fifteen minutes before Reagan had appeared at the convention. He said it was the briefest phone conversation possible, Reagan saying, "George, I'm offering it to you." George said, "Governor, I accept."

I asked George if Reagan had not mentioned Jerry Ford, and he said, "No," and so his impressions about the Ford interview and Reagan's relationship to the effort to include Ford on the ticket were confused and uncertain. We sat there and talked about many matters for about an hour—Pritchard and I, with Gengrich listening—and finally Gengrich drove me back to my hotel.

I am happy to say that I have had no sense of restraint on George's part in his relationship to me arising out of the Broder intervention in getting George out of the presidential race. I was, to some extent, the instrumentality of his withdrawal, and I am sure he was unhappy with me at the time. Nonetheless, in retrospect, it seems certain that if George had not withdrawn when he did, pur-suing instead a spoiler's role by attempting to demonstrate Reagan's weakness in the big northeastern states, he never would have been acceptable as a vice-presidential running mate. I was convinced that a Reagan ticket would not have had anywhere near the universal appeal without George that it does with him. . . . George's presence on the ticket was the best evidence available that Reagan wanted to win rather than to have a comfortable ideological identification. He could have chosen any vice-presidential candidate he wanted, and despite the competitive tensions between him and George, he opted for strength. That au-gurs well for the campaign.

August 3, 1980

I am going to talk today about tax cuts because tax cuts seem to be the daily grist of politics in the Congress at this point. Republicans were dragged kick-ing and screaming into a tax cut gambit by a group which has come to be called the "pragmatic populists"—the leaders of whom are Jack Kemp, Dave Stock-man, and Newt Gingrich [R-GA]. These young and activist people have, to one degree or another, accepted the Laffer curve and have increasingly felt that the destiny of the Republican Party was tied to things which would give people pleasure, rather than to old, painful structures of the past: the need to cut back on the types of government expenditures which permitted the Democrats their constituency politics. The thesis of the pragmatic populists is that if you cut taxes and stimulate the economy, you are much more likely ultimately to balance the budget than you ever will be if you simply try to restrain government expenditures.

To begin with, government is a very conservative institution, and the cutbacks of existing programs come with great difficulty because of the constituency pressures resisting tampering with their vested interests. Resting their case on the 1963 Kennedy tax cut, they claim that adequate reduction of marginal taxes, particularly assuming that the tax burden is heavier than the optimum for the United States, will not result in lost government revenues but will sufficiently stimulate the economy so that government revenues will actually go up, even though government gets a smaller cut of taxation. This group actually finesses the issue of restraining the growth of government, preferring instead to stress the volatile revenue side of the budget and the potential for raising very large sums of tax money if the economic activity is increased by a recapture of the incentives damped down by excessive taxation. Operating quite openly with a group of economists headed by Arthur Laffer,[10] Jude Wanniski,[11] and Irving Kristol,[12] these people have made a philosophical case for achieving fiscal sanity in a way that will not cause pain but pleasure, and they have become siren-song singers for the rest of the Republican Party.

Their first proposal was, of course, the Kemp-Roth tax cut bill, which surfaced in 1978. Kemp-Roth originally proposed a 10 percent cut across the board of all [income] tax rates . . . for each of [three] successive years, compounding out at a 33 percent cut. Subsequent versions have also applied similar cuts to business taxes and have, once the marginal rate of tax was reduced adequately, maintained that level of taxation by indexation.

Kemp-Roth was initially quite a success out on the hustings. The Democrats were deeply distressed by it in 1978, and about halfway through the campaign, it looked as though it would be a tool for major Republican advances in the Congress. The Democrats then got their act together, decided they would start calling the tax cut irresponsible, and by virtue of a concerted drive, the credible

10. Professor of business economics at the University of Southern California.
11. Former *Wall Street Journal* associate editor and promoter of supply-side economics.
12. Cofounder and coeditor of the *Public Interest* and the "godfather of neoconservatism."

incumbents in Congress finally persuaded the people shortly before the election that Kemp-Roth was in fact an irresponsible type of tax cut at a time of high inflation. It actually became a liability in the view of some people like John Rhodes and others who closely followed the changing public mood and were ultimately to be disappointed by the modest net gains we made in 1978.

Not to be dismayed by this turn of events, Messrs. Kemp and Roth continued their campaign with different versions and, by their activism, continued to keep the Republican Party, at least in principle, behind their initiative. I have said many times that I support Kemp-Roth in principle, meaning that I drag my heels on the way to its ultimate conclusion, in that I look at it as rough indexing, with the rate of inflation over a three-year average probably at least 10 percent, and I am not a bit loath to advocate the cutting of taxes, despite inflation and high budget deficits, as long as the total burden of federal taxation reaches the high level it has presently achieved. I am always careful, however, in talking about tax cuts, to say that they must be balanced by effective restraint on the growth of government expenditures, since I fear that the truth about tax cuts is that there is a considerable lag between the cutting of taxes and the generation of the additional tax revenue which results from longer-term economic stimulus. Thus Jack Kemp has looked at me as a nonbeliever, or at least a semibeliever, and there has been tension between us because of my unwillingness to swear absolute fealty not just to the principle but to every detail of the Kemp-Roth promotion. I've always been careful to try to pay tribute to Jack's promotional abilities and feel that his single-mindedness in this campaign has generally been advantageous for the Republican Party, which has had scant reward from the American people for its long record of parsimony in connection with fiscal policy in general.

This past week, George Bush came through on Tuesday and Wednesday, ostensibly on a voyage of goodwill to meet the younger members of Congress with whom he was not familiar. A reception was held at the Capitol Hill Club Tuesday night, to which I could not go because of a staff party, and Wednesday morning he appeared at SOS breakfast. He performed very well there, and I introduced him with considerable pleasure. During the day, he had many photographs taken with members of Congress, a luncheon was held for him by John Rhodes, and a supper was put on at the Alibi Club for a few big shots. I was with him quite a bit and found him very friendly. Dean Burch has emerged as his principal political adviser, and he and George told me of a very friendly reception by Reagan out on the coast the previous week, during which they discussed their respective roles in the campaign and patched the tensions created by the competitiveness of the late primary period.

George confessed himself to be perfectly satisfied with his relations with Reagan, and the two of them agreed that he would not be a Reagan clone but would continue to express the differences that characterized them during the primary. In this respect, George said, "I wouldn't be on the ticket if I agreed with everything Reagan said." He will, of course, acknowledge that Reagan is the head of the ticket and the ultimate arbiter of differences. It appears that he will be spending much of his time in the Northeast, where he did so well in the primaries, and that he wants me to go with him in the plane from time to time for the purpose of helping him avoid the booby traps resulting from constantly changing congressional issues. I should be glad to do this. I am gratified that my friend has an important role and want to help him as much as I can.

October 26, 1980

I sometimes find it useful, in keeping journals, to make entries shortly before watershed events, such as the election forthcoming on November 4. One tends to rearrange one's memory of such events after the fact, and frequently one is wrong on one's predictions, one of the most interesting after-the-fact values of a journal. It is through our errors, through our misplaced expectations, that we learn not to despair before the reason for despairing is known.

I am particularly low at this point of the election because it seems to be following an all-too-frequent pattern for Republicans. We have been ahead of the game, thanks to the tremendous ineptitude of the Carter administration during the past four years. We have seen a president for the first time in history with nothing to say about his record, staking his entire hope for survival on creation of fear about the personality and character of his opponent. Normally, any man who has been in office for four years has something to point to with pride, a remarkable departure for Jimmy Carter, whose entire service in office has been one of drift, indecision, lack of policy, and even lack of decent good luck. On any possible historical basis, we would have to expect him to get his just desserts from the electorate; and yet, as I have spoken in the schools of western New York during the past two weeks, as I have gone from lackluster Republican rally to disinterested service club talk, I have found that, to the extent there is any issue at all, it is Ronald Reagan rather than the failures of Jimmy Carter.

How has he achieved this? His tactics have been deplorable. He has concentrated low political attacks on the personality of Ronald Reagan, engaging in not only devious tactics but outright falsehoods. He has taken advantage of our candidate's incapacity to slander, returning his remarks time and again to slashing and unpleasant partisanship. And yet the people have listened to him. They are convinced, after every war in this century was created during a Democratic administration, that if Ronald Reagan is elected, he will cause war by his statements that America should be strong.

The latest national poll shows Jimmy Carter with 41 percent to Ronald Reagan's 40 percent. In western New York, it is worse than that. While Reagan has cracked the blue-collar strength and the polarized voters of New York City beyond the level of the typical Republican, upstate he is being viewed as much askance as was Barry Goldwater in 1964, when Lyndon Johnson defeated him in our congressional district by a vote of 69.9 percent to 30.1 percent.[13] I have the forebodings of a disaster, even one beyond the simple reelection of Jimmy Carter, and those forebodings I hold tight to my bosom, not daring to share them, but feeling the tension as it rises toward what I'm afraid is going to be very bad news for the country.

The situation, if I can allow myself a glimmer of hope, seems to be uneven across the country. This past Friday I went to Chicago to try to "hedge my bets" with Danny Rostenkowski. Danny is the number-two man on my Ways and Means Committee, a political operative who used to be Mayor Daley's man in Congress and is now Tip O'Neill's man on the Ways and Means Committee. I have had an uneasy relationship with Danny Rostenkowski because I sit on one side of Al Ullman at Ways and Means meetings and he sits on the other, when he comes. I whisper in one ear of the chairman and Danny whispers in the other. It is a tug-of-war between the two of us to see which can hold the chairman's attention and confuse him in the more appropriate direction. The chairman isn't very swift, and I have, during the past year, been using the devious argument with him that he is being used by the Democratic leadership for high-silhouette partisanship in the hope that it will damage him in his district sufficiently so that he will be defeated and Danny Rostenkowski, the Speaker's man, can take over chairmanship of the Ways and Means Committee. Danny denies to me that this is his intention, but he salivates prettily every time he makes the denial. There can be little doubt that he is watching Ullman's race with great interest.[14]

On Friday, politicians that we were, we talked behind the backs of our hands during the hearing about how the races were going around the country. Rostenkowski told me that Ullman was currently ahead, that Corman was up one day and down the next, that [Representative Tom] Foley [D-WA] probably

---

13. Reagan won New York with 47 percent of the vote, followed by Carter (44 percent) and Anderson (8 percent).

14. Ullman lost the race.

would survive by virtue of the massive amounts of money he and [Senator Warren] Magnuson [D-WA] have shifted into the state of Washington following the eruption of Mount St. Helens, [and] that Jim Wright in Democratic Fort Worth seemed to have finally overcome the many petty corruptions with which he is associated and will probably survive.[15] I asked him about [Representative John] Brademas: he said Brademas and every Democrat in Indiana are swept out of office, except for Adam Benjamin, by a Reagan tide there that is running so strong no Democrats can survive.[16] I find this dubious, since Illinois is now several points ahead for Carter, Michigan is neck and neck, and Ohio is also too close to call. And yet there it is: this crazy election finds islands of strong support for Reagan in an eroding political landscape.

For three days each of the past two weeks, I have been campaigning with George Bush, on a theory that I can advise him about tax and economic issues. In fact, I go along to bask in reflected glory, since George is handling issues with all the sophistication and adroitness of a thoroughly experienced and able politician. . . . George is doing very well, but of course, as a vice-presidential candidate, he gets no national press. In the areas into which he goes, he blankets the local news: he always creates a good impression. He obviously is an asset to the Reagan ticket, reassuring to the upper-middle-class types who turn out to hear him and who find themselves very ill at ease with the kind of lower-class appeal that Reagan has brought to his campaign.

My own race has been a lackluster affair. Normally, my opponent is financed by labor unions. This year, the only labor union to endorse him was the UAW, a group traditionally liberal and therefore not normally attracted to a Conservative Party member who claims I am too liberal for the district but one which is upset with me over my refusal to promise protection to the American automobile industry, in addition to my voting against the Chrysler bailout bill. The UAW doesn't have much money at these times of heavy auto layoffs, however, and so the endorsement appears to have a hollow ring to it, since Mr. [John] Owens is not spending any money [and] obviously has none, despite the fact that he would be a good candidate if he were adequately financed. But I have debated him once, will debate him again, and am as yet not inspired with terror at the surge of popular support which he has been able to demonstrate. I really am beginning to reach that degree of arrogance in my reelection campaigns where I am asking for trouble, but I don't expect trouble from Mr. Owens with

15. Foley and Wright won; Corman lost.
16. Brademas lost.

less than two weeks to go and still no name identification campaign of any dimension apparent.[17]

The [Alfonse] D'Amato–[Elizabeth] Holtzman [Senate] race in New York State has been an interesting one. D'Amato defeated Javits by an excessively negative [Republican primary] campaign, trading not on his own qualifications for office but on Javits's age, his illness, and his traditional liberalism. Javits is very bitter about this, feeling that he does not deserve this kind of termination of a very distinguished career as the longest-[serving] senator in the history of the state. I supported Javits strongly during the primary period, feeling that we could not possibly control the Senate, however great the landslide in Reagan's favor, if we threw away the New York seat. At that time, I did not believe D'Amato had a chance to win. Elizabeth Holtzman unexpectedly defeated Bess Myerson and [John] Lindsay [in the Democratic primary], apparently projecting an earnest image which failed to take into account her excessive liberalism. I consider her the most liberal of New York's liberal congressional delegation, and I find it inconceivable that the people of this state would choose such a person at a time when they are yearning for a return to conservative politics at least to some degree.

D'Amato, immediately following his victory over Javits in the primary, raced upstate and tried to establish contacts he had never made there before. There was strong anti-Javits sentiment upstate and always has been, but nobody had any idea who the other guy was, except that he was not Javits. I turned down a request from D'Amato's brother, an assemblyman, to serve as his cochairman for the state campaign, feeling that my credibility would be damaged if I did that after having supported Javits so strongly in the preprimary period. I also told him that I thought it was important to keep Javits in the race [as the Liberal Party candidate], since he would draw votes from Holtzman rather than from D'Amato, and unless [Javits] could draw some votes from Holtzman, [D'Amato] would have to demonstrate an untypical bipartisan appeal to have any chance of winning. Javits has hung in there to this point, but I believe it is only as a result of the deal with the Reagan people: they want Javits to split the anti-D'Amato vote; they want Javits to enhance Anderson's draw on the Liberal line, where Javits and Anderson are the only two candidates; and they want Javits to have some credibility as he goes around to Jewish communities in the large cities of the country campaigning for Reagan. If politics makes strange bedfellows in this case, I suspect it is because Senator Javits cannot face the prospect of

17. Conable won the election with 72 percent of the vote.

going home to live with Marian Javits and would like to get the assurance of an appropriate ambassadorship in the event Ronald Reagan is elected. I wish him good luck in that respect.[18]

One issue causing quite a bit of stir and more than a few tugs and dilemmas is the current discomfiture of Robert Bauman of Maryland. Bob Bauman has been an extremely effective guardian of the parliamentary processes of the House. He is a pristine conservative in both the social and the fiscal sense. He is an orator of some accomplishment and has the saving grace of good humor, although frequently his righteousness submerges it. I had a run-in with him during the last couple of days of the session because I was circulating what amounted to a general statement of support of John Buchanan, my dear friend of sixteen years standing, who came to us from Birmingham, Alabama, where he was defeated by the Moral Majority (despite his Baptist minister status and his very high level of conscience and Christian commitment) in the Republican primary. I, of course, could not turn down John when he asked me to get such a statement to be used in the event he could force his way onto the ballot as a candidate of the WHIG ("We Hope in God") Party in Alabama. He was later thrown off the ballot. I had about forty-six signatures on the statement of support from Republican members of the House when I made the mistake of asking Henry Hyde [R-IL] to sign it. Henry had been associated with John as a member of the Foreign Relations Committee, but evidently, Henry was very offended at John's voting record relative to abortion, where Henry is the great leader of the antiabortion forces. He not only turned me down but went and talked to Bauman about it. Bauman approached me and said that he respected me too much not to tell me in person how much he objected to what I was doing, working against the endorsed and nominated candidate in John Buchanan's district. I told Bob it was one thing to be a tough guy on issues but another thing to turn down a Republican colleague of sixteen years standing when he asked for help "because he got beat in a very narrow primary by an unproven opponent." Bauman not only told me of his disagreement but proceeded to talk with anyone who had not signed my statement of support, and so after six more signatures, I finally had to give it up and tell John Buchanan that the backfires had been lit and I had done all I could.

The next day, it hit the *Washington Post* that Bauman had been charged with soliciting a sixteen-year-old boy for sexual favors and that he was to be permitted to plead guilty to a misdemeanor charge on [the] condition that he take treatment for his alcoholism. Immediately, some of the conservative groups (he was chairman of the American Conservative Union) stated that he was no longer suitable as a spokesman for conservative causes, and we heard every evidence that Bauman was in bad trouble out on the Eastern Shore of Maryland, which is a redneck area. Strangely, Pete McCloskey is his major defender in the House, and his support is coming from similarly unlikely sources. I am sorry for this man, because there can be little doubt that this development is a devastating personal blow to him, but I recall his close association with the pages (of which he was one years ago) and the doubtful nature of his alcoholism (used as a blanket excuse by every wrongdoer in the House in recent years), and I for one will not be able to look at him in the same light as I did before these disclosures of his all-too-damaging frailty.[19]

December 17, 1980
The first Monday in December saw us having our organizing meetings for the 97th Congress. Since John Rhodes had voluntarily declined to run for Speaker . . . a game of musical chairs required the selection of an entire new leadership team for House Republicans. A couple of months ago, I decided that I would support Bob Michel over Guy Vander Jagt for minority leader, Bob's fitting my concept of minority leader better than Guy, in that he was more inclined to day-to-day floor leadership than Guy's more rhetorical, more political, and more studied type of performance. Bob asked me to nominate him, which I did in a somewhat cliché-ridden talk which described him as a good soldier willing to slug it out day after day on the legislative level. I said in my speech that I regretted the partisanship which had developed among the supporters of these two fine men but was convinced that they would put such matters behind them after the election had been held, whoever won, and that we would have a united Republican Party, continuing the momentum of John Rhodes's forging of a cohesive force out of the Republicans during the earlier, sparser period. Bob won the election by a vote of about 103–87, demonstrating how tightly fought and intense it was, his success being based largely on the older members who are not that much indebted to Guy Vander Jagt for his tireless work as a campaign committee chairman.

As to the rest of the Republican leadership selected, I supported every winner, a coincidence not matched by my past performance. I had previously indicated to Bud Shuster that I was likely to support him for whip, but when Jack Kemp

19. Bauman was defeated in November.

was selected as conference chairman, I decided that it was probably appropriate to choose a southerner and switched to Trent Lott [MS], an easier personality, on a secret ballot. Kemp's candidacy for the conference chairmanship was originally my idea, and I believe that my support of him was probably decisive in getting him elected. There was considerable resistance to Kemp as a personality among our colleagues, but I told people like Frenzel I was pushing Kemp in order to get him into the leadership, since I expected him to be talking to Reagan in any event, and I thought it preferable that he speak to Reagan as a member of a collective to whom he would have some responsibility rather than dealing with him as an individual who would be expressing only his personal ambitions and his personal relationship. The other leaders chosen were [Dick] Cheney [WY] for Policy and [Edward] Madigan [IL] for Research, thus completing a whole new cast of characters who I think will be moderate, in touch with all elements of the Republican Party, and well able to deal with a Democratic majority.

The same day that the Republicans organized, Tip O'Neill told the Democratic Caucus his plan to have committee ratios, which sent a chill through me. While he was planning a 5–4 ratio for almost all legislative committees, he announced an 11–5 ratio on Rules and a 23–12 ratio on Ways and Means. Appropriations was to have a 33–22 ratio, in keeping with the tradition of 3–2 on major committees when the divisions are closer between the parties in the House as a whole. The Ways and Means ratio was a big blow to me, because I have had a ratio of either 2–1 plus one or 2–1 against me for the past four years, and the election, which brought the Republicans up to a much closer relationship to the Democrats in the House, led me to believe I would have either a 5–4 or a 3–2 ratio in the 97th Congress.[20]

I immediately sought out Rostenkowski, who had announced his decision to be chairman of Ways and Means rather than whip, and ran into him like a cat on a back fence. Danny will be a tough operative, devious in his statements of position, and I told him that if a ratio of 23–12 was his idea of consensus, it was my idea of civil war. I told him that before I would permit my Republicans to suffer that kind of an imbalance, I would take them out of the Ways and Means Committee and we would meet him on the floor. I told him that we knew more about the tax law than his boys did, and in any battle, I could assure him that he would know he had had a fight. Since I was obviously talking with vehemence and gesticulating wildly as we both sat on the floor together, he later claimed that I had humiliated him in front of constituents who were in the gallery and that I

20. The division in the 97th Congress was 243 Democrats to 192 Republicans.

had been unnecessarily unpleasant and rough. I then asked him if I couldn't get mad at him about this type of unfairness, who should I get mad at? He declined to answer that, but said there were different ways of getting mad. I said that he had taken a high-silhouette leadership position and he had better expect my type of reaction to that type of unfairness. I told him that I would rather be mad at him now than have to spend two years getting even. He vehemently told me that the decision had been made and walked away.

I have been disappointed to find Bob Michel very nervous about approaching Tip on the subject of committee ratios. Bob acts as if he was afraid of Tip and unwilling to take a strong position with him, something which led me to tell Bob's staff that there was bad feedback coming from members of the Ways and Means Committee about his new leadership and his evident dislike of confrontation about such an obviously unfair move by the Democrats. The Ways and Means minority met and discussed committee ratios, telling Bob that our bottom line—the final figure which would determine whether we supported any arrangement he could make with the Democratic leadership—was either a 20–12 ratio or a 23–14 ratio, depending on whether the Democrats wanted a smaller or larger committee.

In fairness to the Democrats, there is more to this matter than a straight power play. Tip O'Neill is known to be very concerned about the departure from the committee of all influential liberals, either as a result of retirement, as in Vanik's case; or through defeat, as in the case of Corman and Fisher; or a switch to another branch, as in the case of Mikva. O'Neill, evidently, over the years has come not to think so much in party terms as in terms of ideological orientation and has been known to say to conservative members of the Ways and Means Committee, "What are you Republicans so upset about? You now control the committee."

My experience is that we cannot depend on conservative Democrats when the chips are down, since in committee, they are more susceptible to party solidarity exhortations than they are on the floor of the House. Even a constructive member like Jimmy Jones is now much more vulnerable as a result of his very close election as Budget Committee chairman.[21] With a 23–12 committee ratio, no additional Republicans would be added to the committee, but Tip would have the prerogative of naming three additional Democrats, at least two of which would be liberals. He looks on this as the only way he can reassert any

21. House Democrats narrowly elected Jones as Budget Committee chairman over liberal David Obey.

degree of control over a committee that otherwise is going to be much more dramatically changed than the Senate Finance Committee is in the direction of conservative policies. Also, a very large part of the Reagan program will be tied up in the Ways and Means Committee, and his one-sided ratio there, plus his control of the Rules Committee, will be the only bargaining tool he has in dealing with a strongly conservative coalition which will dominate the floor of the House. These considerations, which are so important to Tip, are very important to me also, and if his original ratio stands up, I have made an analysis which indicates to me that I will not be able to win any of the closely contested issues in the Ways and Means Committee, even though I was able to do so under a less political chairman with a 2–1 margin against me in the 96th Congress.

It is my hope that we have left Danny a fallback position which will save face for both sides: twenty-two Democrats and thirteen Republicans. . . . Strangely enough, I had support for my resolute stand and my promised unpleasantness from such diverse sources as Russell Long, John Martin (chief clerk of the committee, who has been fired by Danny), and Bobby Shapiro, the retiring staff chief of the Joint Committee on Internal Revenue Taxation. My impression is that if I go public on this fight because of Danny's failure to concede anything, the press will also be sympathetic, viewing it as a Democratic plot to frustrate the will of the people. . . . I don't think Danny wants to start his chairmanship with a badly polarized committee, making it difficult for him to accomplish anything and identifying him as the focal point of resistance to Reaganite changes, most of which are likely to be supported by a wide majority of the Congress, at least until austerity begins to bite.

I have already had several meetings about legislative matters for the 97th Congress. For instance, the coalition supporting 10-5-3 [accelerated depreciation schedules] has met with Jim Jones and me to discuss strategy for pressing this initiative vigorously early in the 97th. We will continue our bipartisan effort, trying to get as much cosponsorship as quickly as possible, assuming that Reagan will be giving his highest priority to an early tax cut. I will acknowledge that ultimately compromise may be necessary. We are going to postpone compromising until the time of enactment, rather than confuse the coalition of support that we have built up by changes which may enhance its chance of enactment. I expect to talk to Bob Dole about this at the end of this week. He and I both share a general reluctance about an unvarnished Kemp-Roth bill, and we are trying to decide on an appropriate strategy for dealing with the administration on it.

I went to a meeting of all ranking minority members with the president-elect at Blair House a week ago, and since I sat very near him, I tried to explain to him that he had some choices to make in potential tax cuts, and that the kind of savings plans and structural changes which many members of Congress favored in the tax-writing committees were trade-offs against straight rate cuts. He looked at Jack Kemp, who was sitting across the table from him and talking to someone else at the time, and said that he actually leaned toward straight rate cuts at this point, obviously sufficiently hedging his bets so that he could talk about it further at some other time. I believe that Bob Dole and I should discuss strategy on this and other matters before we get too far into the session, and that is the reason why Bob is coming to my office on Friday.

A frosty start to the Ways and Means chairmanship of Dan Rostenkowski. Ronald Reagan proves a more formidable character than Conable had expected; despite himself, he is impressed. Conable develops a reputation with the new administration as a "grumbler" and a "pain in the neck." Party loyalty trumps policy ambivalence as Conable shepherds the Reagan tax cut through the House. In his triumph, Conable's relations with Rostenkowski hit bottom. Dick Cheney commits a subterfuge. Next up: Social Security.

This eventful year, highlighted for Conable by his role in guiding, or goading, the Reagan tax proposal through Congress largely intact, also marked the beginning of a gradual decline in Conable's relationship with George Bush, which culminated less than a decade later with a rift between President Bush and World Bank president Conable. As vice president, Bush, mindful of his status as an outsider in Reaganite and conservative circles and perhaps congenitally cautious as well, was overly timid and unassertive in his new role, Conable believed.

Unable to sway Reagan from his uncompromising embrace of the Kemp–Roth tax cut proposal, Conable was impressed by the president's vigor, decisiveness, consistency, forceful lobbying, luck, and, ultimately, effectiveness. Reagan was the only president who grew in Conable's estimation as a result of his conduct in office—but only in this first year.

After complaining to minority leader Bob Michel that Republicans treated the Committee on Standards of Official Conduct (the Ethics Committee) as a nullity, Conable reluctantly accepted an assignment to the committee. One is reminded of Miss Maudie's consolatory remark to the children in To Kill a Mockingbird: *"There are some men in this world who were born to do our unpleasant jobs for us. Your father's one of them."*[1]

February 10, 1981

The year started on a sour note for me, with emphasis on the unfair committee ratio imposed by the Democrats. Congress organized on January 5, and for some

---

1. Harper Lee, *To Kill a Mockingbird* (1960; reprint, New York: HarperCollins, 1999), 246.

period before then, I had been having desultory contacts with Dan Rostenkowski, urging some adjustment of the 23–12 ratio. . . . Rostenkowski continued to perform as expected, taking the position with me that he would be happy to have a better committee ratio but that Tip O'Neill insisted, and when he could get through to Tip, he would try to work something else out. Everybody seemed to be able to get through to Tip but Rostenkowski, and very quickly I decided that he was telling me what he wanted to and was himself responsible for the committee ratio, working closely with Tip to ensure that our committee would be the locus in which any economic counterattack against the Reagan administration could be launched at such time as they felt Reagan's mandate was eroding or his popularity fading.

All the Democrats I talked to, including Tom Foley and Dick Bolling, neither of whom likes Rostenkowski, confirmed that he was in fact the fly in the ointment rather than Tip and that Tip would do whatever Danny wanted. . . . I continue to take a tough and unpleasant personal line with him, clawing at him like a cat on a back fence and making clear that I did not believe what he was telling me. He told me that he resented my unfairness, and I told him the same thing.

The Reagan administration was altogether too deliberate in its organization, leaving us quite nervous about the time lag at the beginning of the Congress. Although his cabinet is second-rate, Reagan has not gone too ideological in his choice of secretaries of the departments, choosing, for the most part, managerial types to whom he can delegate substantial administration and substantial policy formation ultimately. The second and third levels were particularly slow in coming, most of them not even being announced at the time that I dictate this journal entry, and leaving probably a continuing drag into March and April in terms of the administration's capacity to perform normal tasks. We are watching closely to see if Reagan tries to head off possible criticism from his right wing by putting many of them into second- and third-level jobs, just as Carter placed environmentalists and consumerists in second- and third-level jobs, ensuring inefficient administration of the day-to-day function of many of the departments. So far, such ideological appointments are not apparent. Indeed, George Bush seems to be getting more than his share of the appointments, with Jim Baker as chief of staff and David Gergen as deputy chief of staff. I have not had much luck at all in getting jobs for constituents or people I am particularly trying to help, and the process, viewed from my vantage point, of appointing people to high office is quite inscrutable.

President Reagan has been performing well in the early stages of his administration. His people are in constant contact with the Congress, already having better liaison than Carter was able to achieve during his four years in office. . . . Leaders have been called to the White House for conferences quite a bit already, and evidently, President Reagan is participating actively in these conferences. A preliminary meeting was had on economic policy, and although I am in the designated leadership under the rules of my party adopted at the beginning of the year, I was not included. Harry Nicholas complained to Max Friedersdorf, the head of Legislative Liaison, and the next week I was invited individually to meet in the Oval Office with Reagan, [Treasury Secretary Donald] Regan, Bush, and [Office of Management and Budget director David] Stockman to discuss the debt ceiling. I was somewhat chagrined to be asked down in such an important way to discuss a matter of such modest substance and told the president that I thought he should not use up a lot of political capital trying to get through a debt ceiling less than two weeks after he took office. I said the Democrats had to pass it, and many of his own people would be extremely nervous about it, having previously followed a rather rigid pattern of opposition during the Carter administration.

I did suggest to the president that if he was that concerned about losing his first vote and appearing inept, the best thing he could do would be to talk to the American Conservative Union and see that the debt ceiling was not part of their annual rating of the conservative credentials of the members of the Congress. He thought that sounded like a good idea, but I don't know if he did anything about it after that.[2]

I spoke at two Republican conferences on this subject, supporting the raising of the debt ceiling—at the first, in a somewhat light and bantering tone, and at the second, after the secretary of the treasury had made his somewhat strident pitch, telling the members that if they couldn't support Ronald Reagan on something as insignificant as the debt ceiling increase, it signaled very serious troubles for their leader during the coming four years. Apparently, the reports on my talk were good . . . , for I heard that I received a good deal of credit for the one-sided Republican vote in favor of raising the debt ceiling (about a hundred people, as many Democrats as Republicans, voted against it).[3] And the day after the vote, Reagan called me individually to thank me for my part in getting it through. Once again, I told him I didn't think it was that big a deal and that I felt I had not made a contribution of any great substance, assuring him that the

2. The American Conservative Union did not use the debt ceiling vote in calculating its 1981 congressional ratings.

3. The vote was 305–104.

unfair stacking of my committee made it absolutely essential for me to be supportive of whatever he wants during the coming four years if I wished to have any clout, since there is very little that I or my members of the Ways and Means Committee can do individually, unlike Bob Dole and the Senate Finance Committee Republicans.

A couple of weeks ago I called George Bush and told him that he would be a valuable vice president to Reagan only if he continued to know more about what was going on than anyone else in the administration. . . . I told George that we should establish a mechanism for keeping him up with what's happening in the House, since he will naturally gravitate into the Senate orbit otherwise as its presiding officer.

He invited me over to his office in the Capitol Building late one afternoon, while the Senate was voting on confirmation of cabinet appointees, to explore this matter further with me. I suggested that he let me put him on the list of those to be invited to meetings of SOS. He was quite nervous about that, saying that he thought of SOS as a somewhat elite, centrist group and one whose identification might lead other people in the House to resent their not being included. I told him the only alternative was for him to set up a separate group of his own to meet with regularly, but I thought that was worse than his identifying with an already well-established and accepted study group. He finally consented to my bringing it up at the next SOS meeting and discussing with the members how he could take advantage of his former associations in the House to the benefit of the administration. The boys agreed with me absolutely and are now inviting George, although it now appears that he will be able to come only occasionally.

Incidentally, Bob Michel starts off very cautiously. He doesn't seem to want to tangle with the Speaker very much or to take a strong hand with the members on issues like the silly one of the debt ceiling. I asked him if he could appoint me to the Smithsonian board of governors, since I am very anxious to try to meld the Museum of the American Indian into the Smithsonian, and found him unwilling to tangle with Silvio Conte about it, since Silvio enjoys the status of the Smithsonian board even though he doesn't go to the meetings. It seems Appropriations has had that slot for many years, and Bob didn't want to rock the boat. When the committee assignments were announced, I went to him and expressed dismay that the Committee on Standards of Official Conduct had listed as its Republican members Floyd Spence [SC] as ranking member, two freshmen, and three vacancies. I asked him what that meant in terms of Republican concern about ethics, and he laid his hand on my shoulder and said, "Barber, why don't you do it?" Since I had just been chucked off Budget, my tenure there having expired, I accepted, although I expect it will be a nasty job.

February 16, 1981

On Wednesday of this week Reagan is going to address a joint session of Congress to describe his economic plan. . . . I expect the serious work of the 97th Congress will begin shortly thereafter. My great concern, of course, has been the tax part of the package, and this has been the subject of great discussion within the executive branch during the past several days. The leaks I'm getting indicate that the Reagan team is not at all on track with a strategy which can wind up with him getting credit for whatever tax cutting is finally achieved by the Congress. The difficulty has to do with the issue of whether the tax proposal should come to the Congress in one or two packages. Reagan's predilection seems to be for a two-package strategy, the first package to contain something close to Kemp-Roth and depreciation reform, the second to include all other types of goodies of the sort that many individual members of Congress are already committed to. Some time ago—before the inauguration, as a matter of fact—Dave Stockman and Don Regan asked for a meeting with the Republican members of the Ways and Means Committee, which took place in my office and which ended in a Stockman decision that it was not good to go forward with a bare-bones bill of the Kemp-Roth type. The members of the committee were wholly in accord with this decision and agreed to put together a package "not to exceed $8 billion" which could be added to the Kemp-Roth and depreciation measures and which would provide a vehicle with which to move to the Senate in the event the Democrats on the Ways and Means Committee cut the head off the Kemp-Roth proposal.

Don Regan, following that meeting, seemed to have decided that a two-package strategy would be better, for what reason I do not know, although it may be that he has received his orders from the White House. I heard of this last week and expressed my concern, with the result that I was brought down to the Treasury Department and told that while they were going with a two-part package, the president would be sufficiently specific in his announcement of the total contents of the package so that Rostenkowski would not be able to terminate Kemp-Roth abruptly, then move forward with a Democratic bill. My concern was that the members of my committee on my side of the aisle would vote for a bill if it included such things as the elimination of the marriage tax penalty, charitable deduction improvement, expansions of savings packages, further capital gains rate reduction, and something like the Gephardt bill.[4] I am

---

4. Providing a tax credit against income tax for Social Security tax payments.

sure that if such a measure comes out of the House and goes to the Senate, the Senate version will be closer to that than it will to Kemp-Roth. Therefore, I see the probability that the centerpiece of the tax bill will be something the Democrats can claim credit for initiating, unless Reagan describes in great detail the things he can accept as additions to Kemp-Roth.

I thought I had assurances from Treasury that the president's speech would be very specific about the entire package, not just the first part of it. Today, continuing to hear rumbles that the "bare-bones" package was going to go forward, offering the Democrats their opportunity to put together an attractive special-interest-type compendium of tax adjustments, I called Norm Ture[5] and asked him what was happening. He professed great frustration, saying that the White House was going ahead with a bare-bones bill and that Secretary Regan continued to support a much more detailed elaboration of the pieces than Reagan would approve of. I then called Max Friedersdorf to ask him to use his good offices with the president to see that we were not creating a great opportunity for the Democrats to claim credit for the final bill. Max asked me why I thought that, and when I told him that I had heard it from Ture, he expressed great frustration, saying that they had been having extensive debates about the tax cut bill and that Stockman had favored the one-package strategy and had been beaten with Reagan by Regan and his minions at Treasury. He said that he would talk with the powers that be and try to get it changed.

I then called George Bush and expressed the same concern. Tonight at home Jim Baker called me, saying that he understood I was upset and that he wanted to read the specifics of the president's tax speech to me. He then proceeded to read a casual statement that, while Reagan supported some of these other things, including the marital penalty provision, he urged that [they] be postponed until after his economic package had been completed. I told him that I thought it was not affirmative enough, that he needed much greater detail in it, and that I was greatly concerned that we were falling into the hands of the Democrats, not as a matter of principle but as a matter of political strategy. I told him that I regretted spending my whole afternoon making trouble for them, with the president's speech so near its completion, and he said, "Barber, you are the least demanding congressman on the Hill."

On Wednesday I am going to lunch with George Will, and I expect to bare my soul to him on this matter, which is extremely frustrating to me. I did some advance baring of the soul to Neil MacNeil of *Time* magazine this noon at lunch. I'm talking to the newsmen quite a bit, not with an eye to sabotaging the

---

5. Undersecretary of the treasury for tax and economic policy.

Reagan administration but because I think it necessary to talk to them through the press when I'm not getting through well to them in person.

I understand that Jack Kemp is increasingly on the outs not with Reagan himself but with the Reagan staff. I am told that Jack is particularly demanding about matters of great detail and that the White House staff is beginning to do all the things they can to shut off his access to the president. If this is the case, my strategy of trying to get Jack elected chairman of the Republican Conference, which he now is, has proved a bad one. . . . I'm going to have to talk to Jack sometime during the next week about his ambitions to be governor of the state. He has shifted from membership in the Appropriations Defense Subcommittee to ranking minority member of the Appropriations Foreign Aid Subcommittee, telling Bob Michel when he did so that it was necessary, if he was to have any chance of gaining Jewish votes in New York City, for him to develop a position of some publicity relative to foreign aid to Israel.

Dick Rosenbaum[6] of Rochester is also running for governor, having already made a lot of advance soundings and having secured substantial promises of financing well in advance of the beginning of his campaign. He has asked me to talk to Jack to find out Jack's intentions. . . . His adviser John Sears was afraid that my inquiry would tip Jack over the cliff and urge him to run when his natural instincts are so cautious and he is so generally unwilling to take any risks on the way to the presidency. My relations with Jack remain tense and difficult. He seems to believe that anyone who disagrees with him on any detail of his fondly held theories is in fact against him personally. His competitiveness is his own great enemy, and evidently, it is going to bring him a cropper in his relations with the Reagan administration sooner if not later. He is even rumored to be falling out of close relationship with Dave Stockman, a longtime ally of his, as Dave feels the impact of office and receives necessary instructions from on high to compromise and pragmatize his views, formerly ideologically somewhat rigid.

March 30, 1981

We are moving toward some sort of confrontation on the tax bill. Rostenkowski has not been open with me about it. . . . I suggested to him in a meeting about two weeks ago that he give us a vote on the Kemp-Roth part of the bill by starting with the administration's proposal. It is to be assumed that we will achieve something like the 10-5-3 part of the bill, which seems to have a consensus behind it. But the second part of the bill, the 10 percent rate cut for three years

6. Republican state chairman under Nelson Rockefeller.

in a row, has been opposed by the Democrats almost without exception since the middle of the 1978 election, and it is inconceivable that we could get enough votes on the Ways and Means Committee to permit this measure to survive the early stages of the markup.

Rostenkowski is known to be putting together a bill which would have targeted savings plans—exclusions of economic income from taxation, which would reduce people's taxes conditioned on their using the money for savings—and which would have a good deal of attraction across the board politically, regardless of attitudes toward overall rate cuts. I told Danny originally that my boys would like to participate in the putting together of an alternative bill if Kemp-Roth is doomed in the Ways and Means Committee, and that the way for him to permit them to do it—an aid for him when the bill finally comes to the floor—would be to have a vote early on, permitting them to show their solidarity with the president over Kemp-Roth, and guarantee them a vote also on the floor on the president's proposal. He did not answer me directly about this proposed strategy but subsequently went and talked to Bill Gradison at some length about the value of an alternative bill, the virtues of which Bill has been suggesting to me for a long time. . . . My staff at Ways and Means expressed concern that Gradison was becoming too active an element in the negotiations.

I thought it was time to talk to the president about this issue and so suggested to Max that it might be a good idea to have a meeting in which we could explore the possibility of developing an alternative bill that would have the president's name on it, if he is foredoomed in the Ways and Means Committee on the Kemp-Roth part of his original measure. Following that, Dave Stockman invited some five members of the Ways and Means Committee (Duncan, Schulze, Gradison, Frenzel, and me) down to the White House mess to talk about the necessity for an alternative strategy. On Tuesday of last week, Max called me back and said the president wished to meet with me, Regan, Bush, and Stockman on Thursday morning. Tuesday afternoon I looked up Danny again to tell him that I was going to have such a meeting and to try to find out what elements he was likely to push in his alternative bill. He was evasive about this, meeting with me and two staffers, John Salmon (his political operative) and Rob Leonard (the so-called liaison with the Republicans on the majority staff). I talked with Danny for about an hour and a half and was as ingratiating and compromising as I knew how. Rob Leonard later told Pete Singleton, my staff chief on the minority, that he was disappointed that Danny had not been more forthcoming and more specific about the measures he would like to see in an alternative tax bill, which I told him I would propose to the president the following Thursday morning.

On Wednesday morning Rostenkowski held a press breakfast and, in effect, had a press conference in which he announced some of the specific items the Democrats would try to put in the tax bill, including reducing the marital penalty, a reduction in the long-term capital gains rate, a reduction of the maximum tax on unearned income from 70 percent to 50 percent, and some other measures attractive to Republicans. He was quoted as saying that Kemp-Roth was "dead."

I went to the White House as expected Thursday morning and met with Bush and Baker, both of whom advised me that they thought some alternative tax bill was desirable, that they hoped I would be extremely cautious in the way I dealt with the president because he could be expected to be quite firm in his support of Kemp-Roth, and that there was a consensus in the White House staff that the president needed to develop an alternative strategy. It was reported to me, for instance, that Secretary Regan also agreed with this strategy. I had talked to Regan about a week before, asking him to keep in mind the necessity for Republicans to participate in the development of the tax bill throughout its House incarnation, even though it was doubtful that the Democrats would provide enough votes so that Kemp-Roth could pass.

At 10:30 I went in with the president in the Oval Office and the other people I have mentioned, Stockman being the only one absent. As predicted, the president was not only firm but absolutely unyielding in his support of rate cuts. The others sat quiet and uneasy while I explained to the president I had not come to give him tax advice but simply to inform him that it was unlikely that rate cuts as he had proposed, multiyear and 10 percent across the board, would pass in the Ways and Means Committee and that he should be prepared, if he was unwilling to compromise on it, for the press to trumpet his first large administration defeat as a result of the Democratic solidarity on this issue. The president left no doubt of what he wanted, saying, in effect, that if he compromised at this point in the procedure, the bill, by the time it came out of both houses and a conference, would bear no resemblance to his original proposal. He let me know that he expected the Republicans on the Ways and Means Committee to go down fighting and not to participate in the development of an alternative measure. I told him that I could cheerfully do that myself but I wasn't sure all the members of the minority would view it the way I did, particularly with respect to the targeted savings plan that they themselves had cosponsored. He immediately replied that he would help on that and would bring them down three at a time to let them know what he thought their duty was on the tax bill.

The upshot of my conference with the president was that I have the strong impression that he is completely in control at the White House, actually making the decisions himself regardless of staff attitudes, and that he is the president in fact as well as in appearance. He surprises me with his vigor and his absolute decisiveness. It also appears to me, in rethinking the meeting we had, that his staff is not anxious to tangle with him and would prefer to have someone like expendable Conable come down and give him the bad news when it appears that he is not to have his way in dealing with the Congress.

April 2, 1981

On Monday of this week, Ronald Reagan was shot near the Washington Hilton returning from a speaking engagement before a labor group. His press secretary, Jim Brady, was badly brain-damaged by a bullet through the head, and two security officers were seriously wounded. Reagan was evidently lucky, taking a bullet through the left thorax but not damaging his heart. He bled internally extensively and quite possibly might have died had the car not taken him directly to George Washington Hospital, where, after two hours of thoracic surgery, he was pronounced well on the way to recovery and a resilient physical specimen for a man his age.

Inevitably, such an episode plunged the nation into a great bout of self-reproach, and because Reagan bore his adversity with considerable grace and wit, it will add to his personal popularity for quite a period of time. . . . Fortunately, the man who shot him was a white man,[7] young and of wealthy parentage, and no particular social comment can be made out of the attempted assassination. It was a flaky episode, fraught with tragedy but turning out quite luckily, with the possible exception of the permanent brain damage to Mr. Brady.[8]

May 2, 1981

We are now maneuvering for the pattern-setting vote on the first budget resolution, a vote which is expected to occur this coming Tuesday, and the results of which are in considerable doubt. Chairman Jones's budget position is artfully contrived to try to hold the conservatives without losing the liberals. It cuts a little over $4 billion out of defense and adds a couple of hundred million to each of the social welfare programs, conceding to the president three-quarters of his budget cuts. The president's position has changed, through negotiations and

7. John Hinckley, Jr.
8. Brady's brain damage was permanent, though he lived until 2014.

compromise worked out by Delbert Latta, ranking Republican on the Budget Committee, and [Phil] Gramm of Texas, a conservative Democrat and man of economic pretensions who has been active in previous years but never before has been able to arrive at the center of the stage the way he is in this particular issue. The theory is that Gramm will bring a number of southern Democrats with him and that a compromise has been constructed that will permit the president to win the first large vote in the House.

The vote on this first large confrontation appears to be very close, with grumbling from both sides and the initiative clearly resting with the president as he uses his office and his White House environment, not to mention presidential favors like state dinners, to buck up the waverers. I would guess that he is going to win. The night before last, Jim Jones stopped in my office on his way home and asked why the president was campaigning so vigorously and so personally against him on the issue. I discovered that that day the president himself had called some potential Republican candidates for Congress in Jim's home district in Tulsa, Oklahoma, and I had previously heard comments from members of the [Republican] Congressional Campaign Committee that they will target Jones for demise in the next election as a result of his high-silhouette position against the president. I cluck-cluck-clucked with him about this condition, assuring him that he was capable of taking the heat, and was surprised to find as he went out the door that he was saying, "If the president wins this vote, maybe I'll give him the whole ball of wax and vote for Kemp-Roth, being sure that everyone understands that the full responsibility for the future of the economy is then on him."

It is my impression that this attitude may be more common among the Democrats than might be expected. They are in very bad disarray, not used to the fierce kind of presidential lobbying that is being used against them, uncertain what to do about the economy, unwilling to extend confrontation beyond that necessary for their own self-respect, inadequately and nonsubstantively led, and ultimately perfectly willing to put the full responsibility on Reagan as quickly as possible, hoping that he will stub his toe so they can run a traditional negative campaign against him in 1982. Speaker O'Neill is receiving outspoken criticism from his ragtag flock, some of whom are looking for apparently independent positions but are unwilling to support Reagan, and I would guess the difficulty he's having will confirm his vague intentions to retire at the end of this Congress. Jim Wright, unctuous and oily as ever, is having his oratorical powers tested but is being accused of being out of touch with his flock. Tom Foley remains a man of grace and wit but is, of course, politically vulnerable in his own district, and I'm sure he regrets having accepted the responsibility of Democratic whip.

Despite this Democratic disarray, there is beneath the surface considerable disarray among the Republicans as well. This is particularly true of the Republicans on the Ways and Means Committee, who are extremely restive under the president's determination not to compromise. Voluble as I am with the press, I am viewed uneasily by White House people who sense my malaise about multiyear rate cuts, although I frequently make statements to the effect that I have no alternative but to support the president and that I approve of his firm, uncompromising, and very conservative stance "at this point." I am on the tightrope between the president and my sophisticated and activist minority, and so I have to hold open with them the prospect of compromise if I am to avoid open rebellion as they see us moving toward a situation in which they may have to vote no on a lot of the types of proposals they have cosponsored in the past for the benefit of this or that interest group or class of taxpayer.

The situation is very much compounded by Dave Stockman, who continues to make off-the-record phone calls to me suggesting that it is important that we have an alternative in mind when the time comes for putting together the "final tax measure." I am extremely nervous about Stockman's continuing to agitate this issue, since I happen to like him and support his vigorous and intelligent role on the point of the president's program, and I fear that his intrusion into an area of responsibility of the Treasury will eventually bring him a cropper or at least cause bad feeling. Treasury suspects he is agitating a compromise, and indeed, Treasury itself I'm sure is working on contingency plans, but they are determined to make tax policy themselves and so are agitated by his agitation.

Several weeks ago I called George Bush and told him I was nervous about Dave's role and thought he ought to stay out of taxes. George agreed and said he would keep his ears open and talk to Dave if it appeared appropriate, but George himself does not seem to take a strong role, making insubstantial public statements and trying to find out what is happening but not initiating anything himself.

It is my assessment that Rostenkowski's attitude on the president's economic tax proposals will be greatly affected by the results of the vote on the budget this coming Tuesday, and that we should be sure we do have appropriate contingency plans lined up in the event he suddenly initiates tax movement. I have had no further discussion with Rostenkowski at all, and he has obviously been temporizing about taxes until after the meaning of the budget vote is amply demonstrated.

Last Tuesday we had a Republican leadership meeting at the White House, the first I have attended with the full House and Senate leadership in the Cabinet Room with the president presiding. He looked good and showed no ill effects from the shooting. I had ridden down with Bob Michel in his limousine in order to advise him of the difficulties I was having with my Republican minority on Ways and Means. I wanted to be sure Bob understood that I might not be able to hold them in line voting against all the Rostenkowski proposals in his alternative tax bill once the president's rate cut package had been rejected in committee.

Everything appeared to be extremely positive until I was called on to speak and I told the president quite bluntly that I doubted all the Republicans on the Ways and Means Committee would be willing to stonewall the Rostenkowski bill, that this would affect the possibilities of success for his tax package on the floor, and that one of the major concerns I had was that the Senate Republicans did not appear committed to his tax package, thus indicating to my boys that nothing was to be gained by their taking the tough political position that was the president's tax package or nothing.

In effect, I was fingering Bob Dole, who sat down the table a little ways from me and who was upset by my agitating about his porky independence. I also upset Jack Kemp because I referred to Bob Novak's having inserted in one of his columns the gratuitous assessment that it was time for a "Hance-Conable" tax bill, which would constitute the coalition compromise comparable to the Gramm-Latta bill on the expenditure side. Novak had pushed me to try to adopt a formula that he himself appeared to have put together, and Jack had (at the meeting earlier) referred favorably to the extent to which the Democrats were moving toward the president's position on everything, suggesting the possibility of a compromise close to the president's program. I said that I thought talk of compromise would get things out of control very quickly on the tax side, and Jack worried about whether I was attacking him personally in some way, as he always does when there is any degree of disagreement. I later told George Bush on the phone that I disliked being the only jarring note at the meeting, but he encouraged me to speak bluntly at such affairs. George, himself, never speaks bluntly.

May 26, 1981

There has been a great deal of activity on taxes in the past couple of weeks, but that activity has not added up to significant movement in the effort to compromise the conflicting philosophies of the Rostenkowski bill and the Reagan economic program. Rostenkowski's conceptual plan involves traditional tax reform: the jiggling of priorities among interest groups and classes of taxpayers rather than any broad economic change such as the president's effort to reduce tax rates substantially while leaving the tax base as broad as it currently is. Inevitably, we expect some trade-off to come between these two approaches, but it has been our view all along that the ball is in Rostenkowski's court and that the president, following the budget vote,[9] had no obligation to start compromising just because the Democrats control the House and the Ways and Means Committee in which the first steps must be taken.

I will go back to the period immediately following the budget vote. The secretary of the treasury invited me to a tax strategy meeting at the White House at which Baker, Stockman, the secretary, and other unnamed people were present. Their attention had been caught by Rostenkowski's *Face the Nation*[10] performance on Sunday, in which he said he assumed a compromise could be worked out at two years rather than the three years the president wanted or the one year he had been advocating himself. The White House had shifted easily from talking about the three-year package to a "multiyear" package, thus indicating that they were ready to do some compromising on the length of the effective part of the personal tax reduction. After a good deal of discussion, I asked them if they wanted me to feel Danny out about the two-year duration, and the answer was, "No, we want to kick this around and bounce it off the president. We'll let you know."

At noon the next day, a Tuesday, the secretary called me and asked me to tell Danny that a call from Danny to the secretary would be accepted and that he would be grateful if Danny would call him. I asked the secretary if he wanted me to discuss the two-year period with him. He said no, but I called Rostenkowski and told him that a call to the secretary would be appreciated. I said that I had some advice for him, although I could not tell him what the reaction might be to anything he might say. My advice was that what had attracted their attention at the White House was his discussion of a two-year compromise and that he should keep that in mind when he talked to the secretary. I also suggested that he shouldn't make any big deals without being sure that the Senate was bound in, a possibility which bothered me because I knew I would have trouble with my own Republican minority on any deal in which the Senate had not been committed to the final result. Rostenkowski expressed enthusiasm for the opportunity and said he would call the secretary right away.

9. On May 8, 1981, the House approved the Gramm-Latta budget proposal, which anticipated a Kemp-Roth tax cut and was endorsed by Reagan, by a vote of 253–176.

10. A Sunday morning television interview show on CBS featuring prominent political figures.

The next morning, a Wednesday, I received a call from Dennis Thomas[11] at Treasury asking if I had delivered the secretary's message to Rostenkowski. I said that I had and asked if Rostenkowski had not called. [Dennis] said he had not and asked what I thought they should do. I suggested they wait until the middle of the afternoon and if they had not heard from him by then, that Dennis himself should call Danny and ask if my message had somehow gone astray. Immediately following this conversation, however, I saw Danny on the floor and asked him what was happening, and he said nothing. I asked him if he had called the secretary, and he snapped his fingers and said, "Oh darn, I forgot. I was talking to some people when you called and I put it off and I just haven't done it." I said, "I want to repeat to you, Danny, that the secretary would be most grateful if you would call him." As a result, I learned from the secretary that he had called later in the afternoon and was planning to go down there the next day.

He went down on Thursday and called me before he headed for Chicago Thursday afternoon to say that he had had a satisfactory meeting but that nothing had been decided. He said he wanted to meet with me and he felt that it was necessary that he discuss in detail the options with me on Monday morning. . . . The following day, on Friday, I received a call from Bob Dole's office inviting me to a very private luncheon, he said, to be held with Rostenkowski, Senator Long, him, and me. I agreed to attend. The time was Monday noon, and that gave me the chance, I thought, to discuss Danny's options with him with some care before we went to the luncheon. On Sunday morning, Senator Dole was on *Face the Nation* and told forty million people about the private luncheon he was to have with us the next day. He described it as the beginning of negotiations on the tax bill.

Monday morning, I called Danny as planned and spent about two hours with him discussing at some length what I thought was the formula for a good start on negotiations. I suggested that he offer a package of two years of rate reductions, 10-5-3, and reduction of [the] maximum rate of tax on investment income from 70 percent to 50 percent, the package to be accompanied by a second package which would involve some of the targeted saving plans Rostenkowski wanted included in his conceptual bill, but the president [had] to agree that he would sign such a bill during 1981, provided it did not exceed X billion dollars, regardless of what targeted savings plans or equitable adjustments it contained. I told Danny that I thought he should play it to keep the president out of the second package and concentrate on his own economic plan that would be part of the first package. It was my thought that Congress would have great difficulty

11. Assistant secretary of the treasury.

disciplining itself to keep the total cost of the package under a certain size, and the president should have the second package to veto if lack of congressional discipline put them beyond his targets, without endangering passage of the first package, which embodied substantially his entire program with the shorter time period. Danny expressed some enthusiasm for this idea, and I left feeling that he was going to broach it at the luncheon which followed on the termination of our meeting.

We got to the luncheon at about the same time, only to find that Senator Long was going to be a half hour late. It developed later that Long was burned by Dole's announcing the luncheon on television, and well may he have been, because there were at least 200 reporters standing outside the room waiting for developments. There was obviously a high expectancy about the meeting. It was a very nice luncheon, with steak for the three of us other than Dole and hamburg for Dole, but I could not see that anything was being accomplished. I tried to prompt Danny along the lines of the recommendations I had made to him that morning, reminding him that the president did not feel he should make an offer at this time but that the ball was in his court. Even Russell Long told Danny that if he didn't want to deliver the Democratic Party to a handful of conservative Democrats, he should be forthcoming with a plan of his own, understanding that the president always had the option of negotiating with the conservatives if the major party leaders would not take the first step to try to resolve the difficulties. Rostenkowski kept repeating that he had to talk to Jim Wright and "his boys," and it became apparent by dessert that he was not going to make any offers at all that day.

I don't know what Dole had in mind in calling the meeting in the first place or in announcing it publicly over television, but clearly, whatever it was, it never came to fruition to any degree. . . . Wednesday morning I decided it was time to talk to the secretary again. I called him, finally reaching him at the White House, and said that I [had] reluctantly concluded there might be a stall going on, the effect of which would leave us, during the expected markup, with a confrontation over an unvarnished Kemp-Roth bill, and the effect of having that defeated would be to put the ball back in the president's court and make it difficult to keep our boys together. He said that he had come to the same conclusion, that he was at the White House at that time and would talk to the president and see what could be done. I suggested that he go on the *Today* show[12] the next morning and say that he was going to start negotiating with the conservative southerners, since the Democratic leadership in the House had not

12. A weekday morning television show on NBC.

been forthcoming. He said he would get back to me. At 12:30 that day he called again and sounded quite elated. He said that not only had the president agreed but Sonny Montgomery [MS], Phil Gramm, Charlie Stenholm [TX], and Kent Hance [TX] were going to be down at the White House to talk to the tax strategy team at 4:30 that afternoon. He said, "I can assure you that everybody will know they are here."

At 6:30 he called again, even more elated. He said that these four had not only come but had been extremely accommodating, in that they wanted 5-10-10, 70 to 50 percent, 10-5-3, and three minor adjustments. Evidently, they wanted a phase-in of the marriage tax penalty correction and a phase-in of some sort of liberalization of estate taxes. He also said that the group had volunteered to go and tell Danny that they had been to the White House and that they had made an offer but that they would hold off on any agreement until such time as Danny had had a fair chance to negotiate with the White House himself.

The next morning, Danny called and agreed to come down to the secretary's office and talk with him at 11:00. The secretary then invited me to come down at 10:00, essentially to have my picture taken with him for *Time* magazine, but he said also to discuss with me how he should handle Danny, assumed to be ready to negotiate by the leverage and pressure generated by the southerners coming down and making such a generous offer to the White House. I went down and had a nice talk with him but wasn't able to offer a great deal. . . . I have not heard from the secretary since. I have heard from Danny, who called me that afternoon to say that he was not disappointed with his discussion with the secretary [and that] he hoped something could be done, but he couldn't do anything until he had talked to "his boys," something which he planned for the following Thursday. . . . I told him that time was dragging on badly and I thought we would have to negotiate further with the southerners unless we could get some assurance from him that he really was interested in negotiating.

I have great difficulty trying to figure out what Rostenkowski is up to. He may be genuinely undecided. He may be held on a very short tether by his liberals, people like Dick Bolling, who don't trust him at all and are convinced that he wants to give away the store. He may, in fact, be having difficulty with the Speaker, who in a press conference this past week said he expected to have two votes on taxes, one on a straight Kemp-Roth and the other on the Rostenkowski bill. Danny tells me he expostulated with the Speaker on learning of this comment . . . , saying that he did not have a bill but only a concept so far. Rostenkowski's plan may also be part of a collective decision to temporize and dodge until such time as the markup begins, at which time they will try to force

a vote on Kemp-Roth for the purpose of putting the initiative for the first offer of compromise back in the presidential court rather than in the court of the
House Democrats.

The role of Bob Dole also leaves me somewhat nervous. Bob Lighthizer, his
top aide,[13] has been quoted to me as saying, "Rostenkowski and Dole are going
to write this bill; we don't need either the White House or Conable." Dole has
made a number of inconsistent statements. I have heard through the grapevine,
although not from either of the principals, that he and Rostenkowski are going
to meet on Wednesday, the day before the Thursday meeting of the majority
Ways and Means with Rostenkowski. It may be that these two are trying to cut
a deal each with the other. I've always said to both of them that the compromise
bill should be a Dole-Rostenkowski bill, and maybe they are feeling that if their
names are going to be on it, they also should decide the contents.

It was interesting to see the secretary of the treasury's attitude toward Bob
Dole. As I left the picture-taking last Thursday morning, I thanked him for
including me in the picture with the *Time* magazine photographer. He said
with an exasperated tone of voice, "Who did you think I'd have down here to be
photographed with me? Bob Dole? He's got his wife a great job in the White
House,[14] he's had tea in the Rose Garden, he's got all kinds of appointments he
probably wasn't entitled to, and he continues to make demands. He hasn't done a
damn thing for us so far. No, no, Barber, I wanted you down here to build you up
against the day when you will be chairman of the Ways and Means Committee."

One last thing I forgot to mention in my talk about the sequence of events on
taxes up until now was that last Sunday night the president called me at home
and talked to me for about ten minutes. He discussed his speech at South Bend,
where he received an honorary degree from Notre Dame, and then expressed
perplexity over the Dole announcement that there was to be a "breakfast" the
next morning. He said to me, "Barber, you're not going to make any offers at this
breakfast, are you?" I told him that I had nothing to offer and I intended to do
what he wanted me to do, since I had no way of influencing the outcome, not
having the votes, unless he was behind me. He said that he thought it was up
to the Democrats to make the first compromise and he hoped I would hold out
to be sure they had done that. He then asked me what I thought Senator Dole
intended, something which I could not answer, since I was by then perplexed

13. Later US trade representative under President Donald Trump.

14. Elizabeth Dole was assistant to the president for public liaison. In 1983 she was confirmed as US secretary of transportation.

that Dole had announced over television what I had thought up until that time was to have been a private meeting. The president is evidently very nervous about his congressional allies and nervous to the point that, after a long, hard day of traveling and speech making, he would call me at home to find out what I intended and, if possible, what Dole intended.

July 1, 1981

Progress on a tax bill has occurred, but it continues to move very slowly. The basic difficulty is that the Democrats still do not have their act in order and are having to make decisions in caucus one after another, then coming to the committee announcing those decisions and, in effect, voting them through regardless of Republican objections. So far, the dominant figure has been Sam Gibbons, although I do not have any doubt that Dan Rostenkowski is completely in control but is relying on Sam's rather more extensive substantive interest to fill in the gaps in legislation in which Rostenkowski himself has scant interest. The process is particularly frustrating to Republicans, fully confirming my assessment that nothing but trouble for us could come out of the stacking of the committee by a 23–12 margin.

The president's original proposal was a very simple one, based on 10-5-3 of Jones-Conable fame in the way of depreciation reform, and following the Kemp-Roth formula for individual income tax reduction across the board at 10 percent a year for three years. After it became apparent that Rostenkowski was not prepared with an alternative and so was not in a position to negotiate to any substantial degree with the White House, the president switched to a coalition strategy similar to that [which was] effective with respect to budget legislation, adding a series of equitable adjustments to his basic package in the interest of attracting conservative Democrats, and calling the resulting mongrel the Conable-Hance bill.

I have developed a reputation of being a grumbler with the White House as a result of the tightrope I walk between an innocent administration and a sophisticated but totally impotent minority on Ways and Means. I have had to persuade my boys on Ways and Means that I was aware of their frustrations by voicing them in dealings with the White House, and I have done this on several occasions. Most noteworthy was the day on which Conable-Hance was announced. The White House had promised my minority that, before anything was cast in brass on a deal—something many of our minority thought should be done—there would be further consultation with them. We were invited abruptly to the White House the morning of the announcement and told that the goodies were to be added to the bill in order to attract southern Democratic support and that they were to be financed by a major cutback in the revenue loss from the depreciation package: 200 percent declining balance was to be reduced to 150 percent declining balance, and the ten-year write-off of depreciable real estate was to be moved to fifteen years, thus making the package considerably less attractive from the business viewpoint.

I told the president in the presence of the secretary of the treasury that such a move, without adequate preparation of the business community first, would have a very bad reaction. Secretary Regan interjected that he knew something about the business community and that what they really wanted was a reduction in the long-term capital gains rates. I said that this was all very well for a broker to say, but I had been dealing with the business community for a long time, and that I recalled in 1978 efforts to reduce the long-term capital gains rate brought a strong reaction from the Conference Board,[15] then being headed by Reginald Jones of GE and Irving Shapiro of DuPont, who feared that a presidential veto of a capital gains rate reduction would jeopardize their corporate rate reduction. The secretary interjected quite sharply that both Jones and Shapiro were Democrats and that the business community was quite different in its view now. With my minority sitting there beside me, I continued to press the issue and predicted serious trouble with the business community as a result of this abrupt shift on depreciation. That I was right has not been of any particular significance to the White House people. They had to back off within three days and reinstate the original depreciation provision after two days of their watered-down version in order to keep the business community in line, but the idea that I am a grumbler was by then firmly established.

At least my minority heard me negotiating actively for some element of the bill and got the idea that I was not a toady for the Reagan administration but willing to stand up and argue with them and even with the president himself over matters that were within my knowledge. The press has also got the idea that I was less than enchanted with the process and so has described me as "known to be dissatisfied with White House dictation." The result is that I am somewhat gingerly handled by Jim Baker and company, but I am still in full communication with my frustrated minority, some of whom have told me that they will not vote for the bill, even though they do not know what will be in the Democratic bill. Particularly troublesome in this respect is Dick Schulze, who had been offended from the start by the Reagan administration's failure to heed his appointment recommendations. . . . Henson Moore is quite unpredictable

15. A research group consisting of major corporations.

also, trying to negotiate vigorously from his position of weakness, and even my dear friend Bill Frenzel is more interested in expressing his displeasure and his anxieties now than he is in trying to advance the Republican cause as defined by Ronald Reagan.

My relations with Bob Dole have been similarly circumspect. Bob has the votes and appears to have his Senate Finance Committee well under control. I am persuaded that he ultimately will dictate the form of the Republican substitute on the floor of the House, rather than the White House, and so I have called him almost daily or he has called me in order to discuss the evolution of the Senate Finance Committee's bill, now completed and somewhat festooned over the original, simpler mongrel known as Conable-Hance, which the White House wants. Before the Senate Finance Committee started its markup, Bob arranged to have a meeting with my minority in my office, and a number of senators came over, allegedly to consult with my members and to take advantage of their expertise, which, if I may say so myself, far exceeds that of the average senator. We had a good exchange, but I have not seen any particular evidence that the Senate changed provisions in [its] bill which were not supported enthusiastically by our members. One difficulty our members have is that they are sufficiently bright so that there [is] a wide range of views among them, and any impact they might have as a corporal's guard on the Ways and Means Committee is further eroded by the diversity of their views.

To sum up, then, Treasury considers me at this point a pain in the neck because of my grumbling and because of my suggestions for possible changes in the bill because of my unhappy combination of interest and irrelevance. My minority considers me suspect in my loyalty to them, being unwilling to acknowledge their lack of relevance in hoping to parlay a weak position into the kind of impact on the tax bill that any red-blooded American congressman would like to have. My position is somewhat further complicated by press reports of my anxiety and by some of my Democratic colleagues assuming that I am being inadequately consulted by the White House. For instance, Sam Gibbons, who voted for Reagan on the first budget vote, had breakfast with Reagan the other day and dressed him down for failing to consult with me. Reagan said he thought well of me. Sam said, "Thinking well of Barber is not enough. You ought to be taking his advice." The result was that I'm sure Reagan confirmed again the suspicion that I am a grumbler and undependably loyal, judging from my close personal relationship with Sam. With friends like that, I don't need enemies, but I must say that Sam Gibbons, despite the strength of his views and the stubbornness of his independence, seems to give me more respect than agreement. I enjoy Sam for his honesty and directness and for his willingness to admit to error, which he frequently makes. He is an honest man, if abrasive, and I can understand why Tip O'Neill, as a political leader, would not want to have him making the strategic decisions of the Ways and Means Committee as long as there was a possible alternative in Dan Rostenkowski.

The administration is expecting to substitute on the floor a proposal more acceptable to the president for whatever comes out of Ways and Means. The Senate is complicating matters by moving ahead with [its] bill, which has now been completed in the Senate Finance Committee in a form somewhat more adorned and embellished than the Conable-Hance compromise bill. The administration may not realize it yet, but they are going to have to substitute the Senate version for the original Conable-Hance bill. If they do not, inevitably there will be many differences in conference, and Danny Rostenkowski, with his two-to-one Democratic majority in conference, can sit there saying no until the White House either licks his boots or deals directly with him, as they have been unwilling to do since the early part of the negotiations on the first Reagan bill.

I met with Kent Hance last Wednesday afternoon and asked him not to have too much pride of authorship in the bill drawn for us by Treasury, which we put in at my insistence "by request," thus further making Treasury nervous about my loyalty and enthusiasm for the cause. Hance was upset to hear that I was anticipating a later version to be substituted for the one now bearing his name, but I explained to him that if we did not conform more closely to the Senate bill, we allowed ourselves to be victimized by the chairman. I told him to be reassured that the bill finally substituted on the floor, if we are successful in such a strategy, will be called Conable-Hance II, just like Gramm-Latta II naturally followed from the first version.

Rostenkowski has finally accepted the way things are, being pleasant and cheerful with me but no longer anguishing that I will not negotiate with him following his destruction of my independence by the early stacking of the committee. I am not sure he understands yet why I have lost the capacity to be independent, even if he is the author of that loss. At least he accepts the fact that he and I might as well be pleasant if we cannot influence each other.

Perhaps it is time to give some assessment of Ronald Reagan and his administration. Almost six months after he has come to office, I cannot say that a great deal of substance has been accomplished. He has had two very important votes in the Gramm-Latta series,[16] and these have considerable symbolic significance,

16. The two budget resolutions that were the foundation of the Reagan economic program.

as well as pointing the way ahead. It is clear that he controls the majority on the floors of both houses, although he cannot control the processes of timing committee bills generated in the House. Reagan has many more meetings with congressmen than any other president I have served with. He seems to enjoy receiving reports from Congress, and although he says comparably little—and at that, of a general nature—[he] clearly has the intelligence to understand what is going on. He is a superb communicator and, while low-key in his oratory, shows the sense of timing of a polished actor and the shrewdness in his projections that constitute a very important asset in democratic leadership. I would judge that he is still quite popular in this country, although his positions are essentially negative ones and involve very high risks of voter rejection, as his gambles will inevitably be attended with some degree of failure.

So far, he has been extremely lucky. Even now, the forces at work in the economy work against inflation, although they have nothing to do with government policy, and indeed, he has not as yet been successful in imposing any large degree of government policy. He was even lucky in being shot and dangerously wounded, only to survive with remarkable resilience for a man of his age. . . . He is saying the same things now as he said before election, not only confounding the Washington press but delighting constituents who have become increasingly cynical about politicians and their promises. As yet, he is doing what the people want him to do: cut back on government. But as these cutbacks actually begin to bite and cause the hardship which inevitably attends self-denial and restraint, his popularity may suffer a sharp decline because, while people favor economy in government in general, they still think of government as a problem solver and do not wish to cause human hardship by their philosophical restraint.

I am convinced his aides are either afraid of him or hold him in too great an awe. My impression is he is brought into decisions only after they have been virtually made by people like Baker, [counselor Edwin] Meese, and the secretary of the treasury, a very active and loyal man whose political innocence has not been entirely brought to a state of maturity. George Bush seems to be omnipresent, but his influence is not totally delineated. He told me not too long ago that he did not resent the lack of function inherent in the vice president's office and indeed had no time for functions, since he spends more than half of each day with the president. He is increasingly well thought of for his unquestioning loyalty to the president and the grace of his public appearances and sophistication of his views in an administration which is not terribly sophisticated. George stays in close contact with his friends on Capitol Hill, including me, and we are immensely flattered thereby. Nobody fears his accession to the presidency, nor does anyone doubt that he is an important and influential member of the administration. Nonetheless, his touch is a light one, and the oar he pulls uncertain in its power.

August 3, 1981

The passage of the Reagan tax bill on Wednesday of this past week and the conference which followed all Friday night probably provided me with the most significant week of my life, despite the frustrations and failures, which left it as something less than a total personal triumph. It seems significant, in that all the rest of my life had been aimed at these two events: the one dramatic confrontation on the floor, where I was robbed of a major role by the pressure of my colleagues for debate time, [and] the second the cloistered opportunity to put the final and most significant touches into the legislation, despite the circumscribed parameters of the two versions of the bill following the success we had had during the floor confrontation. If our substitutional strategy on the floor had not succeeded, I do not doubt that the conference would have been on quite different subjects than it actually was. But I also do not doubt that it would have been a less acrimonious conference, with the Democrats in a less sulky mood and Danny Rostenkowski not having to prove his manhood to the same degree that he did following our floor victory.

There was, of course, real doubt about the floor victory as the week began. For two weeks prior to that time, the Democrats had had the initiative rather than the administration.[17] Rostenkowski put together his bill with great deliberation and care, getting commitments from those who had previously backed the president on budget issues, as he added each item of special-interest appeal to the comprehensive and conservative bill which was his basic vehicle. I said many times (doubting the ultimate success of our cause) that the Democrats had conceded three-quarters of the battlefield before joining battle, after the pragmatic tradition of the American two-party system, and indeed, it was true. Where a year ago they did not support tax cuts, step by step the majority party had given way to the Reagan initiative, and finally they agreed, with reluctance, first to a one-year tax cut, then a two-year, with a trigger for a third year. Many of their preferential proposals were taken from bills originally sponsored by Republicans,

---

17. On July 23 the Ways and Means Committee had voted almost along party lines—22–13, with Democrat Kent Hance defecting—to send the Rostenkowski bill to the floor. Earlier, and by the same margin, the committee had rejected Conable-Hance, with its three-year, 25 percent, across-the-board cut in tax rates.

and clearly the burden of most of their provisions was conservative rather than in the more traditional redistributive mode of the liberals. Even the weighting or "skewing" of their rate cuts was modest and addressed to those whose incomes were between $20,000 and $50,000, not a traditional Democratic constituency group.

In short, Rostenkowski's strategy was to try to appeal to the same groups who normally would have the support of the president as their primary object. He was clearly using his control of the Ways and Means Committee, his forum for economic counterattack, not to assault Republican principles but to entice Republican votes by boring from within. He not only sought Republican constituencies but tried to outbid the Republicans with respect to interest groups which previously had been a concern only of Republicans. Thus he added to his bill many things designed to lock in on his side the realtors, the home builders, the Roundtable,[18] the small business groups, and the independent oil producers. That he had only partial success, as with the home builders and some of the smaller small interest groups, was more a tribute to the fear these groups have of a new, tough president in the first year of his administration than to any failure of Danny's understanding of what they wanted in the tax bill. Nonetheless, his flexibility in the face of a well-established redistributive Democratic tax tradition and a party which is still two-thirds liberal in the House made it necessary for the president at least to stay in the same small ballpark in his dealings with interest groups whose loyalty is bound to be overshadowed by the pressure of selfish legislative appetites.

Thus, as soon as he seemed to be locked into his bill—something he had delayed as long as possible—Kent Hance and I, and other major actors in the congressional scene, went to the White House and negotiated a final package which included almost everything that anybody's heart might desire. The one item for which I probably had more responsibility than others was indexing:[19] I made clear to the secretary and Jim Baker that I felt that indexing was necessary to attract northeastern support, as long as so much had been done to attract the support of agricultural, small business, and petroleum interests in other parts of the country. The White House had been most reluctant about indexing, perhaps indiscreetly, acknowledging that they supported it in principle although trying to insist that it did not belong in this bill (as though the bill were not inclusive

18. The Business Roundtable is an association of chief executive officers of major American corporations.

19. The adjustment of tax rates in response to inflation.

of all other possible beneficial provisions). By that time, the other items I had been pushing, such as improvement of the day-care tax credits and the charitable provisions of which the White House had been so scornful and skeptical, had been locked in by Senate action, which made it almost inevitable that the White House would finally accept them in order to claim some credit for them. At that stage (a week ago last Thursday), Kent Hance could say with conviction that he knew of only fifteen hard Democratic votes, and I could not assure the White House that there might not be as many as ten Republicans straying across the line, attracted by the weighting of the rate cuts in the Democratic bill and embarrassed by the appeals to oil which represented the final Reagan bid above the Rostenkowski tenders to the Texans.

After the decision was made on Thursday and the bill drawn by Treasury was filed on Friday, we glumly went about our business, meeting with various caucuses on the bill, such as the "gypsy moths" of northeastern habitat and "boll weevils" from the South. On Monday, we still appeared to be in trouble, and I found myself beginning to rationalize the degree of success we were likely to have, saying that the conference would at least be a compromise between three-quarters of Reagan's tax bill and Reagan's tax bill, since it was evident that the Senate was moving with discipline toward the presidential version.

Monday night I flew to New York ... [and] missed the president's speech to the nation on taxes, and so was unprepared for the onslaught of telephone calls which came from all over the country the next day. The president had asked the multitude to contact their friendly local congressman and urge him to support his tax bill, and this appeal coincided with an elaborate organizing effort by the White House to get representatives of the business community to target specific wavering congressmen through the plants in their districts. It is difficult for me to judge how much of the response was spontaneous and how much was organized, but since I had received about a hundred phone calls by noon the next day in my Rochester office, I assumed that a large part was spontaneous. It is unlikely that business groups would have organized the phone-calling efforts to my office to try to encourage me to vote for the Conable-Hance bill. But for one reason or another, many of my colleagues told me that they had received as many as 400 phone calls during the early hours of Tuesday following the president's Monday night speech, and clearly the rolling tide of contacts engulfed many uncertain congressmen and created an environment in which it was easy for them to switch.

The Democrats, having started this period comfortably ahead and confident that the embarrassment of the Gramm-Latta budget votes was a thing of the past, planned no special devious strategy for the Rules Committee, and a straight up-and-down vote on the substitute was the easy result of the Rules Committee deliberations. I testified at Rules, a forum I continue to love and enjoy attending, largely because of Dick Bolling's personal friendship to me. The rule was as expected, but by late Tuesday afternoon, we began to sense that it was possible we were going to win again, despite the Democrats' confidence. They were busy also, and by early Tuesday evening, they began to look glum as they saw their edge being dulled and then broken in the face of the onslaught of phone calls and presidential blandishments. By Wednesday morning, they knew they were beaten. I did not know they were beaten until I saw how many Republicans wanted to speak in favor of the bill.

I was the floor manager, and the shortened debate time (only two hours of general debate after the usual one hour on the rule, then one hour of debate on a liberal substitute, then one hour of debate on the Conable-Hance substitute) proved to be inadequate, at least on the Republican side. I made long lists and ceded, for purposes of control, small blocks of debate time to the various groups, including the boll weevils and the gypsy moths, so that I would not have to decide which of these special caucuses were to speak for their point of view. I had the usual difficult times with some of our more unfortunate and uncertain members, like Mattie Rinaldo from New Jersey and Peggy Heckler from Massachusetts. In fact, I spoke just before the minority leader summed up with a four-and-a-half-minute reprise, and I found that all I had left for myself was three minutes, a terribly inadequate time in which to get into any of the substantial matters which should have been discussed if the merits of the bill were to be talked about at all. I felt that we were clearly ahead on the merits, since Reagan's economic philosophy was still intact, despite all the add-ons, and I would have liked to have pointed out the advantages we had over Rostenkowski's efforts at counterpunching.

When the vote finally came at 6:00, 238–195, forty-eight Democrats had crossed the aisle to vote with us, many of them not the same people who had voted with the president for the Gramm-Latta budget proposals. It was a personal triumph for the president and clearly the most significant victory his administration has had, coming as it did after a thoroughly thought out and carefully put together counterattack by that political craftsman Rostenkowski, who is easy to underestimate. For consolation, the Democrats found themselves saying that now the full responsibility would be Reagan's for the future of the economy. His success illustrated the extent to which this high-silhouette, high-risk president is willing to take responsibility for making permanent changes in an institution which is usually characterized more by inertia and domination by events rather than leadership initiative and the effort to control events and create policy.

I must say that I have grudgingly come to admire and be entertained by the willingness of this president to provide leadership. I had become so cynical about government that I thought all political types were more interested in survival than accepting responsibility for leadership. Reagan, a man who is not all that admirable personally and certainly not all that traditional politically, appears to be a man willing to give leadership of a significant dimension to a country which probably needs leadership more than affection or admiration or political tradition.

The conference convened Friday afternoon at 4:00, an odd time, but a time made necessary by Rostenkowski's refusal to give up a Friday morning date to see his daughter graduate from nursing school. On the House conference committee there were five Democrats and three Republicans, in each case the most senior of House conferees, with the exception of Bill Cotter, who is said to be dying of pancreatic cancer.[20] On the Senate side, there were four Republicans and three Democrats. Rostenkowski was chairman of the conference, it being his turn in the usual rotation between the Senate Finance Committee and the Ways and Means Committee.

Rostenkowski had us meet in H-208, the steamy, small room next to the House chamber, reflecting his prejudice against open meetings. Although the conference was technically open, in H-208 there was room, in addition to members and staff, for only a few reporters and for virtually none of the importunate and disorderly lobbyists who clustered in the hall, sometimes numbering as many as 150 and laying hands on the persons of those conferees unlucky enough to have to leave occasionally for purposes of personal comfort or otherwise. . . . Although at discouraging times during the night we wavered occasionally in our determination, it was assumed that we would go until we had completed the somewhat more than a hundred differences in the two versions of the tax bill, many of which were more imagined than real.

The big issues, as expected, turned out to be oil, commodity straddles, qualified stock options, capital gains holding period, and some of the differences affecting charity. It was assumed we could work out something on day care but that some of the symbolic diversions for the Northeast, like the foolish woodstove tax credit and the virtually unadministrable home heating tax credit, were

20. Cotter died September 8, 1981.

foredoomed. The first thing that emerged as controversy in the conference was the apparent decision of the Democrats in the House that they would recede immediately on the six-month holding period for long-term capital gains in the House bill only, and put therein an effort to reassure brokers whose feelings had been hurt by the interest exclusions inherent in the all-savers certificate. We persuaded them to delay only temporarily in their determination to recede on this issue, but the final result was not unacceptable to me. Early on, we had to face the day-care provisions, and I was humiliated, even though it was only 11:00 at night, to be then so tired and so unable to shift gears that I made an ass of myself when [Senator] Bob Packwood [R-OR] deferred to me to explain it, totally unable to find the sheet which had my talking points ready and suffering mental blocks. . . . After a very fumbling and uncertain performance, the conferees accepted some improvement in the day-care provisions, one of the few things in the bill designed to help poor people. The charitable contributions legislation, of which I had been so persistently and (with the administration) unpopularly an advocate, the provisions of which were in both bills in differing form, was adopted in a not totally satisfactory form after Bob Packwood, the prime sponsor in the Senate, took over direction of the effort before we had time to discuss it in any great detail and offered rather more compromises than I would have offered had I been in control of the conversation.

Step by step, we narrowed the differences until, by 3:00, we had remaining primarily the issues of oil and commodity straddles. Rostenkowski was known to be very emotionally involved in preserving the House version of the commodity straddles, since the commodity market in Chicago is near his district. His version had been worked out by [Marty] Russo [D-IL], one of his operatives on the Ways and Means Committee, and was thought to provide roughly $400 million of tax relief to some 250 commodity dealers. The Senate version, a Moynihan creation, did not provide this windfall for commodity dealers, but in fairness, the House version at least reduced some of the sheltering for other types of commodity straddles and all potential commodity market investors except the dealers themselves.

As to oil, I showed a strong willingness to compromise the amount of the windfall profits tax relief, the only part of the oil provisions that was in conference. I suggested the staff work out a package that would give $10 billion of relief over the next four years, rather than the $16 billion allowed by the House's successful version or the $6.6 billion allowed by the successful Senate version. Eventually, we agreed on a figure somewhere around $11.5 billion in total relief, but then the Democrats on the House conference committee refused to accept any improvement of the depletion law now in existence, insisting that all the relief be put into royalty and windfall profit tax exemption provisions rather than the depletion section.

I became increasingly angry at the refusal to work anything out on this, which I considered primarily a symbolic issue on both sides about which I cared very little. Finally, by 7:00 in the morning, I told Danny in bolder terms that he could understand that I was thoroughly fed up and expected him to use some leadership to get it resolved. When it became apparent that he was unwilling to do this, I moved that the House recede on the commodity straddles, striking him a blow in the gut and making it probable that his future vindictiveness will be aimed at least in part at me. The motion carried, and he lost his chance to perform yeoman service for his commodity market dealers. Although I had reluctantly supported the House version of the commodity straddle provisions in order to keep our coalition together in the Ways and Means Committee, I have felt some relief that I was able to be so effective in salvaging the tougher Senate provisions.

Bob Dole and I then called the secretary of the treasury and Jim Baker told them that nothing could be done about depletion. While we stalled and kept the Democratic House members from walking out, they touched base with many of the members of our southern-Democratic coalition to be sure they understood that we had done what we could to protect their previous oil provisions and then put the total of more than $11 billion in oil concessions into exemption and royalty concessions, the effect of which would be politically acceptable, in that it spread around the benefits to many ordinary landowners and other royalty owners, even though it did absolutely nothing to encourage increased oil production.

At 8:00 we all signed the conference and staggered off, without much sense of mutual satisfaction but sufficiently exhausted so that we knew we had been through something.

In fact, looking back on it, I think we did rather well. Most of the significant things in the tax bill were not subject to the scope of the conference. The matters which survived are not bad. The bill has a lot of garbage in it, but all tax bills do. The Reagan economic program is totally intact and sufficiently clearly understood to have transferred the responsibility for government and for the state of the economy to him more totally than reality should require. In the view of the public, he is totally in control, and if anything will help inflationary expectations and the optimism of the American people over the effectiveness of their government, that should be it.

My relations with Danny are badly damaged, but they have never been good, except for a superficial friendliness. Rostenkowski is afraid of me and feels resentful of my substantive interests and my reputation with the press and with the rank-and-file members of Congress. . . . He was convinced he could detach from Republican solidarity some of the more vocal and brighter members of my minority on the Ways and Means Committee, and he totally failed. In one way or another, I hung in there and became an effective force for change, if only through negotiations with the White House.

Rostenkowski has been resentful of my persistence in referring many of the matters of contention between us back to the stacking of the Ways and Means Committee in favor of the Democrats at the beginning of this Congress. It took him a long time to understand that he had forced me into the arms of Ronald Reagan on substantive tax matters, if I was to have any influence on the outcome of tax legislation in his totally dominated committee. It also took him some time to understand that I had very little enthusiasm for maintaining the prerogatives of the House—if those prerogatives were totally concentrated in his own control of the committee—when the alternative was accepting some degree of White House dictation by a White House with which I had some respect and possibly even a little influence. He knows I felt angry in this conference, and expressed it several times, that the House version (adopted on the floor rather than in the Ways and Means Committee) had to be defended by a 5–3 majority that did not support the House version and indeed [was] humiliated that it had been adopted rather than the product of [its] own labors. For the rest of the Congress, I must live with him as chairman, knowing that he will go out of his way to try to override and embarrass me and that I view him as a bully who stacks the committee and then uses his naked political power to try to frustrate the majority will of the House as a whole. I am sure he will not forget that he has been beaten on the most significant tax measure ever passed by the Congress.

In that respect, I would predict that there will not be a major tax bill again for a long time. The adoption of indexing makes it probable that this measure will have not only a social and a tax impact of considerable magnitude but that its fiscal impact will for some time restrain the growth of government. Indexing changes the whole manner of American taxation. Congress may very well have to increase taxes from time to time, now being denied its fiscal dividend and the craven opportunity of backing into tax increases by default during inflationary times. Of all the elements in the bill, indexing is probably the most significant and probably the greatest source of trouble to politicians of the future. I feel some satisfaction that I participated in its adoption as tax policy for the United States.

What remains, and perhaps it may be difficult to achieve, is long-term reform of the Social Security system. After the vote on the floor with the tax bill, I went over to a very glum Rostenkowski standing in the middle of his supporters, shook hands, and said to him, "You are a good guy, Danny. I hope we can work together to avoid this kind of polarization on Social Security." He said virtually nothing in return and shook hands without enthusiasm. At the end of the conference, probably elated that he had turned back the depletion efforts in our bill, he shook hands with some enthusiasm with Bob Dole and Russell Long but, although I was sitting directly in front of him, did not tender his hand to me. I got up and extended my hand to him, again saying something of a mollifying nature, to which he did not respond except for a perfunctory handshake. From all this, and from his natural competitiveness as well as the edge he has given himself in all the dealings within the committee, I assume that I will continue to have a difficult time as far as Ways and Means is concerned.

But despite his vindictiveness and his competitiveness, Rostenkowski is basically a pleasant man. He enjoys a nonintellectual, comparatively vulgar camaraderie with the people with whom he serves. He is not unintelligent. When they have not been riled by failure, his instincts are friendly. I must make a serious effort at friendliness and must try to plan the campaigns of the future—modest though they may be compared to the immediate past—with an eye to including him and enlisting his cooperation and urging that course on others who have to deal with our committee.

September 21, 1981

A return from the August recess found the Congress in a very different mood from the mood with which we had returned home or to our respective congressional junkets. In the meantime, the folks at home had suddenly become terribly upset about high long-term interest rates. Small businessmen evidently assailed those who stayed around the hustings with doubts, misgivings, and complaints, while the stock market sank in an almost straight line and the bond market fell apart from its already badly eroded condition. Without any means for mutual support during a full month off, members of Congress returned to Washington in full panic, and shouts that Reagan's economic policies are not working filled the air. It seemed irrelevant that the 5 percent opening wedge in what eventually becomes a substantial tax cut had not gone into effect yet and that the budget cuts related to a fiscal year beginning October 1. The American penchant for wanting results immediately, and the ingrained habits of having a high expectancy from changed government policies, worked together for panic and for an erosion of the confidence which had mounted almost to euphoria following passage of the tax bill.

The House Republican leaders had a meeting with Dave Stockman in which he ... informed us of the unhappy statistics which necessitated further [budget] cutting. I made a very strong speech at that time, saying that Ronald Reagan must face up to Social Security, but I hoped he would approach it not from a fiscal viewpoint but from the point of view of achieving long-term reform. I told Dave that if he did not go on the tube and talk directly to the American people, confirming the troubles of Social Security (Wilbur Cohen[21] and Bob Dole are going around saying there is nothing wrong with it), and then accept full responsibility himself for long-term and short-term reform after which the system would be in good shape, he would continue to be demagogued on the issue by Democrats, who would take advantage of the confusing cries to cut Social Security coming out of his administration and the Republicans in the Senate. In fact, Congress will not balance the budget on the backs of Social Security pensioners, and the sooner Ronald Reagan faces up to that and stops thinking about Social Security as a big bank to finance the resolution of fiscal embarrassment, the better off we will all be.

The president does not like Social Security. He closed his mind on the issue back in 1964, when it was somewhat current in right-wing circles to talk about the desirability of making Social Security voluntary. He now thinks of it as somebody else's mess and has refused either to accept responsibility or to understand the nature of the options facing him on this institution. I have made so many unsuccessful efforts to get through to him on this issue that this past week, when we had a Republican leadership meeting, I made no effort to talk to him about the program again. The meeting was largely foreclosed by senators making speeches about the necessity of dealing with entitlements and indicating to the president that they intended to cut defense more than he wanted and that they would not cut the social programs in the light of all the cuts that had already been made in them.

Along toward the end of the meeting, the president made some complimentary reference to Lee Quan Yew, the prime minister of Singapore. I saw my opening then and told him that within the past two weeks, I had been with a group of other congressmen talking to Lee Quan Yew, and a member of the group asked what he thought of Reagan. I told the president that Lee Quan Yew replied that he was impressed and that he would be even more impressed

21. "Mr. Social Security," Cohen was the first employee of the Social Security Board and served as secretary of health, education, and welfare under President Lyndon Johnson.

when the president got Social Security under control. The president made no rejoinder but laughed that I was once again poking him on the subject. In fact, as long as he does nothing on the issue, people like Stockman will continue to see pay dirt in the potential for cutting back on the minimum [benefit], postponing the payment date of COLAs,[22] terminating student benefits, etc. This fiscal approach [of] nibbling at Social Security will confirm the impression people have and [facilitate] the political effort the Democrats will make [to claim] that Ronald Reagan is in fact going to balance the budget by going back on his word not to cut Social Security benefits. I have already seen a bumper sticker which says, "Save Social Security—Vote Democrat."

December 31, 1981

Ways and Means did do a little something as the session drew to an end. Its largest activity was mischievous. Through Pete Singleton, my minority staff chief, I learned of plans to hold hearings in several cities, the first being Baltimore, to study the effect of the Reagan budget cuts. Indirect inquiries (I don't talk to Rostenkowski much directly, although our outward contacts remain affable) led me to believe that this was not the chairman's idea but that Tip O'Neill had ordered all chairmen to hold "propaganda" hearings as a preliminary to trying to recapture the initiative next year. I told Bob Michel this and said I didn't think much would be accomplished by Republicans attending. He appeared to acquiesce but then issued general instructions to ranking minority members to familiarize themselves with what was going on and to take such steps as would minimize the damage. A meeting of our minority was held, and we decided at least one Republican should attend each of the hearings remaining, on the basis of the one hearing already held at Baltimore, where sixteen Democrats and no Republicans had attended, and exaggerated claims of hardship for the poor were left unchallenged. I went as the only Republican at Detroit a week later, missing the Lucullan banquet put on for the Democrats by Mayor Coleman Young the night before and the opening statements by [Douglas] Fraser of the UAW and the two Democratic senators. The rest of the hearing was balanced and quiet, which some attributed to my presence, but I doubt it.

Martha Phillips, my Ways and Means staff troubleshooter, went to the Young dinner the night before and was disturbed by noisy disparagement of me by Rostenkowski in his cups, but all she could quote to me was, "What's a nice girl like you doing working for Old Pigeon Toes?!"

---

22. Cost-of-living adjustments.

I cooperated with the chairman in getting out two little tax bills, the necessity for which was not demonstrated, relating to unemployment insurance for servicemen and other less than central issues. . . . Earlier the same day, this incident occurred: As I was winding up a small bill, Dick Cheney came down the aisle and stood next to me, looking expectant. I said to him, whom I admire, "What are you doing here, Dick?" His response was, "Making history." I asked what he meant, but he was straining to hear something being mumbled in the well by Jack Murtha [D-PA], whom I do not admire, without benefit of microphone on the other side of the floor. Tip brought down the gavel, mumbling himself.

I said, "What was that?" Dick said, "We just raised allowable outside income from 15 percent to 30 percent." We had voted this down, my voting for the increase, by a wide margin the week before, and I told Dick I thought the Republicans should not have been party to such a subterfuge, but evidently, it was a deliberately conceived bipartisan plot, of value primarily to leadership types with high honoraria. It won't help me this year: I have given away over $16,000 to charity, despite my $500 limit on honoraria, and had no more paid speeches pending. I shall be delighted for the extra money next year, but I am ashamed that we continue this type of tactic to achieve what should be honestly achievable. The whole limitation on outside earned income is bad policy—disclosure being the more reasonable requirement for businessmen who should be able to retain their ties to the private sector despite the accident of election to Congress—and illustrative of how we predetermine the makeup of the Congress by foolish ethics rules. We also ensure, however, the presumption that congressmen are crooks by engaging in this type of Murtha-Cheney tactic, and the breast-beating that came about an hour later, when some of our professional consciences discovered what had happened, adequately instructed the press how to make its smirking disclosures. I don't know why I should feel obliged to share the collective guilt for such tawdry episodes when I personally lean so far over backward to follow my own standards, but I have been blaming myself for not having listened more carefully to learn what Cheney and Murtha were up to, since at least I was on the scene at the time.

I had denounced the president's recommendation of a [Social Security] commission, and yet another study, as a cop-out. The president decided on his five nominees early, with Alan Greenspan,[23] a good choice, as chairman. Strangely, Joe Waggonner was one of his choices, along with a predictable in-

23. Chairman of the Council of Economic Advisers under President Ford; later chairman of the Federal Reserve (1987–2006).

surance executive, a knowledgeable woman, and a second nominal Democrat, Sandy Trowbridge of the NAM. Howard Baker announced three Republican senators, tough birds. Bob Byrd announced Pat Moynihan and Lane Kirkland of the AFL-CIO. Tip announced Claude Pepper (!!!) [D-FL], Martha Keys, and Bob Ball. Bob Michel told me privately that I was to be one of his appointments and that he was undecided between Bob Myers (longtime head actuary of SS and then deputy commissioner, although he soon thereafter resigned), whom I had recommended, and Bill Archer (ranking on the Ways and Means Social Security Subcommittee). I tried to discourage him on Archer, who typically had taken a pure position, uncompromising, on the minimum benefit conference rather than help Gradison and me work out a way to force the commission to amount to something. Bill Archer is one of the most brilliant minds in Congress, constantly using his intelligence to find a highly moral, ideological reason for accepting no responsibility for any affirmative action—a total cop-out, pure but useless. Michel finally decided to go with Archer and me.

Although I originally blasted the commission, I now believe it can be constructive, and since it's the only act in town, I'm glad I'm on it. The Democratic appointments make clear that we will not lack game-playing, and I assume that when the report is in, it will be written by Republicans and will be the subject of sharp political attack, since some unpleasant things will have to be done. I am determined, before I leave here, to try to accomplish something in this area.

There were other legislative achievements at the close of the session, unusual and a tribute to Reagan's leadership or more probably to his lieutenants in Congress, but not much noted by the press. Because the continuing resolution, as finally enacted, was to be the controlling budgetary document of fiscal '82, the president needed specific appropriations for both defense and foreign aid, or they would be far below the levels he sought as exceptions to his budget cutting. Both authorizations and appropriations for these areas were passed.

There, Jack Kemp is entitled to the glory for the operative compromise in multilateral aid, with a considerable assist from Henry Hyde. This latter member is an interesting fellow: a former basketball player, his weight must now approach 300 pounds, and his long white hair and florid complexion make of him almost a caricature of the throttle-bottom congressional type. The Hyde amendment is a rigid proscription of abortion; he is arbiter of all antiabortionist effort and, as such, anathema to the women's movement. In short, he is easy to write off as a demagogue, but he is a brilliant orator, courageous in unpopular moderation on foreign aid matters, cheerful in the face of his enemies, of whom he has many, and constantly disclosing a thoughtfulness which is not part of his reputation. I am always astounded at how hard it is to "type" my typical colleagues.

Will the state legislature really redistrict the most respected member of New York's congressional delegation out of a job? After an impressive start, Ronald Reagan dulls, as he is heavily anecdotal and lightly informed. The Gang of 17 fails to hammer out a budget compromise. Is it time to retire? Conable emerges as an unlikely champion of a balanced budget amendment.

Conable's tense relationship with his congressional neighbor Jack Kemp, uneasy at the best of times, worsened as the Democratic-controlled New York Assembly tried to stuff the two of them into the same district. Since Kemp's arrival in Congress, Conable had sought to promote him in various ways, whether into the congressional leadership or into another political office—specifically, the governorship of New York—but his efforts had always been laden with reservations, as Conable privately lamented that Kemp was too thin-skinned, was monomaniacal about tax cuts, and lacked the requisite daring.

Conable was confident he would defeat Kemp in a primary, even though he would be outspent exponentially, but he had no real taste for it. He asked in May, "Why should I fight so desperately for the privilege of standing for two more years in Danny Rostenkowski's rather dark shadow?"

A querulousness crept into the journal. Conable was grumpily impatient with the Republican Right, and he deprecated those who preferred casting nay votes to crafting compromises, especially Texan Bill Archer. Conable's goal, he said, was to "hold the world together," but he was obviously tiring of that task

January 13, 1982

One interesting thing about this president is that he evidently does not think of Congress necessarily in its corporeal sense, but as a group of advisers. Twice in the past two weeks, he has invited the Republican leadership to come to the White House to discuss the forthcoming presidential budget. It apparently has not occurred to him that Congress is not in session or that members of the House might not be available because of their absence from Washington. In each case, he has ultimately had five to seven members of the leadership—not bad for as far-flung a group as the leadership constitutes—and probably reflecting their relative security and sense of responsibility rather than their normal availability at a time of this sort. In each case, we have done almost all the talking at the meeting, and the president has tended to be somewhat less anecdotal than his usual practice. He is extremely skillful at making the person who has last spoken feel as though he has made a good contribution, without in any way committing himself to the point of view expressed. The results of these meetings, then, have been singularly inconclusive.

March 3, 1982

This has certainly been the winter of my discontent. Ways and Means is doing nothing. The House of Representatives is doing nothing. Republicans are splattering all over the ceiling in response to a presidential budget which proposes a deficit of $91 billion, and my efforts to encourage a little silence on the issue pending exploration of the alternatives have made me persona non grata with our more vigorous ideologues. Redistricting is [at an] impasse up in New York, with the Democrats hoping for my inclusion in Jack Kemp's district, while both political parties file maps designed to drive me from the Congress. Despite my relaxed view about future service in the Congress—I could easily walk out of here without a sense of failure or defeat—the mood of uncertainty has made my mood one of impatience, surliness, and general dissatisfaction with my lot.

There have been a number of presidential meetings during the early part of the year, and the pattern of them becomes increasingly clear. The president is very general and anecdotal. Everything said reminds him of something that happened when he was governor of California. Frequently his stories do not appear to have great relevance to the issues at hand. He is lectured by the members of his party about things that he must not do but rarely gets positive advice. He has occasional flashes of resistance to suggestions that are made and obviously is consistent in his intentions. He does not have detailed knowledge of anything and must rely on staff for any detailed briefing we get. His staff, however, does not participate in any substantial degree in the meetings we have, which thus tend to accomplish very little except a restatement of conflicting opinion. He is a very pleasant man.

As an example of the level of his interest and activities, George Bush asked me after a recent meeting to send him one of my doodles. He told me the president had asked him what kind of doodles I draw, since he noticed I was doodling during the meetings. I sent George a simple geometric-shaped doodle on White House notepaper that I had done during the most recent White House meeting. About three weeks later, George sent me a framed and matted elaborate set of five or six little sketches made by the president on the bottom of which the president had written, "Barber, these are doodles—yours was real art"—signed "Ronald Reagan." I have this presidential doodle up on the wall of my office and am convinced that someday it will be worth a lot of money, whether or not this president lives in history. It is a very nice thing to have, but I am astonished by the amount of time lavished on this exchange by these two heads of state in relation to a congressman who cannot really help their destiny in any substantial degree.[1]

March 17, 1982

Strangely enough, Congress seems to be moving toward some sort of a consensus, actually tightening and making tougher the president's budget proposals. This afternoon, for instance, we had a meeting of the joint Republican leadership of the House and the Senate. The dominant force in this meeting was, of course, Howard Baker, unhampered by recent surgery on his knee and, as usual, highly articulate, a moving force, a man of both initiative and judgment and an extremely able group dynamics expert. I have the greatest respect for him and consider him not only a moving force in the 97th Congress but a man whose contributions to government no doubt far exceed his reputation. I did not think him a particularly good candidate for president, because the complexity of his mind made it difficult for him to avoid exploring subjects which need to be presented to the electorate in somewhat stark outline. As the leader of the Senate, however, he is superb. If something is done to rehabilitate the Congress, it is Howard Baker who will do it.

After the leadership meeting today I called George Bush, feeling that I had not heard from him in a long time and that I wanted to talk to him about the general developments in Congress and the growing optimism that something could be worked out that would be at least equivalently tough [as] the president's budget. I've been pessimistic about this previously, feeling that the Democrats had neither a hero nor a program and that the Republicans were splattering all over the ceiling. I also wanted to talk to George a little bit about the balanced budget amendment and get some sense of how he was doing. I thought probably he would be up on the Hill, and sure enough, he was, but when I reached him he said, "Why don't you come up to my house for a drink at about 6:30 tonight and we can talk in private."

---

1. Conable's pen and ink doodles, scribbled to ward off the tedium of meetings, were a prominent entry in that rarest of genres: congressional art.

I agreed to do this and arrived as he came in from the Hill and Barbara came in from Atlanta. We had a nice relaxed talk, and I permitted myself to be persuaded to stay for supper, since my wife was out for the evening. As was usual in the past, George was on the phone a great deal during the conversation, talking among others to his great and good friend Leon Jaworski[2] of Houston, who is apparently dying from cancer and who has been an old and longtime personal friend of the Bushes. George seems perfectly happy and well satisfied with his lot, saying that he feels that he has considerable input with the president. He also feels that the president relies on him to help with the decision-making process when unpleasant things occur. For instance, he had to tell Dave Stockman, immediately following the *Atlantic* article,[3] that he should go in and meet with the president and tender his resignation. Dave thought he was being set up but did it, and the president did not accept the resignation; and George still worries whether he was not adequately tough on Dave and did not take a strong enough position with the president that Dave's credibility was irreparably damaged.

He . . . spoke positively about most members of the cabinet, although not [Secretary of State] Al Haig, whom he considers altogether too bombastic. He was rather stronger on Don Regan than I am and professed great admiration for Dave Stockman's brilliance. . . . He still feels very strong on Jim Baker, saying that Jim provides remarkably high-quality service to the administration and is virtually an indispensable man. He has a very good opinion of Reagan but asked me a great deal about congressional attitudes and seemed to indicate some understanding that Reagan's support in Congress is eroding.

May 9, 1982

I have had a rich, full two months—that is, rich in debate and full of frustration. The major activity of this period was the so-called Gang of 17 activity. After a couple of meetings at Jim Baker's house, one-on-one with Jim Jones, Rostenkowski, and apparently [Senator] Fritz Hollings [D-SC], it was decided that it would be worthwhile for the White House to sponsor secret meetings between representatives of the leaders in an effort to achieve some degree of bipartisanship in reduction of a deficit which, according to Stockman's figures, soared to

2. Watergate special prosecutor; he died on December 9, 1982.

3. William Greider, "The Education of David Stockman," *Atlantic*, December 1981. Greider reported conversations with Stockman in which the OMB director expressed skepticism about the Reagan economic plan.

$180 billion as the expected recovery has not occurred. This was a case of the leadership being ahead not just of the rank and file in the Congress but of the people of the country themselves: the sense of urgency about the budget was nowhere near as great generally as it was among those who watched the figures closely and who realized that $180 billion was a sufficiently large deficit to keep the money markets quivering nervously in paralysis rather than moving toward any degree of recovery.

[A] carefully selected group of people was put together and received notice individually to be at the horseshoe of the Rayburn building to be picked up by unmarked White House cars. The big boys themselves did not attend—Howard Baker, Tip O'Neill, and the president—sending representatives whose actions they could repudiate if the neighborhood brawl blew up into something so messy they wished to walk away from it and accept no responsibility for the mess. From the Senate, the representatives were Bob Dole and Russell Long, Pete Domenici [R-NM] and Fritz Hollings, and Paul Laxalt [R-NV], as a reassurance to the old friends of the president who thought he might otherwise be sold out. From the House, there were seven: Jones and Latta, Conable and Rostenkowski, Michel, Lott, and, representing the Speaker in particular, Dick Bolling. The White House representatives were Don Regan, Dave Stockman, Dick Darman,[4] Ken Duberstein,[5] and, presiding, Jim Baker. It was an affable group, and real efforts were made to attend by all but Fritz Hollings. He appeared to be divorcing himself from the proceedings after the first couple of meetings, although he returned at the end when there was a possibility of agreement.

[At] the center of the stage from the start was Dick Bolling, who relished his role but seemed to have some difficulty deciding whether he was a principal or an agent. This arrogant, egotistical, and brilliant man is a particular friend of mine, for reasons that are not clear to me, but we seem to have an affinity and a respect which each senses in the other. Several times in the course of the deliberations, after he had made a particularly obdurate or opaque commentary, he would turn to me and say, "You understand what I am talking about, don't you?" He, more than anyone else, worried about how to sell the outcome of our efforts at agreement to a fractious and tremendously diverse Democratic majority in the House. We had little doubt from the start that Tip O'Neill would do whatever Bolling agreed to, but we also had no doubt from the start that Tip O'Neill was not in the same position as the president, able to speak purely as a principal when

4. White House staff secretary.
5. Assistant to the president for legislative affairs.

the diversity and suspicion of his party almost created a presumption against the results in secret negotiations with the enemy.

On our side, there was almost a presumption that the president would be able to sell to the unhappy and suspicious conservative freshman Republicans whatever was agreed to, although Trent Lott seemed to represent these people more than others and worried about the growing undertow of mutterment which emerged as leaks began to occur late in the negotiations. Interestingly, the one person in the group identified entirely with the president and supposed to look after his interests was Paul Laxalt, who would have given away the store to get an agreement because of his personal view that nothing would hurt the president so much as a failure to take the steps necessary to reassure the financial markets. Jones and Rostenkowski seemed from the start to be anxious to work something out, although Rostenkowski, whose schedule constantly took him back to Chicago before the time scheduled for the end of the meeting, used to go out saying (after a particularly silent performance), "I can't do anything unless you are willing to knock off the third year of the tax rate cuts." To him, a three-year tax rate reduction was a symbol of his disgrace and his failure last year, and it was the sine qua non of any successful compromise with the president to have it removed or at least postponed.

We isolated three areas for major agreement, none of which were ever achieved: the size of the defense budget cut, the manner in which to cap COLAs for entitlements, and the amount of the tax increase.

The tax negotiations which finally made it apparent that failure was accepted involved offers of such things as possibly moving indexing up to July 1, 1983, instead of having the 10 percent rate cut, an offer which appealed to me because it would lock indexing in place quickly, save some money, and represent to the Democrats some compromise of the third year 10 percent cut. . . . Jim Baker said three times a day, to be sure that nobody would misinterpret his position, that he had not been authorized by the president to retreat in any way on the third year of the tax cut and knew the president to be absolutely locked in cement on it. This was what the Democrats meant when they talked about the "inflexibility" of the president, because that was the one issue on which he proved to be totally inflexible not just in his own mind but in the representations made by his otherwise flexible spokesman during the Gang of 17 discussions.

Incidentally, within the Gang of 17, relations were good. There was comparatively little acrimony or wrangling. We had little doubt that, in an autocracy of which we were the leaders, we would be able to come up with the necessary solution and provide a balance acceptable to all, but as agents, we found our reins too tight. To me, the failure to agree confirmed my view of the great difficulty the Democrats are having as a diverse party. They can coalesce around the negatives, agreeing that they disagree with Ronald Reagan, but their effort to put anything on the table automatically loses them about a third of their membership.[6]

I have also had a great deal of frustration about redistricting. . . . The Democratic map and the assembly put me and Jack Kemp into the same district, with 250,000 from my area and 250,000 from Jack's Erie County constituency, thus ensuring a confrontation between the two of us. I have said to a number of people that I thought I might be able to beat Jack but that I saw very little reason to do it. It would be a meat grinder. He would probably spend $2 million to save himself, and if I won, I would wind up representing an Erie County constituency I do not wish to represent. Destiny's hand is on Jack, while I stand on the downward slope of my career. Why should I fight so desperately for the privilege of standing for two more years in Danny Rostenkowski's rather dark shadow?

About a week ago, we began to get some intimation, from phone calls to Ron Starkweather, that the legislature was moving to accommodate me in some way. I have been talking to all and sundry of the press, saying that if I had either the Republican or the Democratic map as drawn for my district, I would not run again for office. In short, I was engaging in open and vigorous dialogue with the legislature, and apparently, somehow my communication was delivered. I have learned today from a *New York Times* reporter that I will evidently get a constituency made up almost entirely of Monroe County, plus Genesee County and a few fragments of Livingston and Ontario Counties. . . . I doubt it would be as good a district as I currently represent, and [it] would involve the loss of the bulk of my friendly old counties of Livingston, Wyoming, and Ontario.

The upshot of all this negotiation and ultimately success in getting a district I can represent without starting from scratch is that I will be sore pressed to run again and would appear to have been negotiating in bad faith with the legislature if I do not respond to their response to me. I have been afflicted with a high degree of ambivalence about reelection, uncertain what my wife wanted to do, unhappy about the irreversibility of the change if I decided not to run, unprepared with alternative plans for the rest of my life, and quite unsettled about the political prospects for my party. Obviously, the path of least resistance is to run again, and I must make up my mind in the next few days because of

6. Although the immediate efforts of the Gang of 17 came to naught, their negotiations provided the basis for the compromise later in the year known as the Tax Equity and Fiscal Responsibility Act of 1982 (TEFRA).

the lateness of the date. It is in fact extremely late to decide not to run again, since no alternative candidate has been developed, and indeed, no opponent has yet surfaced. All my good friends are quite bemused to find me so indecisive at this elderly stage of life. I have been offered a full- or part-time professorship of political science at the University of Rochester, I have had a number of offers (from law firms) of the six-digit variety, and I do not doubt that I could develop other options quite easily if I vigorously sought to develop them. I have the feeling I am becoming a professional politician, playing the game of politics and no longer performing a citizen-representative role. Tom Benton told me exactly this a couple of weeks ago, causing me to do some rather serious introspection amidst the uncertainty of my redistricting.

May 30, 1982

This past week has been virtually a lost week. We spent the entire time working on a budget, and at the end of the week, Thursday night between 1:00 and 2:00 a.m., we completed the process of voting down all the budget alternatives available to us. It was a most discouraging experience.

On the Republican side, we had a conservative budget group (which had been there all along but had not yet found its designation) emerge into full view of the public. This group—called "Yellow Jackets" because of their having voted some sixty strong "present" (the yellow-colored light in our display board) on one of the votes of the Republican leadership—is made up largely of freshman Republicans not yet attuned to the realities of life in Congress. These people find a natural leader in Bill Archer, the purist who cops out on every opportunity to find modest progress because he would rather be a man of principle, voting no on all issues sullied by compromise. At one point during the debate, the Yellow Jackets were almost unanimous in support of one of the perennial Rousselot amendments, which, using the pencil and the eraser, John constructs, forcing the figures to create a balanced budget. These amendments have been offered over the years and have provided many liberal Democrats with the opportunity to prove their conservative natures to stupid constituents who do not realize that [these Democrats] voted for a technically balanced budget of forced figures only because responsible conservatives like myself could not support it and would therefore defeat any possible enactment.

I wanted to speak against this phony balanced budget amendment but did not seek time until the time had been regulated, at which point John Rousselot controlled the debate for the Republican side; he refused to recognize me, saying that his time had already been used up. Thus I had no way of explaining why I was voting against an apparent balanced budget amendment despite my primary sponsorship of *the* balanced budget constitutional amendment, assumed to be a hot item later this year.[7] I went out and spoke to the press after I had voted against Rousselot's balanced budget amendment, saying that it reminded me of John Gardner's[8] discussion with a southwestern anthropologist who described federal programs as being like the Zuni rain dance: it didn't bring the rain, but it made the tribe feel better. This was widely reported in the press and was viewed as a compromiser's put-down of the principles of the Yellow Jackets, further eroding my standing with this youthful group, who feels they can achieve a result simply by voting for it, regardless of its achievability. I described it to others as being similar to the group's voting to get to the other side of the river and then voting against the building of the bridge, or being unwilling to vote for a reasonable alternative to transport us to the other side.

July 12, 1982

I must confess that I have been proven totally wrong in assuming that Bob Dole could not raise $20 billion in the Senate Finance Committee by a tax increase against which his committee members had been extensively lobbied. I must confess also that I was totally wrong in assuming that it would require a broadly based energy tax to reach the $20 billion. While I'm at it, I may as well confess that I may be totally wrong in assuming that Danny Rostenkowski, if he is able to get a deal and wants to have one, cannot deliver on it. My perception of what's doable and what is not doable seems to have faltered badly in the environment of frustration surrounding service on the Ways and Means Committee by a Republican in the 97th Congress.

It took Dole exactly one week to get out a tax bill which in fact represented what I'd said was not possible: a myriad of cats and dogs shepherded over a great many obstacles and stepping on a great many sensitive toes. Possibly some of these items of business tax increase ("loophole closers") will be turned around on the Senate floor, but I doubt it; it is the assessment of the business lobbyists who come in to talk to me in large numbers nowadays that the momentum in the Senate is such that any salvation for them must be found in the disarray of the House of Representatives.

It is not only the business interests that are tuning up against the tax increase.

7. Rousselot's budget proposal was defeated on May 25, 1982, by a vote of 242–182.

8. Former secretary of HEW under President Lyndon B. Johnson and the founder of Common Cause.

If I read Evans and Novak aright, Jack Kemp is planning to separate himself totally from the president on this issue and lead whatever freshman right-wing Republicans he can get to follow him in an all-out assault on tax increases. Jack has been consistent, having voted against the budget because of the $20 billion of tax increase involved in the $80 billion of deficit reduction.

I called Ken Duberstein, legislative liaison at the White House, and told him it would not be possible to win the tax increase unless the president himself actively engaged in the fight. I told him that I had no great stomach for a tax increase myself and quarreled about the details, but that my goal, as always, was to hold the world together, and I felt the president should be supported if he deemed this an important issue of credibility in the fight against high interest rates. I told him also that the president must stop posturing his rhetoric to support people who do not support him, meaning Jack Kemp, or must acknowledge that he depends on the support of the broad middle ground of both parties on an issue of this sort. Duberstein told me that the president talked four or five times with Jack Kemp before the budget vote and inquired about Jack's vote immediately when he heard of its final passage, even though he was then in Europe. Duberstein said that there was already considerable distance between Jack and the president, not just on this issue but generally, as Jack seeks to try to separate himself from his patron.

I do believe the credibility of the Congress is seriously at stake. Although $20 billion more or less obviously won't have a lot of effect as an isolated fiscal element, the difficulty of raising taxes makes this figure a key element in the confidence people will have that Congress intends to do what is necessary to get a deficit back under control.

August 1, 1982

Dole, operating as senators usually do, with a series of bilateral contracts, got the bit in his teeth and, looking neither to the left nor the right, charged forward with his tax bill until he had not only moved it through the Senate Finance Committee but across the floor of the Senate as well. Along toward the end of the Senate's anguished deliberations, I began to hear rumors that a number of the Democrats were favoring taking the Senate Finance bill directly to the floor of the House, since Ways and Means had been doing nothing in response to the tax mandate of the budget, there to pass it with Democratic support and send it to the president in the flawed condition resulting from Dole's headlong dash. This would not only be a major embarrassment to the president, who was supporting Dole's efforts, but probably to those who would have to live with a rather badly flawed tax law as a result.

I went to Dole over on the floor on the last day of the Senate's deliberations and said to him, "You'd better be careful about what you pass here because we may not even be able to go to conference on it if the Democrats have their way in the House." Dole told me, at that time, it was too late to do anything about it, that the momentum required that he not give way on any single point or he would have to give way on many points, and that he would have to rely on the House to do the right thing at that stage in the Senate's proceedings.

As soon as the Senate had completed the bill, Rostenkowski came to me and said that he would prefer not to do what the rumors had discussed, although a number of his people wanted to do just that, but to take a House version instead to the conference, thus meeting the obligations of the House. I agreed with him, and we sat down to consider a list of possible items to be considered in addition to the Senate bill. These items obviously included some possible tax increases, including some affecting oil; but when the list came out, Rostenkowski was to claim that I had agreed we would pass all measures included on the list and that I would defend them to the end, while it was my understanding that we had discussed these items only as a starting point for discussion so that we would not be marking up solely the Senate bill.

In any event, the day before we were to mark up, Thursday of two weeks ago, Rostenkowski held a late-night caucus of his Democratic members. They were in a rebellious mood, saying that we had no authority to make agreements relative to what the House would do and that they did not like the list he and I had prepared. Word got out that I had made a deal with Rostenkowski . . . , which of course made the oil interests furious with me. Since there was disagreement between me and Danny as to what exactly our deal was, this all was left unresolved, since the Democrats refused to discuss it anyway. So the Republicans never had the opportunity to demonstrate their disarray on the same issue.[9]

Now for the balanced budget amendment. I do not have any doubt of my importance to this effort as a man of alleged reputation as a moderate and a man of judgment. The editorialists are clobbering us rather badly on the balanced budget amendment, and I find many people assuming it is the stuff of extremism. Most people who say that, I assume, have not read the amendment and do not know how many escape valves we have put in it, wishing to avoid

9. The conference committee report for TEFRA, which increased revenue by $98 billion over three years—and which critics frequently alleged to be the largest tax increase in American history—was approved by the House on August 19, 1982, by a vote of 226–207 and signed into law by President Reagan on September 3, 1982.

rigidity or a fiscal straitjacket and preferring to work out a compromise amendment which will create only a greater presumption in favor of fiscal discipline than to accept the probable product of a constitutional convention. The Senate has too long delayed moving their side of the process, and we in the House, with a hostile Judiciary Committee and leadership, have been waiting for Senate debate and passage to create the interest necessary to discharge Judiciary of further consideration of the matter. The Senate has finally acted, and it appears that [the amendment] will pass there by a narrow margin of the two-thirds required. However, once it became a serious possibility, many senators decided that they wished to put their personal stamp on it by offering some further amendment to the proposal, already too complicated as a result of compromise. Pete Domenici—who is being fed stuff by Dave Stockman, a bitter opponent of the amendment who does not dare say so because of Ronald Reagan's support of it—has forced several amendments on the Senate version which will necessitate a conference on the House side and therefore create opportunities for procedural mischief on the part of the hostile people who will dominate the conference or who dominate the House conferees.

I don't know how this questionable effort will turn out, but I fear that the lateness of the hour will make it possible for the whole process to fall between the stools as we rush headlong to get home and have to deal with differing versions in the two houses and, indeed, a totally mischievous House Judiciary Committee. [Chairman Peter] Rodino, who has been having hearings on this issue for five years, has now decided to hold another set of hearings this next week, since our discharge petition[10] now has 184 names on it, and it is probable that if we get to 200, Pete will bring out his own version of such a constitutional amendment in order to further confuse the picture. With all the redistricting that has been going on, it is probable that we will go home sooner than anyone is willing to admit and that the hostility of the House leaders will be effective in preventing passage during the 97th Congress.[11] The 98th Congress is not likely to be friendly to such a proposal, but with our continuing budgetary problems, I think it unlikely that next year's meetings of the state legislatures will not result in at least three more states requesting a constitutional convention, and then the

10. A method by which members of the House of Representatives can bring a measure to the floor without the approval of the committee of referral. The threshold is 218 signatures—a majority of the 435-member House.

11. On October 4, 1982, the House voted 236–187 in favor of the balanced budget amendment, falling shy of the requisite two-thirds majority for passage.

fat's in the fire. I am increasingly convinced that such a constitutional convention would be a devil's playground, and if it only produced a balanced budget amendment, it would produce one with which we would find it very difficult to live here in Congress. Of course, the balanced budget amendment is not the only thing such a constitutional convention would produce, and the process would doubtless be totally disillusioning to an American people [who] have not had to deal with constitutional conventions since 1787.

Conable has a set-to with Pat Moynihan. The National Commission on Social Security pulls one out at the last minute. Congress approves the commission's recommendations, despite the opposition of the Democratic Left and the Republican Right. Conable's resentment of Rostenkowski festers, though he concedes the chairman's effectiveness. An unpleasant task for the Ethics Committee: what to do with two members who had sexual relations with underage pages. Conable reluctantly gives up on public financing of campaigns.

Barber Conable and Daniel Patrick Moynihan were bound by mutual respect, simpatico intellects, and profound historical awareness; they were separated by the demands of party, temperament, and the lasting impacts of upbringing. A story Conable told me wonderfully illustrates the nature of their understanding:

> *[Senator] Jack Danforth [R-MO] had a little Social Security amendment that was stupid and wasn't going to go anywhere. We had a conference on the bill that included this amendment of his. Nobody on the House side wanted it, and not many on the Senate side, but Moynihan gets up and makes a speech about this wonderful amendment. Jack was looking over at us and hoping someone would say something on the House side.*

> *I finally got up and said I hadn't really supported this at the outset, but the more I thought about it, the more I thought it was something we could live with. Pat was sitting at the other end of the semicircle of conferees. He took his pencil out of his mouth, threw it down on the table and it bounced way up. He stalked around the back of the circle, came over and sat in the empty seat next to me and said, "Now, Conable, are you or are you not an unreconstructed conservative Republican Upstate bastard?"*

> *I said, "Now, don't give me a tough time on this, Pat; you supported it." He said, "Yes, but I am not an unreconstructed conservative Republican Upstate bastard."*

> *I said, "Well, Pat, you know it's not going anywhere, and I wanted to give a little vote of confidence to Jack Danforth, a sweet man. Don't worry: none of my boys are going to vote for it."*

> *And he said, "Well, Conable, I want to tell you: if you aren't an unreconstructed conservative Republican Upstate bastard, what good are you?"*[1]

1. Bill Kauffman, *Dispatches from the Muckdog Gazette: A Mostly Affectionate Account of a Small Town's Fight to Survive* (New York: Henry Holt, 2003), 115–116.

April 1, 1983

Let us now consider Social Security, taking the issue through until its resolution. I was centrally involved in this, although the importance of my participation is in some doubt. I had been dismayed by the general fear tactics used by the Democrats in the course of the election campaign of 1982. Pat Moynihan, for instance, despite his having a totally inconsiderable opponent in Florence Sullivan, an assemblyman from Brooklyn who spent only $100,000 while he spent twenty times that amount, and who was a pathetic speaker and candidate generally, felt he wanted to exploit the Social Security issue.[2] Since Pat is my friend and I consider him a man of some quality, I was dismayed by this. I heard radio commercials that he was doing in which he claimed twice to have saved Social Security from cutbacks by Republicans and in which he promised that if the people of New York would reelect him, he wouldn't let "them touch it." It was a demagogic performance making Pat sound like a know-nothing, and I was angry about it. I was so angry that I voted for him with some reluctance and gave an interview to *Newsweek* which was published the week after the election in which I said that he had rendered himself useless to the Social Security Commission[3] by his tactics during the campaign. I said he had engaged in "unconscionable blather" on the issue.

Within a week of the election, we met at a motel in Arlington to see if it was possible for the commission to come up with a resolution of the Social Security financing crisis early in November. At this meeting, Pat came up to me without a smile on his face and said to me, "You, sir, have engaged in an ethnic slur." Well, I said, "Pat, if you're going to engage in blather you've got to expect to be called a blatherer." The conversation went downhill from there, and we were obviously both disturbed at the falling-out we had had. Negotiations of the commission during this three-day meeting were widely televised and largely unsuccessful. We did agree on the dimensions of the problem, finding that the Social Security system had a short-term deficit (that is, between now and 1990) of $150 billion to $200 billion and that it had a long-term deficit of 1.8 percent of payroll. That the commission was able to come up with such a statement of the nature

2. Moynihan won 65 percent of the vote against Sullivan.

3. The National Commission on Social Security Reform, sometimes known as the Greenspan Commission.

of the problem was astonishing, since some commission members, most notably Claude Pepper, had been campaigning two weeks before all over the country on the grounds that there was nothing wrong with Social Security that couldn't be corrected by getting people back to work.

We were able to agree on some other modest matters, such as the desirability of putting everyone at some sacrifice in the resolution of the financing crisis rather than loading the whole burden onto any one group. We were also able to agree that federal employees should be covered by Social Security, although the details were not in any way nailed down due to the fierce opposition of Lane Kirkland, whose public employees unions are now the cutting edge on his AFL-CIO organized labor movement. Beyond that, we were not able to agree at all, and after three days of negotiation, mostly off camera, we adjourned subject to the further call of the chair.

The commission was due to go out of existence, after a presidential extension had been granted, on January 15. It was apparent that no progress could be made without the full participation and consent of the principals, namely, Tip O'Neill and Ronald Reagan. I tried to do what I could about their failure to participate. The first day of the lame-duck session, I did a one-hour special order[4] addressed to the Speaker. . . . I pointed out that it would take us some time to organize the new Congress and that interfund borrowing had been terminated as of January 1, 1983, and therefore the crisis would be on us before July 1. I told him we needed the commission as a shield from the political heat that Congress has run away from so often with respect to the Social Security issue.

My words might as well have fallen into a black hole, so completely did they disappear and so little stir did they create. I then wrote a long letter to President Reagan, telling him that there was no chance of this issue being resolved and that the alternatives for some compromise resolution were so bad that it might be the end of the Republican Party if he did not pick up the phone and say to Tip, "We have got to get together and discuss this as principals." While I take it that my letter was read at the White House, there was no apparent response. As a result, the 97th Congress went to its reward with no apparent progress on Social Security except the definition of the nature of the problem, the one achievement of the commission.

On January 3, when the new Congress was sworn in, apparently Pat Moyni-

---

4. A speech at the end of the day, after the House has completed its legislative business, for which the speaker is granted up to an hour of time.

han came up to Bob Dole on the floor of the Senate and said, "Are we just going to leave it at that and let the commission expire without any further effort?" Bob invited him back to his office, and Moynihan, apparently still smarting under my condemnation of his irresponsibility during the campaign, suggested that I be included and that Bob Ball, the point man for the liberal Democrats and the most knowledgeable about the structure of Social Security because of his fourteen years as commissioner, also be included. The following day, the four of us met in the morning and discussed ways in which a compromise might be achieved. It appeared that all those present wanted to work something out. The result was that Bob Dole called Alan Greenspan in New York, who canceled his afternoon appointments and flew down on the shuttle to see if something could be stirred, at least among the abbreviated group of five commission members who were anxious to see the thing progress further.

After Alan arrived, we had some general discussions which seemed to me not to be major in their hopefulness, but which Alan saw as evincing a spirit of compromise. He called Jim Baker at the White House early in the afternoon and said, "I think we have got something going." Baker said in return that he would send two unmarked White House cars to take us up to the basement of his home on Foxhall Road and that he would meet us there to discuss it further. When we got there, we found Jim Baker, David Stockman, and Dick Darman anxious to discuss further a possible compromise. We made some modest progress that afternoon, and thus began a two-week series of meetings which finally brought forth a compromise. These meetings, and there must have been seven or eight of them, were held either in Baker's basement or in a back room at the Blair House.

The central figures in the discussion were Bob Ball and Dave Stockman, although Alan Greenspan, with good-natured patience, played an important role in holding the discussions together when they fell into difficulty. Baker played the role he always played, pressing for agreement [but] not pressing for any particular type of agreement.

Dole and Moynihan, though important catalysts and necessary to the continuance of the group, said comparatively little. I talked too much but was not a significant factor in most of the decision making and appeared to have only the role of token representative of the House of Representatives. [Senator] Bill Armstrong of Colorado [R], also a commission member, came to a few of the meetings but announced in the beginning that he could not support any compromise worked out with Bob Ball. Ball was as truly a moving part in the negotiations as Dick Bolling had been during the negotiations of the Gang of 17 earlier in the spring of 1982. It never was clear whether he was an agent or a principal, and if an agent, it was never clear whether he was an agent for Tip O'Neill or for Lane Kirkland.

Kirkland took no part in the discussions, holding himself aloof, but we all were confident that Ball was checking everything with him and that he had much more specific demands than Tip O'Neill, who tended to give his confidence to Bob Ball and to think that anything Bob would accept would be acceptable to the liberals of the House of Representatives. Rostenkowski also held himself aloof, expressing his typical resistance to anything that threatened the turf of his committee. Our meetings were generally not long ones, establishing a basic point and then taking it away for consideration by the principals, presumably the president, the Speaker, and the head of the AFL-CIO. The press went crazy, knowing something of this sort was going on and posting watch at all the entrances and exits of the Blair House and the White House. Our discipline was not breached.

There were a number of sticking points on substantive issues. The AFL-CIO wanted an income tax credit to offset any increase in taxes for employees. That was not acceptable to any Republicans. They also wanted taxation of benefits for high-income people or a weighting of benefits against high-income people, about which the Republicans were also very reluctant. Lane Kirkland took a very strong position against any inclusion of federal employees, saying he could not support a report which did that. The Democrats also opposed raising the retirement age vigorously.

As late as January 13, I thought it was still impossible for us to get an agreement and was advising my friends. When the deadline for the commission drew near, however, as our negotiations continued, it was apparent that both sides wanted to resolve the issue. Major breakthroughs occurred the last two days, with the AFL-CIO finally agreeing to a one-year, non-pattern-setting tax credit for the 1984 employee payroll tax increase, the same one originally scheduled for January 1, 1985. No credit was given for the two-year moving up of the payroll tax rate increase in 1990. Lane Kirkland agreed also that he would not oppose the overall report, although he would demur in dissenting views to coverage of federal employees newly hired after January 1, 1984, and we agreed that we would not try to cover any existing federal employees. We also agreed that we would hold off on the issue of roughly 0.6 percent of payroll long term and make a recommendation that this gap be closed either by a payroll tax increase after the year 2000 or by an increase in the retirement age after the year 2000. We also agreed on a taxing of half the benefits of people over a certain income level. This level was left unresolved until the last act of assent, which brought the agreement into being at 3:00 on Saturday, January 15.[5]

After everything else had been resolved, Baker and Stockman said, "There, now we are going to go and talk to the president about this." When they came back at 5:00, they said we had a deal if the threshold for the taxation of benefits could be set at a slightly higher level than the one we had tentatively agreed on. The Democrats quickly assented. We don't know to what extent the president was involved in the negotiations up to that time, but they implied that they had him sign off between 3:00 and 5:00 that Saturday afternoon. The president, however, imposed one other condition: that the commission support the resolution by a comfortable margin, saying that since it was his commission, he did not wish to fly in the face of their recommendation, and he would accept the compromise only if the commission did.

At 5:00 everybody went to work. I was in Blair House and heard Bob Ball discussing the compromise with Claude Pepper, who apparently had come back especially for the purpose. Claude, who is hard of hearing, heard what he wanted to hear, constantly repeating with respect to the delay in the COLA for six months (a $40 million item reducing benefits, in effect) that it was "just a little postponement." Rostenkowski and O'Neill were at the Desert Classic Golf Tournament out in California, and since at 6:00 [in Washington] it was still 3:00 in California, they had to be gotten off the golf course and brought up to date on the solution. Rostenkowski at first said he would have none of it, that the Ways and Means Committee would do its own thing. They wanted me to call him, and I said I was the wrong person to do it. Finally, Jim Baker called him and told him in effect that if he was not willing to sign off on the agreement, the word would go out that the whole bipartisan effort had failed because Rostenkowski was again defending his sacred turf. Danny said, "Let me talk to Tip about it again." Twenty minutes later, Tip called in a strong statement of support for the compromise, refusing, however, to engage in any joint statement with the president.

As to the commission, they were summoned to the Jackson Place office about 7:00 that night and given the outline, if they had not already received it from the White House or other commission members before that time. Armstrong and Archer both objected vigorously, Archer, with his usual purist logic, evoking

5. The commission also agreed to delay the annual cost-of-living adjustment (COLA), which was due in July 1983, until January 1984 and set the date of future annual adjustments in January.

from me a rather emotional speech about how the issue was not the best of possible worlds, but . . . I urged the members to support the resolution as the best of possible real political worlds, whether or not it was in fact a compromise that satisfied anyone. Trowbridge was very helpful, but the battleground involved Bob Beck, head of the Prudential Insurance Company, and Mary Falvey Fuller, a business representative from California. We didn't know how Mary was going to vote until the end, although Bob Beck, a strong and informed conservative, said early that if this is the best we could do, we would have to take it. We hoped to have at least a 10–5 vote, since the president had said the commission must vote by a comfortable margin, but we wound up with a 12–3 supporting vote, Joe Waggonner being the only person to join Armstrong and Archer in their strong objections. The leaders of the Social Security subcommittees of both houses[6] announced their opposition to the compromise at the time the commission report was made available to the press late that Saturday night and on the day the commission was due to expire.

We had left open the issue of what to do about the long-term imbalance, but fortunately, both Pickle and Rostenkowski were predisposed in favor of raising the retirement age. I encouraged them in this, saying that a further tax increase after the year 2000 would be viewed symbolically by the Republicans and would turn a number of potential favorable votes into unfavorable ones. It was apparent from the start that we were going to have more trouble with the Republicans than with the Democrats, particularly the right-wing people who would listen to Archer and Armstrong, Jack Kemp, and the burned freshmen who are afraid to do anything with Social Security.

Ways and Means had hearings on the issue shortly after the Congress reconvened toward the end of the month of January. The hearings were largely informative and noncontroversial, except for Pickle's interrogation of Claude Pepper. Pepper had not taken a position on the raising of the retirement age, and Pickle forced him to acknowledge publicly that raising the retirement age was in fact a benefit reduction, after which Pepper announced his firm opposition to any plan that included a raising of the retirement age, even after the year 2000. I had very unpleasant words with Jake about this, feeling that the more we backed Pepper into a posture of opposition, the less likely we were to get the thing through the House. Jake, however, went ahead and worked out the formula for raising the retirement age, and he and Dan both planned to support it on the floor—Pickle offering the amendment, and Rostenkowski agreeing to vote for it but not tak-

6. The chairmen were Senator William Armstrong and Representative Jake Pickle.

ing a public position. I had great difficulty with our younger Republicans and with Archer and Kemp, not even feeling that I could predict a majority of the Republicans would vote for the proposal. The great bulk of the mail came in opposition to [the] inclusion of federal employees, even though only new hires, after January 1, 1984, were to be included. Most of the people in the country seem to accept the compromise as the best possible under the circumstances.

We had a tense time on the floor. As is my practice, I divided our time fairly closely between those who favored and those who opposed the resolution. Claude Pepper saved his fire for the so-called Pepper amendment, which would raise taxes after the year 2000 rather than the retirement age. He spoke for thirty-four minutes on this issue and then came to me and asked if I could give him some of my time. I was not planning to have much debate on it, since we had already passed the Pickle amendment, which called for the raising of the retirement age but was subject to substitution by the Pepper amendment if a majority wanted to do so.[7] After consulting with my Republican leadership, I refused to give him any of my time and brought the issue to a vote as quickly as possible, substantially foreclosing the large number of Democrats who wanted to rise and use any available time to reassert the Republican determination to cut benefits rather than raising the money in some other way.

Claude wept on the floor when we beat him on this issue; then he voted, after some delay, for the final product, thus assuring that a large majority of Democrats would support it. A bare majority of the Republicans supported it also, and so the issue passed comfortably;[8] went to the Senate, where it was also comfortably passed;[9] and was signed into law by the president with a large ceremony and much congratulation about bipartisanship.

I am personally convinced that if we did not have that issue behind us, it might be the end of the two-party system when Republicans, who handled the issue so badly, went into the presidential election advocating something that could be interpreted as a cut in benefits under the leadership of purists like Archer, Armstrong, and Kemp. In short, I do not see this as a victory for moderation over extremism [but] as a true political compromise achieving a very necessary settlement of an issue too emotional to be handled comfortably

7. The Pickle amendment, which passed on March 9, 1983, by a vote of 228–202, raised the retirement age for full benefits to sixty-six in 2009 and sixty-seven in 2027.

8. The bill, denominated the Social Security Amendments of 1983, was approved by the House on March 9, 1983, by a vote of 282–148.

9. On March 23, 1983, by a vote of 88–9.

or even safely by the Congress. I am convinced that Ronald Reagan would find it very difficult to handle the issue without a major disaster in another election campaign. And, once again, Congress has shown that it will do what is necessary only at the last possible moment and that our system of government is a crisis-activated system of government.

As for myself, I had an extremely frustrating two years [in the 97th Congress]. Rostenkowski, who did not want to be Ways and Means chairman in the first place, could see it only as an opportunity for control. He has little substantive interest and so initiated very little. He took over the staff and put in his own political operatives rather than people who were interested in the tax law. He stacked the committee with a 23–12 edge, despite the close division of the parties on the floor, and saw to it that the people who were added to the committee were docile. He has been easy for me to underestimate because he is not quick, but he substitutes caution, a vindictive personal relationship to those who cross him, an artificial ratio of control, temporizing when he is unsure, and total loyalty to the Democratic Party, despite his constant grumbling about its liberalism, for the brilliance or legislative interest which characterized his predecessors.

My minority continues to be a talkative, aggressive, and intellectually brilliant group, thoroughly frustrated not to have more to say about the course of decision. We have seen little benefit in trying to maintain the turf of the Ways and Means Committee when that meant total Rostenkowski control. As a result, he considers us disloyal to the traditions of the committee, an unpleasant and loquacious nuisance, and politically partisan.

In this environment, I have found it difficult to justify my decision five or six years ago to concentrate on legislative activity and give up any political ambitions, on the assumption that I would be more valuable as a legislator than a politician. Since I at least get consulted by the White House occasionally, not so much for my vote as for my advice on how to handle powermongers like Rostenkowski, I can only assume that my colleagues on the Republican side of the Ways and Means Committee are even more frustrated than I: isolated, uninformed, and totally without bargaining power. I constantly feel as though I am letting them down, but I don't know how to cut them into any more significant action than I have myself. My reputation continues good, but my legislative capacity is crippled, my association with the chairman wary, and my lot one of total frustration. If it were not for an occasional opportunity like the Social Security Commission and the guiding of its report through the Congress, I am sure I would find very little reason for pleasure in my work.

July 1, 1983

I find it somewhat amusing—no, bemusing—that I am now one of the pillars of the Reagan administration. Although I am still not regarded at the White House as a Reaganite, since many of the president's closest supporters recall my prominent position in George Bush's campaign, I nonetheless have been supporting the president much better than his primary constituency. For instance, Jack Kemp has opposed the president on almost every major measure that represents a Reagan initiative since the 1981 tax act was passed. He opposed TEFRA, Social Security, and the balanced budget amendment to the Constitution. In most of these cases, he actually led the fight against the president and took with him a considerable group of the president's most avid supporters. They are constantly convinced that Ronald Reagan has to be saved from himself or from some sinister figure in the White House who holds him captive. The president is still nostalgic about the applause lines that were on his three-by-five cards when he was speaking out on the right-wing lecture circuit, and so echoes sentiments which encourage these people to believe that he doesn't really favor doing the things that are necessary to reduce the deficit.

July 17, 1983

In the perspective of the coming election, the White House now appears to be practically frantic about what has generally been identified as a gender gap. The polls show that women do not accept Reagan as a leader and that they are very resentful of the insensitivity of the Reagan administration to women's issues.[10] . . . However, the White House seems to be embarking on a major campaign trying to change the perception of insensitivity, something that I doubt they can do by cosmetic manipulation.

We have been working on a bill which would crack down on defaulting fathers in child-support cases. The White House, incredibly, thought that this was a welfare problem, not realizing that women do not benefit from efforts to recapture defaults by husbands for the benefit of the US Treasury. I finally persuaded them that this was not the case by my refusal to sponsor their bill treating it as a welfare problem by anything but "by request." They now have accepted a more balanced measure which makes some effort on behalf of women who are not on welfare and are stressing that as great evidence of virtue on behalf of

10. In the 1984 general election, Reagan won 58 percent of the women's vote and 62 percent of the men's vote. Roper Center for Public Opinion Research, "How Groups Voted in 1984," https://ropercenter.cornell.edu/how-groups-voted-1984.

women. The change in White House attitude was made by an appeal by Martha Phillips of my staff to Secretary of Transportation Dole. Liddy Dole apparently understood the issue much better than Margaret Heckler, the secretary of HHS, and so the decision relative to welfare was made by the Department of Transportation rather than the department which is in charge of it. Liddy Dole seems to be something of a plastic woman, but there is steel somewhere within the plastic, and her ambition and understanding combine to make her a much more effective secretary than many of the men in the Reagan cabinet.

This past week I spent a good deal of time in the Ethics Committee,[11] one of the most unhappy assignments I have ever had. A year ago, an unfortunate black page from Arkansas who was in trouble for petty thievery and [was] being sent home for that reason sought to divert attention from his misdemeanors by claiming that he had homosexual relationships with several congressmen and that it was a widespread condition in Congress. In the resulting public furor—which never should have occurred, had the networks checked this boy out carefully before going public with the allegations—Joe Califano was hired to bring about a careful investigation and to report on the state of amorous relations between congressmen and pages. He checked back about twelve years, interviewing many pages and running down every rumor of any sort that was reported to him by what has to be one of the more garrulous groups on Capitol Hill. The result was that it was discovered that Dan Crane [R], a third-term congressman from Illinois and the brother of Phil Crane, had had intercourse in 1980 with a seventeen-year-old female page, while Gerry Studds [D] of Massachusetts was found to have had a relationship with a male page some ten years ago.

Once this information had been confirmed by depositions and ultimately by admission of the parties, the Ethics Committee had to decide what to do about it. In both cases, the relationship was consensual and no harm had been done to the pages involved. In neither case was a public trust involved, except to the extent that the pages could be considered to be wards of the Congress as a whole. The committee was clearly not in the mood for either censure or expulsion, and I took the position from the start that a reprimand was the most serious punishment that should be administered but that the names of the people should be made public. I was convinced that unless they were made public, the names would come out anyway, and it would look as though the Ethics Committee and the House were trying to cover up the disclosures which were the very reason

11. Then known, at least officially, as the Committee on Standards of Official Conduct.

for the probe in the first place, even though they were not related to the original claims by the Arkansas page.

On Thursday, we had about a six-hour meeting, which was agonized, with John Myers [R-IN] the only dissident member of the committee, saying emotionally at one point that he was the only one that cared about the families of the people involved. I dumped on him in a particularly irritated and annoyed way, saying that everyone in the room had feelings and that it was arrogant of him to assume that he was the only caring human being on the Ethics Committee. He was apologetic later, but I don't doubt that this will affect my relations with him, nor do I doubt that word will be out that I am the villain who is more concerned about the reputation of the institution than I am about the ultimate impact on the careers of the two congressmen who exercised such bad judgment. If I could comfortably get off the Ethics Committee, I would certainly do it.

July 24, 1983
I have had a fairly tough time on the Ethics report, being a person with a reputation of being tough, and taking the position from the start that, with respect to misbehavior involving pages, members' names must be at least disclosed to the public. The Ethics Committee reported a recommendation calling for full disclosure and reprimand by an 11–1 vote, John Myers, a Republican from Indiana, being the one dissenter because of his concern about the effect on the family of Dan Crane. Phil Crane and others, including Studds himself, put considerable pressure on me to relent, since I was viewed as one of the leaders of the hard-liners.

However, when the report became known, Newt Gingrich, a man whose own personal life, at least with respect to his marital relations, has not been impeccable, decided to become a hero by urging the expulsion of these two members. A number of people thought the politically wise thing to do would be to take a very tough line with them, regardless of our constitutional authority for expulsion with respect to noncrim[inal] misbehavior which occurred in Studds's case ten years ago and in Crane's case three years ago. By the time the issue came to the floor, Bob Michel was sufficiently concerned about the possibility that these men would be expelled that he moved, as part of his motion to recommit, which he took himself, to upgrade the reprimand to a censure. The censure involves no real difference, as far as the rules of the House are concerned, except that, unlike a reprimand, it requires the members to present themselves in the well of the House for public humiliation by the reading of the reported censure by the Speaker.

With an investigation of drug abuses continuing [and] the probability that the results of this are going to involve charges of racism and certainly are going to involve misbehavior which is technically criminal, it seems to me the House should have left some leeway for tougher action with respect to Crane and Studds, short of expulsion. I could not say this on the floor, however, but I defended as emotionally as I'm capable of doing the report of the committee, thus appearing to be a weak sister for the membership of the House as a whole, while to the membership of the Ethics Committee, I appeared to be the villain with the black mustache.

Crane's was the first motion of reprimand to be moved, and Michel's motion to recommit carried by a comfortable margin, thus requiring Crane to accept censure, which he did with an emotional apology to the House, demonstrating a high degree of contrition. While I voted for reprimand in Crane's case, I changed and voted with Michel for censure with respect to Studds. Although Studds's offense was many years ago, he demonstrated no degree of contriteness at all, and I felt he should not be treated more lightly than Crane. Thus, I switched my vote to one of censure for that reason only, generally preferring a reprimand for both of them.

I went to Michel following the vote and told him that if he didn't like his Ethics Committee, he'd better get himself a new one, upsetting him and causing him in the speech he made on Studds to refer to me by name and to express concern about the necessity of his failing to support the committee recommendation. Apparently, Chairman Louis Stokes [D-OH] did much the same thing with the Speaker, because when I spoke to the Speaker shortly after the episode was over, expressing my severe unhappiness, he referred to Stokes, saying that he hoped he would not get off the committee because of the need for a few strong people on Standards of Official Conduct. I thought better about it after cooling down, and I certainly cannot say that Michel was wrong in judging that unless he took the action he did, the two offenders might have been expelled, a result which would have been unfortunate indeed.

The public seemed generally to side with Gingrich and the tougher penalty, but of course, the public does not know how little difference there is between censure and reprimand, nor can it anticipate what may result from the forthcoming drug investigation.[12] I will have to take a number of depositions on this

---

12. This investigation involved mostly House staffers, although two members—Charles Wilson (D-TX) and Ronald Dellums (D-CA)—were investigated for alleged use of cocaine and marijuana. No official action was taken against either.

during the next month or two, something which gives me heartburn because I would rather engage in the competition of great ideas than spend so much time worrying about the personal behavior of my colleagues.

Rostenkowski seems much more accommodating than he did last year. Perhaps he is maturing in the job, or perhaps I am learning to live with him more easily than I could during the times when I was testing his use of power and being frustrated every time by the strength of his commitment to control. He is a very political leader, unsubstantive as always, but his word is good and his understanding is excellent. His technique of leadership involves heavy use of staff and temporization until he has decided what is the right thing to do. He rarely makes a premature commitment. He has excellent control of his members also, basing it on mutual support, strong commitments, and a vindictiveness that never falters for those who have crossed him. He supports his subcommittee chairmen without exception and expects unquestioned support from them in return for those matters which are outside their subcommittee responsibilities. In the light of such leadership, even Pete Stark has developed a high degree of predictability as chairman of the Miscellaneous Revenue Subcommittee. I cannot say that Rostenkowski's techniques are wrong, but clearly they are frustrating for a minority which is totally cut out of the decision-making process. Had I anticipated the nature of his leadership, I might easily have made a different decision from my decision of five years ago to leave my political ambitions behind and to concentrate on trying to be an effective legislative leader. From my muddy rhetoric, perhaps that was the best decision I could have made, but in light of developments, it is not as clearly a correct decision as it was at the time I made it.

November 2, 1983
The generalized vehicle for advancement of women's rights in the labor force is called the Economic Equity Act. The Ways and Means Committee was to hold hearings on this issue, apparently mostly for show purposes, and the administration had to be dragged kicking and screaming into supporting at least some aspects of the program. I met with the senior staff at the White House, Chairman Dole, and six women Republican members of the House and two Republican members from the Senate. I was the major spokesman for the women in the House and was able to bludgeon the White House staff into accepting a greater degree of flexibility with respect to dependent care.

The following Monday, a portion of this group, excluding Dole and the women senators, met with the president the day before the hearings on the

Economic Equity Act were to be held.[13] This was 5:00 on the day following the Lebanese bombing and the day before the invasion of Grenada. It seems to me singular that the president sat with this group and chatted in an anecdotal way for about forty-five minutes on an issue which was of very little interest to him and which he only barely understood, preparing us then to have a press conference in the White House briefing room about the great support the administration is giving to the women's movement. I said to him at the beginning of the meeting, as the only other man present, that he should know my name was really "Barbara." He then demonstrated the extent of his "time warp" by calling me "Babs" for the rest of the meeting. His performance was quite remarkable, in view of what else was going on at the time, and I have mused about it a good deal since then.

Two of my friends and fellow classmates who have been significant contributors to the deliberations of the House, Jack Edwards of Alabama and John Erlenborn of Illinois, have announced their retirement since the last journal entry. This leaves me, John Duncan, and Bill Dickinson [R-AL] the sole remaining members of the 89th Club who have not announced their retirement or been defeated. I have not discussed the possibility of my own retirement, and nobody seems to be assuming that I might do so, for which I am grateful. Sometime in January or February I will take stock of the prospects and of the situation in the 99th Congress and will make a decision unrelated to any commitment either to continuity or to any other possible employment. I really do not know what my decision will be, but my wife seems to assume that I will stay here until I am carried out.

December 27, 1983

I now appreciate how totally corrupt our farm programs are. . . . Most of them, including the milk program, this next year will be immense. The cost of satisfying the greedy special interests that make up our agricultural community is a cost we can ill afford to bear, both as consumers and taxpayers. But the people who count in this area are people I cannot reach, nor can they be reached by reason or judgment. I shall look forward to the day when the whole process will become so obviously corrupt that public outcry will force our craven collective to chuck the whole subsidy and price-support approach to [the] farm economy. I don't think that day is far off, but I know now that I cannot hasten it.

The same can be said about the state of our electoral system. This year I

13. The bill died in committee.

gave up on public financing as an idea whose time has come and gone, but vast measures and changes of influence which are possibly still not achievable are not likely to forestall the public scandal in the buying of elections by interest groups. Although I sound like the last of the puritans in this respect, and I am so regarded by my more sophisticated friends, I am convinced that representative government cannot effectively survive unless people have some confidence in the capacity of our representatives to vote against those with special interests in pending legislation. I do not blame the lobbyists about the massive sums of money they are contributing to elections, since they are every bit as much or even more the captives of the system than we are. The cycle must be broken somewhere.

A farewell to Congress.

Looking back on his decision to step away from Congress, Conable remarked:

> *As the Republican leader on the Ways and Means Committee, I never could go between two places in a straight line. I always had to try to lay ambushes for my majority colleagues and to achieve what I could through indirection. Without even a remote hope of getting enough votes to dominate, one resorts to whatever stratagems one can find and use. In my own case, however, there was little satisfaction to be derived from devious dealings. I much preferred to move in a straight line, and I frankly did not like being forced to take a circuitous route. This was a major factor, I must confess, in my decision to leave Congress and go on to other things. Twenty years in a minority position finally took its toll.[1]*

April 20, 1984

No politician does anything for just one reason. I announced my retirement in March, and there were many reasons for me to do it. First, I was tired. I have noticed that increasingly I have had a short fuse and tended to lecture my friends, shaking my fist under their noses and behaving in general something like an elderly baby would. I don't like myself very well under these conditions, and there didn't seem to be much prospect that my disposition would improve if I were to stay here longer. Next, I didn't like the political signs. The Reagan administration seemed headed for an uncertain renewal. I don't doubt that the president will win with an almost landslide proportion, but I doubt that he will have coattails or that when all the votes are counted he will have significant tools to govern.[2] I also don't doubt that he will have an extremely difficult economic situation and, as a lame-duck president, reducing capacity to deal with it. Of

1. Barber B. Conable, Jr., *Congress and the Income Tax* (Norman: University of Oklahoma Press, 1989), 6–7.

2. Reagan defeated Democrat Walter Mondale in an electoral vote landslide, 525–13. The Republicans gained fifteen seats in the House in the 1984 election but were still outnumbered in the 99th Congress by a margin of 254–181.

course, his White House will be more pragmatic, with the ideologues leaving almost daily and being supplanted by people who will relate the president more toward government and less toward idea promotion. But he will have a tough time, the vice president will be as puzzled as he is now, and the members of the president's own party will be inclined to run against him and to try to demonstrate an independence of an increasingly unpopular and ineffective president. In short, it doesn't look to me like a good political situation, and I am therefore convinced that the election in 1986 will be an extremely difficult one for the Republican Party generally.[3]

I must say that this year I have been increasingly uneasy about Ronald Reagan as president, since he appears to be no better clued in to the details of governing or the need for his personal attention to affairs of state than he was when he first became president. I go to leadership meetings and find him still sealed inside an envelope of anecdote and elusive as he ever was in a substantive sense. My impression of him continues to be that he is very bright but very lazy. The communication between the White House and the president's supporters in Congress has been bad; the communication between the White House and his opponents has been not only bad but destructive. As his conservative primary constituency has flaked off and opposed the governing decisions he has to make as president, he has increasingly stressed social issues about which there is no consensus and for which many upper-middle-class white Republicans revile him.

But to return to my personal decision. . . . I have some sense from a personal point of view that I would feel as though I were running away or willing my seat to a Democrat if I were to stop in 1986. If I were not to quit now, then I would be at least sixty-four years old and possibly sixty-six years old before I tried to do something else. Inevitably, that something else would be simply the mowing of my lawn back in Alexander rather than the more active options that are available to me if I stop now. Thus, from a personal point of view, there seems to be a tide in the affairs of men indicating that right now my opportunity to stop will leave me with the best possible taste in my mouth and the best possible prospects for the future.

Also, my wife has phased out her job at George Washington University and so does not have to be pulled out by the roots if we leave at this point. She is uncertain what she wants to do and has made no indication of her wishes, but inevitably, before an option for the future is chosen, she must be a full participant

---

3. The Republicans lost four seats in the House in the 1986 election; the 100th Congress included 258 Democrats and 177 Republicans.

372   The Congressional Journal of Barber B. Conable, Jr.

in the decision. I am not sure what her decision would have been if I had tried to get her to walk away from her job two years ago or four years ago, but obviously it would have been more difficult for her then than it is now.

Next, my situation in the Congress is not going to be any easier, since it is apparent that Chairman Rostenkowski is getting better and better control of the committee, using the many devices available to him so to do. Starting with a stacked committee, moving through personal vindictiveness to those who cross him, and finally negotiating an arrangement with subcommittee chairmen whereby he supports what they bring out of subcommittee, whatever it is, in return for their supporting what he wants to do in conference committees, Danny has put himself in a position where he is constantly able to dominate the rather divergent Senate in conference and to do a great deal of real-world legislating in what used to be a forum of give-and-take between senators and congressmen. He has been very nice to me during this past year [and] has acceded to my wishes as a matter of grace on many occasions. He is adroit and understanding when he is interested, although his substantive interests still are far behind his desire to exercise power. The point is that whatever he gives me is a matter of grace and not a true exercise of legislative give-and-take, and I do not have any illusions that this will improve, since he seems to be so successful in the management of the committee. I have no desire to be a supplicant for crumbs rather than a true participant, whether or not Rosty is good to me, and so I can see nothing but growing frustration in the years ahead, before the final crunch comes and he runs for Speaker on Tip O'Neill's retirement.[4]

I have also been increasingly alarmed by the stridency of the younger Republicans. As I have said on many occasions, denying this frustration, they are performing the act of renewal that young people usually do, but they are doing so in a way that is not constructive for the party. They will not support their president, who is ideologically much closer to them than he is to me. Many of them are avid Kemp supporters, willing to accept his panaceas without critical understanding. They give Bob Michel fits. They are not easy to live with and show no signs of mellowing, although I do not doubt that eventually they will accept some responsibility for government and stop posturing over in the corner. Surprisingly few in number in proportion to their stridency, they nonetheless are a very divisive element in our party and somewhat reduce my pleasure in service.

Besides all this, twenty is a nice round number, and nobody can claim that I am "quitting" or "running away." I have been greatly honored to have been able

4. Jim Wright succeeded O'Neill as Speaker in 1987.

to serve so long and in such relatively responsible assignments. My constituents have given me an easy time, and my colleagues have generally been supportive. If I have had the frustrations of being in the minority for twenty years, I suppose those are not equal to the frustrations of being in the majority and still not having an easy button to push, to say this is what I am going to do and to be able to do it without touching a thousand bases. And I am well aware that Chairman Rostenkowski feels even more intense frustrations than I do when, with all his advantages, I still sometimes beat him on close issues. I once thought I might be chairman of the Ways and Means Committee someday; perhaps I should be glad that I have not been. Certainly my reputation has been enhanced by the assumption that I would make a better chairman than those who have served in that role, frequently indulged by those who assume that leadership has something to do with literacy, hard work, and an understanding of the tax law.

Since I have announced my retirement, I have been somewhat surprised at the reaction. Most people accepted it as something I had earned. Only a few asked me to reconsider. My colleagues voted me, in the *U.S. News & World Report* annual poll, the most respected member of the House, as they voted Howard Baker the most respected member of the Senate, leading me to believe that statesmanship is somehow closely related to the announcement of retirement.[5] I have had a veritable outpouring of job offers, based on my reputation and not the expectancy that I could perform well in the many law practices that apparently would like to include me. I have had a total of six political science professorships offered to me, a visiting professorship of law, and an endowed chair at the Harvard School of Government. I have been offered stipends to come and write books at the Hoover Institution, Brookings, AEI,[6] and the Woodrow Wilson Center in the Smithsonian. I have been offered a part-time consultancy with the Conference Board in New York City and part-time consultant jobs to Arthur Anderson and Company and Touche Ross & Co., the leading accountants. A number of corporate directorships have been at least implied, and it is apparent that I could put these many posts together in various ways to have a postretirement life of ceaseless activity if I wish, and major emolument.

I must not make a decision about these before November, if I can keep the offers alive that long, because I do not wish people to speculate about whether I am voting for my current job or my future job. I expect many of the offers to

---

5. Courtney R. Sheldon, "Movers and Shakers in Congress," *U.S. News & World Report*, April 23, 1984.

6. American Enterprise Institute.

evaporate, since there is nothing deader than a dead politician. But at any rate, at this point I am having a good time juggling incoming phone calls and happily wallowing in a pigpen of remunerative options.[7]

7. Conable accepted a position as distinguished professor in the Political Science Department of the University of Rochester, home of his friend Richard Fenno. He also undertook a fortnightly column for *U.S. News & World Report*. In 1986 Ronald Reagan nominated him for president of the World Bank, and he served a five-year term.

Appendix: Key Names

Dramatis personae are sometimes listed under their nicknames, not as an assertion of editorial familiarity but because that is how Barber Conable knew and referred to them. For the most part, the biographical information provided here is limited to the era of Conable's House service.

Brock Adams: D-WA; House of Representatives, 1965–1977; secretary of transportation, 1977–1979

Spiro Agnew: Vice president of the United States, 1969–1973

Martin Agronsky: Host of the political TV talk show *Agronsky & Company*, 1969–1986

Carl Albert: D-OK; House of Representatives, 1947–1977; Speaker of the House, 1971–1977

John Anderson: R-IL; House of Representatives, 1961–1981; candidate for Republican presidential nomination, 1980; candidate for president, National Unity Party, 1980

Warren Anderson: R; New York State senate, 1953–1986; New York senate majority leader, 1973–1988

Bill Archer: R-TX; House of Representatives, 1971–2001; chairman, House Ways and Means Committee, 1995–2001

Leslie Arends: R-IL; House of Representatives, 1935–1974

Bill Armstrong: R-CO; House of Representatives, 1973–1979; Senate, 1979–1991

Skip Bafalis: R-FL; House of Representatives, 1973–1983

Howard Baker: R-TN; Senate, 1967–1985

Jim Baker: Campaign manager, George H. W. Bush presidential campaign, 1979–1980; White House chief of staff, 1981–1985

Bob Bauman: R-MD; House of Representatives, 1973–1981

Abe Beame: D; mayor of New York City, 1974–1977

Tom Benton: Conable's friend and district assistant

Lloyd Bentsen: D-TX; House of Representatives, 1948–1955; Senate, 1971–1993

Michael Blumenthal: Secretary of the treasury, 1977–1979

Hale Boggs: D-LA; House of Representatives, 1941–1943, 1947–1973; House majority whip, 1962–1971; House majority leader, 1971–1973

Richard Bolling: D-MO; House of Representatives, 1949–1983; chairman, House Committee on Rules, 1979–1983

John Brademas: D-IN; House of Representatives, 1959–1981; House majority whip, 1977–1981

William Brock: R-TN; House of Representatives, 1963–1971; Senate, 1971–1977; US trade representative, 1981–1985

David Broder: *Washington Post* columnist

Clarence "Bud" Brown: R-OH; House of Representatives, 1965–1983

Joel Broyhill: R-VA; House of Representatives, 1953–1974

James Buckley: C-NY; Senate, 1971–1977

Dean Burch: Chairman, Republican National Committee, 1964–1965; chairman, Federal Communications Commission, 1969–1974; counselor to Presidents Nixon and Ford, 1974; chief of staff, George H. W. Bush vice-presidential campaign, 1980

Jim Burke: D-MA; House of Representatives, 1959–1979

Arthur Burns: Chairman, Board of Governors of the Federal Reserve, 1970–1978

Phil Burton: D-CA; House of Representatives, 1964–1983

Barbara Bush: Wife of George H. W. Bush

George H. W. Bush: R-TX; House of Representatives, 1967–1971; vice president of the United States, 1981–1989; president of the United States, 1989–1993

John W. Byrnes: R-WI; House of Representatives, 1945–1973; ranking Republican, House Ways and Means Committee, 1963–1972

Hugh Carey: D-NY; House of Representatives, 1961–1974; governor of New York, 1975–1983

Jimmy Carter: Governor of Georgia, 1971–1975; president of the United States, 1977–1981

Al (Elford) Cederberg: R-MI; House of Representatives, 1953–1978

Emanuel Celler: D-NY; House of Representatives, 1923–1973; chairman, House Judiciary Committee, 1949–1953, 1955–1973

Dick Cheney: R-WY; White House chief of staff, 1975–1977; House of Representatives, 1979–1989; vice president of the United States, 2001–2009

Del Clawson: R-CA; House of Representatives, 1963–1978

John Connally: Governor of Texas, 1963–1969; secretary of the treasury, 1971–1972; candidate for Republican presidential nomination, 1980

Jim Corman: D-CA; House of Representatives, 1961–1981

Bill Cotter: D-CT; House of Representatives, 1971–1981

Dan Crane: R-IL; House of Representatives, 1979–1985

Phil Crane: R-IL; House of Representatives, 1969–2005; candidate for Republican presidential nomination, 1980

Al D'Amato: R-NY; Senate, 1981–1999

Dick Darman: White House staff secretary, 1981–1985

Samuel Devine: R-OH; House of Representatives, 1959–1981

Bob Dole: R-KS; House of Representatives, 1961–1969; Senate, 1969–1996; chairman, Senate Finance Committee, 1981–1985; Republican vice-presidential candidate, 1976

Tom Downey: D-NY; House of Representatives, 1975–1993

John Duncan: R-TN; House of Representatives, 1965–1988

Perry Duryea: R; speaker, New York State assembly, 1969–1973; candidate for governor of New York, 1978

Fred Eckert: R-NY; New York State senate, 1972–1982; House of Representatives, 1985–1987

John Ehrlichman: Assistant for domestic affairs to President Nixon, 1969–1973

John Erlenborn: R-IL; House of Representatives, 1965–1985

Hamilton Fish, Jr.: R-NY; House of Representatives, 1969–1995

Joe Fisher: D-VA; House of Representatives, 1975–1981

Gerald Ford: R-MI; House of Representatives, 1949–1973; House minority leader, 1965–1973; vice president of the United States, 1973–1974; president of the United States, 1974–1977

Bill Frenzel: R-MN; House of Representatives, 1971–1991

Max Friedersdorf: White House special assistant for congressional relations, 1971–1973; deputy assistant to the president for the House of Representatives, 1973–1974; assistant to the president for legislative affairs, 1975–1977, 1981

Richard Gephardt: D-MO; House of Representatives, 1977–2005

Bob Giaimo: D-CT; House of Representatives, 1959–1981; chairman, House Budget Committee, 1977–1981

Sam Gibbons: D-FL; House of Representatives, 1963–1997; chairman, House Ways and Means Committee, 1993–1995

Charles Goodell: R-NY; House of Representatives, 1959–1968; Senate, 1968–1971

Bill Gradison: R-OH; House of Representatives, 1975–1993

Phil Gramm: D/R-TX; House of Representatives, 1979–1985; Senate, 1985–2002

Alan Greenspan: Chairman, Council of Economic Advisers, 1974–1977

Robert Griffin: R-MI; House of Representatives, 1957–1966; Senate, 1966–1979

Martha Griffiths: D-MI; House of Representatives, 1955–1974

Al Haig: White House chief of staff, 1973–1974; secretary of state, 1981–1982

H. R. Haldeman: White House chief of staff, 1969–1973

Kent Hance: D-TX; House of Representatives, 1979–1985

Bryce Harlow: Assistant to the president for legislative affairs, 1969–1970; counselor to the president, 1973–1974

Wayne Hays: D-OH; House of Representatives, 1949–1976

Peggy Heckler: R-MA; House of Representatives, 1967–1983; secretary of health and human services, 1983–1985

Jesse Helms: R-NC; Senate, 1973–2003

George Hinman: Executive assistant to Governor and Vice President Nelson Rockefeller, 1959–1977

Fritz Hollings: D-SC; Senate, 1966–2005

Marjorie Holt: R-MD; House of Representatives, 1973–1987

Elizabeth Holtzman: D-NY; House of Representatives, 1973–1981; candidate for US Senate, 1980

Frank Horton: R-NY; House of Representatives, 1963–1993

Hubert Humphrey: D-MN; Senate, 1949–1964, 1971–1978; vice president of the United States, 1965–1969; Democratic candidate for president, 1968; candidate for Democratic presidential nomination, 1972

Al Hunt: *Wall Street Journal* congressional and national political reporter, Washington bureau chief, executive Washington editor, 1969–2004

Henry Hyde: R-IL; House of Representatives, 1975–2007

Andy Jacobs: D-IN; House of Representatives, 1965–1973, 1975–1997

Jacob Javits: R-NY; House of Representatives, 1947–1954; Senate, 1957–1981

Jim Jones: D-OK; House of Representatives, 1973–1987; chairman, House Budget Committee, 1981–1985

Hamilton Jordan: Domestic adviser to the president, 1977–1979; White House chief of staff, 1979–1980

Joe Karth: D-MN; House of Representatives, 1959–1977

Jack Kemp: R-NY; House of Representatives, 1971–1989

David Kennedy: Secretary of the treasury, 1969–1971

Bill Ketchum: R-CA; House of Representatives, 1973–1978

Martha Keys: D-KS; House of Representatives, 1975–1979

Lane Kirkland: President, AFL-CIO, 1979–1995

Henry Kissinger: Assistant to the president for national security affairs, 1969–1975; secretary of state, 1973–1977
Dan Kuykendall: R-TN; House of Representatives, 1967–1975
John LaFalce: D-NY; House of Representatives, 1975–2003
Mel Laird: R-WI; House of Representatives, 1953–1969; secretary of defense, 1969–1973; domestic adviser to the president, 1973–1974
Phil Landrum: D-GA; House of Representatives, 1953–1977
Del Latta: R-OH; House of Representatives, 1959–1989
Paul Laxalt: R-NV; Senate, 1974–1987
Bob Leggett: D-CA; House of Representatives, 1963–1979
Norman Lent: R/C-NY; House of Representatives, 1971–1993
John Lindsay: R/D-NY; House of Representatives, 1959–1965; mayor of New York City, 1966–1973; candidate for Democratic presidential nomination, 1972
Russell Long: D-LA; Senate, 1948–1987; chairman, Senate Finance Committee, 1966–1981
Trent Lott: R-MS; House of Representatives, 1973–1989; Senate, 1989–2007
Clark MacGregor: R-MN; House of Representatives, 1961–1971; White House chief congressional liaison, 1971–1972; chairman, Committee to Re-elect the President, 1972
John Marchi: R; New York State senate, 1957–2006; candidate for mayor of New York City, 1969, 1973
Pete McCloskey: R-CA; House of Representatives, 1967–1983; candidate for Republican presidential nomination, 1972
John McCormack: D-MA; House of Representatives, 1928–1971; Speaker of the House, 1961–1971
Linda McLaughlin: Office manager for Barber Conable
Bob Michel: R-IL; House of Representatives, 1957–1995; House minority leader, 1981–1995
Abner Mikva: D-IL; House of Representatives, 1969–1973, 1975–1979
Wilbur Mills: D-AR; House of Representatives, 1939–1977; chairman, House Ways and Means Committee, 1957–1974; candidate for Democratic presidential nomination, 1972
Parren Mitchell: D-MD; House of Representatives, 1971–1987
Sonny Montgomery: D-MS; House of Representatives, 1967–1997
Henson Moore: R-LA; House of Representatives, 1975–1987
Rogers Morton: R-MD; House of Representatives, 1963–1971; secretary of the

interior, 1971–1975; secretary of commerce, 1975–1976; chairman, President Ford's campaign committee, 1976

Pat Moynihan: D-NY; Senate, 1977–2001

John Myers: R-IN; House of Representatives, 1967–1997

Harry Nicholas: Conable's chief of staff during his entire congressional career

Pat Nixon: First Lady of the United States, 1969–1974

Richard Nixon: President of the United States, 1969–1974

Tip O'Neill: D-MA; House of Representatives, 1953–1987; Speaker of the House, 1977–1987

Bob Packwood: R-OR; Senate, 1969–1995

Wright Patman: D-TX; House of Representatives, 1929–1976; chairman, Joint Economic Committee, 1957–1959, 1961–1963, 1965–1967, 1969–1971, 1973–1975

Claude Pepper: D-FL; Senate, 1936–1951; House of Representatives, 1963–1989

Jerry Pettis: R-CA; House of Representatives, 1967–1975

Martha Phillips: Deputy minority director, House Ways and Means Committee, 1975–1986

Jake Pickle: D-TX; House of Representatives, 1963–1995

Otis Pike: D-NY; House of Representatives, 1961–1979

Dick Poff: R-VA; House of Representatives, 1953–1972

Adam Clayton Powell: D-NY; House of Representatives, 1945–1967, 1969–1971

Jody Powell: White House press secretary, 1977–1981

William Proxmire: D-WI; Senate, 1957–1989

Albert Quie: R-MN; House of Representatives, 1958–1979

Charles Rangel: D-NY; House of Representatives, 1971–2017

Ronald Reagan: President of the United States, 1981–1989

Don Regan: Secretary of the treasury, 1981–1985

Ralph Regula: R-OH; House of Representatives, 1973–2009

Henry Reuss: D-WI; House of Representatives, 1955–1983

John Rhodes: R-AZ; House of Representatives, 1953–1983; House minority leader, 1973–1981

Elliot Richardson: Secretary of health, education, and welfare, 1970–1973; secretary of defense, 1973; attorney general, 1973

Don Riegle: R/D-MI; House of Representatives, 1967–1976; Senate, 1976–1995

Nelson Rockefeller: Governor of New York, 1959–1973; vice president of the United States, 1974–1977

Peter Rodino: D-NJ; House of Representatives, 1949–1989; chairman, House Judiciary Committee, 1973–1989

Richard Rosenbaum: Chairman, New York State Republican Party, 1972–1977; candidate for Republican gubernatorial nomination, 1982

Dan Rostenkowski: D-IL; House of Representatives, 1959–1995; chairman, House Ways and Means Committee, 1981–1994

William Roth: R-DE; House of Representatives, 1967–1970; Senate, 1971–2001

John Rousselot: R-CA; House of Representatives, 1961–1963, 1970–1983

Donald Rumsfeld: R-IL; House of Representatives, 1963–1969; director, Office of Economic Opportunity, 1969–1970; counselor to the president, 1970–1973; ambassador to NATO, 1973–1974; White House chief of staff, 1974–1975; secretary of defense, 1975–1977

James Schlesinger: Director of CIA, 1973; secretary of defense, 1973–1975; secretary of energy, 1977–1979

Herman Schneebeli: R-PA; House of Representatives, 1960–1977; ranking minority member, House Ways and Means Committee, 1973–1977

Dick Schulze: R-PA; House of Representatives, 1975–1993

Richard Schweiker: R-PA; House of Representatives, 1961–1969; Senate, 1969–1981; Ronald Reagan's designated running mate, 1976; secretary of health and human services, 1981–1983

Hugh Scott: R-PA; House of Representatives, 1941–1945, 1947–1959; Senate, 1959–1977

John Sears: Manager of Ronald Reagan's 1976 and 1980 campaigns (until the 1980 New Hampshire primary) for the Republican presidential nomination

Bud Shuster: R-PA; House of Representatives, 1973–2001

Hugh Sidey: *Time* magazine political and White House correspondent

William Simon: Administrator, Federal Energy Office, 1973–1974; secretary of the treasury, 1974–1977

H. Allen Smith: R-CA; House of Representatives, 1957–1973

Robert Stafford: R-VT; House of Representatives, 1961–1971; Senate, 1971–1989

Pete Stark: D-CA; House of Representatives, 1973–2013

James St. Clair: Special counsel to Richard Nixon, 1973–1974

Bill Steiger: R-WI; House of Representatives, 1967–1978

Sam Steiger: R-AZ; House of Representatives, 1967–1977

David Stockman: R-MI; House of Representatives, 1977–1981; director, Office of Management and Budget, 1981–1985

Louis Stokes: D-OH; House of Representatives, 1969–1999

Gerry Studds: D-MA; House of Representatives, 1973–1997

Olin "Tiger" Teague: D-TX; House of Representatives, 1946–1978

Frank Thompson: D-NJ; House of Representatives, 1955–1980

Bill Timmons: Deputy assistant to the president for legislative affairs, 1969–1970; assistant to the president for legislative affairs, 1970–1975

Alexander "Sandy" Trowbridge: Secretary of commerce, 1967–1968; president, National Association of Manufacturers, 1980–1990

Morris Udall: D-AZ; House of Representatives, 1961–1991

Al Ullman: D-OR; House of Representatives, 1957–1981; chairman, House Ways and Means Committee, 1974–1981

Charles Vanik: D-OH; House of Representatives, 1955–1981

Joe Waggonner: D-LA; House of Representatives, 1961–1979

Bob Walker: R-PA; House of Representatives, 1977–1997

Charls "Charlie" Walker: Undersecretary of the treasury, 1969–1972; deputy secretary of the treasury, 1973; lobbyist

John Watts: D-KY; House of Representatives, 1951–1971

Fred Wertheimer: Various positions and ultimately president, Common Cause, 1971–1995

Chuck Wiggins: R-CA; House of Representatives, 1967–1979

George Will: *Washington Post* columnist, 1974–present

Malcolm Wilson: Lieutenant governor under Nelson Rockefeller, 1959–1973; governor of New York, 1973–1974

Jim Wright: D-TX; House of Representatives, 1955–1989; Speaker of the House, 1987–1989

Jack Wydler: R-NY; House of Representatives, 1963–1981

Ralph Yarborough: D-TX; Senate, 1957–1971

Frank Zarb: "Energy czar" and assistant to the president for energy affairs, 1974–1977

Index

Armed Services Committee, 106
Armstrong, Bill, 357, 359, 360
Ash, Roy, 117
auto industry: energy program debate in
    1977 and, 228–229

Bafalis, Skip, 134, 167, 218–219, 228,
    241, 251–252
Baker, Howard, 225, 339, 343, 373
Baker, Jim: budget debate in 1982 and
    the Gang of 17, 344, 345, 346; Bush's
    1980 presidential bid and, 286,
    287; Bush's view of in 1982, 344;
    Conable's comments on in 1981, 326;
    as Reagan's chief of staff, 305; Social
    Security financing crisis debate in
    1983, 357, 359; tax package debate in
    1981, 309, 312, 323, 328, 333
balanced budget amendment debate, 266,
    348–349, 351–353
Ball, Bob, 91, 339, 357–358, 359
Bartlett, Joe, 139
baseball. *See* Republican-Democratic
    baseball game
Batavia (NY), xxi–xxii
Batavia Rotary Club, xxvii
Bauman, Bob, 298–299
Beach, Jim, xxii
Beame, Abe, 178
Beck, Bob, 360
Begich, Nick, 110n7
Belcher, Page, 56
Bell, Griffin, 274n4
Benjamin, Adam, 296
Benton, Tom, 84, 144, 146, 348
Bentsen, Beryl, 267
Bentsen, Lloyd, 51n23, 140
Bernstein, Carl, xxv–xxvi, xxviii
Betts, Jack, 26, 44, 81, 87, 98, 105
Bibby, John F., 45
Bishop, Dick, 84
Blackburn, Ben, 56
Blackmore, Shirley, 144–145
Blumenthal, Michael: Conable's

assessment of as a member of the
    Carter White House, 234; energy
    program debate in 1977, 226, 227;
    resignation from Carter's cabinet,
    274n4; tax reform debate in 1978, 254,
    258–259, 261–262
Boggs, Hale: Conable's comments on in
    1969, 15–16, 26–27; death of, 110;
    elected House majority leader, 57n1;
    John McCormack's retirement and,
    38; tax reform debate in 1969, 12–13,
    14, 17, 18, 19, 20, 21, 24, 26–27
Boland, Ed, 38
Bolling, Richard: budget debate in 1982
    and the Gang of 17, 345; on Omar
    Burleson, 103; campaign finance
    reform debate in 1978, 239; Conable's
    comments on in 1979, 265, 267–268;
    congressional committee ratios issue
    in 1981 and, 305; tax package debate
    in 1981, 320
Botts, Herb, 50
Bow, Frank, 64
Brademas, John, 216, 237, 238, 239, 240,
    296
Brady, Jim, 313
Brezhnev, Leonid, 149n28, 224
Brock, William, 10, 28, 289
Broder, David, 197–198, 266, 268,
    286–287
Brodhead, Bill, 249
Brooke, Edward, 205
Brookings Institution, 14n8, 28, 29
Brotzman, Donald, 94, 99, 112
Brown, Clarence, Jr. ("Bud"), 104, 105,
    232
Broyhill, Jim, 222
Broyhill, Joel: Conable's comments on
    as a Ways and Means Committee
    member, 79, 98; tax reform debate in
    1969, 14, 19, 23, 24
Buchanan, John, 298
Buchholtz, Karl, xxvii
Buckley, James, 50, 51, 210–211

324–325; economic package debate in 1977, 218, 219; meeting with the vice-president of Romania in 1972 and, 83; revenue-sharing debate in 1972, 82, 85; Social Security tax rollback debate of 1978, 241; tax package debate in 1981, 322, 324–325; trade bill and textile quota debate in 1970, 41, 43, 45n15, 52; windfall profits tax debate in 1980, 281

Gilbert, Jack, 13, 14, 18

Gilman, Ben, 177

Gingrich, Newt, 291–292, 365, 366

Glenn, John, 169

Goldwater, Barry, 179

Goodell, Charles, 50, 51, 56, 74

Good Guys dinner club, 117, 121

Gore, Albert, Sr., 28, 29

Gouinlock, Agnes, xx. *See also* Conable, Agnes Gouinlock

Gouinlock, Margaret, xx

Gradison, Bill, 213, 221, 228, 252, 311

Gramm, Phil, 314, 320

Gramm-Latta budget proposal, 317n9

Green, Bill, 45n15, 102, 112, 162, 284

Green, Edith, 142

Greenspan, Alan, 338, 357

Griffin, Robert, 18, 57, 61, 71, 290

Griffiths, Martha: Conable's comments on as a Ways and Means Committee member, 101, 112; considered for Gerald Ford's administration, 142; Joint Economic Committee of 1971, 59, 63; tax reform debate in 1969, 19, 23, 24, 25

Gromyko, Andrei, 224

Gross, H. R., 7

Guarini, Frank, 271–272

gubernatorial elections of 1978: Jack Kemp and, 234–235, 244

Haig, Al, 129–130, 131, 138n15, 344

Haldeman, H. R., 109, 114, 138

Hall, Doc, 56

Hance, Kent, 320, 325, 327n17, 328, 329

Hanley, Jim, 267

Hanna, Richard, 217n2

Harlow, Bryce, 6, 27–28, 58, 93, 118, 141

Hart, Gary, 168

Hastings, James, 7, 122, 177

Hatfield-McGovern bill, 50

Hays, Wayne, 150–151, 173, 201–202, 203

health legislation proposal, 61–62

Heckler, Peggy, 330, 364

Heftel, Cecil, 271–272

Heller, Walter, 60

Helms, Jesse, 206

Helstoski, Henry, 167

Hickel, Walter, 20

Hickey-Freeman suit manufacturers, 35

Higher Education Act (1965), 89

Hinckley, John, Jr., 313

Hinman, George, 142

Hogan, Larry, 134

Holland Purchase Historical Society, xxvi

Hollings, Fritz, 344, 345

Holt, Marjorie, 214, 222, 270

Holtzman, Elizabeth, 223, 297

Home Style, xxiv

Horton, Frank, 141; campaign finance reform debate in 1971, 75; Conable's comments on in 1969, 6; congressional energy conference in 1977, 232; driving under the influence incident in 1976, 205–206; New York City bankruptcy issue and, 177; tax reform debate in 1971, 21

House Ad Hoc Committee on Energy, 231

House Administration Committee, 237–238, 239

House Appropriations Committee, 69, 223, 300, 307, 310

House Budget Committee: budget debate in 1981, 313–314; Conable's comments on in 1977, 221–223; Conable's comments on in 1979,

National Committee on US-China
  Relations, xxvi
National Journal, xxv, 66, 76
National Safety Council, 113
NBC News, 140, 141, 290
New Hampshire primary: of 1972, 80,
  81–82; of 1976, 199; of 1980, 284
newsletter: by Conable, xxii–xxiii, 84, 88
Newsweek, 179–180, 355
New York City bankruptcy issue,
  174–175, 176–178
New York City Seasonal Financing Act
  (1975), 178n19
New York State: Conable and the
  redistricting issue in 1982, 342,
  347–348; Jack Kemp's gubernatorial
  ambitions in 1978, 234–235; US
  Senate race in 1980, 297–298
New York State Republican Committee,
  229
New York Times, 77, 243, 347
Nicholas, Harry, 15, 138, 271; Conable's
  1974 reelection campaign and, 147;
  Conable's appreciation of, 278;
  Conable's relationship with Reagan
  and, 306; Conable's role in the folding
  of Bush's 1980 presidential campaign
  and, 286–287; Reagan's first meeting
  with Conable as president and, 306;
  trade bill and textile quota debate in
  1970, 35
91st Club, 28
Nixon, Pat, 43
Nixon, Richard: Spiro Agnew and,
  93; Air Force Academy speech of
  June 1969, 15; appointments to the
  Supreme Court, 73n20; John Byrnes's
  criticism of, 67; campaign finance
  reform and, 127; China initiative,
  71; Conable on Nixon's relationship
  with congressional Republicans,
  86, 96, 111, 114; Conable's 1970
  visit to the Oval Office and, 42–43;
  Conable's chairmanship of the

Research Committee and, 53–54,
  56–57; Conable's comments to Bryce
  Harlow concerning, 27–28; Conable's
  legislative support ratio with respect
  to, 116–117, 128; Conable's views of
  in 1969, 6, 17–18; Conable's views
  of in 1970, 35–36, 53–54; Conable's
  views of in 1971, 71; Conable's views
  of in 1972, 86; Conable's views of in
  1973, 120–121, 125; concerns about
  George McGovern in 1972, 89;
  decision to mine the harbors of North
  Vietnam, 86; Gerald Ford's pardoning
  of, 145; Gerald Ford's succession
  to the vice presidency and, 117n16,
  118–119; health legislation proposal,
  61–62; invasion of Cambodia and,
  36n7; meetings on the presidential
  yacht, 27–28, 133–134; meetings
  with Republican congressional
  leadership in 1971, 58–59, 60–61,
  62; meetings with Republican
  congressional leadership in 1972, 83,
  93, 94–95; meetings with Republican
  congressional leadership in 1973,
  108–109, 110–111, 114; Wilbur
  Mills and, 70, 115–116; presidential
  election of 1972, 93, 94; proposal
  to reduce the number of cabinet
  departments, 59n6; Republican
  National Convention of 1972 and,
  94–95; revenue-sharing proposal,
  59n5; State of the Union address in
  1971, 58, 59n5, 61n7; Syrian-Israeli
  cease-fire in 1974, 133; tax reform
  and, 16, 18; trade bill debate and, 42,
  52, 115–116; Watergate scandal (*see*
  Watergate scandal)
Novak, Robert, 107, 123, 124, 178, 316,
  350
Nunn, Sam, 262

Obey Commission, 219
Olcott, Ralph, 145